D1598794

THE GOTHAM LIBRARY
OF THE NEW YORK UNIVERSITY PRESS

The Gotham Library is a series of original works and critical studies published in paperback primarily for student use. The Gotham hardcover edition is primarily for use by libraries and the general reader. Devoted to significant works and major authors and to literary topics of enduring importance, Gotham Library texts offer the best in literature and criticism.

Comparative and Foreign Language Literature:
Robert J. Clements, Editor

Comparative and English Language Literature:
James W. Tuttleton, Editor

Eça de Queirós and European Realism

Alexander Coleman

New York University Press. New York *and* London

Copyright © 1980 by New York University

Library of Congress Cataloging in Publication Data

Coleman, Alexander.
  Eça de Queirós and European realism.

  (Gotham Library of the New York University Press)
  Bibliography: p.
  Includes index.
  1. Eça de Queiroz, José Maria de, 1845–1900.
2. Novelists, Portuguese—19th century—Biography.
I. Title.
PQ9261.E3Z617   869'.3'3   79-3011
ISBN 0-8147-1378-5
ISBN 0-8147-1379-3 pbk.

Manufactured in the United States of America

To the Memory of Edward Glaser,
Friend of Portugal

Contents

Acknowledgements

I am grateful to the following friends and critics who took the time to review portions of this study: Priscilla P. Clark, Robert J. Clements, Ernesto Guerra Da Cal, Peter Demetz, Denis Donoghue, Margaret Foley, Danielle Gilman, Kenneth Krabbenhoft, Alfred MacAdam, Dr. Luís de Sousa, Katherine Wallenberg and Ben Webster. I wish to acknowledge with thanks the sage advice of my colleague Wilson Martins, without whose constant encouragement and goading this book could not have been written. All are blameless if any errors or misinterpretations still remain—my obstinacy is at fault. Unless otherwise noted, all translations from the Portuguese or the French are my own; in this regard, I note with appreciation the translations done by Kenneth Krabbenhoft of key passages from the first and second editions of *The Sin of Father Amaro,* texts that have never been available in English before and are difficult to find in Portuguese.

A study such as this often owes its existence to a chance acquaintance or an offhand remark from an old friend; in this case, I can say that Don Jorge Guillén gently inquired of me one day in Cambridge if I had read a short story of Eça de Queirós entitled "José Matias." I said that I had not, but that I would do so immediately; my reading of Eça began after having finished "José Matias," intrigued by what I had found. I have included the story as an appendix to my study of Eça's major novels. It is a masterpiece.

Finally, grateful appreciation is due to José Blanco and the Gulbenkian Foundation of Lisbon, and the Arts and Science Research Fund of New York University, administered by Dean Norman F. Cantor, for generous contributions made toward the publication of the book.

A.C.
32, Rua das Janelas Verdes
Lisboa

A Note to the Reader

According to the agreement reached at the Convenção Ortográfica Luso-Brasileira of 1945, Portuguese spelling has been standardized, with the particular result that Eça's name is now spelled *Queirós*, instead of the Queiroz that he himself used. My book on Eça thus uses Queirós consistently, but at the same time I have refused to change the spelling of titles of texts that use Queiroz; thus the apparent anomaly of having the author's name spelled two ways. I have also used the translator's spelling of the characters in *O Primo Basílio*—"Bazilio" and "Luiza."

1.

Theories for Fictions

1. Portugal and France

Readers outside the Iberian Peninsula do not generally look to Portugal for books to read. The record of translations from Portuguese literature to other European languages is highly erratic, to say the least. Brazilian literature has had better luck. It may well be said that fiction and poetry written in Portuguese are guaranteed a degree of critical silence that is definitive and automatic, above all in the English-speaking world. To paraphrase the snide inquiry of Sydney Smith directed to North Americans in the early nineteenth century, people still ask, "Who reads a Portuguese book?" The answer has to be almost wholly in the negative. But this is the case within Portugal, too. A good example of an author's precariously small audience within Portugal would be the case of the literary fortunes of José Maria Eça de Queirós, born in 1845, and thus scarcely five years of age when Balzac died, a quarter of a century younger than Flaubert, and almost half a century younger than Hugo. He is generally known as the most successful proponent of

1

Realism in Portugal, and this is an understandable fact: since most of Iberian literature lived under the overwhelming presence of the literature of France, he found himself as a young *littérateur* at the University of Coimbra during the 1860s as a protagonist in Portugal of the development of a peculiar and very unique brand of Portuguese Realistic practice. Our reading of Eça de Queirós must begin with the problem of a literature as written in a province of Europe, and the relation of that literature to the massive cultural hegemony of France, England, and Germany during the nineteenth century.[1] It is difficult to identify a readership during that time in Portugal. If, as Georg Lukács and Ian Watt have so convincingly suggested, the European novel represents the aspirations and the social ideals of an ascendant bourgeoisie, Eça de Queirós's readership was a minuscule bourgeoisie, a highly polarized band of readers—the liberal constituency that began to crystallize only toward the middle of the nineteenth century.

The presumptions of basic education in Portugal demanded a command of French language and literature. This was the basic literary diet for readers. English literature occupied a relatively minor role, in spite of the massive economic presence of English capitalism in the political and economic life of Portugal.[2] If the cultural magnetism of France was all-pervasive, this must be understood in the light of the elitist tastes of the meager population in the capitals of Lisbon and Pôrto. After all, the population of entire Portugal at the time of the first official census in 1864 was just over 3,800,000.[3] Lisbon accounted for approximately 225,000, Pôrto only for 86,000.[4] Although demographic outlines are mostly estimates, we might say that the Portuguese middle class during the 1860s constituted no more than 15 percent of the whole population, a class made up of civil servants, army and navy officers, teachers, lawyers, bankers, traders, and students. A good component of the class was, understandably, landowners who preferred to live in the capital.[5] Throughout the countryside, there persisted a home craft tradition along with the production of traditional agricultural staples of rice, cork, and wheat. In spite of the intense efforts toward the establishment of basic industries, the lasting effect of a feudal and agrarian social structure was still evident. Portugal was primarily an agrarian economy, functioning with a chronic scarcity of capital and a permanent deficit in the balance of trade. This situation was to continue throughout the nineteenth century and on through various revolutions, the Republic, Salazarism, and the Revolution of April 25, 1974.

The roots of Portugal's decline from the age of discovery and conquest lie well before the cataclysmic events of the nineteenth century, many of which were to send so many of the members of Eça de Queirós's generation to despair, silence, and even suicide. The loss of Brazil, finally confirmed by the Treaty of Rio de Janeiro of 1825, exacerbated those religious and political divisions in Portugal that were gradually evolving in the wake of the grand Enlightenment reforms of the Marquis of Pombal following the Lisbon earthquake of November 1, 1755, not to mention the dramatic imprint of the Napoleonic invasions in the early part of the nineteenth century. Here again, the culture of France offers a quandary to the Portuguese mind and spirit, as it did for the patriotic Spanish. To be an *afrancesado* was to be in the forefront of the intellectual movement known as the Enlightenment, but it also often implied a series of elements that were alien to Iberian civilization in its most chauvinistic self-image.[6] The horror and fear of Masonry on the part of most Iberian Catholics are a good case in point. At any rate, it is more than probable that the fundamental outlines of the bloody civil conflicts that raged over Portugal throughout the nineteenth century until the declaration of the republic on October 4, 1910, might well be traced to one single event: the inexplicable fact that Don João VI died in 1826, possibly poisoned in his palace at Belém, without deciding between his two sons, possible heirs to the throne. He had two choices, and he chose neither.[7] The eldest, Dom Pedro of Brazil, author of a Benthamist constitution (known familiarly as "A Carta"), found himself to be the rallying point for a brand of monarchic constitutional liberalism. On the other hand, his younger brother, Dom Miguel, living in Vienna under the protectorship and advice of Metternich, was more than anxious to reinstate an absolutist "unconstitutional" regime. At his very worst, we might say that he was an avatar of the "traditional, deeply Catholic, old Portugal, intolerant and superstitious, fanatic and revolutionary." [8] After a savagely fought civil war that effectively crystallized the major ideological divisions within the country between political liberals and religious conservatives, Dom Pedro ascended the throne, and banished his brother from Portugal. But he no sooner began the work of reconciliation of the nation than he died in 1834, leaving the throne to his fifteen-year-old daughter, Maria II. Here begins a uniquely complicated history of uprisings, veiled dictatorships, a Septembrist rebellion, outright despotism, populist uprisings— even an occasional coalition. The constants in this welter of vicissitudes were the presence of the house of Bragança-Saxe Coburg (Maria II, Pedro V, Luis I, Carlos I, Manuel II) until the declaration of the republic in 1910 (the definitive exile of the monarchy) *and,* of course, the generally accepted political divisions in the parliamentary system between Regenerators and Historicals (later Progressivists). Following the English example, these two parties (Eça de Queirós found them almost indistinguishable) alternated in power, although there was an increasing amount of dissidence on the part of socialists in the Proudhonian manner on one side and secret and religious societies on the other. In any case, between 1834 and the end of the monarchy in 1910, there were forty-three elections for Parliament, which makes for approximately twenty months per parliament. As a distinguished historian of Portugal has observed, "In a European context, the Portuguese governments were as stable as any others." [9]

Eça de Queirós was not a politician in the strict sense, nor was he an active participant in the organization of any political party; he left that daunting task to the political activists of his Coimbra generation, the philosopher and poet Antero de Quental, and the brilliantly acute historian and sometime minister Joaquim Pedro de Oliveira Martins. But Eça was, nonetheless, a highly sensitized political animal, and one who was not at all afraid of making literature out of a clearly defined socialistic or even revolutionary program. Born illegitimate, he came from a family of jurists, civil servants; his grandfather on his father's side was perhaps the unique case of a rebel in the family. Early in the century he had a signal role in organizing the liberal uprisings in the North against the Miguelist oppressions of the 1820s, and it is said that he shared exile in Plymouth, England, along with other liberals who were awaiting the arrival of Dom Pedro and his daughter Maria II from Brazil. He was known for his bilious temperament, very much that of an adventurous revolutionary.[10] Eça's father was considerably more circumspect in matters political. But Eça was never far from the anticlerical, rationalist, and positivist mental structures of the Coimbra generation of 1870, that generation so much under the shadow of Renan, Michelet, and Hugo, and so desirous of a new Portugal based upon the industrial revolution, bourgeois leadership, and the parliamentary system.[11]

Eça's major works function within the tenets of Realism, but all such designations end by being deceptive, for his peculiar response to the central impulses of Realism qualifies him, not as a docile follower, but as a synthesist of the various kinds of imaginative bifurcation that Romantic, Realist, and Naturalist theory and practice have come to mean for us. Though it seems foolish to say so, Eça de Queirós's literary allegiances partook of all three tendencies. He did not have an exclusive temperament, but rather one that was comprehensive and contradictory. Within the forty-five hundred pages or so of one of the most recent reprintings of his works, his greatest achievements are much more imposing than what one might consider to have been the predictable provincial or simply imitative response to the central corpus of the then contemporary French literature.

No literate person in Portugal of the time could escape the example of France, and certainly no one with a smattering of Portuguese history could easily brush aside the dilemma that the attractions of French culture so often represented to a cultured reader in Lisbon or Pôrto. France was everywhere in the air, to the extent that Eça could postulate the formula "Portugal is a country translated from the French into slang," only to awaken the fury of the kind of people he always scorned the most—the literary and political chauvinists who seemed to inhabit the salons of Lisbon. He was detested by many Portuguese of his class. His formative culture was imported from France in a wholesale manner; Eça and his inflamed band of friends at the University of Coimbra during the 1860s were acutely conscious that they lived within a marginal country and with an ossified concept of tradition that was fundamentally responsible for the decline and decadence they saw around them. The magisterial presence of France is fundamental in Eça de Queirós's life; yet it was not one he accepted with thanks and grace at all times. In one of his most acerbic fulminations against France, written in 1899 just before he died, he recalls that "I have been accused with acrimony of being a 'foreigner' or an 'afrancesado' in periodicals or in those chunks of printed paper that pass for periodicals in Portugal. And I have been accused of conspiring, by pen and by example, to *deportugalize* Portugal. Well, this is one of those salon errors in which meridional frivolity is so abundant. Instead of being guilty of aiding in the destruction of national characteristics, I was one of the melancholy results of this destruction. No sooner was I born, no sooner did I take my first steps, still in my crochet slippers, I began to breathe France. Around me there was only France." (*OC*, II, 813–14).[12] At primary school and university, "everything French! Some of the lessons were given in French, by illustrious teachers loaded down with medals, who pronounced 'il faut'—ile faúte." As far as literature in Portugal is concerned, Eça is at his most virulent:

> But above all this copying of the French is at its most devastating in my specialty—literature. Just like those ducks that Zola describes so comically in his *La Terre*, there we all are, lined up, slow and uncertain, on the road to poetry and prose, following the French goose. When he heads for the grass, there we go, tottering and flopping, toward the grass. If he stops, beak on high, all of us stop, beak on high. All of a sudden he opens his wings, hops along clumsily, and you have the grotesque parade, clumsy and hopping, confidently scurrying toward a puddle! In imitation of the French goose, we were, in chronological order, Romantics,

Gothics, Satanists, Parnassians, then Realists. All the incoherence, all the affectation, all the extravagance of a literature in decadence, desperate for originality, and unhinging itself in the violent effort to find a new attitude that might stun the reading public, all of these are immediately aped in a serious manner with melancholy gravity (which is the basis of the national character) by honest and ingenuous young men. (*OC*, II, 821)

Eça de Queirós is describing himself, of course, and he is also describing one of the constants of his critical and creative method—the aesthetics of imitation—and this in turn will come to imply the function of plagiarism within Eça's extraordinary fertile creativity. There will be a more detailed discussion of the problem later in our reading of Eça de Queirós, but it might be helpful to read the above passage in the light of his almost magical dependence upon other texts in order to generate his own. As an example, the posthumous novel *A Capital* contains correspondences that mimic the disposition and characters of Balzac's *Illusions perdues;* thus, one can assume that the novel, brilliant as it is, remained unpublished, not only because of the intensely anti-Socialist nature of the work, but because the source of the novel, if you will, is too painfully and amazingly obvious for any nineteenth-century Portuguese reader not to have recognized it.[13]

This late tirade entitled "O Francesismo" is odd, because by the time Eça de Queirós had written it, he was well established, both professionally (as consul in Paris) and in his writing. Yet he felt impelled to publish this extraordinary mélange of exacerbated chauvinism and blind contempt for a culture that was directly responsible for his own creative and critical responses to literature and society. How could he deny that his art was formed in the shadow of France, even drawing much of its grandeur from the contradictory character of his own subjugation to it? As Henry James said of "being" an American, "It's a complex fate . . . and one of the responsibilities it entails is fighting against a superstitious valuation of Europe." [14] The relationship to Europe always took two forms within the imagination of Eça de Queirós: at first a "direct conversion," to use George Steiner's phrase, and later a "great refusal . . . where the European pilgrimage would lead to a rediscovery and revaluation of the home country." [15] Both extremes lie well within the spiritual experience of Eça's whole life. This is why he is so slippery, so difficult to seize. He saw his marginality as a fruitful element in his critique of traditional social structures, and he certainly knew he was marginal from a European perspective. Within their own cultures, it might be said that both Henry James and Turgenev had the same unsettling impressions of their role in the mother country. With his unique perspective as a passionate Gallophile in his youth, Eça came to develop a covert and surreptitious kind of allegiance, even idolatry toward traditional Portugal, a reaction that at the same time generated more than a few ironic deflations of that same culture. Imitation and symbiotic criticism of both France and Portugal are at the heart of Eça de Queirós's singular program for literature as it developed over the years.

We should take "O Francesismo" as representing a completed circle, starting with early allegiance and ending with bitter disenchantment. Not surprisingly, the addictive phase included his years at Coimbra, and his various consulships in Havana, Newcastle, and Bristol. The disappointing realization begins to appear around 1888, at the moment he takes up residence in Paris as consul, a post he will occupy until his death in 1900. As he fulfills his long-cherished dream of permanent residency in Paris, only at that time does he begin to sever the spiritual bond that had sustained him throughout his student years and well into his consular career, his formative years as a writer. As a letter written toward the end of his life shows, the second conviction of Alfred Dreyfus in 1899 was the culminating factor that convinced Eça de Queirós of the error of his youthful enthusiasms.[16] During the final twelve or thirteen years of his life, Eça will remain studiously aloof, indifferent to Parisian cultural life. Apart from the single visit to Émile Zola, he has no contact with French writers or painters, nor will he take any interest in Impressionism, early Gide, Barrès, whatever. Eduardo Prado, Eça's faithful Brazilian friend and possible model for his last novel, remembers him as "Inaccessible. He doesn't attend literary dinners, doesn't go to congresses, nor newspaper luncheons; he doesn't seek out the famous men of today or those of tomorrow." [17] Even the trips to the *bouquinistes* along the Seine were not searches for contemporary literature in French or other languages, but rather a search for old Spanish and Portuguese texts that he would then take home to Neuilly to fumigate, varnish, and preserve. This is not what we imagine to be a literary activist or a critical inquirer, but rather just what Eça de Queirós had described himself as during those years—"petit bourgeois retiré." [18]

One more point from "O Francesismo" might be mentioned. It may well be a banal point, but it is one that can help us understand the cast of the author's imagination as it fitfully related to the central concerns of French culture. "There is nothing more different than a Frenchman and a Portuguese; neither do I comprehend what satisfaction, what joy a Portuguese can think of having as he feeds and bathes himself in the creations of the French spirit. France is a country of the intelligence; we are a country of the imagination. The literature of France is essentially a critical literature. We love, by temperament, eloquence and images above all. The literature of France is, from Rabelais until Hugo, a social, active, and militant literature. By tradition and instinct, ours is idyllic and contemplative. In the end, the symbol of France will always be the rooster, the petulant and shiny rooster who crows brightly with the limpidity of a bugle in the fresh glow of the morning. Our emblem is and always will be the nightingale, mourning in the barely illuminated gloom of groves, the 'lovable and nostalgic' nightingale that made Bernardim weep" (*OC*, II, 822, 823).

To find the source of Eça de Queirós's oscillating opinion of France, it might be best to turn to his earliest writings, both criticism and protoliterature, which he published in Lisbon and Évora newspapers in the years 1866 and 1867, and are now widely dispersed throughout the complete works and the so-called "Forgotten Prose" (*Prosas Esquecidas*).[19] The young Eça, just graduated from Coimbra, a quondam lawyer and occasional journalist, shows himself to be a vessel of contradictory sensibilities, above all in his many responses to French Romanticism. The fact that he responded so vigorously to the political and literary aspirations of French Romanticism gives us some idea of how much complicity there was between his injunctions and his gradually evolving concept of the nature of literature. In this regard, the example of the work of Victor Hugo may well serve as a touchstone for Eça's formative impulses—Romantic, to be sure. "I almost learned to read with the works of Hugo; and each one of them penetrated me in such a way that, just as others can recall epochs of life or states of mind by means of an aroma or a melody, I suddenly see again, as I reread old verses of Hugo, a whole past, landscapes, houses I lived in, occupations and dead feelings. . . . I was really brought up within the work of the Master, just as one can be brought up in a forest. I was brought up with the sound of his Odes, with the broad blasts of his anger, with the vague terror of his Deism, with the grace of his compassion and the luminous mists of his Humanitarianism. All of this towered over me as would a forest; and it conveyed to me, for better or for worse, much of his obscurity, his shadows, and his unjustifiable visions. His hatreds were my hatreds; passionately. I pursued with rapture the lyric flight of his enthusiasms. . . . For me the Master remains exalted and venerable among men. Je l'admire comme une brute" (*OC,* II, 1423–24).

Within this mishmash of asystematic sensibility that was the young Eça who was about to become a Realist, this instinctive taste for the transcendental vision of the absolute was, as he says, "for better or for worse," a fundamental axis around which his first enthusiasms and later discriminations were made. One of the most curious processes in Eça de Queirós's literary development is the gradual erosion of such youthful passions. Eça will regret this abandonment much later, but for the moment, the strength of the quotidian fact gradually begins to work away at such ingenuous allegiances. Nonetheless, the Hugolatry is there, almost never to be extinguished. Too, the strong political implications in the poetry of Hugo, so intimately related to the composition of the *Legende des siècles,* among other works, was not at all lost upon the young author.

Throughout his career as a novelist, the broad political ambitions of the poetry of Hugo were used to combat "the intimate lyricism, which closed up in the heart, doesn't understand any sounds of the universe except the sounds of Elvira's skirts, and makes the practice of Poetry in Portugal a monotonous and interminable confession of the glories and martyrdom of love." [20] Eça de Queirós will associate a poetic ideal more closely with political consciousness than lyric intimacy. He wants poets who "fight for justice, for truth, for the revolution, for the rights of the people. . . . Hugo was the great searcher for the Ideal, the great dramatic poet, and even today, like a prophet, like Dante in the thirteenth century, he is the supreme soul of poetry of this generation." These kinds of poets, Eça will aver, "teach the people, they are the priests of goodness, they are fair, they struggle, they suffer for the free idea." The others—Mallarmé, Baudelaire, Leconte de L'Isle—"are poets full of tedium, of melancholy, who sing of evil, desperation, the infamies of the flesh, Satan, Materialism"; these are "rhetorical poets." [21]

This fantastically doctrinaire view of the Parnassian and Symbolist poets is only the beginning of a delineation of his ideas about the nature of poetry. On other occasions, he will offer a theory of the beginnings of art, of the birth of the imaginative faculty in man. [22] For Eça around this time, music triumphs in the nineteenth century above all for its command of untouchable realities, its transparent expression of what is unfathomable in words.

For him, it is the nostalgia for the infinite that governs music's triumphant power over the other arts; its very lack of representational qualities makes it "the spontaneous voice of all those who, like Don Juan, are resigned, starved of the ideal, nocturnal, ashen-faced by the light of the Moon" (OC, III, 870). These disconsolate listeners consist of "sad and enervated youth," who only commune with "the night, the indefinite, the silence, sadness and evanescence" (ibid.) For Eça, music is the art of the overreacher, the only expression of the Faustian impulse in Romantic man. In the figure of Don Giovanni, symbolic as he is "of life in modern times," one finds "all the hopes, all the religions, all the loves, all the idealism, all the desperation of one's own country. This is what the olympian Goethe felt so profoundly, when he said that Mozart was the only musician capable of comprehending Faust and appreciating Marguerite" (*OC*, III, 871).

Although Eça knew no German, his readings and predilections during these years took on an irrationalist, "musical" atmosphere; he was quite specific in telling us what readings in German literature he carried out in French translations. Most obvious in this regard is the presence of Heinrich Heine. Madame de Staël's *De l'Allemagne*, stories by E. T. A. Hoffman, some works of Jean Paul Richter and Novalis, and of course Goethe's *Faust* in the translation by Gérard de Nerval. One aspect of Eça de Queirós's lyrical substructure is the fact that his Romantic readings were limited to poetry; as a friend observed justly, "he had a phobia of Romanticism which, by a singular contradiction, he adored in poetry, while detesting it in a novel." [23]

2. Romance and Reality

My reading of Eça de Queirós begins with an apparent anomaly—the case of Portugal's most renowned Realist, a mind which, in its maturity, produced some of the most caustic and comic diagnoses of Portuguese society, and a mind which fed upon analysis, documentation, and observation in such works as *The Sin of Father Amaro* and *The Maias,* but which here begins as the lyric fantast of age twenty-one, with a macabre gloss on Heine's "Intermezzo"—a diaphanous beloved, an anguished lover intent upon rejection—all done in an ethereal tone of hypersensitive melancholy of dubious taste: "And when I saw you, I saw no more flowers, nor doves, nor stars: but when I thought of you, I saw you delicate as all the flowers, voluptuous as all doves, luminous as all the stars. At times, alone and silent, I saw your misty eyes passing through the shadow before me, like a legion of rhapsodical inspirations . . . then, your marble-colored arms, then your undulating black hair . . .

finally, above a marvelous background, you appeared above me, serene, perfect, and luminous" (*OC*, I, 571). This text, Eça de Queirós's first published text, is dated 1866.

The beginnings of Eça de Queirós as a writer are here, in one grand outpouring. For the young Eça, the world of fact is evaded by an impoverished manipulation of salon commonplaces; there seems to be no shaping force or power to these divagations. In the text just quoted, the author even evades authorship by use of an ingenuous introductory paragraph: "At the edge of the paper, where one could still see the remains of an old *cantiga,* someone wrote these disordered and strange musings" (*OC*, I, 571). This is an *âme sensible* still without theoretical orientation in literature; he is suffused with indeterminate abstractions.

In another article of the same period, Eça will put forth justifications in the manner of Mme de Staël for the split in sensibility between northern Europe and the Mediterranean; the poetry of the North was the "invisible element" that "took the troubadors, sons of the earth, by the hand to the hearths of the feudal lords: it was the first breath of love which the poor poets of the populace, mystical and sensual, composed for the white castles which they glimpsed from afar in the tournaments" (*OC*, I, 607). Poets of the North, he avers, had to adjust inner feelings to the literary expectations and the formalized poetics of courtly audiences. In the South, the poetry and the *romancero* derive directly from the experience of the people; thus its "profound originality," drawing its power from "popular traditions, climate, the sun, all the meridional vigor," and so too for the vitality of the Spanish theater of the Golden Age, "original, chivalric, energetic, impassioned, full of wild palpitations . . . where lackeys, heroes, saints, winds and galleons speak, where all forms of life mingle" (*OC*, I, 607). Eça in this case seems to disdain rhetorical poetry, preferring the rude, sincere poetry of the people, an odd Arcadian touch by the young critic. Odd for now, that is—Arcadia represents a major ideal in the late works of Eça de Queirós.[24]

The naïve North-South dichotomy reappears in a more virulent form in another essay, "Concerning Painting in Portugal."

Here Portugal is depicted as above all "a nation of struggle, of strength, of material action" within southern Europe, which in turn takes on the form of "the body, the animal part of man, his outward way of being, just as the North represents the vague intimate spiritual feeling—the soul" (*PE*, IV, 276). Within the realm of this southern European *body*, each nation has certain powers and gifts and fulfills certain functions. "Italy and Greece are the exterior perception through the senses, which always translates into the cult of form in an intelligent race." What is the function of art in such a culture, asks Eça, and how does art relate to Portuguese reality? Contemporary arts are in a state of total decadence; poetry is either "sadly arcadian" or colored with rhetorical sentiments; architecture consists of "the perfection of the straight line"; sculpture is nothing but official statuary; music cannot be mentioned, since "we hardly possess two nightingales" (*PE*, IV, 278). Art should study man, "not as he exists under the transformations which fleeting life in society covers him up with, but rather as he should be in nature, in the pure truth of his body and soul" (*PE*, IV, 279).

The nature of that "pure truth" is precisely the basis for all of Eça de Queirós's early writings; in this case, he does seem to prefer what he calls "an equilibrium of soul and form," and this is to be found in the works of Leonardo da Vinci, Mozart, and Goethe. The ideal as described here seems Apollonian— distortion and exaggeration are anathema to him.

If his quest for a mode of expression began with a nearly incoherent parody of the worst elements of the Gothic imagination, all this was accompanied by readings and tendencies that had nothing to do with this nocturnal sensibility. While a student at Coimbra, he underwent an intensive tutelage in the *Cours de logique positive* of Comte, *De la Révolution dans l'église et l'état* of Proudhon, and of course the *Vie de Jésus* of Renan.[25] It was precisely this confusion of apparently antagonistic aesthetic and political principles that Eça recalled in an unusually confessional letter sent to a friend in 1867: "[At Coimbra] there were all theories and all sects among us; there were Republican 'bárbaros' and 'poetic' Republicans; there were mystics who lived out the eclogues of Virgil; there were melancholic and sentimental materialists who proclaimed their theories with a tender languor in their eyes, speaking of vital forces" (*OC,* I, 643). Above all, the cardinal pedagogical figure in Eça's life at this time was the poet-philosopher Antero de Quental, "the great spirit . . . who explicated Proudhon with the serene familiarity of the sages" (ibid.). It may well be said that Eça's instinctive Romanticism received its first critical assault at the hands of Antero's intense advocacy of humanitarian socialism, but it could not have been Antero alone.[26] Coimbra itself was seething with the seeds of a political revolution which soon translated itself into student uprisings, revolts against a tyrannical rector, and a successful boycott of the university itself. As Eça was to remember it later, "in four years, we made three revolutions, if my memory serves, with all the classic elements: manifestoes to the populace, rock throwing or street uproars, a rusty pistol underneath every cape, and fiery effigies of rectors burning away as we executed jungle dances" (*OC,* III, 545). Along with the street actions, there was obviously a veritable torrent of aesthetics, politics, religions, and ideas. "Every morning brought its own revelation, just like a new sun. Michelet was on the rise: also Hegel, Vico, Proudhon, and Hugo, the latter now a prophet and impartial judge of kings. And too, there was Balzac, with his perverse and languid world, and Goethe, vast as the universe, and Poe, and Heine, and I think Darwin even then, and how many others!" (*OC,* II, 1542). Within the ultraconservative and ultracatholic confines of Coimbra, Antero de Quental epitomized a kind of revolutionary and rationalist orientation that Eça gladly admired. But far from only organizing the students and protesting the autocratic behavior of a rector, Antero had previously signaled the beginnings of a literary revolution with his rambunctious and insolent letter entitled "Bom Senso e Bom Gosto," a tract written to the aging Classicist bard António Feliciano de Castilho, translator of Virgil and energetic enemy of Realism in literature. In this provocative and quite aggressive manifesto, Antero voiced exhaustion with, and revolt against, a petrified poetic practice, against the very idea that poetry might be taught in a treatise written by a poet whose political leanings were, to say the least, conservative if not reactionary. In this letter to Castilho, Antero declared war in favor of "irreverent independence of writers who know how to construct their own road, without asking permission from the masters, rather consulting only their own labors and their own conscience. We are making war with the unheard of scandal of an impudent literature which supposed it could circulate without the stamp and the approval of the chancellory of the official grand masters." [27] Although Eça was by nature not one to participate actively in political or literary quarrels, his sympathies were clearly with Antero and a brand of literature that was immediately related to the explosive political happenings of the time. Above all, Eça displayed a marked sympathy for the moral edge of Antero's conception of literature, of the idea that literature and morality were certainly allied. "The protest of Antero was a moral, not a literary protest," he notes approvingly. 'His brilliant letter 'Bom Senso e Bom Gosto' continued, in the realms of thought, the war that he himself had begun against the tyrants, the obsolete pedagogues and rectors, the spiritual *gendarmes* whom he encountered as he penetrated as the free man that he was into the world which he wanted free . . . his attack impressed us above all not for its brilliant irony, but because of its moral content and because of the revolutionary impact of that haughty mockery of the purist tyrant of style and vocabulary."

It is with these multiple and contradictory interests and pressures in mind that Eça can cast out, at least momentarily, the occupants of his Classicist/musical/Herderian pantheon and consider the newest examples of revolutionary aesthetics in France and the United States as typified by Poe, Baudelaire, and Flaubert. For Eça in 1866, these authors are "poets of evil," lurid characters exemplifying satanic delight in decay and dissolution: "These men only see evil: raquitic, broken and rotten bodies, lyrical vegetations which glow as from the depths of an Asiatic dream . . . these men, with their radiant violence, with their despairing ideas, with their ironies, their spiritualism, are in the midst of those modern spirits of today, . . . pale and smooth, like a Gothic cathedral among the ruined houses of a town. They choke in the atmosphere of smoke from the fac-

tories" (*OC,* III, 873). It is the tedium of materialism, insists
Eça, that affects these spirits, and they can escape the suffocation of industrial civilization only by a desperate resort to the
arcane and the world of the unconscious—the world of dreams
and terrors. "Poe's stories are the hallucinatory epic of the nervous system."

In his consideration of Flaubert, Eça sees an Emma Bovary
that few would recognize, "the desolate image of beauty, harmony, perfection, imprisoned by the fat and rude arms of
materialism" (*OC,* III, 876). One could hardly imagine a more
fallacious misunderstanding of Flaubert's intentions, nor a
greater misreading of Flaubert's fictional processes. The young
Eça, still in the grip of critical absolutes and incapable of understanding the objective intentions of Flaubert's portrait, sees
Emma as a seraphic and disembodied representation of
platonic beauty and form. A good gauge of Eça's development
of his own critical understanding in this regard would be to
compare this first substantial mention of Flaubert (dated 1866)
with the incisive and sympathetic account he gives of Flaubert's
techniques in a note written just after Flaubert's death in 1880.
In doing so, Eça gives us not only a testimonial to the genius of
the French master but also a program for his own mature
novelistic practice, as evident in the third version of *The Sin of
Father Amaro:* "his great glory consists in having been one of the
first to give to contemporary art its true basis, breaking it away
from the idealist conceptions of Romanticism, and basing it
completely upon observation, the social reality and the human
knowledge which life offers. No one ever penetrated with so
much sagacity and precision into the complex and intimate motives of human action, the subtle mechanism of the passions,
the play of temperaments in the social ambiance" (*OC,* II,
1118). The transfiguration of Eça's conception of Flaubert can
best be measured by the contrast between the texts of 1866 and
1880, from a naïve idealism to a lucid literary materialism
which strives to see the hard outline of people and things as
they were, and as he saw them.

The 1866 misreading of Flaubert's intentions was not inconsistent with the peculiarly conflictive nature of Eça's literary

allegiances during those final formative years in Coimbra and the first years as a fledgling lawyer in Lisbon. But the confusions and contradictions in Eça's views of the nature of literature and its relation to a society have one constant that never changes throughout his career, and that is the *opaque* nature of his personality, the closed and incommunicative nature of even his most passionate "confessional" confidences to friends. From among the forty-five hundred pages of his complete works, almost none are revealing in the sense that a page by Keats or Chekhov would be. Neither candor nor spontaneity is innate to Eça de Queirós. Furthermore, his was an imagination that was unable to rest contentedly with an easy knowledge of empirical reality; his natural stratagems toward the real never included simple acknowledgment. A much more likely device in Eça's practice would be to make temporary allegiances, momentary calculations. The moving force behind this inability to come to a commodious relation to the world around him was his own evasiveness, the sense that the literate act, and not the physical act, was the one and the unique salvation for the artist. But this was unsettling to him also. As Eça said to a friend one day, "We are turning into printed books. Enough of reading and imagining. We need a bath of practical life. A human action is indispensable—an improbable one, if possible—adventure, the legend in action, the palpable hero" (*OC*, I, 549). João Gaspar Simões put it another way: "Looking around at the real world, he feared to register it in literature. Reality, such as it appeared to him, seemed stripped of literary garments. To represent it such as it was would be to renounce being a poet, an artist, a writer. This is why he adorned it with fantastic, spiritual garbs . . . the world did not inhabit him within; it was he who surrounded the world with that veil which later he will call 'diaphanous' and which by that time was so thick and opaque that reality could not be seen through it." [28]

The "bath of practical life" was not long in coming. Reality ceded to Eça's needs in the form of an editorship of an opposition newspaper in the provincial town of Évora; the generous salary will be paid by friends of Eça's father. At that time, Eça had no formally recognizable political opinions, having recently

art, Eça will give an infuriatingly contradictory elucidation concerning the meaning of gesture and exteriority in society—a
theory of theatrical manipulation of roles which does not at all
fit the grim recommendations just cited, nor of course, any
traces of his earlier Romantic self. This text, dated March 3,
1867, has caused considerable controversy among Eça's critics,
since it has been used to deny or to affirm the integrity or
"authenticity" of feelings in the young Eça.[29] In spite of its
length, it is worth quoting rather liberally. The topic for this
particular column is the yearly carnival, the Shrovetide fair. Eça
inquires whether the orgiastic behavior of the citizenry during
carnival times does not represent, once a year, a "sincere" response to the subconscious impulses within each person. Or is it
just the opposite? He suggestively insinuates that the formality
of daily life as lived during all the days other than carnival time
is the very image of falsity, insincerity, inner denial of how all of
us really are. Eça invents a friend who opines: "We really only
live during carnival time; the rest of the year was the carnival-
esque part of life, the caricature of man. He said that only
during carnival time was it that animality and life were logical,
and that seriousness, solemnity, loftiness, politics, science,
positivistic life were all masquerades. I support this idea. Life is
an immense cavalcade of madmen and clowns." Man lived a
truly animal life in Paradise, after all, in happy passivity, sleeping the just sleep of the plants and the birds; the eternal masquerade began with Adam's fall. As man entered into history,
"each one took up his garment and his pose, learned a few
words, and went through the world rakishly acting out in a
daring way his impudent role. Some people call themselves
poor, dress up in rags, and recite their customary and celebrated sentence: 'I'm hungry,' etc., etc., and go throughout the
world, with the same sun, the same water, the same fruits as the
others who call themselves kings and who call themselves
popes. Others portray themselves as republicans and lovers of
the people; they cut off their beards, take up a cloak and an
ostentatious dagger . . . and begin reciting their litany: 'The
people are suffering! Life is impossible without liberty! Let us
break the chains of the oppressor! Off with the heads of the rich

and the king, damnable and dissolute! Sic Semper Tyrannis!' "
(*PE*, II, 348). "Now, there is one time in the year in which each
figure in the masquerade throws down his symbols and dances,
has a good time, laughs, eats like a beast, drinks like Bacchus.
This time of the year is the only time of his life which is serious. . . . Soon I too am going to cast aside my pen and my
declamations in order to make myself spontaneous and logical
for three days. Then I will take part again in the immense
cavalcade" (*PE*, II, 349).

   In spite of the energetic efforts on the part of Alberto
Machado da Rosa to read this text as if it were yet another
peninsular gloss on Calderonian themes in the manner of the
Spanish master's *Gran Teatro del Mundo* or the English *Everyman*,
there is much to be said for considering such a text as an open
revelation of projective characterization, of purposeful assump-
tion of role and mask. After all, up to now there has been an
Eça as Coimbran dandy, Eça as social revolutionary, Eça as
defender of the family and the hearth, Eça as Baudelairian
satanic. Why not now an Eça who openly affirms these manipulations of masks as a program for life and literature? Is this not
a means for the affirmation of literary consciousness itself, and
is this not the beginning of a process that will lead toward an
aesthetics of irony? What was Eça doing in Évora, really? Are
those fulminations against the injustices of the provincial con-
stabulary or the general ineptitude of the local government to
be taken as newly found and substantiated political orientations? If we are to accept them at face value, and if we are to
accept his oppositionist rhetoric—"We want a lessening of misery, a generalization of well-being"—then we would have to
agree with this one well-intentioned critic who sees Eça's Évora
period as the work of a "young idealist" giving the best proof of
his revolutionary sentiments, the work of a sincerely politicized
critic. On the other hand, it might be more illuminating to
consider the Évora episode, not only as the baptism of fire for
Eça and his tenuous contacts with the Portuguese *povo*, but also
as a useful exercise in the adaptation of one's own imagination
to alternating and possibly conflicting political and literary ambitions, the beginning of an elaborate masquerade. In this

sense, we should assume the duplicity of self in Eça as a standard for his own imaginative manipulations. As one acute observer of this period has remarked, "It is impossible not to be struck by the strange spectacle of a potential ally of Gautier taking a few months off to write like Proudhon. In the *Gazeta de Portugal* he works . . . with a vocabulary compounded of playfully handled romantic clichés and the oxymorons of contemporary French poetry (*sol negro da melancolia*), articulates the finest nuances seeking for the right adjective (although *livid*, *morbid* and *pallid* recur almost monotonously). In the *Distrito de Évora*, the political journalist resolutely prunes his communications of metaphors and burning adjectives, anchors his paragraphs in energetic verbs and massive nouns, and delights in the balanced if not symmetrical sentence structure reminiscent of the Ciceronian oratory of the French revolutionary tradition. In Évora Eça was almost ready to burn what he admired in Lisbon." [30] There may well be the beginning of a rich and possibly novelistic treasure of roles and sensibility here, where a paradoxical integration of warring responses is expressed in equally rich degree of obliqueness, where the writer's own aestheticist isolation functions uneasily with a reductive and typological view of Portuguese society. In imagining a new moral order for Portugal in the future, Eça showed himself to be one of the most energetic and critical members of the Coimbra generation, but never through the means of political action.

The one special link between Eça and the rest of the members of his Coimbra generation lay in the fact that "literary interests were closely allied with social concerns, and Shakespeare, the popular *cantiga*, Heinrich Heine (by way of Nerval, Baudelaire and Proudhon) constituted a paradoxical yet integrated gathering of the Olympic gods to whom one could appeal individually and with equal ease." [31] It seems explainable that Eça, riding herd as he did over such a bizarre combination of intuitions and impulses, felt the need to create a *homo duplex* which might serve as a fictive counterpoise. Later, Eça will realize this program of fictional wish fulfillment by creating the alter ego by the name of Carlos Fradique Mendes, a satanic poet in Eça's youth who is revived much later, in the 1890s, for completely different literary objectives. But here, in his column on literary matters entitled "Comedia Moderna," Eça will timidly put forth his first poet/alter ego/imaginative alternative: the fin de siècle poet dandy Manuel Eduardo who, like his creator, might be thought of as a literary spin-off, thrice removed, from the work of Gérard de Nerval (*O nosso Gérard*), a parodic figure drawn directly from the self-portrait contained in Nerval's poem "El Desdichado." As Eça deftly draws in the details of this fictive *littérateur*, the reader might well recall a few of Eça's own ultra-Romantic persuasions that have been somewhat under cover during the past few months of activity in Évora. As Eça imagines Manuel Eduardo, he notes that "they were two similar spirits: the same practical negligence, the same indefatigable benevolence, the same sense of dedication, the same kind of poetry in the soul, the same gaiety of spirit, the same suave illuminism, the same sadness, the same impassioned heart, the same lover of travel, the same constant and ill-defined disquiet" (*PE,* II, 317).

It does not seem very useful to speak of Eça's 'sincerity,' since one of the dominant assumptions of his mature literary practice is the power and subtlety of his literary duplicity, of how the visionary Romantic adjusts itself to a commitment to the finite and the dominion of fact. Eça's art is above all an art of accommodation; the integrity of his central concerns lies not within the realm of a central core of beliefs but rather in the scrupulousness and probity of the dramatization of his own conflictive perceptions and intuitions. In this sense, his works at least suggest the possibility of a novelistic imagination that is at once nonreferential and dogmatic; his strengths and failures may well be ascribed to such apparently irreconcilable ambitions. "Art is the story of the soul," he will insist around this time. "We want to see man [as he is]—not man dominated by society, benumbed by customs, deformed by institutions, transformed by the city—but free man, situated in free nature, amid free passions. Art is simply the representation of characters just as they are, liberated with their own intelligence and free will, without social shackles. That is what gives Shakespeare his supremacy in art. He was the greatest creator of souls. He revealed spontaneous nature; he unleashed the passions in freedom and showed their free action. That is what is called *studying man*. And that is what makes the grandeur of certain capital characters of Balzac—Baron Hulot, Goriot, Grandet. They realized their destiny, far from human association, subject to free logic and the passions" (*OC*, I, 645).

While gaining at least a presumptive grasp of the possibilities of rendering the "free logic of the passions," Eça will now refine his powers of observation, attempting to understand the "subtle laws of things" to which he will make reference in such a sibylline way in his maturity. It is here that we note once again a confused and contradictory series of impulses. The Tainian imperatives of Race, Milieu, and Epoch are studied in practice by Eça as he gives to the readers of *O Distrito da Évora* some selected translations from Taine's *Voyage en Italie* (*PE*, II, 390–442). As he gradually worked his way through these brilliantly executed translations, it isn't difficult to imagine the young translator and future novelist's response to Taine's adept sketches, with their meticulously observed portraits of cities and customs, executed with Taine's own lyric passion of high emotional tension. In the number dated January 10, 1867, Eça introduces his selections from Taine with significant praise: "This book, of a most profound artistic criticism, with strong coloring, of perfect social analysis, was like a revelation of Italy [to me], of the genius of its arts, of its life and political struggles, of its serene and plastic spirit, of its climate, of its elevated and luminous soul" (*PE*, II, 390). One week later, Eça will continue his effusive praise by citing Taine for his "admirable comprehension" of "the meridional race, its instincts, its simple necessities, its contemplative spirit, its love of form and delicate voluptuousness" (*PE*, II, 394).

In effect, the Tainian "invitation au voyage" incites the reader to witness with him "another climate, another sky, another world," where the Latin race has for once learned to "forget itself" among the natural grandeur of the landscape; the *dolce far niente* of this radiant paradise produces in Taine a surprisingly languorous vision of art and society: "How are men supposed to exhaust themselves by working and producing, when they have these things before their eyes? It is not worth the trouble to have a well-ordered house or to laboriously construct those vast machines which are called a constitution or a church . . . it is enough to look, let oneself live; we pluck the whole flower of life with one glance" (*PE*, II, 392). With such delights available to him, Taine's spirit takes on pagan resonances: "one senses the penetrating mien, the virile strength, the serenity of the magnificent sun, the great God of the air . . . the ancient religion of joy and beauty was reborn in the depths of my heart, with the contact with the landscape and the climate which first brought it into being" (*PE*, II, 406–7).

3. Invitation to the East

In October 1869, after almost two years of desultory literary and legal activities in Lisbon, Eça leaves on a voyage to the Near East with his good friend Count Resende, who will in turn become Eça's brother-in-law seventeen years later. The trip lasted some two months and included not only Egypt but many of the shrines in the Holy Land. The importance of Eça's record of this trip—the posthumously published volume of travel impression entitled *O Egipto*—cannot be underestimated as we try to delineate the stages of his own literary development as an embryonic novelist.[32] The trip was calculated with due Gallic literary precedents in mind, not to mention the ostensible point of the whole voyage—an invitation to 'Monsieur le Chevalier de Queirós' to attend the opening of the Suez Canal, that singular event which accompanied, among other things, the creation of *Aïda* by Giuseppe Verdi. During the preceding two years in Lisbon and Évora, years which mark the ascendancy of Antero de Quental's moral and spiritual authority within Eça's own intellectual cenacle, Renan and Proudhon seem to have been the basic stuff of their readings, but after all, a bit of literary exoticism was welcome relief from such stern materials—works such as Chateaubriand's *Itinéraire de Paris à Jérusalem*, Gautier's *Voyage en Espagne et Constantinople*, Nerval's *Voyage en Orient*, and

Flaubert's *Notes de voyage*. At least one of these texts must have been doubly present, for Eça was fresh from a rereading and complete reconsideration of Flaubert's literary examples. Eça was learning, at last, to see and grasp the imperious lessons of impassivity and minute observation which he simply misunderstood some years before. Too, it is good to remember that Flaubert found nothing in Egypt that corresponded to the Egypt of his imagination; in the company of Maxime du Camp, he was irrevocably led to abandon literary exoticism. Both Flaubert and Eça will make use of Egypt as a grand school of sharpening perceptions, where specificity and the weight of objects contemplated come to the fore. As Flaubert wrote to Jules Cloquet from Cairo, "Le détail vous saisit, il vous empoigne, il vous pince et plus il vous occupe, moins vous saisissez bien l'ensemble; puis peu à peu cela s'harmonise et se place de soi même avec toutes les exigences de la perspective." [33] For Eça, the impact of the East had an equally bracing and tonic effect. From the very first pages of the rewritten diary (ordered and compiled by Eça's son and not published until some twenty-five years after Eça's death), the implosion of things and persons seen surges forth in a rush of descriptions, observations, and recorded conversations. Freed for the first time from the calculated culture, religion, and social traditions of Portugal, Eça finds in the Orient not only something new but also an unleashing of his imaginative powers, above all because the East was more ambiguous, chaotic, and nondirective. In the Orient as he saw it, you don't have to visit anything, because everything comes up to you; you only have to open up your eyes. For the first time, he envisages the possibility of an unprogrammed imaginative life; the streets of Cairo will be the key to this uncovering of what was formerly only furtive and latent in his mind.

"Those who have never left the straight and monotonous streets of Europe cannot conceive of the colorful and luminous unconventionality of the cities of the East. . . . In Europe, the streets are straight, flanked by broad façades, as somber and inexpressive as the face of an idiot. The people are banal and gross, dissipated and exhausted by the tedium and the difficulties of life; their clothing is dark, meager and frugal. . . . Everything is correct, rigid, clearly outlined, measured and well behaved. . . . Everything is fine with these well-behaved creatures except the imagination. . . .

"In the [European] city, the imagination is perpetually repelled. The imagination lives only from the life of other beings: it needs to alight on external things and extract from them, just as does a bee from a flower, all the dreams that the objects contain. . . .

"Nevertheless, for the imagination of a European, there is still a free region, abundant and full: Cairo . . .

"All races, wardrobes, costumes, languages, religions, beliefs, and superstitions are to be found there, in those narrow streets. In any small café in the Coptic or Moslem quarter, one sees Arabs, Turks, Nubians, a man from Samaria, Persians, Albanians, Bulgarians, a Jew, an Indian, an Abyssinian, an Armenian, an Arab from Magreb. . . . A Greek makes the coffee, a Bedouin sings in the middle of the room, a Frenchman takes photographs, an Englishman observes, an American takes notes" (*OC*, III, 718–720).

Just as the places, events, and observations give Eça a new imaginative commitment to the chaos and welter of an indeterminate reality, he senses another set of responses in the delta country around Cairo, where "Everything surprises us, as if we were to enter an ancient world . . . those elongated lines, that transparence of colors, the serenity of those horizons, everything makes us feel that we are in a world that has disengaged itself from the contradictions of life, and which has entered . . . into immortality" (*OC*, III, 705). Above all, Egypt becomes an instrument that aids in the eradication of Romantic mystery: "Not one tenebrous shadow, not one mystery on the horizon, not a bit of melancholy tints! Everything is vivid, precise, clear, keen . . . there is no place for legends nor mysticisms" (*OC*, III, 768). And finally, there is the deathly brilliance of the Egyptian sky; it is "of a lugubrious and terrible solitude . . . immobile, eternally blue always, it is a desert, it is a wilderness. The sky of Egypt is an idol: it observes all disquiet, all desires, all tediums—impassively, implacably, and blue. It gives nothing, it says nothing to the poet, to the farmer, to the traveler, to the beggar. It is like a sky of stone. It seems made of lapis lazuli. It annoys one because of its stability and its empty perfection. It is the most terrible of deserts: it is a desert of abstraction, a supernatural desert" (*OC*, III, 772).

There are other extraordinary moments in *O Egipto*, such as Eça's first uncovering of the fragile aestheticist basis for his revolutionary social ideas. The lessons from Coimbra undergo a serious revamping during the journey; in a Turkish bath, far away from the anguish and struggle of civilization, in a place where "initiative and individuality melt away," an astonishingly salacious Eça de Queirós begins to appear: "I confess that in the Turkish baths, under the magnetic pressure of the masseur, listening to the water dripping in the hookah, I decided that all vices and all crimes were natural, rational and legitimate! I wanted to be a caliph, I wanted to sleep on divans of satin, enveloped in the aroma of aloes and the perfume of roses. . . . I would eat delicious, spicy things, I would order that the stomachs of my slaves be cut open in order to examine the disposition of their entrails, I would cut off the heads of Abyssinian women in order to feel the warm blood of those hot-tempered women of the Nile, I would drape pearls over my hounds, I would forget my people, and I would order that all bodies that were not divinely beautiful be tossed into the Nile!" (*OC*, III, 787). The earnest revolutionary transfigures himself into a fin de siècle sybarite for a moment; these moments will reappear in the most unusual and surreptitious ways in the later novels set in the East; the fantasy in the Turkish bath is a unique "first" for Eça's imagination. After leaving Cairo, Eça and Count Resende visit the pyramids of Gizah, along with the temples and ruins of Memphis. After attending the opening of the canal at Suez, they leave for Palestine, Syria and Lebanon, returning to Lisbon via Alexandria on January 3, 1870.[34]

O Egipto is probably one of Eça's most instinctive and subliminal works of nonfiction, with its torrential accumulation of detail and the exuberant descriptive style. No reader of Eça should pass over this immensely revealing document, for, as one observer has put it, "[The trip to] the East was his farewell to fantastic and Romantic lyricism." [35] The Eça who traveled through Egypt and the Holy Land will gradually take on the mature cast of mind that he was to express in his later novels, that of the practical humanitarian positivist, a fervent student of the Renanian program of demystification of the life of Christ, a flighty creator whose definition of the function of the literary imagination has irrevocably changed. For the new convert to Realism who was Eça de Queirós by 1870, and in spite of an odd moment or two in a Turkish bath, the new program relates to a disciplining of the Romantic imagination, subjecting it to the impositions and even dictates of the social critic and the social satirist. Eça's literary youth is now relegated, as he was to say on another occasion, to the realm of a "romantic and marvelous museum." [36] But again, all of this must be deduced from the luminous brilliance of Eça's descriptive texts in *O Egipto*. There is almost no mention of his own inner life; there are no theoretical disquisitions upon the nature of fiction or literature in general. *O Egipto* is thus not only an untheoretical precursor of a whole register of fictional procedures to be found in the later novels and stories, but it is also a direct precedent for Eça's first formal theoretical declarations made in June 1871 after his return to Lisbon. This is the epochal declaration entitled "Realism as an Expression of New Art." [37]

On arrival in Lisbon, Eça found his friends in the Cenacle, as guided by the energetic mentor who was Antero de Quental, to be in a high state of ebullient critical warfare against aesthetic and political traditionalism. Under Antero's guidance, a series of public lectures was devised, aimed at the creation of a revisionist program of reform of all aspects of Portuguese life. The first lecture was to be given by Antero, entitled "Causes of the Decadence of the [Iberian] People"; the second, a severely critical overview of contemporary Portuguese literature, to be given by Augusto Soromenho. Eça was called upon to give what ended by being a two-hour improvised lecture on Realism, and subsequent lectures were to be given on such topics as the reform of education and "The Critical Historians of the Life of Jesus," a lecture which presumably would have diffused the work of David Strauss and Ernest Renan to a wider public in

Portugal. This last scheduled lecture by Solomão Sarraga was arbitrarily suspended by governmental prohibition, since the announced topic was "antagonistic to the doctrines of the official religion of the state." As a whole, the lectures themselves and the subsequent political and social scandal caused by the government ban have come to represent the decisive entry of the Coimbra generation into the literary, political, and artistic life of Portugal; specifically, Eça's lecture marks the opening salvo for Realism in Portuguese literature.

Antero de Quental's rather ambitious announcement for the series of lectures set the high reformist tone that was so much a part of the pedagogical nature of the whole generation:

> We wish to open up a forum where the ideas and the creations that characterize this moment in the century are given expression, with a special emphasis upon the social, moral, and political transformation of nations.
>
> We wish to link Portugal with the modern movement, making it thereby a product of the vital elements of which all civilized humanity partake.
>
> We wish to acquire knowledge of the events taking place in Europe.
>
> We wish to stir up public opinion concerning the great questions of Philosophy and Modern Science.
>
> We wish to study the conditions of the political, economic, and relgious transformation of Portuguese society. [38]

Eça's particular response to the central corpus of French Realism has, up to now, been expressed only in a partial and quite unsatisfactory fashion. Here, in the Casino lecture, he had an opportunity to give an account of a movement that in France was already developing away from the shadow of Balzac. The lecture also gave Eça his first formal opportunity to present a revolutionary *and* moralistic aesthetic that he broadly and liberally drew from the otherwise conflicting and contradictory aesthetic theories of such diverse works as Taine's *Histoire de la littérature Anglaise* and Proudhon's *Du principe de l'Art dans la Révolution et dans l'Eglise.* In France itself, it would be difficult to imagine a more bizarre union of diverse aesthetic principles, but in his Casino lecture, Eça is clearly intent upon picking and choosing for his own curious purposes. To that end, he will combine to his own satisfaction, if not ours, Proudhon's philosophical idealism along with a concerted admiration for the work of Flaubert in literature and Courbet in painting. Eça's knowledge of Courbet was rather indirect. Three paintings will be commented upon by Eça, works that he could not possibly have seen; for the descriptions in his lecture, he appropriates Proudhon's highly prejudicial and wayward descriptions to be found in *Du principe de l'Art* . . . . Although this might well have been an almost fatal handicap for the fledgling lecturer, Eça had no choice but to bring together the figures of Proudhon and Courbet. It should be kept in mind that many French critics who wrote articles on Realism in literature also wrote commentaries on Realism in painting—Baudelaire, Gautier, Zola, the Goncourts, and Duranty himself can all be included in this group. Eça was an intense reader of the *Revue des Deux Mondes,* and he was aware of the intertwining fortunes of the two genres. In his lecture, Eça always uses the terms "Naturalism" and "Realism" almost interchangeably, as so many French critics of the period did also. Either term functioned similarly in French literary and artistic criticism during the period 1840–60; either term represented "an exact imitation [lit., calque, copy] of nature as it is, without choice of subject, and without idealization or intrusion of the artist's personality, emphasizing the material rather than the spiritual aspects of nature." Both terms represented and were synonymous with "materialisme" and "positivisme," and were directly opposed to "idéalisme," "rêverie," "fantaisie," "poésie," "imagination." [39]

Armed with his idea of truth in art and motto—"Death to Imbecility!"—Eça found a new mission for himself and his burgeoning art. As he later recalled those years," I got the idea for a very elevated, very lively [literary] campaign, in which irony is radiantly placed at the service of justice, where each hard blow makes a majestic truth surge forth, a campaign where the demolition of everything emphasized an education for everyone." In the first of many "Barbs" (*Farpas*), Eça began to wage this severely condemnatory campaign against the dormant and paralyzed condition of Portugal. In the first of these *Barbs,* entitled "The State of Portuguese Society in 1871," published just a few days before his Casino lecture, Eça gave a preview, in corrosively satiric terms, of what was to come in the lecture. He begins with an acerbic catalogue of Portugal's mental exhaustion:

> The country has lost its intelligence and moral conscience. Traditions have broken down and people have become corrupt. The only ideal in life is convenience. There is no principle that is not denied, nor institution that is not mocked. No one respects himself. There is no solidarity among the citizens. No one believes any longer in the honesty of politicians. The middle class debases itself day by day with inertia and imbecility. The people live in misery. Public services function vaguely with a sleepy routine. The contempt for ideas gets worse every day. All of us live at random. Perfect, absolute indifference from top to bottom! All spiritual and intellectual life has stopped. Tedium invades the soul. Our youth wander about, aged before their time, going from a secretary's desk to a café table. The ruin of our economy grows and grows and grows . . . commerce is wasting away, industry grows weaker. Wages are going down. Incomes are going down. the State is considered . . . a thief and treated like an enemy. This is not existence, this is an expiation. We do not wish to be accessories to this universal indifference. (*OC*, III, 959–60)

After a lurid condemnation of political life, the degradations of journalism, and the empty rhetoric of the Lisbon theater, Eça begins a scrutiny of the present state of Portuguese literature:

[Our] literature—poetry and novel—is without ideas or originality. It is conventional, hypocritical, extremely dishonest. It doesn't express anything—neither the collective tendencies of society nor the individual temperament of the writer . . . as a result, it does not understand its own time, and no one understands it. Our literature is like a Gothic troubadour who wakes up from a sleep of centuries in a beer factory. It talks of the *ideal,* of *ecstasy,* of *fevers,* of *Laura,* of *roses,* of *lyres,* of *spring,* of *pale virgins*—meanwhile, the industrial world (manufacturing, positivistic, practical, experimental) asks a question, half astonished and half indignant: What does this fool want? What is he doing here? He's an idler, take him off to the police! . . .

The novel is the apotheosis of adultery. It studies nothing, it explains nothing; it doesn't draw characters nor outline temperaments, it doesn't analyze passions. It has no psychology, no action. Pale Julia, married to burly António, hurls the conjugal manacles at her husband's face and faints lyrically into the arms of Arthur, who is disheveled and gaunt. In order to move the sensitive reader more deeply and in exculpation of the unfaithful wife, António works, which is a bourgeois ignominy, while Arthur is a loafer, a Romantic glory. Honest women have been weeping the tears of their own sensibility on account of such whorehouse dramas as this since 1850. (*OC,* III, 966–67, 968–69)

4. The Casino Lecture

But this is nothing if not a prologue to Eça's improvised declarations given on June 12, 1871. Although there is no text as such of Eça's Casino lecture, it can be reconstructed by annotating and comparing the accounts given in Lisbon newspapers over the subsequent ten days. The audience was stunned to see this agent of a literary and political revolution appearing in the dress of an elegant diplomat: "Irreproachable buttoned-up frock coat, high collar, white vest, satin tie, glossy shoes, gray gloves." A revolutionary dandy, it would seem.[40]

The lecture apparently began with the fundamental point of the whole series of lectures: revolution itself was a permanent fact of the times. Artists, on the other hand, have traditionally relegated the concept of revolution to the realm of political change, that is, the disruption and reorganization of society. In other words, art has up to now been untouched by the upheavals of society, and this was due to the pernicious nature of escapist Romanticism of the brand that he so brilliantly flayed in the passages quoted previously from "The State of Portuguese Society in 1871." For Eça in June 1871, freshly impressed as he was by his rereadings of Proudhon's *De la Révolution . . .* and *Du principe de l'Art . . .* , the very concept of revolution must be imposed forcibly upon the realm of all the arts, from whence it was mistakenly exiled at the beginning of the nineteenth century.

The turn of the century was a moment where reaction, restoration, and the literate sensibility found an uneasy and, to Eça's mind, an unhealthy alliance. He insists that revolution must be an aesthetic principle; art cannot be isolated from society. It is related to the progress and the decadence of societies and is even reflective of it. Art must be embedded, as it were, into the matrices of the society which gives it birth. Nineteenth-century art has disobeyed this fundamental principle, and this opposition to the spirit of the times is the source of its weakness. "Our conscience is being formed by [revolution]. It is the soul of the nineteenth century. And meanwhile, our ideas about art are still the old ideas of the past. Revolution is everywhere except in art . . . art represents and sustains Reaction." [41] Art must be democratic if it is to be of our times; it must be antiheroic. "Down with heroes" becomes, for the chastened dandy, a battle cry for the creation of analytic literature in Portugal. Any dissociation between artistic and social ideals signals the past decadence and decline, and *that* past is precisely the state of Portuguese literature which he depicts to his audience. He will insist that they themselves are victims of this ostentatious decadence of the imagination, since they support and even purchase Romantic works—that is, the works which go against the grain of the times. Art should not be elevated to spheres it has no share in.

Now, how and with what means can art and literature be made to express and incarnate the ineluctable wave of history? Eça's anti-Romantic stance does not attempt to excuse the sins of Classicism; quite the contrary, the sterile imitation of Aristotelian principles in the drama, the plague of Portuguese bucolic poetry, the nostalgic and sentimental poetics a la Chateaubriand call for severe condemnation—"Christianity to be played on the piano," he says.

According to Eça, Romanticism took another, more ominous turn. "It gave the word to the plebeian spirit; it is the same thing as saying that it created passion and its expansion. Style felt aggravated; Romantic style finally became apopleptic. At last, artists broke the molds of French literature and sought materials from all nations—they exhausted everything, took leave of the reality of the present-day world. All writers fled from their times; each one sought refuge, accompanied by a disdain for work, morality, the family, Science. . . . In this way, we arrive at the worst of things—Art for Art's Sake." [42]

The recent explosion of the Paris Commune is the key to this new public spirit in the arts, says Eça. On the one hand, such politicians from the Left as Camillo Pelletan and such pamphleteers as Henri Rochefort (Communard in 1870, but anti-Semite in the Dreyfus case) consistently criticize all falsity in society, and do so in the name of truth. The ideal seems to be: paint reality such as it is. There is no future for the arts except through the tenets of Realism/Naturalism. What is Realism? It is above all an antidote, a new broom, a cleanser of souls, and the sign of a return to psychic health. It is not a formal system, but it is the general philosophical basis for spiritual conceptions that are of this time and of no other. It is a law, a map, an agenda of human thought in the eternal region of the beautiful, the good, and the just—this is the new region for the practice of all the arts. It is not just a mode of expression; it is not trivial and overly detailed; it is not "photographic." As Eça considers it, it is something else—it is above all the negation of art for art's sake, and it accompanies the abolition of rhetoric, "the epilepsy of the word"; it is and should represent a critical analysis whose only aim is "absolute truth." Above all, it is the "anatomy of a character and a critique of man, so that we may know ourselves better and . . . so that whatever is evil in society may be condemned."

Flaubert's art, once again, becomes a misunderstood and deformed ideal; it is not that he is unsympathetic to Flaubert's practice insofar as he can grasp it, but he seems oblivious to, and unconscious of, any aspect of *Madame Bovary* which does not fall within the scope of his stern and quite un-Flaubertian views of literature at the time of the lecture, with those heavy emphases upon the aims of art that relate to morality, truth, and justice. The larger implications of *Madame Bovary* as a whole—Emma's inability or failure to find any situation worthy of her vocabulary, or Flaubert's intense effort to define the reality behind his heroine's vaporous concepts of bliss, passion, and ecstasy—all these are questions that are suffocated by Eça's pedagogical manias.[43] So, too, for the fundamental problematic of *Madame Bovary*—does language have its source in life? Is life really behind language?—these are not touched.[44] The gap between the instructional impulse in Eça's theoretical declarations and the unleashed fantast that appeared in the Cairo Turkish bath and will occasionally make surreptitious reappearances through his fictional life is a quandary without resolution. There is no resolution here, because Eça's backing and filling denotes an untenable critical and novelistic proposition—the marriage of moral inculcation and imaginative invention, the marriage of preaching and romance novelistics. These various demands do not adjust themselves easily to each other.

Eça might well have kept in mind Flaubert's remark about Sainte-Beuve and Taine: "They do not pay sufficient attention to art, to the work in composition, to composition and style; in brief, what makes for beauty." [45] Eça should also have kept in mind the kind of easily made loopholes in Taine's theory of epitomization which aided Taine to unchain Shakespeare from any determinants at all: "all comes from within—I mean, it forms his soul and his genius; circumstances and externals have contributed but slightly to his development." [46]

Even taking into account Eça's broadly characterized terms, neither is there mention of the provocative campaign carried out by Flaubert against the deceits of language—its arbitrariness, its oblique and inexpressive nature.[47] Nor is there any mention of the ideally abstract nature of Emma's dreams coexisting with the banality of Yonville. Eça sees in Flaubert only what he instinctively felt was a part of himself—*o artista vingador*—the implacable manipulator of the scalpel, the pedagogue with finger poised, ready to expose the poverty of domestic banalities, including of course its "frightful entourage of hallucinations, repentances, terrors, debasements, shame, or ruinations." All is paraded before the reader's eyes, insists Eça, "oozing squalor and decay, as frightful as the sight of a ghost from which we instinctively recoil with revulsion and horror. Thus is Realism in art made manifest . . . principally by such an intuition of morality, justice, and truth that the author imposes and which he achieves." [48]

Eça sums up the essence of his lecture with an imposing program for the future of Portuguese letters. Realism must be of our time, he affirms, but Portuguese writing of the nineteenth century has so far been of any and all times except that of actuality. Only with the portraiture of contemporary experience and a study of the "science of temperament and character" can this new art be created, an art modeled upon the ideals of corrective justice and liberative truth, an art that does not fear the intrusions of a certain degree of moral rigidity.

As examples, the three works of Courbet are analyzed and commented upon: *Le retour de la conférence, Un enterrement a Ornans,* and *Les Casseurs de Pierres.* Eça's audacity is considerable. Since he improvised the lecture from notes, we have no way of knowing the precise terms he used in his descriptions of these works. A journalist who was present laconically mentions in his account that "the three works were described meticulously, and it was affirmed that they were immortal works, all inspired by the governing principle of the new art: Justice."

What is clear from the discussion at hand is this: Eça imposes moralistic intentions upon the paintings that are singularly missing from an objective scrutiny of the paintings themselves. This manipulation of Courbet by Proudhon was later denounced by Zola in his *Mes haines:* "Proudhon, avec son manque complet de sens artistique . . . veut un moraliste en peinture . . . Il faut que je distingue entre les idées de Proudhon et l'artiste auquel il applique ses idées . . . le philosophe a travesti Courbet." [49]

The program announced by Eça was essentially a passionate demand for a social ethic in literature, and this in turn will demand an ironic scrutiny of traditional social structures, a grand plan for the demythification of Portugal; above all, it will demand the destruction of the Romantic fallacy. The work of fiction will become an expandable container for the reality of Portugal, and this task implies not only one of selecting details among an infinity of possibilities but an examination of the criteria behind the selection. The Casino lecture gives us the theoretical *donnée* for the future execution of the three versions of *The Sin of Father Amaro.* The youthful fantast will willingly cede to a mimetic literary aesthetic which is tinged with moral energies. Eça will, of course, continue to attempt to retain a sense of fidelity to the diverse and contradictory nature of reality, but the central concerns of the Casino lecture will be the axes that govern his reformist temper around this time.

Eça's tortured sense of his own artistic weaknesses dogged him incessantly throughout his life; this self-doubt is more than likely related to his own inability to find or create a novelistic technique that would consistently encompass the dualities and contrasts that always flowed out of his works. Much later in Eça's life, a friend and admirer recorded a painful instance of his dilemma. The interlocutor, Alberto de Oliveira, was visiting Eça at his home in Neuilly, and had just complained rather insolently to him about the failure of the whole Naturalist movement in literature. In effect, Alberto de Oliveira might well have been referring not to Zola, but also to some aspects of Eça's own Naturalistic phase, that is, the second version of *The Sin of Father Amaro.* Oliveira lamented the fact that Eça's great creative talent, "instead of creating freely works of fantasy that would not be limited by narrow precepts, had instead let himself be fettered to plots in which one always sensed the impatient and imprisoned fluttering of wings. To my great shock and shame, Eça agreed with me! He recognized that, in effect, although Naturalism did contribute toward the disciplining of his imagination, it also condemned him to repress, many times without benefit, the impulses of a true Romantic, which at heart he always was." [50]

It is here that Eça's imaginative powers will be constantly called into question, above all by himself. At times, the satiric mode forces him to withhold, suspend, or falsely reconcile the wealth of reality in order to achieve the condemnatory moral edge to which many of his works aspire, a kind of ethical deus ex machina. Rich pluralism is often sacrificed to a dogmatic critical perspective, that "sacred irony" with which he later undermined the presumptions of the stagnated reality that was "his" Portuguese society. Irony is a weapon with which he will attack not only exhausted traditionalism and chauvinism but also the remains of his political radicalism, which he fondly recalls from the Coimbra days. His is a brand of irony which illuminates the fictions by which people live. This lurking didactic note within the structure of his imagination, above all as it relates to what he regarded as the racial deficiences of the Portuguese character, prevented him from exercising the full options that an untrammeled Realist might otherwise enjoy.[51]

5. Fiction and Its Personages

A bundle of contradictions, then. His achievements reflect his wavering and uncertain estimation of the task of a novelist, and above all of his imprecise and contradictory theorizations about the nature of the novel. Eça will agree with his French contemporaries and predecessors that a character's behavior is something more than a set of aleatory responses. Action is always symbolic in his work. At the same time, character might be thought of in another way not to the liking of Eça. In this contrary understanding of the nature of fictional character, it might pull away from the implications of a fixed, coherent personality which is normative in tone, a limiting fixation. These kinds of characters posit a kind of *discontinuance* of personality by means of a definition of their fantasies and their desires, embodying reactions against the milieu rather than actions preceding from social determinants.[52] This would be a fictional character that is clearly antithetical to the Tainian and Eçian precepts. The world of Eça's first distinguished novel, *The Sin of Father Amaro* (3d ed.), is congenial to the idea of personality *continuance;* it has a coherent view of the self, because the ordering principle of the fiction itself forces and coerces reality into a significant form, a struggle between anarchic desire and social custom.[53] For Eça at this time, the reductive character in literature is generally the character that is closest to a sociological type. Writing to a friend as late as 1888, Eça finds himself capable of making the following affirmation: "In Portugal there is only one man, and he is always the same, whether he takes the form of a dandy, a priest, a secretary, or a captain. He is an indecisive man, weak, sentimental, goodhearted, a babbler, 'takes it easy'; this man hasn't an ounce of character nor intelligence that withstands circumstances. This is the man that I describe, underneath his diverse costumes, whether it be dress coat or cassock. This is the true Portuguese, and the man who has made the Portugal that we see around us" (*OC,* II, 1648).

Can any observer imagine a more alarming view of human nature for a novelist? Eça's characters and his situations will more often than not be governed by this kind of reductive idea of character. In the same way, Eça will not at all fear the implications of a thesis novel. In commenting upon the novels of Benjamin Disraeli, Eça will mention the fact that some "of his novels are pamphlets in which the characters constitute living arguments, conquering or succumbing not according to the logic of temperaments and the influences of the ambiance, but according to the needs of the controversy or the thesis" (*OC,* II, 553). There is scarcely a glimmer of disapproval in such a statement, because a thesis was a natural thing for Eca de Queirós as practicing novelist.

There are reasons for Eça's singular lack of conscious self-scrutiny. It may well go back to an earlier expressed theory of comedy, of the ways in which irony may be manipulated for burlesque and satirical effects. Any novelist must know that an overdone arrangement of types may turn the novel into a parade of preordained tics and manias. If the characters or the types do not surprise us, following E. M. Forster's elegant exposition in his *Aspects of the Novel,* then something is probably amiss in the novelistic aesthetic itself. This is why he is so singularly discontent over the years with his own characters and his own abilities. His theory of humor may well be at the heart of the matter. For Eça, it is "holy irony" which liberates the observer from routine, "from the adoration of false gods and false devils, from the mystifications of politics, meager ambitions, small luxuries, from infatuation, from the melancholy slavery of the political parties, from social superstitions and transcencent commandments. It is irony which, making us free, makes us just men" (*OC,* II, 1380). This is a key point; his instinctive preference for literary types derives directly from the urgent necessity and functionality of *directed* humor or critique within his novels. Laughter, for Eça, is "the oldest and still the most terrifying form of criticism" (*OC,* II, 1383). Criticism, when produced by the godlike laughter of a Rabelais, a Cervantes, or a Lesage, produces a unique unmasking, a revelation which is the essence of the novel of social criticism—it obligates the reader "to see truthfully." In Portugal above all, the people see only falsehoods, "because of the passive acceptance of imposed opinions, because of the extinction of the critical faculty . . . the public see what they are told to see" (*OC,* II, 1383). Satire should make us laugh at the idols, "revealing the mannequin underneath." In Évora, Eça became convinced of the fact that life was above all a performance, an act in the drama that is man living in society. He admitted this in his letter to Conde de Arnoso: "In order to enjoy the life of a society, we must take part in it and be an actor in its drama; otherwise, a society is nothing more than a succession of figures without meaning which pass before our eyes" (*OC,* II, 543). An observer of Eça's work put it in a quite different, even contradictory way: "Convinced that he would never have anything to contribute from the realm of his own personal life, he would explore an art of social customs which would attempt to translate and explicate the complete soul of a people." [54] The artist is precisely this investigative consciousness that is capable of looking behind the uniform or the dress in order to expose the generic type underneath. "I am an artist, nothing more; my political criticism is commonplace. Besides, for a novelist, Constitutionalists, Socialists, Miguelists, and Jacobins are all social products, good for Art when they are typical, all of them equally explainable, all equally interesting" (*OC,* II, 1387).

All of the foregoing, while an unlikely program for a fledgling Realist, would be at least understandable if the author himself was content with such prescriptions; if his theories regarding irony, humor, and types were more or less concordant with his actual novelistic practice; and above all if he found real satisfaction in the methodology he so energetically proposed on so many different occasions. But the conversation with Alberto de Oliveira is not at all atypical; Eça was tortured by what he felt to be the inadequacies of his own writing, by his inability to make his characters live, as it were, on the page. "Balzac loved his Valérie," said Taine in his great essay on Balzac. We sense and perceive the fastidious combination of reverence and parody that went into the making of Flaubert's Emma. As James said of Balzac, "it was by loving them—as the terms of his subject and the nuggets of his mind—that he knew them; it was not by knowing them that he loved." What is the general relation between Eça and his characters? It is not that he hated them all but it is true that he is unable in many novels to move his characters from within, since he does not participate in their reality except as the distanced observer always viewing from above, from a critical stance.[55]

Eça's characters are not free to act themselves out; he generally *does* force his will upon them; *The Maias* may well be an exception. Eça was aware of this, and anguish is not too strong a word to use to describe his own bafflement on this matter.

"By the way, what did you think of the section from *Cousin Bazilio* published in the *Diário da Manhã?* Idiotic, don't you think? 'Ce n'est pas ça. Ce n'est pas ça, du tout.' The style is limpid, it has energy, transparence, precision, *'netteté.'* But there is no life in it. It lacks 'vigor' [*poigne*]. The characters—you will see—do not have the sense of life that we have; they are not exactly 'des images decoupées,' but they have a gelatinous musculature . . . unquestionably, there are some good scenes, a few good touches . . . but it is a small skill, the skill of a 'métier'; all in all, I'm an imbecile. And the sad thing is that I despair because of it. I will never do anything like *Père Goriot,* and you know of the melancholy in such a instance—that word 'never!' I construct cardboard worlds. . . . I don't know how to make 'flesh in the soul.' How is it? How should it be? Still, I don't lack technique [*o processo*]: I have it, better than Balzac, Zola, and 'tutti quanti.' Some little thing is missing within, the small cerebral vibration; I am an irremissible imbecile." [56]

One year later, he writes to Ramalho concerning the draft of the first chapter of the posthumously published novel, *A Capital*. This time, the same hesitations, the same paralyzing self-doubts: "Did you read the first chapter of *A Capital?* What did you think? It seems bad to me; and the rest of the book—you will see—worse. It is cold, it is depressing, it is artificial, it is a laborious mosaic. One could praise the *corecçao,* but the absence of life is to be lamented. The characters are all stuffed, and I hate them so, that if they had any blood in their veins, I would drink it. I am an imbecile; I 'sense' what I should do, but I don't know how to do it." [57] These very personal texts may be taken many ways, of course. They may even be elaborate mechanisms to elicit contrary praise from Ramalho—who knows? But the point seems clear enough. Eça's novels are not what one might call "self-developing organisms." Very often, the reader becomes uncomfortably aware of authorial intrusions and intersticed commentary that is at variance with whatever degree of inner existence the character has managed to establish on the page. This is so not only because of the strongly dialectical nature of Eça's attempts at novelistic portraiture but also because of the way these characters function with regard to his own self. In an odd moment in a letter to Ramalho, Eça says that "at times, I don't know how I have any courage left to understand my characters' difficulties, when I have to observe them through the density [*espessura*] of my own troubles" (*OC,* III, 520).

A confusion between theory and practice is one of the few accountable consistencies in the work of Eça de Queirós. Although Eça's ambitious program related to the social aims of literature will bring him increasing renown as the master portrait painter of a society in decadence, this satirical impulse will deny him the possibilities of a more autonomous and less mimetic kind of literature. *Cousin Bazilio* is a case in point. Having completed the work, he was fully aware of the faults inherent in the plot organization—the arbitrary manipulation of the letters by the servant Juliana, the unconvincing denouement that is contained in the deaths of the two female protagonists. Juliana dies of a convenient aneurysm, while Luiza ends her days mysteriously comatose from an undiagnosed illness that removes her from the scene. It seems that the latter disappearance is meant to be a stern punishment meted out by the author for the immorality and inanity of her adventure with Cousin Bazilio. These capricious events, imposed as they are upon the fabric of the novel by Eça, destroy the sense of coherent evolution and development of the tale. This was a private concern of the author, but it became the subject of an acrid public critique of the work, written by the Brazilian novelist Machado de Assis (1839–1908) and published in Rio de Janeiro on April 16, 1878.[58] This is a massive condemnation, and it wounded Eça deeply, above all because he knew it to be true on the whole. Not only does it condemn the structural flaws of *Cousin Bazilio;* it also questions some of the basic tenets of Naturalistic practice. Of course, Eça was "a faithful and extremely fanatic disciple of the Realism propagated by the author of *L'Assommoir,*" according to Machado de Assis. His review begins with the embarrassing but justified assertion that *"The Sin of Father Amaro* [second edition] is an imitation of the novel of Zola, *The Sin of Abbé Mouret.* Analogous situation, same tendencies; different milieu, different denouement, identical style." These are tendentious remarks of course, and have caused no end of critical controversy, but the details are unimportant, really. Having implied artistic dishonesty on Eça's part, Machado de Assis then launches into an acute exposition of the structural deficiencies of *Cousin Bazilio,* accusing the author above all of an inability to give inner life to Luiza. The moral dilemma of the work as it stands is simply unbelievable. According to Machado, "she is a negative character, and in the realm of action created by the author she is more a puppet than a person of moral sensibility. I repeat, she is a puppet; I don't mean that she doesn't have nerves or muscles—she hasn't anything else, she has no passions nor remorse, conscience least of all." Without will, without that missing "little thing" (*coisinha*), Luiza is, for Machado de Assis, "inert matter." A reader can only feel nothing, he suggests. In order for someone like Luiza to be a magnetic character for a reader, Machado feels that "her own tribulations should have come from herself, whether she be a rebel or a repentant woman, whether she be remorseful or curses everybody; but for God's sake, give me a woman of moral sensibility!" Machado then goes to the heart of Eça's characterization of Luiza: "It seems that Sr. Eça de Queirós wanted to give us a heroine who was a product of frivolous education and indolent life. Nonetheless, there are indications which give us the impression, at first glance, of a salacious intent. The reason for this lies in the sense of fatality in the works of Sr. Eça de Queirós. In other terms, his unrelenting Realism—physical sensation." For Machado, Luiza is an externalization of the peculiar vices of "all Portuguese women" which Eça was so careful to describe in his *Farpas.* Machado accuses Eça of writing a sardonic critical essay and calling it a novel. He also implies that Eça pretended to be a moralist while including scenes that many readers took to be pornographic. Eça received Machado's critique with uncommon magnanimity: "In spite of the fact that it is adverse, almost 'reverse,' and of having been impelled by an almost partisan hostility toward the Realist school, this article still honors my book because of its refinement and because of the talent with which it is written. It almost makes the book better." [59] Still, Eça must have been infuriated by the accusation of plagiarism and must also have been affected by the full thrust of Machado's assault; it was too accurate to be denied. In a letter to Ramalho Ortigão of January 17, 1878, Eça was surely aware of the faults of the book: "I know the large defects in *Cousin Bazilio*, and I will be very careful never to repeat them." [60] After the Machado article, something will radically change in Eça's practice, if not in his novelistic theory. Never again will he try to openly evolve or develop "scientifically" a moral or social thesis; he will go underground, as it were, and attempt a brand of fiction in which the weaponry is hidden and surreptitious but no less coruscating in its effect. Sexual encounters will be described more obliquely, too.

There is one other document written by Eça concerning the critique of Machado de Assis. Wisely left in manuscript, it is a truculent and ironic reply to Machado, dated 1879 and written in Bristol while he was consul there. [61] Simply put, this text was ostensibly designed to be a prologue to the third version of *The Sin of Father Amaro*, this final version published in 1880. It brings alive again the basic arguments of the Casino lecture: "It is only through the laborious observation of reality, the patient investigation of living materials, the Benedictine accumulation of notes and documents, that durable and strong works are constructed. . . . Modern art is all made of analysis, of experiment, of comparison. The inspiration of old which created a novel in 15 feverish nights is today an obsolete and false way to work. The new muse is the experimental science of phenomena." After defending himself rather dubiously against Machado's accusations of plagiarism, and pointing to Zola as "one of the most prodigious artists of our time," Eça will return to the exemplary art that served him so well in the final section of the Casino lecture—the art of Courbet as interpreted and transmitted to Eça by Proudhon. But in contrast to the Casino lecture usages, Eça will here make use of an artist he considers anathema, Jacques Louis David. Proudhon, in his *Du principe de l'Art* . . . , vol. III, condemns the depiction of Napoleon by

David. "Devant l'immensité de cet homme, l'Alpe semble s'abaisser et se reduire à la dimension d'une taupinée. On le voit, David a fait tout ce qu'il a pu pour idealiser son héros; il n'y manque même pas un certain romantisme." In the 1879 unpublished preface, Eça will arrange in the same manner an "idealistic" version of Napoleon, an ideal man soon to be un-horsed by Realistic scrutiny: "The idealist painter rolls up his sleeves and puts together this painting: a mountain pinnacle, and on this pinnacle a horse with the heroic proportions of Phidias's horse, rearing up on his hind legs. On this horse, Napoleon with arms and legs showing, looking like a Roman Caesar, with a crown of laurels on his head. In the background, clouds; below, a signature." The Realist, on the other hand, would have "read history, consulted the accounts of the time, studied the Alpine scenery, the uniforms of the epoch." He would have given us a "Napoleon on a mule, smothered in furs, with an otter skullcap and blue-tinted glasses because of the glare of the snow . . . suffering and defeated." Which would we have preferred, the first, who invented the scene or the second, who painted it for you? The idealist gave you a *falsifica-tion,* the naturalist a *verification.* The entire difference between Idealism and Naturalism is right there" (*OC,* III, 915). In the realm of literature, Eça seems to affirm the same conflicts be-tween the imaginative fantast and the detailed mimetic artist; thus, if an writer wishes to portray a young woman from the Lisbon bourgeoisie, the idealist will draw her according to his loose borrowings from Goethe, Lamartine, Balzac, and Chateaubriand. On the other hand, the realist who goes and observes her will "study her profile, manners, voice; he will examine her past, investigate how she was brought up, study the environment in which she lives, the influences over her, the books she reads, the gestures she uses" (*OC,* III, 916).

6. Portugal from a Distance

Eça de Queirós was an almost permanent exile from his country during his mature years. Diplomatic posts in Havana,

Newcastle-on-Tyne, and Bristol will finally culminate in his appointment to the consulate in Paris on September 20, 1886, a post he will continue to occupy until his death on August 16, 1900. Having completed the first two versions of *The Sin of Father Amaro* and *Cousin Bazilio* in Havana and Newcastle, Eça will begin to voice serious preoccupations about what effects this state of exile might have on his own writing. In essence, he asks himself: How can an ostensible Realist function in permanent exile from the reality to which he is allied and from which the literature is bound to evolve? It is an anguishing dilemma for Eça; in a letter of April 8, 1878, he describes the obstacles he is facing as he begins to plan the ambitious project of his *Cenas Portuguesas,* a projected series of some twelve novels. Some of these were published posthumously; others such as *The Maias* organically grew into one massive Balzacian portrait of Lisbon society. At any rate, the project was not going well in 1878, and the reasons are painfully clear: "I am convinced that an artist cannot work at a distance from surroundings in which his material for art are to be found. . . . I cannot depict Portugal in Newcastle. In order to write any page, any line, I have to make two violent efforts: disengage myself entirely from the impression which I get from the society around me and then evoke, by means of a tension of reminiscence, the society which is far away. This makes my characters less and less Portuguese, but they are not more English because of this; they are beginning to be *conventional;* they are converting into *a manner.* . . . So I find myself in an intellectual crisis: either I go back to the environment in which I can produce, by the experimental method—that is, return to Portugal—or I will have to surrender to a purely fantastical and humorous literature. It still remains to be seen whether or not I have an artistic intelligence" (*OC,* III, 520).

Eça will never return to Portugal except on generous vacations from the consulate. The dilemma expressed in the letter to Ramalho Ortigão will never be resolved in a satisfactory manner; quite the contrary, it will become more acute and torturous as the years pass. An increasingly disenchanted view of French society begins to enter Eça's critical writings, a view that reached its culmination after the second conviction of Captain Dreyfus, and this in turn will produce an increasingly idyllic and uncritical image of traditional Portuguese society. How does Eça justify this new "purely fantastical and humoristic literature"? What will the theoretical justifications be for this apparently inexplicable "rebound" from the now abandoned theories of humor, caricature, and satire? As always with Eça, there will be considerable sleight of hand, much evasion. A typical document that symbolizes this volte face is his prologue to *The Mandarin* written to the editor of *La Revue Universelle* and dated 1884. This gives a precious insight into Eça's indeterminacy. *The Mandarin* will be of interest to the editor, Eça avers, not because it reflects in any way what used to be known as "analytical and experimental" techniques. Quite the contrary, "this work of mine is concerned with dream and not with reality, since it is invented rather than observed; it seems to me [therefore] to represent faithfully the most natural and spontaneous aspects of the Portuguese spirit." [62]

Keeping in mind Eça's enthusiastic predilections and condemnations announced with such passion over the years since the Casino lecture, it is difficult to imagine a greater critical transfiguration than this. True verisimilitude to Portuguese society lies not in the factual description of the country and its people but in invention and dream—*this* is the only route to the Portuguese soul: "Minds so conditioned must necessarily feel removed from what is characterized as reality, analysis, experimentation or objective certainty. Fantasy, in all forms from song to caricature, is what attracts us; thus in our art we have produced above all lyricists and satirists. Either we have our eyes raised to the stars while we listen to the pulsing of our hearts, or if we by chance lower our eyes to look at our worldly surroundings, we can only laugh bitterly. We live by emotion, not by reason."

Eça cannot deny that he and the Coimbra generation were engaged in a revolt against precisely *this* view of the Portuguese "soul," what with its fatal marriage of nostalgia, *saudade,* and unbridled rhetoric. But for Eça de Queirós in 1884, things have changed. He remembers himself as having taken up the cudgels for Naturalism, not out of inner impulse toward any kind of literary, artistic, or political reform, but because "we imitate France in everything . . . our whole civilization, especially in Lisbon, gives the impression of having arrived the day before in packing cases from Bordeaux." Slaves of an alien aesthetic, he and his generation took on the trappings of Naturalism, "not out of natural inclination, but out of a feeling of literary duty—I almost said of public duty. For the honor of modern Portuguese letters, we tried to put in our works much observation, much 'humanity'; but in studying our neighbors . . . it turned out that we soon regretted those times when it was permissible, without being old-fashioned, to celebrate handsome knights in shining armor. The time for wandering in the woods of fantasy was gone—alas!"

The Mandarin will be a work cast in another mold. It will, "at least for a single small volume," be a happy occasion for a release from "reality, modernity and banality, . . . the inconvenient submission to truth, the torture of analysis, the impertinent tyranny of reality." Having finished the work and after having corrected the proofs, Eça announced that he "may get back on the sidewalk and resume the serious study of man and his eternal misery. Happy? No, my dear Sir—resigned." [63] This sense of "resignation" to the pressures of reality is a key critical moment for Eça. From now on, his advocacy of Realism and/or Naturalism will become increasingly tempered by an ever expanding mythification of Portugal, its people, its history, its society. In other words, he seems to suggest that if we are to be faithful to the "reality" that is Portugal as it is, we must adjust thereby, on the grounds of fidelity to "the facts," our descriptive practice to include formerly scorned purple patches and pathetic fallacies. Too, Eça will begin to acknowledge, both in his readings and in his own writing, a more passive response to reality. Two years after having finished the prologue to *The Mandarin*, Eça will write a highly complimentary prologue to a book of short sketches entitled *Azulejos*, written by Count Arnoso. This prologue, dated June 12, 1886, presents us with an even greater modification of his earlier views. The years of exile are beginning to have their effect.

This alternative tendency in Eça marks the beginning of a certain softening of critical rigor toward Portuguese reality. This has its charm and allure—it is a graceful kind of idealism—but it does tend to erode his formerly unswerving complicity with what is real and contemporaneous around him. One does sense a growing impoverishment in his constricted world view, accompanied by an expansive and highly illusory reevaluation of Portugal. But maybe not—this is possibly too gross a characterization for a process and a "conversion" which elaborates itself fitfully over a period of fifteen years until the author's death in 1900. For now at least, in June 1886, Eça derives a newly found satisfaction from Arnoso's descriptive abilities, his "fugitive, winged and caressing way of painting things in *blue and white*. Without you [Arnoso] being alien to the essence of life and reality, it does not seem to be in your tastes and temperament to dig down to the core with the acrid curiosity of passion . . . you well understand the usefulness and the beauty of going down to the somber essence of life, of uncovering the rhythm which determines everything; but you rightly consider it more attractive to remain on the surface" (*OC,* II, 1438). Arnoso, as seen by Eça, combines "a tenuous and resigned melancholy" with a "timid and faded, but still visible brand of irony." The book "combines poetic grace with human truth," and it "satisfies the need for idealism which we all have in our hearts," while still fulfilling the "dry curiosity toward the real which our positivist education gave us" (*OC,* II, 1440). Eça then begins to speak of art in a way he would never have permitted himself to do in the days of the Casino lecture or the various versions of *The Sin of Father Amaro.* Art, he says, poeticizes our existence; it is a permanent part of us; it offers to us "the only possibility of realizing life's deepest desire—which is to be not completely extinguished by death." Art gives us fame, too—"that relative immortality." Finally, art extends our temporal passions and beliefs; it is relived in the imagination of the viewer, the listener, or the reader. This is the promise that art gives to all artists: "Art is everything because only it is permanent—and all the rest is nothing" (*OC,* 1441). The eternity of a people lies in a single book; we have all forgotten the names of the ministers and the politicians of France in 1856, but we know everything about Emma Bovary, even the kind of dress she put on to meet Léon at Rouen.

Eça's gradual disenchantment with the novelistic possibilities of any kind of dogmatic Realistic practice will also lead him to reconsider his characterological system—typical of his insights into certain "types" in Portugal is his discussion of *o brasileiro*. This is the character, much abused by the Romantics, who leaves Portugal as the reluctant and melancholic emigrant but who returns to Portugal in a few years with patent leather shoes, finely dressed, and confident; in due course, this character builds an ostentatious palace, entertains the local politicians and the clergy, generally manipulating the locals so that he may be dubbed a baron. Eça now recognizes that such type casting of the Romantics was not due to their repugnance against the class system or the riches of society; rather, it was a dramatic exploitation of Romantic dualism, where the soul implacably was divided from the body. The same man who was characterized as the "sad emigré" as he left Portugal is quickly subsumed into the gross *brasileiro* upon his return. Eça will insist that "the man who sweats" is not automatically vulgar and coarse and that the "poetic man" is not inevitably superior, aesthetically or personally. "The *brasileiro* (who is as Portuguese as *vinho verde*) should be saved for literature from the spiteful hands of the Romantics. There is no other way for a writer who wishes to grasp the social implications represented by the phenomenon of *o brasileiro* but to break down the conventional image . . . and to make him a human being again who suggests a substantial chapter of recent Portuguese experience." [64]

In arguing for the destruction of the idea of a literary type in Portugal and at the same time reconsidering the true nature of the character of the nation, Eça does bring about an unusual change in the function of character and humor in his novels, above all the writings during the final Paris period of 1888 to 1900. Both as an essayist and as a novelist, a suave and gentle brand of imaginative pastoralism will begin to suffuse his work; the world of the machine is gradually made into the world of the garden—Portugal becomes a distant and luminously envisioned *locus amoenus.*

Dürer's *Melancholia* serves as Eça's emblem for his growing disenchantment with many things—civilization itself, the city, all knowledge, all science, and rational inquiry. In a late essay of 1891 entitled "The Decline of Laughter," he will adumbrate a series of variations on this theme, criticizing "the man of thought who constantly seeks the realities behind appearances because of the fanaticism of his critical and scientific education. This is the man who sees the sky only as a complicated combination of gases; he uncovers in the soul only a crude functioning of organs. He knows what portion of phosphate each tear contains, and while contemplating two splendorous eyes full of love, can only think of the two hollows in the skull behind those eyes. This is the man for whom all heroic sacrifice can be explained by egotistical motives, . . . who loses a dream with each step, and who finally doesn't know where he is going and who he is . . . this man can only be a melancholic" (*OC*, II, 1479–80). Eça then considers the cosmic disillusion of Dürer's figure and then exhorts him with a simple but nonetheless ominous counsel: "Abandon your laboratory, go back to Nature, don't complicate your life with so many machines, don't split hairs with so much analysis, live the good life of a provident father who tills the land. If you do this, you will reconquer the august domain of laughter, with health and liberty" (*OC*, II, 1480).

These apparently innocuous recommendations signal a radical alteration in Eça's world view. The word "civilization" comes to be used in a pejorative way. It not only takes on echoes of a hypersensitive and overly cultivated soul, but it directly describes Eça's feelings toward the city—his sense of inauthenticity, idle desperation, and tedium—the latter the inevitable result of scientific progress and growing self-consciousness, so he will say. Eça will abandon diagnosis and those magnificent pictorial dramatizations of Lisbon life which culminated in *The Maias.* His later novels will represent a literature of stasis, where the values tend to evolve into undynamic, possibly uncritical structures. This process can be traced, as we are about to do in this study, if Eça's work is examined chronologically, from *The Sin of Father Amaro* and *Cousin Bazilio* to *The Maias*, and on through *The Illustrious House of Ramires* and *The City and the Mountains*. In the latter two works, and in such essays as the above-mentioned prologue to *Azulejos*, "The Decline of Laughter" or "Positivism and Idealism," Eça's imagination has reordered itself. Formerly, we might say that he was intent upon fusing social observation and imaginative invention; now, and all through the 1890s, he begins to give way to the temptations of the religious and historical romance in literature, one that is profoundly nostalgic and conservative in its imaginative elaborations. What was formerly a hateful brand of stagnation and intellectual torpor is now viewed more positively, let us say; it is a model of political and cultural stability. Eça's imagination took on a static cast as he became a pessimist and even a quietist in his relations to the world about him. He was, of course, profoundly conscious of his own anachronistic imagination, and will even turn this anomaly into a seriocomic historical romance—*The Illustrious House of Ramires*—especially as this "reverted" imagination contrasted with the immediate and pressing world of society in turmoil. *This* is the spectacle which he became increasingly incapable of witnessing, even from the enclave at Neuilly. Instead of the acerbic and even venomous tone of the earlier novels, we sense a cast of the imagination that has arrived comfortably at a resting place, one that instinctively sought solace from the flux of the contemporaneous in the past. But this is a brand of the past that has very peculiar and private meanings to Eça in his decline—it is rigorously preindustrial, prebourgeois and semifeudal, intimately related to the values of a landed aristocracy—that is to say, the values that he was to share with the ancient lineage of the family of Emilia de Resende, whom he was to marry in 1886. This is a strange sight for all students of Eça; here we have the contented diplomat in Paris, repentant of his earlier barbs and arrows slung at Portuguese society, now an aging pastoralist, aloof as much to the Paris of the 1890s as he is to the reality of a Portugal in social ferment.

The past *was* a fatal invitation to Eça toward the end. Similar to many neopastoralist exercises which ally themselves to possibly reactionary political stances, Eça's social vision of Portugal was a redone and artificial vision of the past, distant in time and space, with the violence drained out of it. In this sense, it was all too available for whatever historicist fantasies he wished to create out of the materials of the past. In this sense, the past has no defense at all. The Portugal of his imagination, lovingly recalled and reconstituted in his study in Neuilly, has the same aura of the ideal domain as did the cosmopolis that was Paris, as imagined by a languorous and bored Eça de Queirós long ago in Lisbon, Leiria, and Évora. The distance created the ideal; the residence in the ideal brought disenchantment.

With the whole problem of the Portuguese national character weighing increasingly upon his exiled consciousness, Eça began to transform his vision of Portugal into a reelaboration of the pastoral mode, one which might be related to ideas of permanence, order, status quo, and suggestive also of moral and political retrenchment.[65] In French literature, the city/country dichotomy was comically summed up by Flaubert in his *Dictionnaire des idées reçues*—"People in the country better than those in towns. Envy their lot. In the country, anything goes—sloppy clothes, practical jokes, etc." [66] Unfortunately, such an author as Maurice Barrès would remain supremely unconscious of the imbecility of such commonplaces. In his *Les Déracinés* (1895), the two kingdoms conflict in the incarnations of uprooted, virginal students from Lorraine who meet their fate in the moral sewer that is Barrès's vision of Paris. It was André Gide who put the matter to rest in his review of the novel, where he neatly pointed out the banality of these mechanical contradictions and the infantile nature of such antiurban mythologies. As Gide indicated, the novel itself could not have existed had not Barrès brought himself and his characters into the fragmentary and inciting world that was Paris—"Peut-être pourrait-on mesurer la valeur d'un homme au degré de depaysement (physique ou intellectuel) qu'il est capable de maitriser . . . ce qui exige de l'homme une gymnastique d'adaption . . . quant aux faibles: Enracinez! Enracinez!" [67] This might be fruitfully applied to the strange process that so insistently accosted Eça during the

Neuilly years. Isolated in Paris and magnetized by an increasingly archaic vision of nonurban Portugal, he ends his days by limiting to an extreme degree the intuitive richness he had so laboriously achieved with the amplitude and nondogmatic scope of such a work as *The Maias*. In Gide's terms, late Eça was *faible*.

If we take the last two novels as an organic whole, it might be possible to understand how the pastoral imagination, in its reductive drive toward what is characteristic in the Portuguese national character, had to exclude, by some intrinsic necessity, desire and sexual passion in the characters. In the last two works, desire becomes suffused with the historical vision. The subversion of social order that passion brings is extirpated, above all because Eça has intentionally abandoned the world of the analytical novel and has cast his luck with the more fanciful possibilities of historical and pastoral romance, where the grand perversions and horrors of *The Maias* could not possibly be accommodated.

Another matter: his late occasional writings evidence a critical reevaluation of organized religion; to be more specific, the role of progressive social action within such bodies as the Church of England or the Roman Catholic church. As always, Eça himself will have nothing to say that is clearly revelatory on this subject, but it is easy to see that the rich variety of references to the church in his late essays contrasts notably with the near absence of such discussions in earlier essays, with the possible exception of the inevitably anticlerical references that accompanied the writing of *The Sin of Father Amaro*. A good example of Eça's altered motivations might be his essay entitled "Positivism and Idealism" of 1893, a work which succinctly and definitively notes the demise of the whole political and literary ethic which governed so much his own and the Coimbra generation's responses to society. The youth of today, he says, are engaged in a "reaction not only against politics, but against the general structural of society, as it was created by scientific positivism" (*OC*, II, 1496). The essay intensifies its polemic as it enters into a discussion of the increasingly negative response of all readers to the tenets of Naturalism, all while coolly dispatching the cherished dogmas of the Casino lecture: "In literature, we are witnessing the disrepute of Naturalism. The experimental novel, of positivistic observation, all constructed on the basis of documents, has come to an end (that is, if it ever existed except in theory) . . . everyone now prefers the novel of the imagination, of sentimental or humoristic psychology, of archaeological (and prehistoric) resurrection. Even the novel of cape and sword is in vogue, those with marvelous imbroglios, just like in the days of D'Artagnan" (*OC*, II, 1496). Things have changed in the same way in the realm of philosophy. The free thinkers are on the way out, undergoing as they are a crisis of late-nineteenth-century rationalism.

Why so much disillusion and disenchantment with a world that was so energetically empowered with revolutionary pragmatism just a few decades before? For Eça, this is a problem that goes well beyond the precincts of literature. This new mood is, in his view, healthily retrograde; it is a return to the first principles of a newly revitalized life of and for the spirit. In a word, the young generation is in revolt, not just against Zola, but against Comte; Guizot; the industrial revolution; and above all, the ultimate enemy of religion and the Bible, Charles Darwin and that nefarious work entitled *The Origin of Species*. The message of this Tolstoyan generation is clear enough; this is Eça's formulation:

> It is another and renewed desire to discover something more in this complicated universe than might and matter, a desire to give to civic duty a higher sanction than that furnished by the civil code, to conceive of an exalted principle which would promote and realize in the world that fraternity of souls and equality of property which neither Jacobinism nor political economy has been able to achieve. . . . In sum, this new generation senses the need for the divine. Certainly, science did not break its promises, but it is also true that the telephone, the phonograph, the combustion engine . . . are not sufficient to give peace and to make these young souls happy. Furthermore, they

suffer from that lowly and zoological level to which science has reduced man, deprived by it of the ancient grandeur of his origins and of his privileges of spiritual immortality. (*OC,* II, 1498)

In this indirect defense of the younger generation, Eça is attempting to formulate a response to his conclusions regarding the theory of Naturalism in general, and Darwinism in particular. This response, which has an urgency that suggests not only sympathy but overt acceptance, is related to his growing horror of Darwin and the attendant determination to block off the spiritual cancer that led his mentor, Antero de Quental, to commit suicide some two years before, in 1891. In the necrological note composed in memory of Antero, Eça will note that the "Naturalistic imagination" can only "affirm that life, in its empirical form, is the murky struggle of dark forces. In its philosophical and intellectual form, life is nothing more than the egoistical contemplation of these instinctive struggles. Therefore there is nothing except the void, confusion, and universal uselessness" (*OC,* II, 1553).

The falsity of Naturalist theory resided in its misunderstanding of the role of the imagination in human life, Eça will suggest. The rebellion of the young is caused above all by the "brutal and unrelenting manner with which positivistic science treated the imagination, which is just as inseparable and legitimate a companion of man as is his reason." This treatment ended in a complete divergence between reason and imagination. Man was left shut up in a bright, cold laboratory with a frigid wife named Reason. Man was bereft; he began to pine and "dream of that other companion, so jolly and inventive, so full of grace and luminous impulse." And so we have a revolt which is not a revolt at all, but a spiritualist reaction, and Eça is a willing participant. The attractions of Christianity are related to the solace given by poetry and dream. Man needs his dreams, insists Eça, above all because reality has lost the possibility of being real and poetic at the same time, such is the bifurcation imposed upon man by the ethic of Darwin and Bounderby— the reality of the industrialized urban nightmare so carefully registered by Zola and Dickens. Above all, the blame must be laid upon the modern city, which is the source of his victimization, his sterility, his sense of nostalgia and loss: "The strident tumult of the cities, the heightening caused by a cerebral life, the immensity of industrial power, the brutality of the democracies, all these things necessarily lead the most sensitive and imaginative men to seek out the refuge of religious quietism— or at least to try to find in dream an alleviation from the oppression of reality" (*OC*, II, 1501).

Christian faith a la Schleiermacher comes to signify one possibility for the anguished and tortured spirit of the times. The world will be refreshed and purified by this "strong wind of idealism." As for literature, it will gain a more transcendental, even metaphysical view of reality; it will give a mystical touch "to us, makers of prose or verse; it will be a positive benefit and a great consolation" (*OC*, II, 1501).

Eça will touch on the realm of the spirit on many occasions in the next few years. He will record a visit to a spiritualist center in Paris and will pay high compliments to Pope Leo XIII for the spirit of Christian social action called for in his encyclical *Rerum Novarum* (1891). Too, Eça will make a passing acquaintance with Turgenev, Dostoevski, and Tolstoy by means of Count Melchior de Vogüé's *Le Roman Russe,* as recorded in the essay "O Bock Ideal." In many ways, Eça's newly critical assault on Realism and Naturalism and his increasing sympathy toward the church may well be due to his fervent acceptance of some of the key thoughts to be found in the brilliant and highly reactionary prologue to *Le Roman Russe,* one of the most lucid and amusing assaults on Realism and Naturalism in literature.[68] This prologue might be worth talking about for a moment, since Eça seems to be in such sympathy with much of its argument. For de Vogüé, Realism and democracy are synonymous: "The new art seeks to imitate nature in its unconsciousness, its moral indifference, its lack of choice . . . it expresses the triumph of the collectivity over the individual, of the mob over the hero, of the relative over the absolute." In this 'century of microbes,' mechanistic rationalism is everywhere to be seen, reality has been scrutinized and satirized; evolution has triumphed. There reigns a veritable *ivresse* of science and the dominion of fact. And yet, we are now in a moment of disenchantment—ignorance has reappeared in different guises, political reform has done little to give people greater liberty, oppressed as they are by 'natural laws' and 'material fatalities.' Man seeks recourse from such mechanistic oppression . . . "the old instincts come alive again; man seeeks above himself a superhuman power for recourse; but no One is there anymore." With the exaltation of the individual comes the inevitable accompaniment, caused by a very instructive contradiction: universal doubt. De Vogüé envisions a Christian revolution, a divinization of what was formerly a wholly dogmatic, terrestrial political program: "The world has been subject to a ferment for nineteen centuries—the gospel—and the latest revolution emanating from that gospel is the triumph of it and the definitive arrival of the Messiah." Within the realm of any intellectual activity that might be termed 'realist,' a fatal error has blinded all its practitioners—they are ignorant of the "mystery which subsists beyond rational explanations." Man is a duality; the divinity gave life to inert matter, and that divine breath is the Spirit itself, the element that is both verifiable and impenetrable, something which makes all rational explanations of reality insufficient. For de Vogüé, no greater testimony can be had than the work of Flaubert himself. He is the exemplar of the exhaustion of any post-Romantic literary ideology. Flaubert verifies and affirms, for all to see, "the inanity of the pathetic idols to which literature so indiscriminately offered itself: human passion elevated to the level of the divine, the reformation of criminals, the liberalism of Béranger, the revolutionary humanitarianism of 1848." We find ourselves, not surprisingly, "like squirrels in a cage," at the end of the nineteenth century with that one unique and "grotesque Iliad of nihilism, *Bouvard et Pécuchet.*" This is the work which tells us where progress, science, and immortal principles have brought us. For our redemption from this morass, we must acknowledge "a higher grace," a "sense of the divine." It is only by recognizing the transcendental nature of man that the new generation can, "tired of puerile inventions and hungry for the truth," truly find the Way and the Life.[69]

Eça's peculiar attention to this work is revealing of the directions of his spirit. There is no discussion whatsoever in "O Bock Ideal" of the literary import of de Vogüé's magnificently orchestrated attacks against democracy. Eça is interested only in the religious ramifications of de Vogüé's antirationalist and antiscientist bias. "The so-called 'Light of Science,' ever brighter and higher, only serves . . . to show us how infinite and inaccessible is the enormous metaphysical darkness which surrounds it." After defining the new spirit of the age as having been impelled by a "muffled spiritualist reaction against the materialism of the times," Eça repeats with considerable fervor de Vogüé's most messianic pronouncement: only the spirit of the Gospels "will give to the democracies that exalted moral direction, that spirit of goodwill and sacrifice, those forms of love and renunciation, which are the only things that can bring the classes together, protect the interests of justice, and combat the tyranny of money and bring to fruition the ideal of equality on earth."

Eça then repeats de Vogüé's basic preoccupation: Who or what is this authority which might transform the world in an age of materialism? It must be the church—the Roman Catholic church. Eça openly confesses to his newly found sympathy for the social mission of the church: "Who else except the church would be capable of giving a divine mission to contemporary democracy? Doesn't the church emanate from the people, isn't it run by the people, living with the people, in perpetual communion, thinking and feeling with them? Isn't the church the greatest *disinterested* entity? Because it was born in the Temple, ejecting the moneychangers—it was there that it expressed its complete disdain for money [capital]." [70]

Puttering through the bookstalls on the Seine, increasingly debilitated by chronic diarrhea and stomach upsets, Eça's writing toward the end will be subjugated to an imaginative reworking of this final resolution of his own political and literary quandaries. Examining his *processo* from the Casino lecture on, there are a few constants, but they are *very* constant—one of them must be his progressive disenchantment with France, and, even worse, the *idea* of France, intimately related as it was to his own increasing distaste for the egalitarian values promulgated by the Revolution's example. Although he was able to solve paradoxically his increasing distaste for France's example by his own imposed isolation in Neuilly, Eça's imaginative directions turned toward the archaic universe that was his *idea* of Portugal. The progressive and even revolutionary instincts of his youth transfigured themselves into a Franciscan benevolence toward the world.[71] As he gradually lost the socialist illusions of his youth, they were replenished only fitfully by his increasingly diffuse concept of a fictionalized Portugal. As a reader of Eça has observed, "Neuilly was the sepulcher in which the robust personality of this great revolutionary of Portuguese letters began to decompose."[72]

Notes

1. The best discussion is to be found in José-Augusto França, *Le Romantisme au Portugal* (Paris: Editions Klincksieck, 1975), pp. 125–29.
2. Ibid., p. 27.
3. A. H. de Oliveira Marques, *History of Portugal.* (New York: Columbia University Press, 1976), II, p. 19.
4. Ibid., p. 20.
5. Ibid., p. 25.
6. Ibid., p. 33: ". . . leurs amis idéologiques étaient devenus les ennemis de leur patrie."
7. The tragic nature of João VI's indecision and its cataclysmic effect upon nineteenth-century Portuguese history was best summed up by the Portuguese historian J. P. Oliveira Martins, whose two-volume *Portugal Contemporâneo* (8th ed. [Lisboa: Guimarães Editora, 1976], p. 33) begins with this stunning opening paragraph:

1—*A morte de D. João VI*

S. M. fora a Belém comer uma merenda. Era nos primeiros dias de Março. Quando voltou ao palácio achou-se, à noite, mal—cãibras, sintomas de epilepsia—Vieram médicos: o barão de Alvaiázere e o valido cirurgião Aguiar. No dia seguinte (5) o estado do enfermo piorou, e o rei decidiu-se a despir de si o pesado encargo do Governo. A 7, a *Gazeta* publicava o decreto nomeando a Regência, presidida pela infanta D. Isabel Maria cuja bondade merecia as graças particulares do infeliz pai. <<Esta minha imperial e real determinação, afirmava o decreto do dia 6, regulará também para o caso em que Deus seja servido chamar-me à sua santa glória, enquanto o legítimo herdeiro e sucessor desta coroa não der as suas providências . . .>> Mas quem era esse legítimo herdeiro? D. Pedro, o brasileiro? D. Miguel, no seu desterro de Viena? Nâo o dizia o rei moribundo, que toda a vida se achara indeciso, e acabava como tinha existido, sem uma afirmação de vontade, entre flatos, na impotência de uma morte oportuna.

8. de Oliveira Marques, *History*, II, pp. 58–61.
9. I am following the schematic description in ibid., pp. 54–77. The quotation is to be found on p. 53.
10. Good insights into Eça's extraordinary grandfather, Joaquim José de Queiroz e Almeida, can be found in Rocha Martins, *Os Românticos Antepassados de Eça de Queirós* (Lisboa: Inquérito, 1945). Having been a magistrate in Brazil during the early 1820's, the grandfather brought back to Portugal a retinue of servants (some of them former black slaves) who were to care for the infant Eça during the first five years of his life until the grandfather's death in 1850 at the age of seventy-six. Eça's father did not marry Eça's hard-hearted mother until four years after the birth of the child; he did not recognize Eça as his legitimate son until Christmas Day 1885, just six weeks before the *mariage de raison* on February 10, 1886, a ceremony which *neither parent chose to attend*. Eça's strong sense of attachment to his grandfather over the years was hardly equalled by his troubled feelings toward both his mother and his father. The relationship was formal, not to say chilly. The grandfather may well have served as the model for the affectionate portrait of Afonso da Maia in Eça's masterpiece, *The Maias* (1888). In sum, Eça's childhood was that of a familial outcast; there are echoes of this emotional trauma throughout his work. See Chapter IV, Note 125.
11. de Oliveira Marques, *History*, II, p. 39.
12. All quotations translated by the author are taken from the three-volume edition *Obras de Eça de Queiroz* (Pôrto; Lello e Irmão, 1966), hereafter referred to as *OC*. When other translations of Eça's works into English are used, they will be so noted. There is another complete edition in the process of publication, done with the highest degree of scholarly scruple. Unfortunately, it is still incomplete as of this writing. I refer to *Obra Completa*, Organização Geral, Introdução, Explicações Marginais e Apêndices

de João Gaspar Simões; Fixação do texto de Helena Cidade Moura (Rio de Janeiro: José Aguilar Editora, 1970).

13. See the minute and exhaustive examination of the relation between Balzac and Eça in the essay entitled "Imitação Capital," to be found in António Coimbra Martins, *Ensaios Queirosianos* (Lisboa: Publicações Europa-America, 1967), pp. 289–378. In his short essay on *A Capital,* Valery Larbaud not only gives us a succinct résumé of the plot but tells of the delights of discovery: "Je l'ai acheté [*A Capital*]; je pensais en lire, à coups de dictionnaire, de dix à vingt pages chaque jour; au bout de quatre jours je l'avais terminé: 573 pages de texte absorbées avec voracité, sans une panne, sans une seconde de découragement. Je savais lire le portugais! Et je venais de lire l'oeuvre d'un maître, d'un des grands romanciers européens du XIX e siècle." Valery Larbaud, "Écrit dans une cabine du sud-express," *Oeuvres,* ed. G. Jean-Aubry and R. Mallet (Paris: Gallimard, 1957), p. 949.

14. There is a good discussion of this point in George Steiner, *Tolstoy or Dostoyevsky,* rev. ed. (London: Penguin Books, 1967), p. 36ff.

15. Ibid.

16. "[With the second condemnation of Dreyfus], the last but still persistent remains of my old Latin love for France died. . . . Its purported Humanitarianism and Messianic ideal of social justice is a mere *réclame,* constructed by Romantic literature. . . . In no other nation can one find such a *large mass* of people who so unanimously desire the condemnation of an innocent." "Letter to Domício da Gama," September 28, 1899, in *OC,* III, 671–72.

17. As cited in João Medina, *Eça de Queiroz e o Seu Tempo* (Lisboa: Livros Horizonte, 1972), p. 57.

18. "Letter to Oliveira Martins," April 26, 1894, in *OC,* III, 635.

19. The "Forgotten Prose" (*Prosas Esquecidas*) now comprises five volumes, and must be read in addition to the "official" three-volume edition published by Lello e Irmão of Pôrto: Eça de Queirós, *Prosas Esquecidas,* I–V, edição organizada por Alberto Machado da Rosa (Lisboa: Editorial Presença, 1965–66). Hereafter, these texts are referred to as *PE.*

20. Medina, *Eça de Queiroz e o Seu Tempo,* pp. 78–79.

21. *PE.* II, 273–74.

22. I am indebted here and elsewhere to the excellent overview of Peter Demetz, "Eça de Queiróz [sic] as a Literary Critic," *Comparative Literature,* XIX, 4, pp. 289–307.

23. Luiz de Magalhães, "Uma Página Anónyma de Eça de Queiroz," *In Memoriam* (Lisboa: Parceria Antonio Maria Pereira, 1922), p. 256.

24. See Demetz, "Eça de Queiróz as a Literary Critic," p. 291.

25. Ibid., pp. 296–97.
26. The best index of the impact of Antero upon Eça de Queirós may be suggested by noting the passionate advocacy of Antero's example as contained in Eça's own necrological note, now entitled "Antero de Quental," and to be found in the collection of essays *Notas Contemporâneas* (*OC*, II, 1540–65).
27. An exhaustive documentary study of this topic, the so-called *Questão Coimbra*, is to be found in *Bom Senso e Bom Gosto* (Textos integrais da polémica), Recolha, notas e bibliografia por Maria José Marinho (Lisboa: Portugália Editora, 1966–70), I–IV.
28. João Gaspar Simões, *Vida e Obra de Eça de Queirós*, Nova edição, refundida e acrescentada com um índice onomástico de toda a obra do escritor (Lisboa: Livraria Bertrand, 1973), p. 137.
29. The controversy is eloquently aired by Alberto Machado da Rosa, in his impassioned "Nota Bibliográfica" to *PE*, V, 9–155; above all, 48–50.
30. Demetz, "Eça de Queiróz as a Literary Critic," pp. 293, 295.
31. Ibid., p. 295. See also Mario Sacramento, *Eça de Queirós: Uma Estética da Ironia* (Coimbra: Coimbra Editora Limitada, 1945), 52–57.
32. The full title of this key text is *O Egipto: Notas de Viagem*, edited by Eça's son José Maria and finally published in 1926. It is contained in *OC*, III, 673–820. See also Jean Girodon, *"O Egypto* d'Eça de Queiroz," *Bulletin des Études Portugaises*, XXII (1959–60), pp. 129–86, where Eça's heavy borrowings from books on the Near East variously authored by Théophile Gautier, Gérard de Nerval, Edmond About, Maxime du Camp, and others are convincingly documented. Eça's travel diary is, in many ways, a record of his voyage through books bought and borrowed.
33. See Enid Starkie, *Flaubert* (Harmondsworth, England: Penguin Books, 1971), chap. XIV, "The Eastern Trip."
34. Recently, Eça's notes and other sketchy materials from his trip to the Near East have been published as *Folhas Soltas* (Palestina, Alta Síria, "Sir Galahad," Os Santos) (Pôrto: Lello e Irmão, 1966).
35. Gaspar Simões, *Vida e Obra*, p. 222.
36. Ibid.
37. The student of Eça's exoticism is urged to consult the extraordinarily perceptive work of Ernesto Guerra da Cal, *Lenguaje Estilo de Eça de Queiroz*, I, *Elementos Básicos* (Coimbra: Por ordem da universidade, 1954), esp. subsection 2 of chap. VI, "El exotismo histórico y la cultura cosmopolita. El exotismo geográfico y el tema viajero."
38. Fidelino de Figueiredo, *História da Literatura Realista (1871–1900)* (São Paulo: Editora Anchieta S.A., 1946), p. 19. The principles behind the Casino lectures, and probably the choice of lecturers,

was formulated by Antero in collaboration with his friend José Fontana, a peripatetic Socialist who had aided Karl Marx in the founding of the First International (London, 1864). Fontana may well have served as a foil for Eça's satire on revolutionary programs in the aforementioned novelistic gloss on Balzac's *Illusions Perdues, A Capital*. See César Oliveira, *O Socialismo em Portugal (1850–1900)*, Pôrto: Edicão do autor, 1973. *A Capital* is to be found in *OC*, III, 19–285.

39. Bernard Weinberg, *French Realism: The Critical Practice, 1830–1870* (New York: The Modern Language Association, 1937), pp. 102–3. See also the brief and succinct history of the term "Naturalism" in Levin, *The Gates of Horn*, pp. 71–73.

40. Eça's lecture is available to us only through journalistic notes, which have been collated and synthesized in Antônio Salgado, Jr., *História das Conferências do Cassino* (Lisboa: n.p., 1930[?]). Similar résumés are given in Antônio Cabral, *Eça de Queiroz: A Sua Vida e a Sua Obra*, 3d ed. (Lisboa: Livraria Bertrand, 1945), pp. 148–53. The government's view of this "lecture series" is best dramatized by the ensuing parliamentary debate, now available in *As Conferências do Casino no Parlamento:* Apresentaçao e notas por José-Augusto França (Lisboa: Livros Horizonte, 1973). It is impossible to resist quoting the marquis of Avila, minister of the realm and principal instigator of the ban. Here is his rationale:

If the illustrious Deputy were in Paris, and had the responsibility of the government against the Commune, he would understand that it is a question of combating an enemy which declared war against the family, society, and God; an enemy which set fire to monuments, libraries, the collections which represented the progress of civilization and the arts, that utilized kerosene to obtain its objectives . . . and when they cannot make a frontal attack upon a society, recur to lectures (*conferências*) by means of associations. This is an enemy which desires the abolition of marriage, family, property, and which preaches atheism. (França, *As Conferências* . . . , p. 100)

Eça's most underrated work, *O Conde de Abranhos*, may well be a fictional portrait of the Marquis of Avila and others of his mentality. See *OC*, III, pp. 287–405.

41. Salgado, *História das Conferências*, p. 53

42. Ibid., p. 54.

43. "Emma tests each episode in her life in the light of the language she has learned from books." Leo Bersani, *Balzac to Beckett* (New York: Oxford University Press, 1970), p. 142.

44. Ibid., p. 143.
45. Harry Levin, *The Gates of Horn* (New York: Oxford University Press, 1963), p. 13.
46. Ibid., p. 10.
47. Leo Bersani, *A Future for Astyanax* (Boston: Little, Brown and Company, 1976), p. 96.
48. Salgado, *História das Conferências*, p. 56.
49. See the excellent analysis of Eça's views of Courbet in Jean Girodon, "Eça et Courbet," *Bulletin des Études Portugaises*, XXIV (1963), pp. 89–101. The Zola quotation is on page 93 of this article.
50. Alberto de Oliveira, *Eça de Queiroz; Páginas de Memórias* (Lisboa: Portugália Editora, 1945[?]), pp. 55–56.
51. The definitive treatment of this subject is to be found in Sacramento, *Eça de Queirós*. See note 31, above.
52. This whole paragraph owes much to Bersani, *A Future*, pp. 51–73ff.
53. Ibid. pp. 52–53.
54. Sacramento, *Eça de Queirós*, p. 80.
55. This statement rests on some conclusions in Robert Garis, *The Dickens Theatre* (Oxford: At the Clarendon Press, 1965), pp. 33–34.
56. *Novas Cartas Inéditas de Eça de Queiroz*, ed. Alvaro Moreyra e Bricio de Abreu (Rio de Janeiro: Editora Albra, 1940), pp. 7–8.
57. Ibid., p. 49.
58. The article was originally published in *O Cruzeiro*. The following comments use the transcription of Alberto Machado da Rosa, in his *Eça, Discípulo de Machado?*, 2d ed. (Lisboa: Editora Presença, 1964), pp. 209–23.
59. As quoted in Simões, *Vida e Obra*, p. 398.
60. *Novas Cartas Inéditas*, pp. 14–15.
61. This long essay has been reprinted in *OC*, III, 907–16, under the title "Crítica e Polémica: Idealismo e Realismo" (A propósito da 2ª edição de *O Crime do Padre Amaro*).
62. Eça de Queiroz, *The Mandarin and Other Stories*, trans. Richard Franko Goldman (Athens: Ohio University Press, 1965), p. 4. It goes without saying that the terms of my discussion owe much to Harry Levin's *The Gates of Horn* (New York: Oxford University Press, 1963), especially Chapter II, "Romance and Realism."
63. Ibid., pp. 4–7.
64. Demetz, "Eça de Queiróz as a Literary Critic," p. 302.
65. This might be termed "Reactionary Pastoralism," following the lead of John Seeleye, which contrasts itself notably with "Revolutionary Pastoralism," "posited on a salvational, mystical, transcendental notion of a future, not a present state." See his "Some

Green Thoughts on a Green Theme," *TriQuarterly* (Winter/ Spring 1972), pp. 576–638.

66. Gustave Flaubert, *The Dictionary of Accepted Ideas*, trans. Jacques Barzun (New York: New Directions, 1954), p. 25.
67. André Gide, *Prétextes* (Paris: Mercure de France, 1963), p. 32.
68. "O Bock Ideal" is to be found in *OC*, II, 1534–39. The work of de Vogüé was highly popular in France, serving as it did as an introduction to the Russian masters who were just beginning to be appreciated in France: Vte E.-M. de Vogüé, *Le Roman Russe*, 19th ed. (Paris: Librairie Plon, 1927). De Vogüé's introduction is only one of the many signs of a reaction against Naturalism in general: the so-called psychological novelists of the day (Anatole France, Maurice Barrès, Pierre Loti). As a touchstone for this "movement," one might recall the ferociously antipositivist novel *Le Disciple* of Paul Bourget (1889).
69. de Vogüé, *Le Roman Russe*, pp. xiv, xxi, xxii, xxiv, xxxii–xxxvii.
70. "O Bock Ideal," *OC*, II, 1537–38.
71. This is necessarily an oversimplification of a highly complex problem, that of Eça's final vision of social justice and social revolution. For the moment, it would be best to note, along with Jaime Cortesão, that Eça's final novels were accompanied by political essays and *Legends of the Saints*, one of which, "São Cristovão," gives clear evidence of the permanence of Eça's still persistent ideal of social revolution.
72. Gaspar Simões, *Vida e Obra*, pp. 658–59.

2.

Amaro and Bazilio

1. The Making of Two Novels

The years between 1870 and 1880 are at the heart of Eça de Queirós's literary development. Not only will he publish three separate versions of *The Sin of Father Amaro*, but also the novel which many readers sense to be Eça's most heightened Flaubertian phase—*Cousin Bazilio*. We should include also the novel which, in many ways, brought a new direction to his writing—*The Mandarin*, published in July 1880. Eça's energies were at a uniquely sustained peak during those years, a fact which is not entirely evident from the published works. During those years, an immense amount of effort was put into two masterpieces, which for various reasons (including his own doubts about their worth) were never published during his lifetime—*A Capital*, based upon an exquisitely elaborated transfiguration of Balzac's *Illusions perdues*, and the already-mentioned *O Conde de Abranhos*, an acid portrait of a constitutionalist politician, based vaguely on the career of precisely the same gentleman who closed down the Casino lectures in 1870. Supposedly written by the count's valet, this work, is a mock hagiography which ends by being one of Eça's most corrosive and amusing portraits of a national type. Also worthy of mention is the unfinished fragment *A Catastrofe,* a work which had a singularly bizarre history and which might have been one of his greatest single achievements had not a series of events, not exactly flattering to Eça, intervened to discourage him from continuing on with this apocalyptic vision of an invaded and plundered Portugal. Too, much journalism for Portuguese and Brazilian newspapers and reviews—some satirical sociopolitical commentary from *As Farpas* (The Barbs), now collected under the title *Uma Campanha Alegre;* and other, more considered and equanimous pieces now available under the titles of *Cartas de Inglaterra,* to mention one of the more distinguished collections of essays.[1]

As noted, his career as *déraciné* did begin with the short stay in Leiria. In a letter to Eduardo Coelho, Eça notes that "I write to you from my administrative exile; I am as bored as homeless Ovid and François I in captivity" (*OC,* III, 495). It was understood that this duty in Leiria was a kind of obligatory preparatory prelude to a distinguished diplomatic career, as arranged, more than likely, by his well-connected father. Still, it must have been difficult for Eça to accustom himself to the modest surroundings of the town—the world of sacristans, priests, civil servants, interminable sessions of whist, the atmosphere of muffled salons. In addition, much of the time was spent consulting bulky treatises on international law and political economy in preparation for the consular examinations. To while away the time, Eça seems to have carried on a delicate affair with a local baron's wife, a woman given to considerable flights of imagination in the way she organized her social life. During carnival time, she gave an elaborate masked ball and invited, naturally enough, her intimate friend Queirós, who marshaled every sartorial talent in the town to make a Cupid's costume for himself, replete with wings of silk Cambray. His entrance was, by all accounts, a sensation. After dancing a quadrille, Eça and the baroness retired to an adjoining salon, where they were surprised by a forewarned coachman and house painter of the Baron. They proceeded to accost Eça and sent him tumbling down the front stairs of the mansion in summary fashion. The whole episode is recounted in parodic detail in *The Maias,* Chapter IX.

Although Eça gave every evidence of detesting Leiria and removing himself from the provinces as soon as a consular appointment was available, Leiria remains as an inexhaustible mine of characters and situations for the novelist. He must have been a keen listener and enthusiastic student of local scandals and lurid anecdotes. The two basic situations that Eça was to develop in *The Sin of Father Amaro* and *Cousin Bazilio* owe at least some of the provenance to actual happenings in Leiria that took place about that time. An industrious admirer of Eça's work notes that the possible models for both Amaro and Bazilio were objects of opprobrium well known to Leiria folk. The seducer priest really did exist—he was renowned not only in Leiria but in surrounding parishes which he also served. According to the local legend, a young lady named Amélia or Maria Amélia developed a grand passion for this cleric, and a surrepitious affair continued for a while until the priest abandoned the clergy and took this Amélia to Lisbon, where he was able to support her.

Also, the possible source for the character Luiza, of *Cousin Bazilio,* seduced in her husband's absence and aided by a conniving maid, was a sensational case of adultery in Leiria just a few years before Eça's arrival. Her fate was evidently not much more fortunate than that of her fictional counterpart, who dies of brain fever at the end of the book. The young matron from Leiria was banished from her home by her outraged husband and was shunned by all decent people of the town. She finally ended her days in a hovel a few kilometers from Leiria, sustaining herself as a seamstress.[2]

These matters offer no special key to the two works in question, in the same way that nothing is gained by denigrating the achievement that is *Madame Bovary* by bringing up the arresting story of the wife of a Normandy Doctor, Delphine Delamare, who took poison in 1848 leaving behind an unpaid bill from the circulating library in Rouen along with massive debts that required the public auction of furniture to satisfy her creditors. Just as Flaubert made use of this *donnée,* so too did Eça make use of local scandals. They were the base materials for a novelist who at that time was just beginning to formulate the critical and novelistic principles that went into the Casino lecture of the following year. The stories about these proto-Amaros and proto-Luizas, along with the forced ejection of Eça from the masked ball and his boundless ignominy because of it—all these topics are a part of an incipient process that was just beginning to function.[3] We know that he was beginning to respond to the principles of Realism, such as he understood them, but the process of character development was tortuous for him, as we have seen. In Eça, observation was only the beginning of a long and involved process which, when deciphered, might reveal how strong a force French and English novels exercised upon his imagination. His capacity for free invention was lamentably weak, and he knew it. On the other hand, his ability to transfigure other patterns, as it were, was unusually strong and productive. This process, evident to a considerable degree both in *The Sin of Father Amaro* and *Cousin Bazilio,* has given rise to innumerable articles and even book-length pamphlets concerning Eça's so-called plagiarism; in an author of the proportions of Eça's reputation and renown, this would seeem to be difficult to sustain. But the fact of the matter is that Eça's imagination *was* erratic and discontinuous. What is more to the point would be to consider Eça's sources as becoming wholly his own, of how a previous text turns into another text, without changing too many words! [4] It is with some relief that we note that the French scholar Jean Girodon, in his deft essay on Eça de Queirós and *Madame Bovary,* notes that while it is not inexact to say that Eça was the principal exponent of the Realist school in Portugal, the reader should consider this fact as something of an accident, something imposed upon Eça for reasons that might now seem extraliterary. M. Girodon's characterization of the genuine Eçian tone in literature seems accurate and satisfying: "Objective observation, impassivity, documentation with scientific pretensions, were never in his line at all; even in the most impersonal portions of his work we sense him to be present always, and it is this presence which is his greatest charm." [5]

This contradiction points to an ambiguity and even duplicity in his own literary principles. But in the early 1870s at least, Eça seems temporarily convinced that the novel must make some kind of moral order out of social anarchy, and it is this stern principle which guides much of the first revision of *The Sin of Father Amaro* and most certainly the elaboration of *Cousin Bazilio*. There is a sense of coercion in many of these pages, and there are good reasons for a reader's sensing some degree of pressure from the author. Let us look at some of Eça's letters, written during the various rewritings of *The Sin of Father Amaro* and *Cousin Bazilio*. They are cogent documents, and quite surprising thoughts for an apparent Realist. In a letter to Teófilo Braga of March 12, 1878, Eça fears that *Cousin Bazilio* will suffer the disapproval of the revolutionary iconoclast that was Braga at that time: "it was quite possible that you, seeing that *Cousin Bazilio* diverges from such combative art as *The Sin of Father Amaro* (because of *Cousin Bazilio*'s theme and elaboration) would disapprove of it. For this reason your approval was an agreeable surprise to me." After making a catalogue of the characters and the social types that these characters were to represent in the work, Eça will insist that "A society constructed on those false bases is not one based upon truth; attacking it is a duty. And on this point I believe that *Cousin Bazilio* is not completely outside of the realm of revolutionary art." Referring once again to his characters in the novel and now including the hapless Father Amaro, Eça avers that they all deserve "a sound beating administered by all men of goodwill." Further, "we must slash away at the world of the bureaucrats, the world of sentiment, the world of literature, the world of the farmer, the world of superstition, and with all due respect for the institutions which are of such ancient origin, we must destroy false interpretations and false achievements which a rotten society gives to them. Don't you think that such a labor is a just one? . . . If there was ever a society that demanded an avenging artist [*o artista vingador*], it is this one!" (*OC*, III, 515–18).

In another letter written just two weeks later, Eça will thank his correspondent, Rodrigues de Freitas, for his review of *Cousin Bazilio;* he is even more than thankful for de Freitas's comments on Realism in general: "What I deeply thank you for is your general defense of Realism. My novels are of no importance, it is clear that they are mediocre. What *is* important is the triumph of Realism, which even today, unknown and vilified, is still the grand literary development of the century, destined to have a lasting influence on society and customs. What do we want to do with Realism? . . . we want to take a photograph (I was almost going to say 'caricature') of the old world of the bourgeoisie—sentimental, devout, Catholic, world explorer, aristocratic—and then expose it to the derision, the guffaws, and the contempt of the modern and democratic world—to prepare the ruin of this old world. An art that has these aims . . . is a powerful auxiliary of revolutionary science." [6]

These statements, lacking in nuance as they do, must be read with due cognizance of the character of the correspondent. In the case of Teófilo Braga, a mind of energetically synthetic abilities and eventual author of the eleven volume *History of Portuguese Literature* and many socialist tracts (*and* future president of the Republic in 1910), Eça brandishes a literary program that he knew Braga would approve of; as for the letter to Rodrigues de Freitas, it must be read as a grateful acknowledgment of the author to an unknown journalist. Neither correspondent could expect from Eça the kind of expressions of doubt concerning the aims of Realism such as those reserved uniquely to his longtime friend and sometime collaborator Ramalho Ortigão. The letters of Eça to Ramalho of 1877 and 1878 show an author fully conscious of the failures of his own literary dogmatism, precisely those which have been governing the composition of the second version of *The Sin of Father Amaro* and the already completed *Cousin Bazilio*. On the matter of *Cousin Bazilio*, Eça seems unusually distressed. With comments such as the following, it is difficult to take seriously the heroic revolutionary statements shown in the letters to Braga and de Freitas: "You must have received *Bazilio* by now. As you will see, it is mediocre. Except for two or three scenes, *written recently*, the rest (written two years ago) is what the English call "rubbish" . . . it was not publishable; it should have remained in boxes, just like those piled-up canvases in ateliers which evince the painter learning his trade." [7] This must be read with some caution. The structure and execution of *Cousin Bazilio* was a process that took many years, quite possibly beginning prior to even the first version of *The Sin of Father Amaro*. Why this obfuscation? It is not a question of a failure of memory, nor is there an open attempt to deceive a good friend. But there is a gross confusion in Eça concerning the ends and the means of his writing, to whom it should be directed, what it is for, the relation between art and social reform. Rather than obfuscation, let us say that confusion seems to reign. Perhaps the key to all this lies in what may have been a happy slip of the pen in Eça's letter to Rodrigues de Freitas of March 30, 1878, cited above. In the passage quoted he mentions the ideal of photography and then says, "I was almost going to say 'caricature.'" Surely, no matter how talented the practitioners of photography and caricature may be, it is impossible to relate in any fruitful way the two genres—it would make for a confusion, let us say, of the art of Atget and that of Daumier.

In this period of Eça's literary development, there were accommodations available to him. Eça saw caricature as univocal, without debilitating subtleties which might muddle the clarity of the critical attack. In the early novels, he will insist upon their critical yet objective nature, just as his journalistic "Barbs" will give him ample opportunity to lash away at the paralyzed society he saw around him. However, Eça is forced to diverge from his potential mentors in French literature, since Flaubert, the Goncourts, and Zola himself "rarely recur to laughter and comicity to express their theses in a work of art." [8] Eça will carry on an odd parallel practice for a considerable length of time— on the one hand, the journalist who thinks of himself as an objective dissector of society; on the other hand, an aspiring novelist who wishes to make use of the genre as an instrument of social inquiry and reform—portraiture with sermon.

There are even more conflictive and complex issues at hand here. Irony and literary radicalism do not seem to meet at all comfortably during these years. After all, irony should uncover a pluralistic vision of society; it may well imply an easy confluence between aesthetic detachment and moral imperatives, either of which may lie hidden within the structure of a fictional discourse. In Eça, irony will imply a kind of negative artistic freedom in which his juvenile commitments will be later withdrawn (in the 1880s and 1890s) in the name of ampler perspectives and a greater panoply of voices. But the Eça of *The Sin of Father Amaro* I and II and *Cousin Bazilio* is decidedly not an ironist; the conquest of irony, to use Mario Sacramento's phrase, is a long process of initiation, one which will gradually erase the open moral imperatives of these first two works.

It might be useful to look at how Eça's journalism and fiction responded to the univocal view; the themes which make up most of the obsessive patterns in his journalism often reappear in the guise of a fictional character. Often the characters become the agents of Eça's own journalism, pummeling away at society from the more expansive and inviting realms of "imaginative" fiction. A cursory glance at these journalistic "Barbs" (*Farpas*) might help us understand why Eça was so bereft of a sense of irony and grace when evolving the not at all oblique dramatizations of character in *The Sin of Father Amaro* and *Cousin Bazilio*.

In his preface to the collected "Barbs," Eça notes that the primary aim was "to provoke laughter," as well as to force people "to see in a truthful way" the world around them. "In Paris, a great painter told me that 'the masses see falsely.' This is true in Portugal, above all. Because of the passive acceptance of imposed opinions, because of the extinction of the critical faculty, because of the prejudices that form a part of the examination of anything, the [Portuguese] public sees what it is told to see." (*OC*, II, 1383). In this sense, laughter brings us to the ideal of *justice*, that that ideal must be the prime mover of the new art of the nineteenth century—criticism through laughter, reasoning through irony.

Eça's own contributions began in June 1871, with the already mentioned "Study of Portuguese Society in 1871" (see pp. 33–34). This is the text which is reflective of every sociological and political presumption that will in due course propel the social critique of the first two attempts at fiction. There is one element of this "Barb" which should not go unnoticed, and that is the dramatization of immobility, the idea of an overwhelming tedium and torpor taking over everybody and everything. " 'I'm bored!' is the chorus heard everywhere. Spirits are empty, the senses unsatisfied. Gradually, with the will weakened and the body enfeebled, man wants only to *distract himself, to kill time.* But doing what? Reading? He doesn't read a book of science, literature, or history; instead he reads Ponson du Terrail, and from a lending library! . . . Conversation has been extinguished. No one has original ideas of his own, but they do have four or five sentences made up a long time ago and which get repeated. After that, everyone yawns. Four people meet in a café; after five minutes of whispering trivialities, each one of the conversants is trying to figure out how to get rid of the other three. . . . What has been lost in all this is the sense of citizenship and that of a nation. In Portugal the citizen has disappeared. In the whole country there is nothing more than a heterogeneous congregation of inactivities which bore each other. It is a nation made for a dictatorship—or one to be conquered" (*OC,* III, 973).

These comments obviously apply to the particular society of which he was a part, one wholly governed by instincts of male supremacy, and one which was impervious to such unheard-of ideas as the dignity of women. But women are so fundamental to Eça's life and literature that he cannot fail to take up an inquiry into their state. By March 1872, some ten months after the initial "Portrait of Portuguese Society," Eça will begin the scrutiny of the seemingly invisible element of Portuguese social structure—women. The date of this "Barb" is most important, since by then Eça had probably completed the first draft of what was to become *Cousin Bazilio* and certainly had finished the first version of *The Sin of Father Amaro.* So by March 1872, Eça's indagations into the character of Portuguese women will have a close relation to the fictional counterparts that will appear later uner the names of Amélia in *Amaro,* Luiza in *Bazilio,* not to mention the rich gamut of secondary characters—the Gansoso sisters from *Amaro,* the "liberated" Leopoldina of *Bazilio.* As always happens with Eça's theorizing, the arguments are incisively expressed but hardly full of nuance. He begins his inquiry with preliminary comments, then launches into a collective portrait of a Portuguese woman—any woman, all women:

"Let us examine the general type that is the unmarried young lady from Lisbon. She is skinny, pale, stuffed into a puffy dress, with a thick, laboriously done coiffure, taking such little steps with such an air of fatigue that one can hardly understand how she might ascend any hill in Lisbon, not to mention Life itself. The first salient sign is her anemia . . . rachitic, bloodless, fleshless, without vital strength—some suffer from nerves, others from stomach troubles, others with chest pains, but all have the chlorosis which attacks those beings which are deprived of the sun. . . . And to see them on vacations! If they have to mount a horse, what fright, what squeals, how many Pater Nosters murmured! On board a passenger ship, English and French girls want to go up on the deck, gaze at the sea, feel the humid breeze; meanwhile, the Portuguese girl is below, whimpering, praying, taking her broth. Hence, her lack of activity, her unfortunate 'passivity.' A Portuguese girl has no initiative, no determination, no will. She has to be ordered and governed. If she is not, she remains on the median of life, arms lowered, irresolute, and in a state of suspension. During any danger, a family crisis, a difficult situation, she prays. Her abstract faith tells her that only God can inspire her, give her the decision already made, the exact idea; in the end, they always follow their maid's advice" (OC, III, 1201–5).

"In Portugal, women are excluded (by habits or by laws) from public life, industry, commerce, literature—practically everything. They remain in possession of a small world, their natural element: the family and their own toilette. So that when ladies meet and converse, their talk revolves, like butterflies within a glass-enclosed candle, around two supreme topics: clothes and love affairs. The child with good hearing and curiosity absorbs, like a sponge sucking up water, all that she hears around her. Now, what are the facts that such conversations among mother, aunts, friends, or any visitor offer to the young child's curiosity? That so-and-so was just married, that someone else separated from her husband, that the dresses of yet another do not at all jibe with her low income, that Sr. X is courting her, but that he already has a mistress who is an actress . . . always the affairs, the clothes, the scandals, the gossip, the history of passion. What is the result of all this afterwards? Well, we have young ladies of fifteen speaking with great authority on marriage, dowries, adulteries, and abductions, pointing out that a particular comedy is outrageous or that a particular novel is immortal" (*OC*, III, 1208–9).

"There are many ingenuous people who suppose that the fear of a catastrophe is of great consideration to any woman. This is puerile naiveté. Nothing has a more profoundly attractive enchantment to a woman than a catastrophe. It satisfies the most violent desire in the soul—to tingle with excitement. Today, in this world of stimulation, the trivial, a pair of slippers, tranquility, a toothpick in the teeth, plebeian virtues, all these are to be avoided. Everyone demands turmoil, sensations, and shocks . . . all literature—theater, novel, and poetry—educate in this sense only: to tell us how to shudder, how to experience intensely. We who are now moralizing [9] together wrote a deplorable novel which united literary insignificance and moral sterility—*O Misterio da Estrada de Sintra*. What is this book? It is the idealization of catastrophe, the terrifying enchantments of the calamities of love. Above all, a love that is unlawful and guilt-ridden. The dangers and the tragic finale are as attractive as a delicious abyss. The husband who kills his wife, intending to give just punishment to sin, actually brings passion into poetic relief. . . . Drama is the ideal of all of us. To act out that drama is our perdition. Through drama we desire death and commit evil. Through drama we throw ourselves into violent destinies. Men have many ways to act out a drama—war, revolution, duel, books, and even (unhappily for many impresarios) theater itself. Women confined as they are to the world of feelings—have only one recourse—love!" (*OC*, III, 1213–14).

If these observations are instructive in any way, they do point up a few constants which become unspoken presumptions when subjected to fictional development in *The Sin of Father Amaro* and *Cousin Bazilio*. One element of these constants might be the very nature of *accidie*, paralysis and stasis in early Eça—it is dynamic, it is the one absolutely fundamental theme of these works. From boredom and *accidie* come all the complications and ruinations in the novels. Within this context, Eça will speak of the pernicious nature of the act of reading, of how a text makes more evident the enormous distance between the inventions of the imagination and reality. In his portrait of the Portuguese female adolescent, Eça will mention, with obvious distaste, what he considers to be a precocious and "false" imagination, the febrile and unhealthy product of a banal reality and the uncontrolled verbiage of an incipient mass culture—that of the lending library. It is no idle coincidence that Eça's model reader of literary junk is a borrower, not a buyer of books; so too is Emma Bovary, so too is the infinitely idle Luiza of *Cousin Bazilio*. Eça's realities are immensely self-effacing; there seems to be almost nothing to them, in spite of a few set scenes in each of the two novels. However, this thinness of things and people gives even more ample room for the author's intrusive depiction of the agents of desire—the vulgar Marianic literature of the bourgeoisie in *Amaro*, the romances that enchant the bored Luiza in *Bazilio*. Books are the one dynamic element in Amélia's suffocating ambiance. As for Luiza, the delusions and fantasies drawn from literature are the only counterbalance to the bourgeois contentment of her husband and his friends. Literature becomes the moving force that produces "drama" amid "tedium," and this makes us think of Flaubert in an even more intense way than before.

Eça mentioned the novelistic collaboration with Ramalho Ortigão—the novel called *O Mistério da Estrada de Sintra*. There is a unique moment in that novel, where an afflicted Countess vents her rage against a Portuguese version of Don Juan—the same kind of character that Eça will later elaborate (or was elaborating in a parallel fashion at that time) into such ruthless seducers as Father Amaro or Cousin Bazilio. Eça makes the Countess speak in terms that are strikingly similar to the language of the "Barb" of March 1872. The subject is not torpor or *accidie* but just the opposite—the temptations of "danger," "variety," "new sensations" in the Quierosian sense. The Countess is implacable: "That unworthy type known as the *conquistador* must be demolished by means of ridicule, caricature, the horsewhip, and the local police force. The *conquistador* is not an attractive figure; he possesses not one iota of attractiveness, good bearing, grandeur; as a man, he has no education, honesty, good manners, wit, *toilette,* ability, courage, dignity, or simple cleanliness—and he can't spell" (*OC,* III, 1408–9).

The Countess then proceeds to recreate imaginatively a typical sequence in the life of a woman, beginning with boredom of a kind which leads inevitably to seduction and even more inevitably to catastrophe, remorse, and guilt. In this process, there is a necessary and basic element—the hardworking bourgeois husband against whom the wife plots and schemes. She herself takes her own situation and tells us, "My husband is an honest, sympathetic, hardworking, and affable gentleman . . . he works, he works, he works. He earns his daily bread and the clothes for all seasons with long and boring hours of work performed with exhaustion and tedium . . . he is fair-minded, a good and dedicated man. He sleeps soundly because his exhaustion is justified and unsullied. . . . So what do I do? I bore myself. Just as soon as he leaves, I yawn, open up a novel, argue with the maids, yawn again, open the window, look out. A young man passes by, with good bearing and robust, a blond or a brunet, imbecilic or mediocre. We look at each other . . . I am enchanted . . . I smile at him . . . I get a letter written without wit or grammar. I go mad. I hide it, I kiss it, I reread it, I despise life.

"He sends me some verses—verses, my God! And then I forget my husband, his sacrifices, his goodwill, his labors, his sweet disposition. I no longer care about the tears and the desperation that lie in the future; I abandon probity, decency, responsibility, family, social correctness, relatives, the children—my children! Everything is conquered, swept along by a wayward sonnet copied from some book or other!" (*OC,* III, 1407–8).

Such passages, drawn as they are from both his fiction and his journalism, bring up some recurrent concerns. As we read the successive variations of these themes both in *The Sin of Father Amaro* and *Cousin Bazilio,* these unvarying impulses will find themselves distributed among a considerable number of female characters. Without being too reductive, it would seem that Eros inevitably takes on an indecorous pose in Eça's fiction, one that haplessly reflects the humiliation caused by the passions.[10]

Rare is the fictional work of Eça de Queirós which is not moved by the dynamics of adultery; neither lover nor mistress escapes the atmosphere of repugnance and simple distaste that so often accompanies the paradoxical process of "divinization" with which Queirosian passions so often invest themselves. Among the conflicts between social stability and individual desire, the process we are about to outline—the making of the three versions of *The Sin of Father Amaro* and the writing of *Cousin Bazilio*—is emblematic of how obsessive mental structures gradually filter into the stratagems of each character and how, in sum, social stability becomes the ultimate presumption behind the making of his major fictions.[11] As for the elusive tensions of the individual against an overwhelming and highly authoritarian social structure, Eça's own solution and fictive projections do nothing to encourage the view that would make him a sympathetic apostle of the imaginative self triumphant over the world; quite the contrary—the treacheries *against* the imagination seem to be all-encompassing in his novels. In this sense, lovers are typical victims; since they are imaginative generators of the selves that they think they love, they are automatically victims of Romantic delusions.

2. Three Versions of a Crime

Eça de Queirós's first major published achievement in fiction, the first edition of *The Sin of Father Amaro*, did not have an easy gestation. The writing of the work was a singularly tortuous, even devious procedure. Most readers of the work as it is presently available in the Portuguese edition and the translation into English have good reason to assume they are reading a definitive, organically contrived novel—such is the impression that its careful elaboration gives. But this is not the case. *The Sin of Father Amaro* hides its erratic and wayward development under the surface of the reassuring and heavily laid on social panoplies typical of the French novel of its time. As it is currently available to us, the prologue the author composed for the edition that is now considered definitive presents a circuitous and highly debatable defense against the accusations of plagiarism which were made by Machado de Assis and others; this, in turn, only complicates and even prevents our understanding of how the novel was to grow in length and development. But even that prologue is part of the complex program the author often was to indulge in—a subtle twist of the truth and the resultant bafflement of the reader typifies the case of an author who often found that he had to cut his losses, erase the clues which might lead his readers back to the sources in other literatures.[12]

In sum, the novel we read today is the third edition of the work, finally published by the Lisbon publishing house of Ernest Chardron in 1880. Prior to this edition, Eça published two radically different versions of the work, the first in the *Revista Occidental* early in 1875; the second dating from the following year, a "definitive edition," according to the author. This second edition, considerably rewritten and containing additional scenes, was the subject of the lucid review by the Brazilian novelist Machado de Assis, that critique which had such a profound impact upon Eça. Thus, the "definitive" edition is the second edition, but it is not at all definitive in the light of the final revision published in 1880. The second edition was subjected to yet another amplification, very probably under the aegis of Machado's critical intuitions.[13] The rewriting of the third, definitive edition will take some three years; the principal characters—Father Amaro and Amélia—undergo transfigurations in motivation and impulse, and they show an increasingly critical stance on the part of the author toward his two protagonists. Too, the relation between self and society is gradually adjusted throughout the three versions in the sense that the atmosphere of Gothic romance which lurks so noticeably throughout the first version is gradually replaced by a more balanced novelistic analysis of the mental structures and customs of a provincial Catholic society.

The history of the three versions of *The Sin of Father Amaro* is, in a sense, one part of the literary history of Eça de Queirós between the years 1871 (the date of the first mention of such a project) and 1880, the date of the doubly "definitive" version.

Intervening between the second and third versions of the work loom two events that were to impose themselves upon Eça to the extent that he will reconsider a text done twice already. These events might be described in the following manner: (1) the extraordinary success of *Cousin Bazilio,* published as it was between the second and third editions of *The Sin of Father Amaro,* and (2) the bizarre attempt by Eça to blackmail the Portuguese government into making a direct payment to him in order to prevent the publication of a text that might be considered seditious, above all if it were published by an author who was a distinguished consul then resident in England. In due course, this strange course of events will be described, but suffice to say for the moment that the outrage and stupefaction of his friend Ramalho Ortigão (charged as he was by Eça to forwarding and personally presenting this impossible scheme to the appropriate minister) stopped the author from proceeding any further with this insane plot. As we shall see, the letter from Eça to Ramalho dated November 10, 1878, shows the author in a state of considerable derangement as to the propriety and the efficacy of his scheme and makes us question the honesty and good faith of Eça de Queirós, not for the first time and certainly not for the last.

Thus, we have the first two versions dated 1875, the intervening controversies both literary (*Bazilio,* the Machado critique) and personal (the blackmail attempt). Then appears the final and most imposing *Amaro* of them all, the edition of 1880. For these reasons, the text cannot be considered as a single entity; rather it is a palimpsest of conflicts between literary theory and practice over almost a decade, reflecting as it does the temporary reconciliations between doctrines and aesthetics in each successive version. The typically Queirosian self-dramatization, unique in its shading and at times subtle distancing, varies throughout the three versions. The questions that arise as we examine the substructure within the final version are not idle critical quandaries; they relate to the manner in which Eça patterned the most obsessive themes which were to haunt him so persistently throughout his creative life.

In random fashion, and making no case for the priority of

one pattern over the other, we would have to mention how often his texts revolve around the games of love and marriage; the fundamentally illegitimate nature of both love and passion, symbolized by the recurrent suggestions and instances of incest; the many guises under which the metaphor of the "orphan" haunts his characters—types without the accommodations of place in society, wihout the protective aura of parental recognition, without a "home" for the psyche—this in turn will imply the critical nature of Eça's attitude toward Portugal, his apparent home. At all times he is inconsistent, at various times malevolent, unjust; at times uncritical and simply sacharrine.

All of these blatant topics seem to be variants of Eça's most primitive fixations and concerns and their exorcism in literature. Rarely spontaneous or effusive in life or in literature, Eça knew the sciences of dissimulation as did few other imaginations of his time; in his works, love is criminal, impossible, or simply incestuous. It is Wagnerian in its engulfment and in its destructiveness. The articulation of this tabu within the confines and within the images of bourgeois society is of the essence in his fictions—no other theme, no other metaphor or idea can compete with the constant repetition, over and over, of this maddening and ultimately depressingly misogynistic view of the nature of women and the nature of love.[14] And aside from being expressive of whatever inner concerns did propel these themes, Eça was well aware of the necessity of a certain éclat and sexual scandal to increase the sale of a book; he often consciously adjusted his texts toward the salacious for precisely that purpose, as Machado de Assis pointed out with such precision. In brief, his protagonists participate equally and tragically in the act of social conformity *and* in the act a "good" society calls tabu. Therein lies the drama; they are strung out between two realms. As Leo Bersani has put it, "the hero of realistic fiction supports a novelistic structure which includes his expulsion from the viable structures of fiction and of life. . . . Both the reader and the society within the novel stand in fascinated awe of those figures who embody that secret excess or violence which perhaps prefigures a structural explosion but which also awakens the self-preserving energies of a stable order. The hero is simultaneously an invitation and a warning." [15]

It might be instructive to consider one of the many early instances of an obsessive theme in Eça, a moment to be found in the pages of that earlier mentioned novel written in collaboration with Ramalho Ortigão. Published as an epistolary novel between July 24 and September 27, 1870, in the Lisbon journal *Diário de Noticias*, it was finally published in book form in 1884. In the later edition, it was accompanied by an exasperated prologue written by the two authors, alleging that the novel was "without plan, method, literary tendency, documentation, style, retired as we were in the glass tower of the imagination." Speaking for Ramalho and himself, Eça characterizes the work as "execrable; neither one of us, either as a novelist nor as a critic, would wish such a book on our worst enemy" (*OC*, III, 1271–72). Nonetheless, there are a few moments (we have already noted the Countess' condemnation of Don Juans) that contain, in embryo, much of the passionate flare of Eça's critical, literary, and personal dilemmas. Not six pages into the novel, just after the two protagonists have been abducted without explanation on the road to Sintra, the following question is asked of one of the kidnapped characters: What is to be done with a distinguished lady of Lisbon society who finds herself with child during the period that her husband has been away on business— for the past year? The gentleman cooly responds, recommending an immediate separation, and, if the woman has the means, a voyage to America or Switzerland with her lover. On the other hand, if the woman in question is poor, she should buy a sewing machine and languish in the sordid conditions that inevitably will be her lot. Either rich or poor, he avers, such women will die off quickly, either in a cottage on the border of Lake Leman or in the most miserable ghetto of Lisbon: "Everybody dies just the same, of consumption or of tedium, in the exhaustion of work or in the ennui of an idyll" (*OC*, III, 1280). Fair enough, we might say, although it does seem odd that an idyllic cottage outside Geneva would produce a mental disease as fatal as the rampant tuberculosis of a ghetto. But for Eça, this is the law. Idylls are preludes to the death of the heart and the soul.

But the text does not end with this dispiriting analysis. What about the child? What of the social consequence of passion? These are other matters and bring the author and his character to an even more icy prescription for the destiny of the illegitimate child: "As soon as he is separate from the family and the law, the child is a miserable wretch whose misfortune is attributable, in large part, to society, which has not yet managed to define the responsibility of clandestine fathers" (*OC*, III, 1280). Much of *The Sin of Father Amaro* lies inert in those few sentences, since in all three versions of the novel the newborn child inevitably takes on the guise of an innocent yet fatally subversive threat to the norms of a society, and these norms cannot be broken—they must be sustained at all human and inhuman cost. The child "outside of the law," to use Eça's phrase, draws upon a potential magnetism, darting across the constraints of life in society, offering a potential affinity to all that is alien to order—inchoate passion. This is to say that the child suggests the contrary structures of anarchic desire, and it must be done away with.[16]

This is the passionate secret theme in Eça's work; it reappears in vexing guises, sometimes with blinding clarity and frankness, at other times hidden behind an occasional mention. Let us look at another instance. At approximately the same time that Eça and Ramalho were composing, at considerable distance from each other, that epistolary novel known as *O Misterio da Estrada de Sintra,* Eça had written a considerable number of pages of text entitled "The Story of a Graceful Body," which may or may not still exist in the trove of his papers that still await publication. If it does not exist, it may have been subsumed into the many versions of *The Sin of Father Amaro;* it may have been destroyed by Eça in the early 1870s; or it may be the draft, still extant, that is now known as the rough draft outline of *Cousin Bazilio.*[17] Finally, and not at all last in the series of possibilities, "The Story of a Graceful Body" may be the short story now known as "A Fair-haired Girl." In any case, the matter of this prototext is worth pursuing, since, in many ways, both *The Sin of Father Amaro* and *Cousin Bazilio* are essentially the same works, written under the same dogmas and literary credos. Concerning this "Story of a Graceful Body," Eça's good friend Jaime Batalha Reis gives us the invaluable and only clue in his memoir, dated 1903: "One day he came to show us— Antero de Quental and me—the first draft of a novel entitled 'The Story of a Graceful Body.' It was a major work, so long that it took several nights to read. I believe it was his first effort in the so-called 'naturalist' or 'realist' vein. If memory serves me, the basic idea of the book was more or less the same as that of *Affaire Clémenceau*, by Dumas *fils*. The work itself, however, largely betrayed the influence of Gustave Flaubert's method in *Madame Bovary* and *L'Éducation sentimentale*" (*OC*, I, 568).

There is nothing more than this tantalizing recollection, from around the autumn of 1870, the work of Dumas fils having appeared in serial form in a Pôrto literary review beginning with the January 20, 1870, number.[18] Other references by Eça to Dumas fils do not at all contradict the impression that Batalha Reis vaguely recalled. Eça *had* written a draft of a novel, and that work was written very much under the combined circumstances of his own "irregular" and "illegitimate" birth and the similar fate of Dumas fils's protagonist, also illegitimate, also a slave of the passions. Just two years later Eça will describe Dumas fils as the "Saint Thomas of the bedroom . . . the doctor of dirty clothes" in this essay, or "Barb," of October 1872: "Dumas fils compiles his information by night, with crook and lantern, sidling along connubial walls, secretly snatching everything that issues from the bedroom: hairpins, rumpled sheets, fusty bedpans, and telltale rags. His knowledge is based on what he scavenges from the trash" (*OC*, III, 1248).

In the same essay Eça is once again constrained to question the fate of an adulteress: "it was a matter of deciding in cold blood, with casuistry and elegant grammar, whether or not a husband should murder his wife. Thumbing through the Bible with a cigar in his mouth, M. Dumas declared: 'kill her!' Others, folding razors and placing them away in their pockets, generously stated: 'don't kill her.' Certain jokesters declared, between a gag and a beer: 'he should have killed her all along!' Whereas others, opining that the issue must be studied further with the aid of dictionaries, cautioned: 'don't kill her yet'" (*OC*, III,

1249). A similar dialogue occurs in the second chapter of *Cousin Bazilio.* The hapless playwright Ernestinho is trying to bring his play to an end, one that would be dramatic and outrageous, but at the same time one that would answer to the theater manager's demand that "the husband . . . pardon the wife." In the salon, Luiza's husband, the solid engineer who is soon to absent himself in order to enable his wife to engage in an affair with Bazilio, is asked his opinion as to how Ernestinho should finish this "play within a play." The answer is pure Queirós, that is, pure Dumas fils: " 'Not by any means! Never! I am for death! Entirely for death! It's essential that you kill her, Ernestinho! . . . I'm talking seriously, and I'm a tiger [*uma fera*]. If the husband is deceived, I'm for death. I don't care if it's in an abyss, a room, or the street—but she must be killed. Could I consent that, in such a case, a cousin, a person of my family and blood, could lower himself to pardon like a sissy? No! Kill her, I say. Why, it's a family principle. Kill her at once!' . . . They all protested at this outburst of Jorge's, calling him a 'wild beast,' 'Othello,' 'Bluebeard,' and so on. He only laughed, peacefully filling his pipe. Luiza sat crocheting in silence." [19]

As for adultery in general, Eça will find nothing in Portuguese society to restrain those deadly passions brought on by "amorous idealism," that delirium to which the Countess, Amélia, and Luiza all fall victim. As we know, Eça will recommend in that "Barb" concerning young ladies' educations that they undergo a severe regime of physical exercise, consisting of at least two hours of waltzing per day—a beneficial activity which works as a "sweet medicament against anemia, pallor, and hot flashes. It is above all a fatiguing excercise. Any woman who does not exhaust herself flies off into worlds of the imagination" (*OC*, III, 1255). Eça is not saying this with tongue in cheek; he does believe this, his characters are the result.

The unpublished "Story of a Graceful Body" must have been related to adultery and illegitimacy, to the treacheries of a beautiful woman, since these are the obsessive themes of the novel by Dumas fils. Even the most cursory reading of that work can only confirm the correspondences between *Affaire Clémenceau* and the nascent thematics of *The Sin of Father Amaro* and *Cousin*

Bazilio. It would seem that Batalha Reis's recollections were at least minimally accurate. *Affaire Clémenceau* attracted Eça for what it offered in the way of a fusion between known experience—the ignominy of being an unrecognized bastard son—and literary resonance. Both Dumas fils and Eça were illegitimate sons; both Amaro and Luiza are orphans. In pre-Freudian terms, Dumas fils is able to make these tensions available to Eça in a gripping, manic monologue: "My true crime, that for which terrestrial justice will never pursue me, and for which I will never forgive myself nor those who pushed me to do it—do you want to know what it is? It is of having doubted, of having blushed at times because of my mother." Within the mind of Clémenceau, Dumas fils traces the consequences of this confusion between any woman and a mother—a retributive, vengeful relation to the woman that will be later his wife, a *belle dame sans merci,* exemplar of "the three vices which were to undo that woman first, and then ruin me also: l'impudeur, l'ingratitude, la sensualité."

Affaire Clémenceau is written in the form alluded to by the subtitle of the work: 'Mémoire de l'accusé.' The narrator is Clémenceau himself, imprisoned and accused of the intentional murder of his wife Iza, née Dobronowska. Briefly, the novel describes a talented and hypersensitive Clémenceau, hounded since his illegitimate birth by the condemnation to which society unthinkingly and automatically has subjected him: "I was therefore thrown out of the community because I did not have a father, which in the eyes of the other children [his school-mates] was something equivalent to the plague or scurvy." The child is insidiously ridiculed by a fellow student, André Minati, who will die a gruesome death later in the novel, and who will be found to be the brother of the dreaded Iza. Clémenceau's obvious artistic talents are encouraged by one M. Thomas Ritz, whose son Constantine becomes a good friend. Clémenceau becomes an esteemed sculptor under Ritz's guidance, but an artist of more than a little priggishness and subject to a good dose of Proudhonian theories concerning the morality of art. "Do you know what art is? It is the Beauty within Truth; following that principle, art is created out of absolute laws which you

vainly seek in Nature itself." At a masked ball, Clémenceau sees
Iza for the first time, and the process of divinization begins:
"For me, it was not a young woman, it was not a child, it was not
a woman, it was Woman: Symbol, Poem, Abstraction, Eternal
Enigma."

Clémenceau becomes the lover and the sculptor of Iza, whose
mother is a different kind of exemplar—possessiveness and arriviste opportunism: "In Poland as in France, money is the big
thing." Iza marries Clémenceau. Iza's seraphic beauty is accompanied by a tempestuous and capricious character; a vicious child, her beauty (as eternalized by Clémenceau's
sculptures) bring him fame and misery. Fearful of the physical
effects of pregnancy, she does everything to avoid having a
child, but one is born nonetheless. Did she wish to rid herself of
the child by killing it? Probably—"She did not dare to suggest a
murder to me, but she thought of it, I am certain." An anonymous letter apprises Clémenceau of Iza's daily infidelities; Constantine Ritz convinces him to abandon her and rusticate for a
few years in Italy, consoling him with such thoughts as "These
kind of women are not on the earth for the intimate joys of
conjugal life. One should sing of them, paint them, cast them in
bronze, make love to them—but marry them, never! They are
lacking in everything—dignity, a sense of decency, conscience,
knowledge of what is good, a feeling for the family, of duty and
of maternity, love itself—all these things are a closed book to
them. Their only mission to shine and to reign." While in Italy,
Clémenceau receives another anonymous letter, this time an-
nouncing a passionate affair between Iza and his good friend
Constantine. Returning to Paris, Constantine confesses the
truth to Clémenceau; Iza proposes faithfulness to him once
again, all the while affirming her contempt for men in general:
"Do I know them, these men? Have I looked at them? What are
their names? I don't even remember. I had an evil spirit, doubtless. I was thirsty for new sensations. But, in my heart, I only
loved you." [20] After making love to Iza again, Clémenceau
plunges a dagger into her heart. End of *Affaire Clémenceau*.

Since we speak only of a text which may have served as a
possible source, substance or counterpoint to Eça's "Story of a

Graceful Body," anything that might be said about this proto-*Amaro* or proto-*Bazilio* can only refect the inner sympathy between the text of Dumas fils and those of Eça which were being written around that time. Some of the desperate, even Dostoevskian, tone of the murderer's confession may well be reflected in passages from Eça's future novels, not to mention the determinist presumptions in the Dumas fils work, theories for which Eça had a notable weakness. In the words of Clémenceau, "Free will disappeared starting with Cain. Cain is no longer master of all his actions; he must submit to his pro-creator. The father was guilty, the son is a criminal. The physiological transmission having been begun, the hereditary fatality imposes itself and is not interrupted. As is the father, so is the son." [21] These presumptions may seem elementary, even primitive for a mind of such apparently refined and subtle temperament as that of Eça, but it would seem that the "Story of a Graceful Body" may well have reflected such ideas; certainly, *Amaro* and *Bazilio* are not exempt from such gross presumptions. But again, all conjecture about the "Story of a Graceful Body" is just that—conjecture.

In the early 1960s, Eça's eldest daughter typed out a long manuscript of some eighty pages, with the first page missing and a few other pages either out of order or missing entirely. This manuscript is one Eça's unpublished papers that still lie in a trunk at the family estate, A Quinta de Santo Ovídio. This text gives every evidence of being a rough draft of *Cousin Bazilio*, the work published in February 1878, well after the appearance of the first two editions of *The Sin of Father Amaro*. This draft, which has not been published but which has been meticulously described by the French scholar Dominique Sire, offers a few details of extreme interest. A secondary character such as Leopoldinha is existent in this draft, and the same for the gentle family friend, Sebastião, who attempts to mediate between the absent husband and the erring wife. The cliché-ridden Acácio, one of Eça's most finished and devastating characterizations, carries the name of Major Pimenta in this manuscript. In this earlier version, he lacks the Dickensian pomp and gesture which Eça will give to the figure as Counselor Acácio in the final version of 1878. Whole chapters of this draft, which have just come to light, remain almost untouched and went directly into the final version—the dreadful soirée of Chapter II, the reading of Ernestinho's theater piece, the condemnation by Jorge of an adulteress, along with the shocked reaction of the rest of the guests in the salon. Also included in the final version are such scenes as the arrival of the seducer cousin, the description of the squalid Paraiso, the blackmail by the servant Juliana, who has purloined the mistress' letters to her amorous cousin. On the other hand, this draft contains no material at all which corresponds to the last six chapters of the 1878 *Cousin Bazilio*. But what of the principal protagonists? They are there in this draft, of course, and they behave in roughly the same tragicomic way that they do later. What is intriguing is the fact that in this hasty and unedited version, *the figure of Luiza is named Amélia, and the seductive cousin is not named Bazilio, but João Eduardo*. Of course, Amélia will become the seduced innocent of the three versions of *The Sin of Father Amaro*, while the figure of João Eduardo will be transfigured into Amélia's rejected lover—the liberal freethinker whose sincere love for the girl will be thwarted by the odious Father Amaro. What is even more fascinating about this manuscript is the fact that on page 40, approximately halfway through, the name Luiza begins to appear, without at all annulling the appearance of a figure called Amélia. Eça is referring to one character concept under two different names. On page 45, the name Amélia is crossed out and is replaced by Luiza. This Luiza will carry on to the end. What conclusions might be drawn from these tantalizing pages? I leave it to Mlle Sire: "Therefore, *Cousin Bazilio* could have been written prior to *The Sin of Father Amaro* . . . in a word, could not this ms. be 'The Story of a Graceful Body,' and could it not be contemporary to [the first version of] *The Sin of Father Amaro?*" [22] Whether we have the "lost" first fiction of Eça is not at all clear; what we do have is incontrovertible proof that *Bazilio* is either contemporaneous with, or prior to, even the most primitive draft of the first edition of *The Sin of Father Amaro*, written between 1871 and 1875. This might encourage us to read both works in a parallel fashion in order to comprehend more fully Eça's literary apprenticeship as a novelist.

Another common thread throughout these works, and one that gave an even greater astringency to Eça's thematics, was undoubtedly his reading of Proudhon. For the purposes of both *Amaro* and *Bazilio,* the Proudhon we now recognize as the precursor of socialist alternatives to Marx and one of the founders of modern sociology—*that* Proudhon is barely visible within the contexts of the three versions of *The Sin of Father Amaro* or *Cousin Bazilio.* Another aspect of Proudhon's writings—his ferocious misogyny—furnished Eça with a program around which the characters of his novels may well have gained an imposing degree of consistency, if not believability. Though Proudhon would have been the last to admit the intrusions of literature into his myopically didactic program relating to love and marriage, it is not impossible to discern in Part IV of his *De la Justice dans la Révolution et dans l'Église* an embryonic series of situations, characters, and observations by Proudhon which the Eça of the early 1870s could not possibly have passed over without noting their inherent possibilities for novelistic realization. Without pretending to give an organic view of Proudhon's total effect on Eça during the Coimbra-Lisbon-Leiria years, a few elements of that hysterical tract entitled "Amour et Mariage" deserve comment, above all as oblique accompaniment to Eça's dark and grimly retributive views on the matter of *A Venus Tenebrosa.*

For Proudhon, marriage and the family become the foundations of justice, the microcosm which represents the societal religion of humanity. Love must be subordinated to this justice; it cannot and must not be allowed to overpower the imperious demands of the family and the ménage. The bond of familial love, insists Proudhon, is threatened by the idolatrous divinization of Romantic love, which in turn undermines the structure of the family first and then goes on to destroy the whole structure of civilized society. Poets and novelists are guilty of a mindless celebration of this inebriative caricature of the love that should not reign in the home and that brings depravation to our youth—that is, those most susceptible to this fanciful idolatry. The lover, impelled by her or his Bovaresque readings, "dreams of an intimate, continuous, inviolable and eternal union, lost in solitude, far from men and things." Love, in Proudhonian terms, is born of "being in a state of heat, an organic and repugnant fatality." Only through marriage can it be transformed into the source of our own humanity and responsibility toward society. Lovers who love outside marriage, whether simply unmarried or, what is more likely, adulterers and adulteresses, fatally isolate themselves from society and resign themselves to their instincts. all with the aim of possessing each other. What are the implacable consequences of such social irresponsibility? asks Proudhon: "The lovers possess each other; the soul has felt joy, the flesh is satisfied, the ideal has taken wing. A movement that is the reverse of the first, and just as inevitable, reveals itself. The cycle of abatement has begun. In vain does the imagination attempt to retain the soul in a state of ecstasy. Reason awakens and is embarrassed; from the deepest depths of the conscience, liberty show its ironic laughter; the heart becomes undone; reality and its consequences— pregnancy, childbirth, the mother's nursing—all combine to make the ideal grow dim."

Following this parodic view of love and marriage, Proudhon assures us that the arrival of the inevitable children can ameliorate this distressing collapse of the Romantic ideal, "but such reprises can never equal the first explosion in quality and in power." [23] Christianity is the guilty party in this divinization of love, because of the pernicious use within Christian society of the falsely exalted language of mystical love. Exorbitant Mariolatry causes the corruption of innocent and well-meaning adolescents and causes the corruption of the ideal of priestly celibacy itself. Proudhon sees this around him everywhere; above all it stems from a corruption of language and action which is at the source of the degradation in behavior within the church itself, visible above all in provincial parishes and provincial parishioners.

But it is not only the language of popular pamphlets and such novels as George Sand's *Lélia* which bring on these catastrophes; it is also due to such works as the apparently innocuous *Paul et Virginie*, "a so-called pastorale which should be on

the index of all families." Proudhon makes no distinctions between "honest novels" and "obscene works"—all literature is a
panderer in disguise; all literature produces temptations which
cannot be alleviated either by "work, reading, walking, or cool
drinks of any kind." The worst excesses are suffered by young
seminarians and nuns, in which case the "zeal of religion and
the fervor of mysticism produce the same effect as platonic
love." [24] In many senses, we are at the heart of the substratum
of all three versions of *The Sin of Father Amaro.* These sections of
De la Justice . . . , with their acute and passionate analyses of
the hypocrisy, the slippery moral standards and the general
clerical corruption of the church must have had a due effect
upon Eça's moralistic imagination. This is what he read in
Leiria, and this is the atmosphere which was to become the
reference point for the drama of passions that is *The Sin of
Father Amaro.*

Such anguished protestations only dramatized for Eça a suffocating reality—the melodrama of the "laws of nature" and the
impositions of celibacy in the church and order in society. As
one of Proudhon's tortured priests exclaims in the testimony
contained in *De la Justice* . . . , "for me, approaching as I am
the age of sixty, I am beginning to enjoy a bit of calm. If I had
to begin my life as a priest over again and return to being
twenty-five years old, I would rather be shot right now!" [25]

3. *Chronology of* The Sin of Father Amaro *(First Edition).*

Before taking up his post in England, Eça handed over the
primitive version of *The Sin of Father Amaro* to the *Revista Occidental,* a new magazine whose secretary was his good friend
Jaime Batalha Reis, with much of the daily editorial work in the
hands of Eça's old Coimbra classmate and sometime admirer,
Antero de Quental. This was not an ideal choice. The letters to
Batalha Reis concerning the publication of the first version of
The Sin of Father Amaro are worth looking at, since they explain
and clarify the murky prehistory of the text and partially explain Eça's implacable drive toward a more perfect version,

which will bring forth two more versions of the novel, all with the same title, though the texts are so radically different. But the question remains: Why do Eça's actions and intentions regarding this primitive manuscript seem so baffling and even inexplicable?

The reasons are not hard to find. Eça left the manuscript of *The Sin of Father Amaro* with Batalha Reis for publication in the review, that is for sure. This is the version that may well have been begun in Leiria in 1870, continued in Lisbon, and most certainly finished in Havana during his first consular appointment. But there was one understood proviso—that the manuscript was to be handed over to Batalha Reis not in order to be printed "as is," but as the basis for rough galleys, which in turn would be elaborated, rewritten, and completely changed by the author while in residence at his new post in Newcastle. The correspondence illuminates what will be a Queirosian constant in his mature working methods—primitive galleys as the basis for major adjustments to the text. Here is Eça to Batalha Reis, dated Newcastle, January 6, 1875: "My dear Batalha: What's Father Amaro up to? I've been waiting for him to arrive in an envelope, flattened out and clad for publication, having put his crime behind him. I have waited in vain. Do you have other plans for the novel vis-à-vis the magazine? Has the laborious birth of the magazine suffered some kind of setback? Has it been impossible to convert into print the romantic scribblings of which that realistic account has been made? If this is not the case, send me the proofs." [26]

Within a few weeks the requested galleys arrived and were sent back to Lisbon on February 8, but with a stern condition: "It is indispensable, it is absolutely necessary that I review some of the second set of galleys or the page proofs. The changes I made are important and complex. The very style of the work is fastidious and mannered to begin with, full of little subtleties and ultimately sensitive to punctuation. If we add typographical errors to it we'll have made a lamentable mess." [27]

Eça not only sent the galleys back encrusted with extensive emendations, but whole new chapters were included, with the request that they be intercalated, if at all possible, into the primitive text. But Eça's impressive assiduousness ("I have revised those proofs with a sublime degree of care") was in vain. Without waiting for a round of proofs from Eça, the *Revista Occidental* appeared on February 15 with the first three chapters of the uncorrected first galleys. Time was pressing, it is clear. No matter what the explanation, it was an ungracious move on the part of the editors.

Eça's first set of galleys could not possibly have arrived before the already planned publication date of the first number. His volcanic reaction against these manipulations was not long in coming, but Batalha and Antero persisted in their dreadful botch. The final text as published included neither major nor minor adjustments to the texts which Eça had so carefully executed in the galleys sent from Newcastle on February 8. Worse, what *was* published was actually a truncated version in which the enumeration of the chapters leaps from IX to XI, then from XIV to XX, followed by XVII through XIX, followed by an unnumbered chapter, then XX through XXII, chapter XX being repeated twice.[28] Quite a debut.

This first number of the *Revista Occidental* arrived in Newcastle during the third week of February. The ensuing salvo came in the form of a terse cable, then a vituperative letter (cable, February 26): "Stop publication novel send proofs published installment outrageous I will not authorize publication rest before reviewing proofs"; (letter, February 26): "I give you the rough draft of a novel and instead of publishing the novel you publish the draft! . . . We agreed that I would correct the proofs; otherwise, what I gave you was nothing more than a shapeless, senseless thing. But you don't wait for the proofs; you publish the shapeless, senseless thing. It's truly outrageous!"

Eça soon divined the identity of the true maker of this editorial mishmash—none other than the ultimate Proudhonian of letters and maximum literary moralist, Antero de Quental. It was Antero's "moralizing scissors," to use the phrase of Ernesto Guerra da Cal, which pruned the more scabrous sections from the draft of the novel. Eça is not to be consoled: "I'm sick with rage. If Antero were here I'd throttle him. . . . Antero is the greatest critic on the peninsula, but he knows as much about art as I know about mechanics. To have Antero overseeing the publication of *Amaro* is simply too horrible. I most emphatically request you not to send me that odious magazine. . . . Butchers! The Devil take you! May you roast in Hell, you hoodlums! Did your excellencies not perceive that the first chapter was incomprehensible? And for a simple reason: columns were missing! Entire columns were missing, you monsters! Assassins! May Satan swallow you whole!"

Nonetheless, more defective numbers of the *Revista Occidental* continue to arrive indifferently; by April 23, Eça is still unable to contain himself; he begins a conciliatory letter to Batalha only to end with more explosive invective: "each issue of the magazine to reach me is a fresh dagger blow! I reel, I faint, I send you the choicest oaths by the south winds! Licking my chops with delight I think up tortures for you: impalement, flaying alive, drawing and quartering. The last issue above all! Am I an ass? Are you? Careful—If I decide to abuse you, this letter of conciliation will turn into a diatribe of hatred." [29]

Two more numbers were to arrive after this missive, with the usual defective enumeration of chapters and similar disregard of Eça's laboriously corrected galleys. In due course, he will request Batalha to send back the unused, amplified galleys so that the book might appear in the form of a nonserialized bound volume; this will be the much-vaunted second edition of the work, which subsequently was published in Lisbon in 1876, with a short preface by the author. In a letter to Ramalho from Newcastle dated, March 1, 1875, Eça strikes a rather resigned tone over the whole affair. [30] This second edition is much more than a mere amplification or simple publication of the corrected first galleys which never saw the light of day. New characters are introduced, not only are episodes amplified, but in some cases whole new sections are introduced. It is another book, with another technique and another literary orientation. Later in this chapter we will discuss the rather peculiar dissimilarities between this edition and the primitive draft Eça so imprudently handed over to Batalha Reis and Antero de Quental. For the moment, the revealing short preface to the second

edition will give us a short list of alterations and transfigurations of the primitive version. As is often the case with Eça's
critical declarations, this text is as much an obfuscation of the
facts as it is a clarification: *"The Sin of Father Amaro* comes out
now in book form, rewritten and transmogrified. Part of the old
structure was torn down to make way for the new. Many chapters were rebuilt line by line. New chapters were added, the plot
was reworked and expanded, the characters made more
rounded and refined. In short, the entire work is more
polished. By the same token, *The Sin of Father Amaro,* such as it
appeared in the *Revista Occidental,* was a sketch, a makeshift
edition. What is published here is the completed work and the
definitive edition." [31]

So far so good. Here we have a succinct résumé of the major
changes effected within the text. However, when Eça begins to
describe for us the theoretical and critical change of stance
underlying the making of this second edition, he falls into what
must be termed open misinterpretation, if not outright decep-
tion. As we shall see, there are understandable reasons for this
literary sleight of hand: "In style and characterization, as well as
certain aspects of the plot and the dialogue, this new work
retains many of the old version's faults, as is to be expected.
Traces of partisan literary obsessions that played an important
role in the original conception of the book are still present. In
terms of pure art, they are regrettable. Nevertheless, as these
defects are attributable to the very concept and the logical concept of the work, complete elimination of them would entail a
radical reworking of the idea and the form of the novel." [32]

Nothing could be further from the literary reality that is this
second edition of *The Sin of Father Amaro.* If anything is to be
said about the critical theory that lies subjacent in the second
edition, it would be to the effect that this rewriting and amplification denote an Eça who has willfully removed the last vestiges
of descriptive Romanticism and who, with equal force of will,
has subjected himself to a scabrous brand of Naturalist practice.
The preface announces a text that has liberated itself from
"certain preoccupations of a school and party," but it is precisely this text—the second edition—which gives us Eça's most

brutally Naturalist novel. In spite of Eça's assurances, the *Revista Occidental* version shows no doctrinaire rigor, as does the second version. From the point of view of literary theory, the first edition is a passionate, even naïve text, a subliminal outburst from a young writer. The question remains: Why does the author describe the primitive text in terms which could not possibly correspond to the text? Further, why would he similarly distort the primary characteristics of the revised text, in a mirrorlike reversal which any knowledgeable reader could easily discern? The answer may well lie in the simple allegation that Eça protests too much. The second version *is* an unusual example of literary partisanship; it, and not the first version, reflects all too clearly the "school and party tendencies" mentioned in the prologue; it is precisely this element which unleashed Machado de Assis's devastating critique of this, the second edition. And it is this critique which caused Eça to engage in distortions, misstatements, and evasions of facts and dates in the published and unpublished prologues to the third edition of 1880.

Let us look at Machado's 1878 critique once again; it is not only a lucid exposition of one of the major defects of this revision, but it is also an open accusation of plagiarism—the purported *Urtext*, Machado will insinuate, is Zola's *La Faute de l'Abbé Mouret*. The accusations have some relevance to the general tenor of the revisions undertaken by Eça for the second edition, and it is clear that Machado's allegations touched him to the quick, exacerbating his already unsure view of his own work. Furthermore, Machado does not try to hide his distaste for the doctrinal defects of this second edition: "It is relentless, consistent, logical Realism taken to obscure and childish extremes. We witness the appearance in our language of a straightforward, vigorous and unwavering Realist determined to make his chisel ring on the marble of yet another literary school which, in Mr. Eça de Queirós's eyes, was but a ruin and an outworn tradition. For the first time we saw a book in which indecency (for let us use the proper term; we are attempting to refute the man's doctrine, not his talent—even less the man himself), in which indecency and baseness were examined with particular fondness and described with item-by-item precision. . . . As regards the story itself, and the episodes which embellish it, they are the greatest attraction of *The Sin of Father Amaro*. They smack of forbidden fruit." [33] Eça's response to the general tenor of these charges was not to appear until the publication of the third version in 1880, and even then, the published prologue to this version will be a heavily truncated version of the extensive and devious response (in draft form) which was never published in his lifetime. Before examining the formal and the thematic variations in the three versions, it might be useful to look at this argumentative response to Machado, which Eça's better judgment induced him not to publish. After some preliminary roulades, Eça launches into a series of declarations which ought to give pause: "When I published *The Sin of Father Amaro* for the first time, I had an incomplete knowledge of provincial Portugal, of the devout life, of the motives and manners of clerics. Afterward, having visited the locale in a methodical and lengthy way, and having perhaps observed things better, I simply redid my book upon this new basis of analysis. . . . *The Sin of Father Amaro* was written in 1871, read to a few friends in 1872, and published in 1874 [sic]. The book of Sr. Zola, *La Faute de l'Abbé Mouret* . . . was written and published in 1874 [sic].[34]

In the words of João Gaspar Simões, there is "manifest confusion" in these declarations; this is the most generous way of explaining away what are simple misstatements of facts. Since the novel is set in Leiria and Eça spent those uncomfortable months in Leiria during 1871, it is more than probable that a rough draft of the *Revista Occidental* version *was* written at least partially in Leiria, but it is manifestly untrue that the author had any more opportunities to complete his "incomplete knowledge of provincial Portugal," since Eça left for Cuba in November 1872 and returned only fitfully to Portugal during vacations from the consulate. The subsequent revisions contained in the editions of 1876 and 1880 owe nothing to a more profound observation of provincial mores. On the contrary, the revisions were related to a desire to sharpen the style of the work and, even more important, a wish to make the work conform more exactly to a preconception recently acquired concerning the nature of literature and the aims of Realism itself—for him, literature must be a critical discipline. As he was to say so often, "The idealist gave you a *falsification;* the realist gives you *verification.* Therein lies the difference between idealism and Realism: the former falsifies, whereas the latter verifies" (*OC*, III, 915). João Gaspar Simões has explained the impulse behind the revisions quite succinctly: "The penchant for critical analysis and social-mindedness in his work became more fundamental to Eça the more he removed himself from the arena of political and social action, in the strict sense of the word. One might call this a compensatory mechanism. Seeing in print a work of his characterized more by the 'abstraction of innate fantasies' than 'the study of real phenomena' displeased him for this very reason. The first version of *The Sin of Father Amaro* derives more from an abstraction of his personal experience in fact than from observation made into literary Realism." [35] With regard to Eça's insistence on the "metaphysical impossibility" of his having been influenced by the work of Zola, it must simply be said that it is not a "metaphysical impossibility," but a simple reality. The expanded description of the mass in Chapter VI of the 1876 version surely owes something to the magnificently orchestrated mass in Chapter II of Book I of *La Faute . . .*, while the burial of Amélia in Chapter XXVII surely owes something to Chapter XVI of Book III of *La Faute. . . .* But these are minor matters, not at all related to the extraordinary evolution of this text.

4. The Story Itself

There is a nucleus of a story in all three versions, but it is fair to say that the 1875 version published pell-mell in the *Revista Occidental* is tonally the least fastidious, the most spontaneous and subliminal text Eça ever allowed into print. It is the text that is most touched with the remains of Romantic plenitude and innocent ecstasy. As Eça's good friend Oliveira Martins was to describe it, *"The Sin of Father Amaro* was the only novel that

came out of Eça's guts; all the rest are humoristic works." While
the latter part of the statement is debatable, surely Oliveira
Martins was correct in noting a visceral, confessional quality to
the writing which subsequent revisions were to mitigate, all in
response to Eça's increasing control over his ironic stance before self and society.

Portuguese society is barely visible in this first, truncated version. One of the centers of the text is surely Father Amaro
Vieira himself, a hypersensitive melancholic who finds himself
named to serve in the provincial cathedral parish in Leiria, a
town that might be imagined as the Portuguese equivalent of
Flaubert's Rouen. But Leiria had, in Eça's vision, a distinctly
more impoverished and suffocating air, what with its inevitable
conflicts between ultra-Catholic majorities and Voltairean liberal minorities a la Homais, along with a full complement of
gossips, useless functionaries, aged but still lusty spinsters, all
guided by a considerable case of well-fed but shabby clerics of
surprisingly liberal sexual mores. The world of Leiria is a sharp
initiation to the naïve young priest. This "first" Father Amaro is
drawn by Eça as handsome, guileless, and self-effacing, without
stratagems or worldly ambitions, and certainly without an
openly sexual sensibility—a potential sensualist, yes, but still
without awareness, without consciousness: "The priest hung his
head over the soup bowl and blew on his spoon, eating in silence. The light outlined him clearly. His small head, with its
close-cropped black hair and salient tonsure emerged from a
high, tight collar. His complexion was pale, and his skin had a
delicate quality. His nose was small and straight, his eyes large
and black, and his long eyelashes revealed a sensitive, anxious,
and curious nature." [36] After some initial reluctance on his
part, Father Amaro boards at the home of Sra. Joaneira, and
there he meets her daughter Amélia, a young woman of some
twenty-two years. Given Eça's rather jaundiced and sardonic
ideas about the education of young women in Portugal, Eça
makes her into the classic case of the results of a Catholic
education—a woman whose own sexuality has yet to be recognized. "She had always lived in a religious environment. They
had taught her the catechism and dogma and told her of divine

retribution. Consequently, God seemed to her a barbarous, violent thing that allotted suffering and death to all. It was necessary to appease Him through fasting and prayer, attending the novena, loving priests, taking communion, reciting the rosary, and paying attention to the sermons. . . . Sometimes, when she went to bed, she felt guilty if she had forgotten to say the Hail Mary. She did penance, fearing that God would smite her with fevers or make her slip on the stairs and fall." [37] This is the embryonic personality that one observer has called "rather vegetative," [38] and it is true that Eça has given the future mistress of Father Amaro an excessively passive nature, without awareness. Her personality is due to the mechanical application of hereditary factors, one of the weakest aspects of his literary Naturalism. Such descriptive passages as the following will soon disappear from the subsequent versions: "She was emotional by nature. She had inherited certain sensibilities from her father . . . as a child, Amélia had been entranced by the grandiose rites her mother had shown her. She felt boundless love for the crucified Jesus, the statues of the saints and the stories of martyrdom. Sometimes, in church, under the magnetic influence of the organ, the incense, the penetrating voices of the priests and the splendorous altar, she broke down and cried." Eça will make of Amélia a passionate reader of popular romances, those peopled with noble chevaliers, passionate ladies cloistered behind high convent walls, inquisitors in deep dungeons interrogating weeping sinners, with crucifix in hand.[39] Between Amaro and Amélia, Eça will establish a paradigmatic situation—priest and virgin woman, "father" and daughter—which will prevail throughout the rewritings. One should note also the hypertrophic sentimentality of the descriptions, their morbid and indeterminate sensuality. Within this superheated atmosphere, Eça brings Amélia and Amaro together in a suicidal passion. Eça carefully registers the fateful union of carnality and religion, a favorite topic of his social criticism. Needless to say, he will quickly abandon (in the revised versions) the kind of treacly rationale that he gives to Amélia in the first version: "She maintained that love was not a sin. His priesthood blessed it: through His priest she was loving God. It may look like a sin, but it was God who willed it. God writes straight in crooked lines. Nevertheless, she felt now and again that perhaps it was a sin; in those moments, terrified, she loved Amaro all the more. To forgo paradise only intensified her pleasure and her love. It meant suffering for him, longing for him, crying out for him. At the same time, the sacrilege of their rendezvous, their evil and horror, made her enjoyment both bitter and sweet, abrasive and sublime." [40]

This vertiginous passion will culminate in the inevitable melodrama—Amélia becomes pregnant and gives birth under circumstances of considerable anguish and mutual recrimination. The birth of the child brings tragic consequences, for not only is Amélia dishonored according to ancient Iberian code, but the possibility of marriage is perforce excluded. Amaro sees his potential ecclesiastical career as fatally compromised; not only will Amélia conveniently expire due to the trauma of the birth, but Amaro himself will drown the child in a genuinely horrific scene at the end of the novel.

A passionate union of temperaments gradually converts itself into the most intense kind of conflictive drama on the social plane; Eça is here re-creating within his imagination precisely the same elements which made his own illegitimate birth a tale so dramatic, so "novelistic." In fictive terms, the desire that formerly went mute and unexpressed with the strictures of a provincial society has now taken living, dynamic form, and this realization—the child—becomes the ruinous testimony to the breaking of the tabu. In this sense, the child must be destroyed, just as desire must be destroyed, "with a brutality both shocking and eminently logical." [41]

The death of the child is a hysterical denouement. Since this text is not available in English and has been rarely seen in Portuguese, and since Eça obfuscated the raw emotional stress of the scene in later versions, it might be useful to quote extensively from this telling passage:

> Amaro was aware of the soft, gently crying thing he held bundled in his arms. He started running down the terrace and soon came to the road.

At that moment, however, the touch of his infant son upset his plans—his orderly unshakable plans: to leave the child at someone's door, abandon him, give him up forever. What if dogs should attack him or the cold air do him in? What if no one heard! The child could cry all night and then die alone, like an animal, frozen stiff! Or leave him in the fields, in the damp grass! Abandon him! It was so cold. But he could not turn back. Dionysia had no milk. How could he take him to the city and shamelessly admit: "Look at this child—he is my son." He could not. He could not. So he remained alone on the dark lane, trembling, stricken, neither advancing nor retreating, almost numb, listening to the faint, shrill, whining cries that rose up from beneath the cloak. . . .

If he left the child there, in the fields, everything would come out. . . . And if he killed himself? There was the river, gently murmuring. It ran deep at that spot, beneath the oscillating reflections as shiny and delicate as reflections on steel! The child no longer cried. He reached under the cloak to touch it: it felt cold. If only it were dead! Dead. . . . Suddenly like a roll of thunder, the idea of killing it took possession of his mind. To kill it! To kill it! He no longer had thoughts, consciousness, feelings. He acted instinctively, like an animal. He was afraid, so afraid. His fear was carnal, savage, vile. He stood on the riverbank where there were canebrakes. He thought he heard footsteps. He knelt down, placed the child on the ground, and opened the cloak. The swaddling clothes stood out white against the dark earth. Nearby was a large, mossy stone, wet and heavy. He took it, placed it next to the infant, and bound everything tightly together into a heavy bundle that would sink. He thought he heard the child, his son, softly crying. In front of him was the water, dark and faintly sparkling. A few bent reeds trailed in the water, making them quiver. Tense, his breath rasping in his throat and teeth chattering, Amaro let go of the bundle. It went

pshah! and the water flowed calmly on. He did hear
steps. He broke into a desperate, cowardly run. [In his
room] . . . he calmly lighted the lamp. He looked at it
for a moment with moronic attentiveness. Then suddenly, he threw himself face down on the bed and
there remained, immobile." [42]

Few texts of Eça will carry this weight of melodrama, and even
fewer will reflect the febrile and subliminal tone of the descriptions. All is action, without premeditation or calculation. In the
version of 1876, Eça is able to register an even greater intensity
and complexity within Amaro as he kills the child; at the same
time, there is a touch of the crass Naturalist which disappears
completely in the third version of the work. The revised scene
begins at approximately the same moment as the first version:

The child was not crying. He felt it beneath the
cloak. The flesh seemed cool to him, like the flesh of a
dying man. If only it were dead! He lowered his gaze
and uncovered the child. There was a weak cry, like
the shrill squeal of a rat. It was alive. All at once, for no
reason, the thought occurred to him: Kill it! Kill it
now! He was not reasoning or thinking ahead. He had
but one idea. It was a solid, almost painful presence
inside his head: Kill it! It was the answer to everything!
All of his fears and anxieties, all of the danger and
recrimination would be finished! A horrible, savage
selfishness overcame him. The infant meant danger to
him, and also evil, dishonor, infamy, sin, and crime.
And he felt fear—a vile, carnal fear. Fear that they
would find him out, denounce him to the bishop, turn
their backs on him in public; fear that they would
throw him into a dungeon, shut him away, shivering
with fever in the depths of a cellar. These ideas
pricked him like kicks from a horse. He thought the
infant was a hateful thing whose purpose was to accuse
and villify him, to starve him, to do him in! He would
have liked to strangle it with his bare hands. He looked

around. There was a small canebrake rustling in the
wind. At his feet the water sparkled dimly. He knelt
down, laid the child on the ground and opened the
cloak. The swaddling clothes and the towel stood out
white against the dark earth. He got up stiffly; his hair
was standing on end. The infant cried. Suddenly he
knelt down, took hold of a large rock, and placed it on
top of the child. He tied everything together into a
tight bundle, snatched it up in a jerk, and threw it into
the water. It went pshah! A few frogs jumped in
fright. Amaro stood still, petrified, staring at the river.
He crouched down to listen, leaned farther over the
water, and instinctively immersed his hand. The cold
made him shiver. He jumped up, blankly looked
around, and suddenly started running along the river.

   When he entered his house the cathedral bell was
chiming two o'clock. He felt his way up the stairs. The
candle on the table was burning. He went over to it.
There, still rolled in its mailing wrapper, was the *Diário
Popular* which he had brought in that afternoon. He
opened it automatically. He began reading the first
line of the lead article: "No news in the political realm.
The latest decision of the honorable Minister of the
Navy. . . ." He reread those words two times, then
ten times, then over and over again. He made an effort
to remember who was in charge of the navy.[43]

   The text from the second edition is paradigmatic in many
ways, since it is not a rewritten text but one which has been
re-created and even superimposed upon the primitive version.
The former instability and blind terror of the early Amaro is
here replaced by one who is still moved to kill the child instinctively, but who now enters into a dialectical discussion, as it
were, within himself. He ponders the consequences in a more
rational way. What was formerly a telegraphic description of
irrational motives becomes, in this version, a reasoned attempt
to justify the death of the child in view of Amaro's own place in
society and in view of his ecclesiastical career. In effect, society is

called in to marshal its own justifications within the febrile imagination of Amaro. This new Amaro has lost his inner waywardness, we might say, and has gained a more submissive and conformist relationship to authority and to traditional society and its mores. Too, there are stylistic adjustments which would have been unthinkable to the Eça that wrote the earlier version—for instance, that repulsive expression which tries to convey the sound of the child's whimpering: "the shrill squeal of a rat." This is a kind of reductive leveling which denotes another view of human existence. Amaro's tears disappear, and so too do the formerly inevitable chattering of teeth. The rock which weighs the child down, so portentously described as a "large, mossy stone, wet and heavy" in the primitive version, becomes the more modest but equally lethal "large rock." The crime itself occupies some two long paragraphs in the primitive version, while the return to his rooms is dispatched in just two short lines. In the revised version, the infant is killed with a more frightening economy of gesture, but the ensuing paragraphs, including the catatonic reading of the *Diário Popular,* are developed with painstaking care. In sum, the ambiance begins to move into the motivations for the actions of the cleric; he begins to reason with an eye to his future, a process which the terrified naif of the first version would have found both despicable and unthinkable.[44]

One *does* have the impression that a thesis is beginning to impose itself upon the novel. Unquestionably, the second version is decidedly more anticlerical in its formulations of the quandary represented by priestly celibacy, and this is underlined by the disappearance in the second edition of the only priestly colleague (Cónego Silva), who is saintly enough to avoid the endless gourmandizing and general sensuality of the other parish priests (Dias, Natário and Brito).

But there are other aspects of this revision which suggest to what extent Machado de Assis's accusations have some validity. After all, we are not attempting to trace sources; what is of interest is the fact that the *presumptions* of this new text have been altered, and the optical view is often more lurid and scabrous. Let us take as an example the most grisly scene ever written by Eça in any circumstance—the moment when Amélia's former suitor, João Eduardo, sees her cadaver in the process of being prepared for the coffin by bored and callous attendants:

> João Eduardo looked on all the while as if magnetically attracted to the scene. He could only make out half of the room, a cluttered place into which death had entered without warning.
>
> Inside a dully reflective brass basin, pieces of cloth were soaking in water. A starched ruffled skirt hung from a window latch. On top of the table, at the base of the mirror, were combs and hair pieces and the glittering metal hook of a garter. To one side João Eduardo saw the legs of an iron bed. From the headboard, which he could not see, came a vivid, warm, yellowish light, as if from enormous candles. He imagined that the corpse was in that bed.
>
> The man who was lining the casket stood up, brushing fibers of wool from his hands.
>
> "Come on," he said. "Let's stretch her out."
>
> João Eduardo felt an intense, painful, irresistible curiosity. He moved and looked again . . . he recognized her at once. . . .
>
> Her pallid face was scarcely discernible amid the bright candlelight, the whiteness of the satin shroud, the crown of roses, and the veil that framed her head. The slightly open mouth, with its blackened lips, was the only trace of darkness. Her arms lay against her sides, with the hands resting on the mattress. The fingers were somewhat twisted. The heavy, close-fitting shroud vaguely outlined the shape of her breasts, her joined legs and the bulge of her knees, which were slightly raised. It also revealed her feet, in heavy, squat shoes of yellowish satin, not quite touching. Amidst the lights a horsefly droned monotonously back and forth over the body.
>
> The gray-haired woman in the black smock drew

near. She noticed that the sleeve of the shroud had come apart at the seam near the shoulder. She took one of the huge pins she carried stuck in her bodice and plunged it into the corpse with great effort, fastening the satin sleeve to the shoulder.[45]

I leave it to Alberto Machado da Rosa to describe the atypical nature of this kind of grotesquerie: "in all of the vast opus of Eça de Queirós there is nothing as harshly realistic as the handling of Amélia's corpse in the second version of *The Sin of Father Amaro*. The entire episode is an offensive autopsy of horrors." [46]

5. Bazilio, *Machado de Assis*.

The events that intervened between the second and the third editions of *The Sin of Father Amaro* create the dominant assumptions that guide the final revision of 1880 and the rapid writing of *Cousin Bazilio*. But as always, Eça is mightily unsure of his own powers and of the direction and general tenor of his writing. In a letter of November 7, 1876, Eça forcefully urges Ramalho to write a critical essay on the second edition of the novel; but he also evinces considerable doubts about the nature and quality of the revisions he has just completed. "I need counsel, direction; I need to 'know myself'—in order to persevere and develop what is good [in my writing] and to avoid the bad, or modify it, disguise it. But isn't it exactly that which is the most difficult thing? . . . So, tell me what you think is good and bad in this new *Amaro* . . . the books that I am about to write are conceived and executed with the same idea—*more perfect in their elaboration, more misanthropic in their conception* [italics mine]." [47]

In effect, in a letter to his publisher of February 1877, he announces that he is hard at work on "Cousin João Carlos," evidently an early title for the work now known as *Cousin Bazilio*. In April 1877 he is drafting the final copy; the manuscript is sent in two installments, one of May 17 and the other

June 15. In effect, *Cousin Bazilio* was written in an incredibly short time—possibly as little as three or four months. Is it possible for such a lengthy novel to be written without the aid of the draft discussed above? Probably not. *Cousin Bazilio* has all the appearances of a hurried redraft, subject to little revision. Unlike the two versions of *The Sin of Father Amaro*, it will never undergo any successive rewritings.

One of the elements that must have forced Eça to such an inordinate, slapdash effort was more than likely his exhaustion with the "bestial" Amaro as revised. A new kind of discipline, another approach to *Amaro* was clearly in the offing. This time, Eça will make use of a masterpiece of Flaubert—*Madame Bovary*. So much has been written about the "influence" of Flaubert in Eça's work that it behooves us to examine, at least in a summary fashion, the apparent correspondences between the French masterpiece and Eça's *Cousin Bazilio*. Again, Eça's process—the drawing upon another text as a kind of mirror for his own elaboration—is a key to his way of writing. In the instance of Madame Bovary, the parallels *are* striking. "The same two motifs are employed: extramarital affairs and consequent financial pressures on the two women; the same motives within these heroines: the desire to replace the prosaic world of reality with the glittering world of Romantic illusion; the same terrible revenge taken on both by that scorned world of reality. The basic differences in temperament between the two heroines, given similar motivations and similar situations—Emma, headstrong and energetic; Luiza, timorous and languid— become indicators of the debt of the creator of one to the creator of the other, when we see Luiza acting in dissonance with her basic temperament but in consonance with the temperament of Emma (the whipping of the Banker Castro)." [48] In both cases the unfaithful wife is punished for her infidelity, although the deaths are caused by differing motives. But there are other similarities; in no particular order, we might mention that there is the same desperate attempt to flee with the lover, the abandonment by the lover via a letter, similarly organized love nests—Léon's rooms in Rouen, the grim Paraiso acquired by Bazilio, similar coach rides, similar attempts by the two ladies to stave off ruin by seeking help from gross moneylenders—M. Lleureux and M. Guillaumin in *Madame Bovary*, the repulsive Castro in *Cousin Bazilio*. And of course, both Emma and Luiza are voracious readers of fantasy-laden Romantic fictions. In a few instances, Emma and Luiza seem to be made out of the same words:

Madame Bovary:

But when she saw her reflection in the mirror, she was astounded at her appearance. Her eyes had never been so large, so black, nor of such depth. She was transfigured by some subtle change permeating her entire being.

She kept telling herself, "I have a lover! A lover!" . . . So she was finally going to possess those joys of love, that fever of happiness, of which she had so longed despaired. She was entering into something marvelous where all would be passion, ecstasy, delirium; she was enveloped in a vast expanse of blue, the peaks of emotion sparkling in her thoughts. Ordinary existence seemed to be in the distance, down below, in the shadows. . . . Then she remembered the heroines in the books she had read, and the lyrical legion of these adulterous women began to sing in her memory.[49]

Cousin Bazilio:

She went to look at herself in the mirror. She thought her skin was lighter, fresher, and she had a moist, tender look in her eyes. . . . She had a lover, she did!
. . .

Immobile in the room, her arms folded, gazing fixedly, she repeated: "I have a lover!" . . . it seemed that she was finally entering a higher and more interesting existence, where each hour had its different enchantments, each step led to an extasis, and the soul was covered by a radiant light of sensations.[50]

What seem to be glaring coincidences have led critics to the belief that Emma and Luiza are national doubles of each other, the typically Queirosian appropriation of a Flaubertian model. Such inferences are misguided, not only in the specific instance of Luiza, but in the more general area of the organizing principles of Eça's fiction. We are confronted with the enigma and the mystery behind Eça's borrowings from other literatures. The borrowed elements are there, for sure, and cannot be denied. But they *do* undergo a sort of sea change and become quickly acclimated and assimilated into the peculiar structure of Portuguese society and Eça's theory about that society. In a short essay of 1954, Francis Steegmuller was one of the first of an increasing number of sensitive critics who have noted how Eça animates his characters obliquely through other models, by a sort of literary refraction: "You have certainly read—or if you haven't you'll read it some day for the sake of your own pleasure—*Cousin Bazilio,* the realistic, subtle, and sensual novel about Luiza, that Portuguese Emma Bovary, so charming in her own right, so like and yet so unlike her French counterpart. Like Emma, Luiza destroys her marriage and her life by following a chimera—in her case, the memory of a youthful attachment which seems to her more glamorous than her status as wife of a government-employed engineer. Emma Bovary, on the contrary, is haunted not by a memory but by an aspiration toward a romantic never-never land, a future in which all her repressed potentialities will find fulfillment. One is ruined because she looks back to a past whose glamour has become degeneracy, the other because she strives toward a future that is impossible, self-contradictory." [51] This is a sensible discrimination, and we might add a few more to it—after all, should we speak about the implications of the title? Why wasn't the title *Cousin Luiza?* The center of gravity in *Cousin Bazilio* is not Bazilio; it is Luiza. Bazilio is just as banal as Rodolphe or Léon, but his name gives the book its title, because Eça was determined to expose all Don Juans, all seducers, according to the wishes of the Countess in *O Misterio da Estrada de Sintra*—"the conquistador . . . must be demolished by means of ridicule, caricature, a horsewhip, and the local police force." Eça obeyed the Countess' injunction with admirable but nonetheless unfortunate rigor. The title does not correspond to the text, and it is a measure of the moral direction of the work that the contradiction between the text and its title never seemed obvious to Eça. Bazilio is the surface agent of the book, let us say; he is the catalyst for Luiza's downfall, but he is not the psychic center of the work. We should rather say that Luiza, through Emma, is at the heart of the novel, somewhat à contre-coeur. Such a possibility was cleverly formulated by a recent observer of this anomaly: "It is the nature of things which make Emma suffer; it is the nature of Emma which makes Luiza suffer, for she has not a nature of her own, that is, a consistency and wholeness of personality." [52] This is surely a part of the problematic achievement of Eça in Cousin Bazilio. We sense the presence of Emma in Luiza, but oddly enough we also perceive that Luiza "is the exact contrary of Emma." [53]

Luiza is a fundamentally satisfied creature; she knows what surfeit is. Although she is a reader of Romantic fiction, the act of reading does not impel her to realize, in the Quixote/Bovary pattern, the vocabulary of the imagination. She does not attempt to erode the power of the real by a fancied world. She is a happy occupant of her trusting husband's bed, and he in turn does not have that bovine air of Charles Bovary, trusting and loving, it is true, but incompetent, a drone, a heavy weight on Emma's life. It is Charles's goodwill and tolerance which form a part of Emma's impulse against him—her own imaginative impoverishment is the profound activator in the novel. On the other hand, Luiza finds herself haplessly betraying her absent husband for two reasons only, and they are meager: the fortuitous arrival of the once loved Cousin Bazilio, and the even more fortuitous exit of her husband for the purposes of a business venture in the South. As one observer has put it, this is a good example of Eça's "crystalline psychology." The remark is obviously not well intentioned toward Eça, of course, but there is good reason for disappointment. Flaubert would never have approved of such theatrical ruses as part of the plot machinery, although it must be said that the death of Charles's first wife is exceedingly fortuitous—how else would we have met Emma?

But the point remains: Luiza has none of the thirst for the future that impels Emma into the arms of Rodolphe and Léon; she does not sense the distance between the daily life of the word—the word as representative of objects—and its nonreferential possibility, the word as object, where the word is free to represent experiences not containable within the constrictions of the mimetic process. In sum, that situation where the word becomes a world elsewhere, a cosmos in itself. This sense of estrangement in Emma's imagination forms the nucleus for the "Quixote" pattern in her life.[54] This is the *donnée* which begins the meticulously described decline into isolation which is one of the basic Flaubertian processes visible in the work. The ball at Vaubyessard is a tantalizing affair, because it is the first instance in which Emma's readings begin to take on the forms and contours in a transfigured reality. As a creature of print who is in the process of being hypnotized into action by print, Emma takes on the roles of fancy with a sense of revenge against the grinding materialism which has been imposed upon her, and from which she is temporarily rescued—first by literature, then by her two lovers. But in the case of Luiza, although her readings are superficially similar, Eça is not able to reproduce the gradual changes effected by the act of reading, and *that* is the essence of the Quixotic process in Emma's imagination and temper. Emma loves in an insane and headlong way; Luiza has an affair. The readings have not rubbed off on her.

In Flaubert, reading brings forth a series of ideas. Whether they are admirable or loathsome, it makes no difference. These ideas become images, and these images become imaginative landscapes, possible locales for the imagined life in the future; in turn, these images and landscapes become banalities, lairs of moral decline when realized or when concretion is attempted. For Emma, life is composed of imitation and reproduction of imitation, and there is no way to sort out, from a qualitative point of view, which might be better or worse. As Mary McCarthy has observed of Flaubert, "all ideas become trite as soon as somebody expresses them." [55] From this, *Bouvard et Pécuchet* and its accompanying *Dictionnaire des idées reçues* can not be very far off.

There are other matters, too. As is well known, the maid Juliana purloins the love letters of Luiza and Bazilio, and proceeds to make use of them to better her own hideous state within the house and to extract an impossible sum of money from her mistress. In due course, the family friend Sebastião arrives at Luiza's home with a policeman and forcibly obtains the letters. In effect, she has been saved from the ignominy the letters represent. However, she contracts a mysterious and vaguely described malady and dies in the arms of her husband Jorge, while the now absent Bazilio lounges in France, well away from the *mêlée*.

Well and good; but if we consider the deaths of Emma and Luiza, it is not difficult to perceive that they pertain to an entirely different set of circumstances and motivation, not to mention differing intent on the part of the respective novelists. "Emma does not die to make a point or a moral lesson, nor does she die to prove the folly of Romantic love." [56] Rather, she dies to show, in as surreptitious and as oblique a manner as possible, the folly of a world dominated by Napoleon III and his agent, M. Homais, the local harbinger of progress and science, another example of a voracious and star-struck reader. Luiza *does* die to make a point, and that is just the trouble. But she does not disappoint us entirely. Eça is able to imbue her with a considerable degree of inner drama, all within the confines of his implacable program. Still, she lacks a proper plenitude; she is too obviously an agent in a pattern to which she must conform. The fault lies, of course, in Eça's contradictory flightiness; the lack of contentment with the finite; and worst of all, the lack of a commitment to the real. This may be the reason why, as if in compensation, this novel, describing as it does a very small affair, is so lengthy.

Luiza's death does not come with the sense of inevitability and implacability which accompany the final moments of Madame Bovary—Emma's acquiring the poison from Justin, Homais's silent and passionately helpful assistant; her long and frightful agony, her final convulsion. We can even understand why Homais would insist on watering Charles's geraniums on the next page. But Emma dies because her world has come apart. Luiza dies only became Emma has died, and thus Eça carries out implacably the "parallel which her creator has so assiduously traced between the *burguezinha* of Lisbon and the gallant rebel of Normandy." [57]

There is another aspect of *Cousin Bazilio* that has often intrigued those readers who seek a theory of types to be found in all of Eça's novels. He will insist that the major figures in the book are not intended to be drawn and were not drawn from within, but rather as gesticulating caricatures drawn from without. In a letter to Teófilo Braga, Eça gives us a catalogue of the types he has presented in the salon scene of Chapter II, and then he tells us what they represent: "Official formalism (Acácio), the small-minded sanctimony of an abrasive temperament (D. Felicidade), brainless literature (Ernestinho), acrimonious discontent of a bored bureaucrat (Julião) and, at times, when it is convenient, a poor goodhearted man (Sebastião). A social group in Lisbon is made up of these dominant elements, with just a few modifications. I know at least 20 of such circles in Lisbon" (*OC*, II, 517). As always, we are taken aback by this gross critical language, coming as it does from a novelist who professes to be intrigued by people and how they got to be what they are. But fictional actuality at this stage is generic, not individual. It is for this reason that Eça envisions his characters as types, and this is why he was so fascinated by national caricatures such as Monnier's Joseph Prudhomme or Dickens's Pickwick. Eça loved to use ritualistic figures. After all, many of the "Barbs" composed by Ramalho Ortigão were actually satiric portraits of windbag politicians whose only capabilities lay in their endlessly inflated oratorical performances. One of Ramalho's parliamentary characters, the Senator Assunçao, produces a discourse of such outrageous imbecility that Eça is moved to congratulate Ramalho for the depiction: "But above all, the discourse of Assunçao! It's extraordinary! It's immense! Send me the whole thing! Send me two! Send me his portrait! Is he your invention? Isn't he somebody created by Dickens? Could it not be an unpublished work by Molière? Did such a parlimentary session take place, was such a speech really made? Well, then; we must be extraordinary! Does this mean that we are a great people? Do we actually possess, alive, a type like that, not only equal but superior to the great funambulesque types that other countries have? . . . Spain has Sancho Panza, France has Prudhomme, England has Pecksniff and so many others, without forgetting the immortal Pickwick, but those types are in novels, theater, and poetry; we have our Assunçao alive, in the flesh!" (*OC*, III, 510–11).

This is one part of Eça's characterological designs; out of this intent comes Counselor Acácio in *Cousin Bazilio,* a magnificent example of the consistently grave expression of vapid cliché. When asked why he did not marry, the Counselor will parry off his inquirers with such replies as: "It is a very great responsibility both before God and before society"; "the weight of years and the white hairs on my brow forbid it"; "It is long since the fires of passion became extinct in me, my dear friend"; and so on. Just as he loves to portray such drones of officialdom as Acácio, Eça is also more than anxious to dramatize the more malevolent and vengeful characters he has observed in such a society as that of Lisbon. For instance, the character of the servant Juliana in *Cousin Bazilio* probably owes her existence to the probing portrait drawn by Ramalho Ortigão in his "Barb" of April 1876, around the time Eça began to redraft the work. Compare Ramalho's insight with the venomous character of the servant Juliana; they are quite similar: "Just barely tolerating her position as a maid, and considering it a fatality from which she will try to escape at the first instance, the Portuguese maid, in the depths of her humiliation, revolts and conspires. Since life bores her, she tries at times to bring about a crisis which would bring a solution to her problem. She covets things, she schemes, she plots, she gets a lover, she lies, she steals, she plays the lottery . . . if she were to discover a small romantic secret, a criminal intrigue, how she will make them pay for the possession of that weapon! She begins by observing the lady of the house and the men who visit her at home. She begins to suspect the doctor who pays visits. She listens at the door, spys through the keyhole. If she doesn't uncover anything, she becomes irritated, becomes haughty, petulant, and insolent." [58]

This is a Juliana in skeletal form. She is one of the few at-

tempts at a truly proletarian character in Eça, a kind of malevolent creature lurking through the corridors, looking for anything, any bit of information with which she might blackmail
her rich masters. But in general these kinds of characters were
not at all Eça's forte. He is congenial only with the high trappings of the constitutionalist monarchy, the bureaucratic somnolence of the ministries, the world of the businessman and
trader. In spite of the intense pedagogy in favor of social revolution with which he was imbued since the Coimbra days, it is
very difficult, if not impossible, for him to create any character
that is, in any sense, a *worker*. Functionaries, yes; workers,
never. The world of the arriviste was his world, and there are
no other worlds in his texts.

One of the many anomalies of the Portuguese culture Eça
wanted to depict and which he represented so acutely was the
fact that, until 1875, there was no collective symbol or national
type which alluded to the Portuguese people at large—a myth
on the order of a John Bull or an Uncle Sam. In France, Monnier's Prudhomme traces his birth and ascendancy to the structures of the society of Louis Philippe: profoundly antiheroic
and antirevolutionary, the living symbol of a middle class that
was solidifying its hold upon the governing structure, a spirit
that would continue with Guizot, Lammenais, and countless
other "representative men." In England, the figure of John
Bull dynamically exemplified the matchless destiny of the em-
pire; in the United States, the lanky, patriarchal, and always
stern figure of Uncle Sam represented in an effortless way the
overwhelming political and diplomatic power of unleashed
post–Civil War capitalism. In this sense, Uncle Sam held sway
over the American public through his unique melding of political power and the financial sovereignty of the robber-barons.

Each one of these symbolic makers of history were testimony
to an urban civilization, commercial and industrial. As well as
being representative of their cultures and their political structures, the images were profoundly pedagogical, inculcating
ideals and stimulating action as well as being allusive to a historical past. But there were no mass culture types in Portugal. The
one national type that was available to Eça was precisely one

that he could not exploit—the recently drawn figure of Zé Povinho, a creation of the superbly talented cartoonist and ceramicist Rafael Bordalo Pinheiro. The birth date of Zé Povinho is symptomatic of the state of social consciousness of Portugal in the late nineteenth century. He was first sketched by Bordalo Pinheiro on June 12, 1875 (the same year as the founding of the Portuguese Socialist party, by the way). The name Zé Povinho is essentially untranslatable; it might be said to mean "Joe Little People." As drawn in numerous cartoons after 1875, he is depicted as a short, squat figure wearing a porkpie hat. He has a broad mouth, an infectious smile, rotten teeth, and a bulbous nose—he is not a light drinker. Zé has a good number of holes in his clothes and his shoes are heavily patched. He is the fate and destiny of Portugal visualized, the eternal citizen of Parvonia.[59]

Zé is an unreconstructed peasant, but not at all a peasant enjoying the fruits of his country labors. Quite the contrary, Bordalo Pinheiro's cartoons always show this kind and generous creature as the victim of a Lisbon society that has no intentions of giving him and his class the portion—the deserved portion—of the riches of a new society. Zé is marginal, conserving his rural costume and his illiteracy, never adapting himself to the world of the factory, but still essentially submissive, passive. He exudes country honesty, forthrightness, and candor. Up to his death in 1904, Bordalo Pinheiro will ring endless variations on this type. Sometimes he is depicted Gulliver style, trampled over by a procession of Portuguese kings and queens; at other times, as a saddled horse being mounted by the king and beaten with poles by Progressive ministers. In the long tale of England's political domination over Portugal, Zé Povinho will always be drawn as the peasant, that is, Portugal, with empty hands and empty pockets, but with justice on his side; John Bull and the other representatives of Europe and America are inevitably shown with bursting paunches and overbearing manner. One of the most moving of Bordalho Pinheiro's cartoons is that of June 29, 1882, showing a woman sobbing against a wall, pointing to a slogan—"We have been sold out!" Zé is shown as a shocked witness, hands raised in horror. Even after the artist's death, the figure had taken on such representative power that he continued to be drawn throughout the twentieth century. A cartoon published in a Lisbon paper of November 8, 1975, shows the two principal contenders for power—the socialist Mario Soares and the communist Alvaro Cunhal—on their knees on either side of a confessional, with a stern Zé Povinho of the cloth preparing to hear both penitents and all issues. The caption reads "Reckoning with the People" ("Contas ao Povo").

I bring up the history of this "national character" only to note that it is precisely this kind of agent of collective and populist consciousness that Eça will not be able to exploit in his fiction. He is blind to a whole range of social experience, as Dickens was not; both Eça and Dickens function as dramatizers of traits. However, neither author is attracted to tragic depths. Robert Garis has pointedly commented on this matter in the case of Dickens: "All of Dickens' attempts to register the inner life are in one way or another, demonstrations by exception to the rule that we do not ordinarily think of him as someone that very often wondered what it was like to be another person." [60] Since both Eça and Dickens were consummate actors and histrions, declaimers of their own fictions, there seems to be some conflict between their ability to intuit a multivocal work in fiction and their fascination with national traits and caricatures. In spite of his most strenuous efforts, Eça achieves an autonomy of character only intermittently and inconsistently.

On April 16, 1878, Machado de Assis published the first of what would become a two-installment commentary on Eça's work to that date. It will be the most painful experience at the hands of a critic that Eça will ever undergo; not even the ill-intentioned and vicious comments by Pinheiro Chagas and Fialho de Almeida concerning *The Maias* of 1888 will have anywhere near the effect that Machado's keenly reasoned criticism will have upon the author that was Eça de Queirós. After 1888 and the publication of *The Maias,* whatever aesthetic developments and transfigurations occur in Eça's work are not at all due to his critics; rather, these changes will respond strictly to a series of altered dispositions within Eça's imagination. On the other hand, 1878 will be a year that changes the whole complexion of Eça's fiction; not only will he execute a dramatic volte face, but he will gradually obliterate the principles that lead to the dogmatic resonances which we have been discussing in such works as the first two versions of *The Sin of Father Amaro* and *Cousin Bazilio.*

The Machado comments on the second version of *The Sin of Father Amaro*, already reviewed above, were more than enough to incite Eça into writing the retaliatory document (thankfully not published at the time), which is now entitled "Idealism and Realism" in the *Obras Completas* III, 907–16.

Although Eça took the opportunity to reply to Machado's critique, one could never take the reply as open acknowledgment of the essential validity of Machado's comments. Eça was incapable of such a public avowal. He will, however, give gracious compliments to Machado's article, "which by the elevation and that talent with which it is written honors my book, almost augmenting its authority." [61] Eça could not venture beyond those generous thoughts. Why not? After all, had not Eça been expressing similar thoughts in his letters to Ramalho from Newcastle? No, he will still attempt a defense "of the school [which my works] represent and which I consider as an important element of moral progress in modern society." Admit nothing, that is. The rule of the hour seems to be: *keep one's distance!* The main objection of Machado to the plot structure of *Cousin Bazilio* is simple and devastating—the use of the deus ex machina: "And here we arrive at the capital defect of conception in the novel by Sr. Eça de Queirós. The situation is drawing to a close, because the husband is about to return from the South, and Bazilio begins to get bored with the situation; he will return to Paris either because of Jorge's impending return or because a friend is instigating him. At this point, a servant intervenes. She is Juliana, the most complete and truthful character in the book; Juliana is tired of serving meals, she sees the means to get rich overnight. She obtains the letters: it is a triumph, it means riches. [After a series of threats by Juliana] . . . one day Luiza is unable to contain herself; she tells everything to a friend of the family (Sebastião), who in turn threatens the servant with arrest and prison; he gets the letters back. Juliana succumbs of an aneurysm; Luiza, who had already been suffering because of the lengthy menace and the threat of perpetual humiliation, expires a few days later.

"A perspicacious reader will already have seen the incongruence of Sr. Eça de Queirós's conception, and the inanity of the character of his heroine. Let us suppose those letters had never been discovered, or that Juliana didn't have the maliciousness to get hold of them, or that such a servant would never have been employed, or any other excuse of the same stripe. The novel would be over, since Cousin Bazilio would continue on his way back to France, and Jorge would return from the South; the two gentlemen would return to their former lives. In order to forestall such circumstances, the author invented the servant and the episode of the letters, the threats, the humiliations, the anguish, and then the illness and the death of the heroine. How is it possible that such a lucid mind as that of Sr. Eça de Queirós did not see that such a conception was the least congruent and the least interesting thing imaginable?

"If the author wanted to teach something (since we have seen that Realism also inculcates social and apostolic vocations), or demonstrate some thesis with his novel, we must confess that he did not achieve his aim, unless the thesis or the teaching is the following: In order to have peace in a home during an adultery, one must choose one's servants well. . . . I say, if you are going to write a hypothesis, give me a logical, human, truthful hypothesis. We all know that the spectacle of great physical pain is distressing; nonetheless, it is a normal maxim in art that such a spectacle in the theater moves no one; there, only moral anguish is of value. Well now, apply that maxim to your Realism, above all as the effect is proportional to the cause, and you cannot ask me to be moved in exchange for an equivocation.

"And now let us pass on to the most serious aspect, the most grievous flaw: it would seem that Sr. Eça de Queirós wanted to describe for us a heroine that was a product of a frivolous upbringing and an indolent life; nonetheless, there are traces in the book that would make one assume, at first glance, a salacious intent . . . . Readers of good faith try to defend the book, saying that some scenes could be expurgated, so that only the moral or social thought that engendered the work would remain. They forget or pay no attention to the fact that the salacious character of the work is precisely the marrow of the composition. Some episodes are cruder than others. Of what use would be the elimination of some parts? We could not eliminate the tone of the book. Now, the tone consists of the spectacle of ardor, amorous demands, sexual perversions. When a fact does not seem sufficiently characterized by its own term, the author adds another one that is inappropriate. Speaking of a coal seller standing at the door, the author says that she exhibits a 'bestial pregnancy.' Why bestial? Naturally, because the adjective gives more bulk to the noun and the author does not sense the sign of human maternity; he sees an animalistic phenomenon, nothing more."

Two weeks later, Machado will continue his commentary, this time on the basis of a few subsequent articles by other hands, protesting against the virulence of his attack; one observer felt, for instance, that Machado had seen absolutely nothing of "worth" in *Cousin Bazilio*. But Machado de Assis will not relent; he will insist upon his admiration for the "artist," the style, Eça's ability to observe, and he will insist no less on his conviction that this great artist is being undermined and even ruined by the literary conceptions to which he so blindly adheres. Machado's final paragraph sums this up in a definitive finale; he will never comment directly on any other work of Eça de Queirós: "As far as Sr. Eça de Queirós and his friends on this side of the Atlantic are concerned, I will repeat that the author of *Cousin Bazilio* has in me an admirer of his talents, but an adversary of his doctrines; I am desirous to see him apply, by different means, the forceful qualities which he possesses. Furthermore, if I do admire also the many gifts of his style, otherwise vigorous, it still is excessively complacent; above all, it is external, it is superficial. His fervent friends may be shocked by the way I feel, and by the frankness with which I am expressing it. But how can criticism be anything else?" [62]

In the earlier part of the first article, Machado had accused Eça of being a gross plagiarizer; he then proceeded to accuse

Eça of being a blind follower of the worst excesses of French Naturalism. All of this is bad enough. But his comments on *Cousin Bazilio* are even more devastating and contemptuous. Machado implies that, under the guise of a "moral lesson" or a "revolutionary work of art," the work is, in effect, a bedroom farce bordering on the pornographic. Above all the scenes in the Paraiso—the champagne kisses, the not at all subtle description of cunnilingus among other details, all these things brought forth an even greater burst of Machado's fury, above all because of the calculation and literary cynicism which must have motivated the writing of such scenes. What other object can such scenes have, implies Machado, than the selling of books? Why drag in Proudhon, when the book is so obviously salacious? So much for literary socialism and the moral improvement of the masses! Speaking again of Eça's motives, what of the "calculated cynicism" of such postcoital gestures by Bazilio as "He twisted his mustache with the greatest satisfaction. Now that he had taught her a new sensation, he would have her in the palm of his hand!" The same impression of insensitivity and mechanical behavior lies behind the final lines in *Cousin Bazilio*, at the moment when he returns to Lisbon and learns of Luiza's death. This is his reaction: "What an idiot I was! I could have brought Alphonsina along with me after all!" [63]

Another kind of analogous wisecrack (*dito análogo*) brought the second edition of *The Sin of Father Amaro* to an end; in the third edition, such final fillips will disappear. All in all, there is a good case to be made for the view that Machado's two-part critique marks a turning point and a major crisis of novelistic aesthetics for Eça. But another kind of crisis was brewing, this one not at all related to literature, really, but one directly connected to Eça's economic difficulties, which were constant and implacable.

On November 10, 1878, just six months after reading the articles by Machado de Assis, Eça will write a lengthy and intricate letter to Ramalho; it is a revealing document. Naturally, the Machado piece is never mentioned, but it has had its effect.

Eça has taken on what now must have seemed the hateful task of rewriting, in painstaking fashion, what he once called the "definitive" edition of 1876: "I should say to you that the third edition of *The Sin of Father Amaro* is a new novel; the only thing left from the version you read is the title. Line by line, it is undergoing such a transformation that this new version is as different from the first as *Don Quixote* is from Voltaire's *Henriade*. . . . Am I doing the right or the wrong thing—redoing an old novel? I obeyed a kind of instinctive call, and the fact is that you will see a 'strange work.' "

Eça's letter to Ramalho also contained an enclosure, a letter to the minister of foreign affairs, Andrade Corvo. He asks Ramalho to read the letter, approve of it, and then pass it on to the minister with the understanding that Ramalho will act as agent for Eça during this transaction. The letter Ramalho was to have passed on was an open attempt on Eça's part to blackmail both the minister and the Portuguese government generally. The plan, if it can be called that, is worthy of the overworked and conspiring Juliana: Eça had written a work— "The Battle of Caia"—which was to force the extortion of monies. Although only a fragment of this piece has been published, the general outlines and intent are clear. The work describes the invasion of Portugal by Spanish and Italian troops, and in turn gives us a vast fresco of Lisbon in a state of anarchy: churches overflowing with penitents, chaotic bands of volunteers attempting to hold back the invading hordes, banks and the market in a state of collapse, panic in the ministries; a whole civilization is on the border of the ultimate catastrophe; the dreaded *Finis Portugaliae*. Eça's letter explains to Ramalho how the text in question will help him obtain a princely sum from the Portuguese government:

> The idea came to me one afternoon [in Newcastle], in the salon of a lady's home; she was playing the favorite gavotte of Marie Antoinette on the piano; I, petting a dog in the sunlight. All of a sudden, without cause or provocation, I recall . . . the idea of this

book just as I am describing it to you. . . . "What a scandal it would cause in Portugal!" I went home to begin drafting this scandal. Simply put, this is what I want to do: I want to give an electric shock to the enormous dormant pig that is Portugal. You will say: "What shock? You fool! You can give it all the shocks you want to with your book, but the pig is going to sleep. Destiny maintains it in somnolence, and whispers to it: 'Sleep, Sleep, my pig.'"

Well and good, but I am going to tell you what I plan to do and not what the country will do; naturally, Portugal will continue to sleep. But outside of the scandal, I want money. If *Cousin Bazilio* sold, why should not "The Battle of Caia"? Keep in mind that risqué [*picantes*], lugubrious and voluptuous episodes will not be lacking; "épatants? Pas si bête." It will have everything—"un salmis d'horreurs." Does the bourgeois love a good orgy scene? It will have it, but this time it will be his own daughter who is raped, in his own home, by that brutal Catalonian soldier in the employ of the "Dragons from Pavia." So, if the book sells, why shouldn't I speculate and try to pay my debts? *Donc*, let us sum up: electric shock to the pig, money to the baby [I am the baby].

Now, why did I write to [Minister] Corvo? Because this is a serious thing; I am an employee of the government, and such a book is a grave matter . . . and this work represents capital to me . . . if he forces me to not use my capital, he should pay me for not using it. Don't you agree? Perhaps you don't consider this as strictly moral. I answer back along with Darwin: "In the struggle for life, to be weak is almost to be guilty." [64]

The plan, as evolved by Eça, becomes even more fantastic as the letter progresses. He tries to coach Ramalho, directing him to respond in certain ways in case of possible protests from the minister. In effect, Eça is threatening the government with the publication of a text that may well be obscene, salacious, and a political bombshell to boot. The government must pay for Eça's silence—this is the reasoning.

Although Ramalho's response to Eça's plan has never been published, the contrite letter of November 28 gives some idea of the outrage and bafflement that Ramalho must have expressed to Eça by return mail. Gleaning bits and pieces from Eça's self-defense, we assume that Ramalho had successively characterized the author of Cousin Bazilio as a "blackmailer, a sycophant of the minister, a man lacking in any moral sense, a budgetary thief, an intolerably mushy character," and so on.[65] (The language is Eça's.) What was worse, Ramalho must have implied that Eça has been writing with one eye cast upon a minister's approval in Lisbon; furthermore, that the task of being a consul is not worthy of a true artist, when Balzac and Dickens had made their living by the pen, as it were. There also seems to have been some reference to Eça's monetary avarice and lack of financial discipline. All these accusations are conjectural, of course, since we are inferring them from the energetic but limp responses of a very chastened Eça de Queirós.

In the words of a keen observer of this lamentable affair, "these documents cast doubt on the moral integrity and the aesthetic coherence of the writer during this epoch. They even justify the insinuation of Machado de Assis that Queirosian Realism is a sensationalistic exploration of what is sordid and obscene. According to the language of the letter, he is hardly inspired by the slightly perverse desire to "shock the pig" and the bourgeoisie; instead, he is animated above all by the need to earn money, just as he earned it with Cousin Bazilio: in exchange for opulent scenes of debauchery." [66]

The results of these successive shocks administered by Machado de Assis and Ramalho Ortigão are not long in coming. "The Battle of Caia" will never be published. O Conde de Abranhos, the devastating portrait of a classically corrupt constitutionalist politician, will be left in draft form, never to be published during Eça's lifetime. The corrosive text known as A Capital, with its highly cynical view of socialism and revolution, will also remain in manuscript. The reprimand has made its effect. Eça will never again attempt to use literature as a means to produce a desperatley needed windfall. After 1878 he expects little money from writing and will isolate himself from the alluring idea of a lucrative work of art. He begins the task of revising and expanding the second edition of *The Sin of Father Amaro* and never again speaks of "scandals" or "sensations" in relation to his artistic intent. The texts that were planned to be executed with "muita pimenta" are either abandoned or gradually reworked into such a masterpiece as *The Maias.* Writing becomes divorced from income, and Eça enters into his artistic maturity, happily and unhurriedly. As he was to say many years later, "Art is everything because only it endures—all the rest is nothing!"

6. The Sin of Father Amaro (*Third Edition*)

As did the previous versions, the novel begins with a setting in the provincial town of Leiria. Father José Migueis, the parish priest, has just died what can only be called a portentous and symbolic death—"a full-blooded, overfed man, known among the clergy of the dioceses as the Prize Glutton," he dies of apoplexy, gluttony, and general surfeit. Few parishioners regret his death, and the funeral is sparsely attended. From the beginning of this now carefully integrated novel, the central images— alluding as they do to carnality and excess—take on the most myriad forms. At times it is seen through enthusiastically painted set pieces a la Courbet, describing the gourmandizing by the lascivious clerics of Leiria; at times, a frank depiction of sexual desire and its consummation. José Migueis, the rancorous priest who appears in the novel only to die in the first few pages, sets the tone for these variations. He is emblematic in another way. Despised by others and contemptuous of these same others, his isolation from the communities he ostensibly serves suggests a sense of alienation and inhumanity. It is the priest's dog, Joli, who obliquely reflects the fate of this crank: after his master's death, "none of the other priests wanted the unhappy Joli, and they drove him off with the tips of their umbrellas. The dog, his suit rejected, howled all night on the streets. One morning he was found dead by the wall of the Misericordia. The driver of a dung cart picked up his body, and José Migueis was definitively forgotten." [67] Father Amaro is chosen to replace Father Migueis, by means of the intervention of a favorably inclined Minister of the Interior. On the advice of Canon Días, his former spiritual advisor in the seminary, Father Amaro is placed in the home of Sra. Joanneira, a well-proportioned *beata* who rents rooms to lodgers and who commands a circle of highminded ladies in Leiria. Her daughter is named Amélia, a girl of twenty-two, "good looking, well-built, and much sought after." In due course, Amaro will discover that Senhora Joanneira is the mistress of Canon Días, and this discovery of sexual realities in the ecclesiastical realm begins to corrode the moral structure of Amaro's seraphic personality. As the Canon confesses to a colleague, the abundance of food is the signal for a wealth of other kinds of gifts: "Not a day passes that she doesn't send me her little present—a plate of rice, a dish of jelly, a beautiful black pudding! Yesterday she sent me an apple tart. If you could have seen it! The sauce was like a cream! . . . Then, placing his outspread fingers on his chest, 'These are things which touch one's very heart. . . . It's not for me to say, but there is no one like her.' " [68] Eça articulates the implied meaning of these declarations with succulent descriptions of the good *beata*'s cooking. The general atmosphere in the house of Sra. Joanneira is one of a happy, chaste ménage which disguises a meticulously concealed arrangement. Eça takes real delight in producing these homey spaces, with their dense, cozy air. These are the spaces of emotional repression and constraint, relieved by occasionally furtive satisfactions:

> In the middle of the dining room, covered with dull wallpaper, the brightness of the table, with its snow-white cloth, the china, the shining glasses reflecting the strong light from the lamp with its green lampshade, gave an air of joy to the whole room. From the tureen came the savorous odor of the soup: in a large dish a plump chicken, smothered in white, juicy rice, and

surrounded with large sausages, had the succulent appearance of a dinner fit for a *morgado*. In the glass-doored cupboard, placed a little in the shade, shone the brightly colored chinaware; in a corner underneath the window stood the piano, covered with a faded satin cover. There was frying going on in the kitchen; and a pleasant smell came from a basket of newly washed linen. The priest rubbed his hands with glee.[69]

One of the many constants in the construction of plot in the novels of Eça is the use of mutually responsive, refracting characters; that is, characters who are set into the structure of the novel so that they may reflect, obliquely or in caricature, the actions of another. The death of the obese and repellent Father Migueis brings a vacancy to Leiria that Father Amaro fills; in turn, his spiritual advisor, Canon Días, welcomes him into the circle of *beatas* in the house of Sra. Joanneira, the Canon's cook and mistress of long standing. Amaro, in turn, already morally vitiated, will ease himself into the comfortable state of being the surreptitious love of Sra. Joanneira's daughter, Amélia. The parallels at the outset of the novel do not stop with these elements, which might seem fortuitous at first glance. In the novel, the appearances of moral order, clerical chastity, and disciplined religiosity within Leiria and the microcosm of the boardinghouse reflect only the visible surface of an apparently moral social system. This structure is immediately belied by the sexual relationship between the Canon and Sra. Joanneira, and it is also accompanied by another character that exemplifies the moral disease of Leiria—Joanneira's sister is also an occupant of the lodgings, "half idiot and paralyzed for the last ten years." Much later in the novel, just as this sister is in the process of dying in atrocious agony, Amaro and Amélia kiss for the first time at the same moment of her death. Too, Amaro and Amélia make love in a garret just above the rooms where the idiot daughter of the bellkeeper lives. No character in *The Sin of Father Amaro* is ever "alone," from the point of view of novelistic structure. Eça constructs "pairs" of characters which function dialectically and symbiotically within the movement of the action as a whole.[70]

If *The Sin of Father Amaro* were nothing but a drama of illicit passions carried out in the foreground, accompanied by vaguely filled in sketches of a stable societal structure, the work would hardly have gained the length of a long short story or a novella. But the third version is one of considerable length, and there are good reasons for this inordinate expansion. The greater length is not due to an inner expansion of the emotional realms within the characters; if anything, there is something of a diminution of impulse in both Amaro and Amélia in this third version. The expansion of the work is probably due to a change in Eça's view of the relation between self and society. The new concept of this revision is based upon the fact that the actions of the characters are much less impulsive and personal, much more reflective of the objective, collective direction of the society at large. This third *Amaro* is a frieze, a panorama of Portuguese society in the provinces. The concept of frieze governs the placement and function of the characters: they are secondary, above all in comparison with their function in the earlier versions. The balance between individual desire and the stolid power of a society has been tipped in favor of continuance, "order," and emotional stability.

Even the most ambitious portrait of a society must begin with the portrait of the individual within the society. The Father Amaro of this last revision is a coherently structured character. In a critical sense, Eça has loaded the dice with a series of determinants which "form" him. Amaro Vieira is born in Lisbon in the house of a Marqueza. His father is a valet, his mother a chambermaid. He is an orphan by the time he reaches his sixth birthday. The Marqueza, herself a widow and forty-three, has taken it upon herself to impose upon the young Amaro the only road she considers fit for the child—the priesthood. "His yellow face and thin body asked for the destiny of a recluse for which he had been chosen: he was already attached to the things of the chapel, and his great delight was to nestle at the feet of the women, to cuddle in the warmth of their skirts and listen to them talking of the saints. . . . Amaro was, as the servants described him, 'a warmed-up corpse.' He never played, never jumped about in the sun. He got to be very nervous and subject to fears, so at night they let him have a night light and put him to sleep at the foot of the children's old nurse. The other servants made him girlish." [71] As the young Amaro observes the priests who come to visit the Marqueza, he sees them as clean, fine people, taking snuff from boxes, receiving gifts on silver trays. The priestly vocation, if any might be discerned in Amaro, is directly related to conformity and ascension within society. It is, moreover, hardly an asexual temperament. "In his cell was a picture of the Virgin, reposing on the sphere and crowned with stars . . . in pausing to contemplate the print, he forgot the sanctity of the Virgin, seeing in front of him only a pretty blonde girl; he loved her; he sighed for her and as he undressed he turned and looked lewdly at her over his shoulder; in the daring curiosity of his imagination he even lifted the chaste nails fixing the blue robes of the Virgin and supposed delicious forms and white flesh." [72] Amaro is baffled by the quandary represented by the apparent contradictions between the adoration of Mary and womanhood itself—what is vulgarly known as the madonna/putanna complex: "What being was this, then who in spite of all the theology, was enthroned over the altar as Queen of Grace, and afterward cursed in brutal terms?" These divagations end by demoralizing the young priest; in his last year of studies, "after the heavy services of Holy Week, as the hot weather began, he entered the infirmary with a nervous fever." [73] Through the intervention of the Marqueza, he receives the desired appointment to the cathedral at Leiria, but the interview in the sumptuous home of his dowager protector leaves him with more than a few traces of Bovaresque longings. "Amaro was lifted out of himself. He envisaged a vague, superior existence, of romance taking place over luxurious carpets, or in padded coupés, with airs from operas, melancholy and in good taste, and love scenes of exquisite enjoyment." [74]

The atmosphere of Leiria was one which Eça de Queirós had studied with a gimlet eye and intense fascination. As he already had done in the salon scenes of Chapter II of *Cousin Bazilio*, Eça presents in this third edition of *The Sin of Father Amaro* another purposefully unappealing cross-section of the spinsters and bachelors of Leiria. They are brought together by Sra. Joanneira to present the new curate, the recently arrived Father Amaro. The cast of characters is not at all auspicious: the Gansoso sisters, Joaquina and Anna; Dona Josepha, the canon's sister, "a withered creature, crookedly formed, with shriveled, cider-colored skin, and a hissing voice," João Eduardo, the young Homais of Leiria, an intense and ultimately unsuccessful suitor for the hand of Amélia; finally, Arthur Couceiro, a toothless poet and musician who brings a macabre atmosphere to the vocal serenade in which the evening soirée culminates. "Arthur sang to draw tears, with a vacant, wandering look; but in the intervals, during the accompaniment, he smiled all round—and in his dark mouth one saw the stumps of his decayed teeth. Father Amaro, as he sat under the window smoking, contemplated Amélia, who was absorbed in that morbid, sentimental melody. Against the light her fine profile had a luminous line." [75] Amaro falls in love with Amélia and loses no time in lending Amélia a small pamphlet, "a pious little work written in an ambiguous lyrical style, almost obscene, which gave to the prayer the language of lust. Jesus is invoked in the terms of the avid, eager desires of sexual appetite." [76] After surprising Sra. Joanneira and the good Canon in bed, Amaro becomes all the more calculating and determined in his desire to possess the young Amélia. She begins to belittle the pretensions of the very earnest João Eduardo as the amorous intensity of Father Amaro increases; but the tortured priest in turn is plagued by wrathful fantasies done with more than a touch of a Romantic Torquemada: "he would give people to understand that the mother [Sra. Joanneira] was a prostitute. He would put terror into her heart! Cover her with mud! And in the cathedral, as the people came out from mass, he would gloat as he saw her pass, wrapped in her little black shawl, shrinking with shame, shunned by all, while he, deliberately taking up his position at the door, would stand conversing with the wife of the civil governor and joking with the Baroness of Via Clara! During Lent he would preach a grand sermon, and she would hear people in the shops and in the Arcade saying: 'What a great man is Father Amaro!' " [77]

The embittered João Eduardo here becomes an agent of the structure and motivation of the work; this impassioned, thwarted admirer of Amélia shares not a few of Eça de Queirós's Proudonian orientations regarding the church, the clergy, and the possible divinity of Jesus. Just as Father Amaro represents to João Eduardo the essence of a lax and eminently traditional priesthood—that is, a danger to civilization and liberty, an intriguer with luxurious habits, "eternally conspiring to bring back the world to the darkness of the Middle Ages"—the figure of Jesus becomes, for João Eduardo, the paradigm of the Christian revolutionary, "a poet, a revolutionary, a friend of the poor." [78]

In order to undermine the forces of ignorance represented by any priest, and Amaro in particular, João Eduardo composes a severe diatribe entitled "Modern Pharisees," a philippic that is published anonymously in the local paper, with gross allusions to lecherous priests and innocent virgins, all ending with a comically ominous warning: "Take care, black cassocks!"

Amélia has, meanwhile, accepted the suit of João Eduardo, but the engagement is ended, since the anonymous authorship of the article "Modern Pharisees" has been revealed. His social and civil service career in ruins, João Eduardo begs for advice and consolation from Dr. Gouvea, a mind of decidedly Darwinist persuasions who sends the hapless adolescent on his way with the following peroration, one of the most subversive passages in all the works of Eça de Queirós, but not at all atypical:

> "Ah!" said the doctor, "what a beautiful and wonderful thing is love! Love is one of the greatest forces of civilization. Well directed, it could lift up the whole world and be sufficient to cause a moral revolution." Then, changing his tone, "But listen. Be well aware that sometimes this is not love, this is not in the heart. The heart is a term which usually serves us, for decency's sake, to designate another organ. It is precisely this other organ which is the only one interested, in

the majority of cases, in affairs of sentiment. In those cases the grief doesn't last. Good-bye, I hope it is so with you." [79]

João Eduardo receives even less balm from his friend Gustavo, the firebrand printer: "what one should occupy one's mind with was not love, but trying to bring liberty to the people, freeing the worker from the claws of the capitalist, finishing with monopolies, working for a republic!" [80] In a state of rage, João Eduardo proceeds to assault Father Amaro in the public square; he, in turn, refuses to prosecute the deranged lover and becomes a sainted hero, an "innocent victim of an atheistic attack." After considerable machinations, Amaro and Amélia become lovers; the inevitable pregancy occurs, with the even more inevitable hysteria and recrimination. Amélia gives birth to the child in the country house of Canon Días's sister, then dies in spite of the energetic ministrations of Dr. Gouvea. Amaro then efficiently hands over the child to an ominous old woman, a "weaver of angels," who promises to care for the child; the infant dies within a few hours.

In the final chapter of this third revision, an oblivious and now wholly obtuse Amaro is found chatting with other priests and nobles of the town a few years later, inquiring about the latest horrors of the Paris Commune that are being reported to the Lisbon populace by telegraph. Amaro asks of a count: "does your excellency think that these ideas of republicanism, of materialism, could spread here among our people?" The count responds with a broad gesture of contentment: "While we have respectable clergymen like you, senhores, Portugal will maintain with dignity her place among the nations of Europe! Because religion, my dear senhores, is the base of order!" [81]

The most striking change between this finally "definitive" version and the earlier ones is, of course, the matter of the child's death. In this sense, the title of the novel as translated into English is highly misleading. Eça surely would have disapproved of the implications of personal sin, because the original title makes no such suggestions—it is simply *O Crime do Padre Amaro*. Still, Eça never altered the title during any one of the revisions, although the nature of Amaro's crime differs so radically between the second and the third versions. In the first two versions, the child dies a victim of the impulsive terror of Amaro. The motives in the second version are less related to hysteria than they are to cool calculation, but the crime is the same—the child is drowned. In the third version, the "crime" is one that would tax any Western legal tradition—rather than an overt act, we have sleight of hand; the murder is removed from the surface of the text; the child is delivered to the "weaver of angels"—that is, a woman who disposes of unwanted children by neglect and purposeful abandonment. What was a crime of desperation and terror in *Amaro* I and II becomes a dehumanized exchange of monies and an infant in *Amaro* III. The appearances are maintained, and Amaro's career continues on its course unperturbed. The priest is no longer the direct agent of the child's death, and in this sense the moral opprobrium is deflected from Father Amaro toward society itself. He is now a symbol of the moral decay of a declining society. José Augusto França sees the moral displacement of *Amaro* III as evidence of a new set of assumptions in Eça's writing: "If the act of Father Amaro continues to be considered a crime, even though the crime no longer exists, it is because the concept of the crime is displaced, passing from the individual level toward the social level—this is the lesson, the moral of this story." [82] In this version, the figure of Father Amaro is infinitely more diminished. He has lost the instinctive, unstable, and erratic personality that made the first two versions so much more the delineation of a sensual consciousness than a portraiture of society's strictures over the individual. Eça has, in effect, carefully preordained all the elements in this new version, all while eliminating the sexual sensibility which moved the characters in such a nonreflexive way in the earlier versions. For instance, surely it is not a happenstance that Eça describes his protagonist as without sexual experience in the first two versions, while the Father Amaro of the final edition has had, as a matter of course, a rather grim affair with a shepherdess while officiating in the parish of Ferrão, to which he was assigned just after ordination. Too, it is part of the literary program of this "definitive" version that this new Father Amaro would be a creature of reason and cynical calculation. For instance, upon learning of Amélia's pregnancy, Amaro, in the earlier version, is without a plan or a solution, a trapped priest contemplating suicide. In the final version, the prospect of suicide is not mentioned, while emphasis is placed upon the possible scandal and opprobrium that might befall him: "Just imagine the scandal! The mother, the neighbors! And if they suspect me, I'm lost. I won't wait to hear what they'll say, I'll run away! . . . I want to avoid a scandal. What else could I want?" [83] While the earlier Amaros were nonauthoritative and relatively immune to the temptations of an ecclesiastical career, this new Amaro is something of an outward ritualist, reveling in it—a sophist of moral relativism. Also, it would be impossible to consider the creation of the first two versions as an act of social criticism—this was simply not a part of Eça's program. But the open social satire contained in the final pages of this version leads us to the conclusion that Amaro and Amélia have taken on a collective resonance in the author's mind. This requires us to redefine the nature of the literary reality implicit in this third version, a situation where all phenomena and characters within the novel are identified by the contours which limit and define them—it is these exterior elements which constitute their exact inner selves. [84] These contours are heavily accented in the revision of 1880, and it is thus that the text is heavily imbued with a not at all latent anticlericalism redolent of the satiric jabs written a few years before in *As Farpas*. Thus, the theme of gluttony and surfeit becomes an almost endlessly repeated connective device thoughout the novel; Father Migueis dies of overeating in the first few pages, while much of Chapter V is dedicated to the Pantagruelesque meal served by the Abbot of Cortegassa to Amaro, Canon Días, and the two invited guests, Fathers Natário and Brito. After eating well beyond any limit, the drunken priests take a late afternoon walk which is interrupted by the shouts of Father Natário:

> "You donkey, can't you see? You beast!" It was a turn in the road. They had collided against an old man

leading a sheep; Natário stumbled forward in a
drunken rage and threatened him with his closed fist.
"I hope your honor will pardon me," said the old man
humbly. "You beast!" bellowed Natário with flaming
eyes. "I'd like to smash you with a hatchet!" The old
man stammered, he had taken off his hat, one saw his
white hair; he appeared to be an ancient farmhand,
grown old in his work; he was probably a grandfather.
Cringing down, red with shame, he shrunk into the
hedge beside the narrow cart track to let the reverend
fathers, jovial and excited from the wine, pass on their
way.[85]

As one commentator has seen this episode, "the incident is
symbolic of one of the aspects of the 1880 version: the priests of
Leiria lack the most elementary Christian spirit and civic conscience; they do not worry about the misery of the people nor
show even a shadow of compassion for the humble. They identify ecclesiastical interests with those who enjoy riches and power . . . that is to say, reaction." [86]

Other social types are worked into the fabric of the novel in
an explicit manner. It is not hard to discern in such figures as
the good Abbot Ferrão or the demagogic socialist Gustavo a
purposeful intent—to broaden the social canvas and make the
book, in Eça's own words, more "human, "warmer," while
paradoxically more "objective." Amélia loses that vegetative
somnolescence of the earlier versions, and becomes a more de-
monstrably passionate and assertive being, above all in contrast
to the ferocious rationalisms of this new Amaro. Machado de
Assis had accused the figure of Luiza in *Cousin Bazilio* of being a
puppet, and the same may well be said for the Amélia of the
earlier versions. In this final version, she attains the consciousness and inner drama of a moral exemplar who is at the same
time compelling in her excruciating dilemma. What strikes the
reader of this magnificently executed revision is the meticulous,
impassive quality of the elaboration, accompanied by a continually resurging and evolving series of social and sexual tensions.
Within and below the surface of this novelistic frieze, we sense a

reality that has been transposed into nonreferential complicity with the most intrusive and demoniacal components of Eça's private dilemmas—the first masterpiece produced by an artist on uneasy and fractious terms with his own inner demons.

Notes

1. *Uma Campanha Alegre,* can be found in *OC,* III, 955–1266; the *Cartas de Inglaterra* are in *OC,* II, 497–608. The latter book has been gracefully translated into English by Ann Stevens as *Letters from England* (Athens: Ohio University Press, 1970).
2. See Júlio de Sousa e Costa, *Eça de Queiroz: Memórias da Sua Estada em Leiria 1870–71* (Lisboa: Livraria Sá da Costa, 1953).
3. For *O Primo Basílio,* I am using the English spellings adopted by the translator for the (incomplete) English edition: *Cousin Bazilio,* trans. Roy Campbell (New York: The Noonday Press, 1953).
4. As Jean Girodon so rightly points out, "the study of an author's sources is in no way literary criticism." Nonetheless, Eça's insistent plagiarism is so glaring that it is impossible not to take it into account. Two of the more recent contributions to the abundant literature concerning Eça's borrowings are to be found in Jean Girodon, "Fiches Queiroziennes," *Bulletin des Etudes Portugaises,* XXVII (1966), pp. 189–220, and António Coimbra Martins, "Imitação Capital," in *Ensaios Queirosianos* (Lisboa: Publicações Europa-America, 1967), pp. 289–378.
5. Jean Girodon, "Eça de Queiroz et Madame Bovary," *Biblos* (1949), p. 211.
6. *Cartas de Eça de Queiroz* (Lisboa: Editorial Aviz, 1945), pp. 49–50.
7. *Novas Cartas Inéditas* (Rio de Janeiro: Editora Alba, 1940), pp. 13–14.
8. João Gaspar Simões, *Vida e Obra de Eça de Queirós,* 2d ed. (Lisboa: Livraria Bertrand, 1973), p.396.
9. The reference is to Eça's older *confrère,* Ramalho Ortigão (1836–1915).
10. This is the argument elaborated by António Coimbra Martins in his definitive treatment of eros in Eça: "Eva e Eça," *Bulletin des Etudes Portugaises,* XXVIII–XXIX (1967/68), pp. 287–326.
11. One of the many points made by Carlos Reis in his *Estatuto e Perspectivas do Narrador na Ficcão de Eça de Queirós* (Coimbra: Livraria Almedina, 1975), esp. p. 78.
12. I am, of course, referring to the truculent prologue which Eça wisely decided not to publish and which is now available in *OC,* III, 907–916.

13. See Alberto Machado da Rosa, *Eça, Discípulo de Machado?* 2d ed. (Lisboa: Editorial Presença, 1964).
14. Coimbra Martins, "Eva e Eça," pp. 324–25.
15. Leo Bersani, *A future for Astyanax* (Boston: Little, Brown and Company, 1976), pp. 69–70.
16. See ibid., chap. II, "Realism and the Fear of Desire."
17. This is the plausible thesis sustained by Dominique Sire in the article "Une Première Ébauche du Roman *O Primo Basilio*," *Bulletin des Etudes Portugaises et Bresiliennes*, Nouvelle Série, XXXIII–XXXIV (1972–73), pp. 245–64.
18. José-Augusto França, *Le Romantisme au Portugal* (Paris: Klincksieck, 1975), p. 675.
19. *Cousin Bazilio*, p. 37.
20. Alexandre Dumas fils, *Affaire Clémenceau* (Paris: Michel Lévy Frères, 1872). The quotations have been translated by the author from pp. 50, 90, 29, 89, 105, 125–26, 203, 259–60, 347.
21. Ibid, p. 145.
22. Sire, "Une Première Ébauche," pp. 254–55.
23. P.-J. Proudhon, *Oeuvres complètes*, vol. VII, entitled *De la Justice dans la Révolution et dans l'Église*, part IV (Paris: Librairie des Sciences Politiques et Sociales, Marcel Rivière, 1935). Quotations translated by the author are from pages 22 to 24.
24. Ibid., pp. 130–31.
25. Ibid., p. 128.
26. *Eça de Queiroz e Jaime Batalha Reis; Cartas e Recordações do Seu Convívio*, ed. Beatriz Cinatti Batalha Reis (Pôrto: Lelloe Irmão, 1946), p. 19.
27. Ibid., p. 21.
28. For an exhaustive description of this débâcle, see Ernesto Guerra da Cal, *Lengua y Estilo de Eça de Queiroz*, Apéndice: Bibliografía Queiroçiana, I (Coimbra: Por Ordem da Universidade, 1975), pp. 17–20.
29. Batalha Reis, *Eça de Queiróz e Jaime Batalha Reis* . . . , pp. 23–27, 31. Trans. Kenneth Krabbenhoft.
30. See *OC*, 509–12.
31. Eça de Queirós, *O Crime do Padre Amaro*. Edição organizada por Helena Cidade Moura, baseada nas Versões de 1875, 1876, 1880. (Pôrto: Lello e Irmao, 1964, 2 vols.) I, pp. xxvii–xviii. The texts from the first two versions that are translated below are drawn from this definitive edition; I have depended upon the trustworthy Flanagan version for the translations from the 1880 *Amaro*: *The Sin of Father Amaro*, trans. Nan Flanagan (New York: St. Martin's Press, 1963). The most exhaustive comparison of the three versions of the novel is to be found in Maria Luisa Nunes, "Techniques and Functions of Character Drawing in the Three Ver-

sions of *O Crime do Padre Amaro*," diss., City University of New York, 1973.
32. *O Crime*, I, p. xxviii.
33. Machado de Assis, "Eça de Queirós: *O Primo Basílio*," as reprinted in Machado da Rosa, *Eça, Discípulo de Machado?*, 2d ed., pp. 210–11.
34. *OC*, III, 908, 909.
35. Gaspar Simões, *Vida e Obra*, p. 357.
36. *O Crime*, I, p. 43.
37. Ibid., p. 168.
38. Nunes, "Techniques and Functions of Character Drawing," pp. 228–47.
39. *O Crime*, pp. 282–84.
40. Ibid., II, p. 192.
41. Bersani, *A Future*, p. 66. See also the conclusions drawn by Maria Luisa Nunes in her examination of the three versions, "Techniques and Functions of Character Drawing," pp. 504–37.
42. *O Crime*, II, pp. 425–28, 432–34, Trans. Kenneth Krabbenhoft.
43. Ibid., pp. 420–25, Trans. Kenneth Krabbenhoft.
44. Nunes, "Techniques and Functions of Character Drawing," pp. 198–222, 454–79.
45. *O Crime*, II, pp. 458–59, Trans. Kenneth Krabbenhoft.
46. Machado da Rosa, *Eça. Discípulo*, p. 118.
47. *Novas Cartas Inéditas*, p. 3.
48. James R. Stevens, "Eça and Flaubert," *Luso-Brazilian Review*, III, no. 1 (May 1966), p. 61.
49. Gustave Flaubert, *Madame Bovary*, trans. Mildred Marmur (New York: New American Library, 1964), p. 163.
50. *OC*, I, 985, 984. This passage was not translated in Roy Campbell's version; it is for this and other reasons that I describe this translation as unreliable and incomplete.
51. Eça de Queiroz, *The Relic*, trans. Aubrey G. F. Bell (New York: The Noonday Press, 1954), n.p.
52. Stevens, "Eça and Flaubert," p. 54.
53. Girodon, "Eça de Queiroz et Madame Bovary," p. 222.
54. I am referring to the suggestive chapter entitled "Technical Problems in Stendhal, Cervantes and Flaubert" in René Girard's *Deceit, Desire and the Novel*, trans. Yvonne Freccero (Baltimore: The Johns Hopkins University Press, 1965), pp. 138–52.
55. Mary McCarthy, Foreword to *Madame Bovary* (New York: New American Library, 1964), p. xv.
56. Stevens, "Eça and Flaubert," p. 53.
57. Ibid., p. 61.
58. As cited in Vianna Moog, *Eça de Queirós e o Século XIX* (Rio de Janeiro: Editôra Civilização Brasileira, 1966), p. 229.

59. These comments are based upon the superb introductory essay by José-Augusto França in his *Zé Povinho 1875–1975* (Lisboa: Livraria Bertrand, 1975), pp. 7–21. See also *Zé Povinho Fez 100 Anos* (Lisboa: Centro de Artes-Plásticas dos Coruchéus, 1976).

60. Robert Garis, *The Dickens Theatre* (Oxford: At the Clarendon Press, 1965), esp. chap. III, "Dickens and the Inner Life."

61. As cited in Gaspar Simões *Vida e Obra*, p. 398.

62. Machado da Rosa, *Eça, Discípulo*, pp. 212–23.

63. *Cousin Bazilio*, p. 343.

64. *Novas Cartas Inéditas*, pp. 29–30.

65. *Novas Cartas Inéditas*, p. 39. Letter to Ramalho dated November 28, 1878.

66. Machado da Rosa, *Eça, Discípulo*, pp. 242–43. The financial situation of an accomplished writer in France was a matter of an entirely different cast. See Priscilla Clark, "Stratégies d'auteur au XIXe siècle," *Romantisme*, Nos. 17–18, 1977, pp. 92–102.

67. *The Sin of Father Amaro*, p. 8. I am indebted once again to Nunes, "Techniques and Functions of Character Drawing," for some of the conclusions drawn in this section.

68. *The Sin*, p. 11. See W. P. Rougle, "The Role of Food in Five Major Novels of Eça de Queirós." *Luso-Brazilian Review*, 13 (1976) 157–181.

69. Ibid., p. 16.

70. It should be added that these "pairs" within the novels of Eça might also be termed, as has António Coimbra Martins in his brilliant essay "Eva e Eça," *witnesses*, as well as "pares galantes" reflecting the low actions of the "pares burlescos." *Bulletin des Etudes Portugaises*, XXVIII–XXIX (1967/68), pp. 298–99, 307.

71. *The Sin*, pp. 21–22.

72. Ibid., p. 25.

73. Ibid., pp. 26–27; See n. 125, Chapter IV.

74. Ibid., p. 35.

75. Ibid., p. 46.

76. Ibid., p. 56.

77. Ibid., p. 78.

78. Ibid., p. 90.

79. Ibid., p. 162.

80. Ibid., p. 166.

81. Ibid., p. 351. See the comments of Nunes, "Techniques and Functions of Character Drawing," pp. 494–503, on this, the Chiado scene which brings this third version of *The Sin of Father Amaro* to a close.

82. França, *Le Romantisme*, p. 679.

83. *The Sin*, pp. 249–50.

84. Machado da Rosa, *Eça, Discípulo*, p. 133.

85. *The Sin*, p. 65.

86. Machado da Rosa, *Eça Discípulo*, p. 283.

3.

The East of the Imagination

A few things can now be said about *The Sin of Father Amaro* and *Cousin Bazilio* that might well have been out of place if brought up on prior occasions. If we think of these works as constructs of an observed society in which human will and passions were subjected to a unitive vision on the part of the author, we must note a rather severe imbalance between this compelling vision and the possible but not yet realized plenitude of the characters enveloped by this vision. Shall we say that neither works are humane, in the fullest sense of the word, and that neither work reflects, even to Eça's own satisfaction, the peculiar literary sensibility that was his? Both depend upon certain mechanisms; the virtues and the vices of the characters are, it is implied, the products of the mass determinant which is society itself, and Eça in turn has felt compelled to relate his earnest literary principles to that single central vision of man in society. But really, it is not at all clear that he was innately sympathetic to any central vision for any length of time and with any consistency; Proudhon, Hegel, Marx, and Jesus pass through his works at times interchangeably and confusedly. This is why we get this sense of vacillation and doubt in his theoretical pronouncements over the years. Each one of those occasions, be they essays, polemics, or letters to friends, was considered by him to be holding actions good enough for the time in which they were written but nothing more than that; the Casino lecture most certainly did announce a few principles that served as the bases for the three versions of *The Sin of Father Amaro* and *Cousin Bazilio*. But by 1880, the Casino lecture had done its work, and the ideas there expressed were of limited and rapidly waning interest to Eça. In many ways, we might think of the first two novels as forcibly centrifugal works of literature. They criticize Portuguese society; they banish sublime erraticism and individual prerogatives from the surface of the text; and they allow only a brand of behavior that functions well within the constrictions of the physiology of Naturalism. In this sense, those two texts leave no room for the reader's imagination, nor for a glimmer of the sublime or the infinite; they are texts in which the finite and the empirical become utterly irrelevant to Platonic realms.

Now, the world of private disorder was never one that Eça was comfortable with for long, either in literature or in life, but surely he did long for the fictional freedom to elaborate a more imaginative brand of fiction. The two works written and published between 1880 and 1887—*The Mandarin* and *The Relic*—are so divergent from the worlds of Amaro and Bazilio that it might be useful to review those aspects of his earlier literary impulses, precisely those which were purposefully set aside, so that the truth of the new art of Realism might prevail in Portugal, if belatedly.

Setting aside a part of one's own imaginative self might seem to be a rather odd way to begin a literary career, but Eça's hand was firm. During his most dogmatic and instructive phase, Romanticism was subliminally related to poetry, and poetry was inimical to the practice of democratic literary dogmas. For the novelist Eça de Queirós, Romanticism was the realm and the dominion of a deviant and perverse imagination. In *The Sin of Father Amaro* and *Cousin Bazilio,* it is this leftover brand of shabby Romantic practice that offers the most inviting targets for Eça's barbs, and these are realized in the figures of Luiza, Acácio, and Couceiro, among others, who are all variants of a single delusion, one that is an intimate part of the author's own lyric substance. With an implacable execution, Eça offers the counterbalancing truths of science; he accommodates himself to the frightful visions offered by the social and literary Darwinists. Neither *Amaro* nor *Bazilio* are fantasies or romances; they are not allegories of the human condition—they are novels in the prescriptive sense.

This is a matter that deserves comment, if only because it is so obvious. Up to now we have been speaking of Eça as a novelist, using the term as we know of it in contemporary critical discourse in English; but this is not at all a sure thing. Much of the confusion concerning Eça's contradictory and almost unrelated responses to society in literature stems from the fact that we might understand him better if we think of him after 1880 as a romancer and not as a novelist. In Portuguese, the terms "romance" and "novela" have come to be almost synonymous; in Spanish the situation is quite different, although the term "romance" is rarely applied to long works of fiction and is used to refer to the octosyllabic folk poetry of the *romancero*. In Spanish and Portuguese there is manifest confusion concerning the two terms. In Spanish and at times in Portuguese, "novela" is a catchall term in which the most disparate kinds of long narrations mingle indiscriminately. In this sense, *Don Quijote de la Mancha, El Amadís de Gaula, O Crime do Padre Amaro, Little Dorrit,* or *The House of the Seven Gables* might be referred to as "novelas." The genre known as the "romance" does not now exist as a genre concept in Spanish or in Portuguese, although it accurately does describe some forms of fiction before Cervantes in Spanish. In English, however, there is a fundamental distinction between the romance and the novel, and this distinction might well explain how Eça used his readings in English literature after 1880 to embark on a new way of thinking about the nature of literature. *The Mandarin* and *The Relic* are a literary volte face, above all because they must be read as romances, not as novels. The American critic Richard Chase gives us the classic distinction: "The novel renders reality closely and in comprehensive detail; the people are in explicable relation to nature and to each other, to their social class, to their own past. Character is more important [in the novel] than action and plot. By contrast the romance, following distantly the medieval example, feels free to render reality in less volume and detail. It tends to prefer action to character, and the action will be freer in a romance than in a novel, encountering, as it were, less resistance from reality. *Being less committed to the immediate rendition of reality than the novel,* the romance will more freely veer toward the mythic, allegorical and symbolist forms [italics mine]." [1] Most authors (but not the novelist that was Eça de Queirós in 1880) would have agreed with that archromancer (admired by Eça during the Coimbra days) Edgar Allan Poe when he called the then beginning Realist trend "pitiable stuff, the depiction of decayed cheeses." Romance and novel have always coexisted rather uneasily, above all during the final half of the nineteenth century in England and France. However, as those literatures gained in analytic power and mimetic fidelity to a society in the throes of change, that is to say, as the novel gained precedence over the romance, fiction lost a world of "fine fabling," to use Robert Louis Stevenson's term. The world of the romance denotes the genre that was not at all killed off by Cervantes; on the contrary, it flourished in England and later throughout all of Europe under the name of the Gothic sensibility, in the work of Eça's beloved E. T. A. Hoffmann, Baudelaire, and Heine, among others.

Few authors have doubted about themselves as did Eça de Queirós; his long exile from Portugal will make him into a brand of writer that was not at all on the horizon during the earlier years. This "disengagement" from the Portuguese scene also accompanies a real sense of suffocation and saturation on his part, since he is, after 1880, an author now profoundly at odds with the expressive means that served him so well in the first two novels. Is it not true also that the Queirosian tone and temperament were only intermittently discernible during those works, as he himself was to admit ruefully? Why not then abandon, at least for the moment, the long novel, with its careful study of the Lisbonese bourgeoisie? This is what he will do in

The Mandarin and *The Relic*—create a literature which gains a considerable degree of latitude in its relation to contemporary reality, one that does not aim at a minute fidelity to the possible, but rather uses the tools of the imagination to expose and dramatize a series of moral dilemmas, all under circumstances of the author's own choosing. In this sense these will be works redolent of the quest theme, done with a marvelous atmosphere and even including a few picaresque elements—a literature anachronistic for its time but still presaging the radical amplification of fictional possibilities that we all recognize in post-Realist practice of the twentieth-century novel. I am referring to a concept of fiction that is not naïvely bifurcated between reality and fantasy, or fantasy unleashed from reality, or of reality crushing something frail and fragile called fancy. Eça's new orientations, brought about as they may well have been by the increasing alienation from the fabric of Portuguese society, gradually evolved into a concept of fiction in which a natural and unforced fusion of both worlds is apparent; political and sociological relevance is set aside; parody and satire come to be the covert structures for Eça's lifetime ambition— the demolition and reconstruction of Portuguese society. Texts become both moral and verbal icons, not constructions reflecting mimetic concerns. Voltaire's *Candide* might serve as an example.

The preface to *The Mandarin* is, as we have seen, Eça's fundamental manifesto. No other critical text by him has quite the capital importance of this letter/preface/pronouncement. In a way, it announces the fictions to come, works done with "fine sentence[s]" rather than "exact notion[s]." For that reason, he suggests, Stendhal is neither pleasing to the Portuguese in general nor to Eça in particular; this apparently inexplicable lapse is expressed in the most stealthily adroit way: "Were we to read Stendhal in Portuguese, we should never be able to enjoy him; what is considered exactitude with him, we should consider sterility . . . what charms us is excessive emotion expressed with unabashed plasticity of language." [2]

Eça seems to be carrying out a critical dialogue with himself, a scrutiny of his library. The results of this exercise are already evident on the first page of the prologue: I have been on the wrong track, I have not been true to myself or my culture, he seems to be saying. This will lead, naturally, to a less critical kind of writing, at least from the point of view of Antero de Quental, Teófilo Braga, and the rest of the Coimbra firebrands. "Fantasy, in all its forms from song to caricature, is what attracts us; thus in our art we have produced above all lyricists and satirists." How does he explain away his former writer's self? It is easy: "we undertook this noble task [that of Realism] not out of natural inclination, but out of a feeling of literary duty—I almost said of public duty." All of the elements of this program were laboriously carried out, but it was in vain, he implies: "We tried to put in our works much observation, much 'humanity'; but in studying our neighbors, small *rentiers* or petty employees, it turned out that we soon regretted those times when it was permissible, without being old-fashioned, to celebrate handsome knights in shining armor. The time for wandering in the woods of fantasy was gone—alas." The Portuguese artist, and Eça himself, "suffocated in the atmosphere of reality, modernity, and banality. If he could not occasionally take off into the blue, the longing for chimeras would soon kill him." This carefully adjusted argument—a literary reneging, in effect—carries with it a clever caveat. Eça proceeds to ask for *temporary* license to unfetter the imagination, as it were; to let it soar in the world of romance that had been so unjustly buried under the oppressive weight of the "new art." This is the meaning of the acutely placed adverb "occasionally" in the sentence above, and this is affirmed by the following justification: "Thus, *at least for a single small volume*, one no longer accepts the inconvenient submission to truth, to the torture of analysis, to the impertinent tyranny of reality. . . . One can make sentences march across the white page like processions advancing with cadenced steps among bouquets of roses, across sun-filled plazas; then, the last page written, the last proof corrected, one can leave the street, get back on the sidewalk, *and resume the serious study of man and his eternal misery.* Happy? No, my dear Sir—resigned [italics mine]." [3]

In passing such a negative review of the "pettiness of character, banality of conversation, poverty of sentiment," what else could Eça be referring to but precisely his own characters— Luiza, Bazilio, Amaro, the Gansoso sisters, just to name a few. They fulfill the negative prescription which he now so rotundly condemns. Both *The Mandarin* and *The Relic* offer not an "asphyxiation" by reality but rather a luminous, alternative world untrammeled by the impositions of moralized art. After correcting the galleys for *The Relic,* Eça will return, as he promised, to the "study of man and his eternal misery" in his masterpiece *The Maias;* but this time the study will be much more than merely "serious" (*severo*) but rather richly hued and broadly compassionate, the artifact of Eça de Queirós at the height of his powers.[4]

By the way, *The Mandarin* is preceded not only by the letter/preface, but also by a prologue in the form of a truncated dialogue drawn from an "unpublished comedy":

> First friend (drinking cognac and soda, on a terrace under the trees, at the seashore):
> "Friend, on these hot summer days that dull one's wits, let's rest from the bitter study of human reality. . . . Let's take off for the realms of Dream and wander among those romantic blue hills on which stands the abandoned tower of the Supernatural, and where fresh mosses cover over the ruins of Idealism. . . . Let's give way to Fantasy!"
> Second friend: "But temperately, friend . . . with moderation!
> And as in those wise and delightful Allegories of the Rennaissance, *let us be sure to include an unobtrusive morality.* . . .[italics mine][5]

Perforce, this must be a literature that is not *entirely* inventive and invented; it must still include the possibilities of an "unobtrusive" moral lesson. What is the lesson that is to be taught? Well, it must be related to the morality of *survival* itself; both works continually exploit the metaphors of monetary enrichment, surfeit, debauchery, and projective guilt: luxury turns to horror, and quickly. These books might be taken as moral dissections, by Eça himself, of his desperate avariciousness during those years, caused as it was by his consistent impoverishment while consul, and also having engendered the wild plotting and scheming which culminated in the plan to blackmail the Portuguese government in the episode of *A Batalha do Caia,* to be followed by Ramalho's stern reprimand. In effect, *The Mandarin* might be thought of as some kind of literary expiation for the depraved financial drama which finally drove Eça to such fantastic extremes—a catharsis.

The subject of *The Mandarin* brings all these possibilities together in a dilemma which, aside from enjoying a hoary lineage in European literature as an exemplum of ethical quandary, effectively transfigures Eça's inner disquiet into an inviting and insidious invitation. Here is the theme:

> In the depths of China there is a Mandarin richer than all the kings told of in Fable or History. Of him you know nothing, neither his name, nor his appearance, nor the silk of which his clothes are made. In order for you to inherit his uncountable fortune, all you need do is to touch this little bell on the book right at your side. In the deep confines of Mongolia, the Mandarin will hardly even sigh. He will indeed be a corpse; and you will see at your feet more gold than the greed of a miser could ever imagine. You, who read this and who are a mortal man, will you ring the little bell? [6]

This is to be a *conte philosophique* in the manner of Voltaire. But the moral dilemma offered by Eça's version of the Mandarin theme carries with it other intriguing ramifications; that is to say, those related to a brand of expiatory literature which might reflect both the moral and artistic perplexities of which Eça found himself captive during the early consular years. The fable is suggestive also of a few other echoes. Both *The Mandarin* and *The Relic* are indicative of moral pressures, in spite of their purposefully jocular appearances. The expiations in these works are comic, but we should note at the same time that they are subtle dramas of hypocrisy; guilt; and temporary, if uncritical, remorse. The literary precedents were not very far from Eça's imagination. For instance, in *Le Génie du Christianisme* (1802), Chateaubriand will suggest, as did Rousseau, that the distinction between good and evil is inherent in man, and that evil is automatically repugnant to the conscience of all free men. It functions independently of society's threats of punishment and incarceration; it does not feed upon society for its moral acuity or probity. In order to express these home truths, Chateaubriand formulates a rotund praise of the power of the "inner voice," and the theme of *The Mandarin* is announced: "O Conscience! Are you not a phantom of the imagination, or man's fear of punishment? I ask myself: If you could, by one stroke, kill a man in China and inherit his fortune in Europe, with the supernatural conviction that nobody would ever know anything of it, would you carry it out?" [7] There are echoes of this not only in Rousseau but also in Balzac and in minor texts of Sidney Smith and Annie Edwards. In France, the tradition of the Mandarin theme culminated, well before Eça, with texts of Dumas fils (again!) and Henri Monnier's *As-tu tué le Mandarin?* The fable, in most of its guises, offers the prospect of untold riches in exchange for the most minimal action possible—in this case, touching a bell, making it sound for just a moment. The means of administering the violent death from afar is inoffensive, and in any case, the distant victim is decripit; at any moment he will succumb of a natural death. Guarantees of impunity and anonymity only add to the allure of the temptation. In Eça's particular formulation, the victim cannot possibly know anything of his murderer at a distance, since Eça's Ti Chin finds himself in the deep confines of Mongolia, ignorant of the existence of Europe, of Portugal of course, and certainly of the hapless bureaucrat to whom this unique proposal has been made.

As was the case in the first two novels, there are considerable parallels between these texts and Eça's own diplomatic or bureaucratic experiences. It is not irrelevant to point out that while consul in Havana Eça found himself responsible for the fortunes of thousands of Chinese laborers who had been im-

ported in a wholesale fashion from the Portuguese colony of
Macao. These unfortunates came to Cuba in order to further
the construction of railroads and to work in the infamous sugar
plantations. Upon arrival in Havana, Eça found these good
"Portuguese" citizens in a state of total feudal servitude and
exploitation. Eça not only took it upon himself to better the fate
of these laborers; he also wrote a major indictment of this neglect and abandon. By attacking the Cuban plantation system
and the exploitation of the Chinese, Eça brought to himself
a considerable degree of notoriety; had he desisted from his
protests and taken a more leisurely view of this ma-
nipulative management, it is more than likely that he would
have left the island of Cuba a rich young diplomat, lauded by
the Cuban establishment. But he did not envisage this or apparently consider this possibility. He attacked, in his reports to
Lisbon, the system that was so cruelly exploiting the Chinese.[8]
Eça's contacts with the Chinese were something more than that
of a literary tourist; the subject was close to him for many reasons.

Eça's hero in *The Mandarin* is, like Eça, an impoverished
bureaucrat and, just as Eça was, an aging bachelor who "always
enters rooms with the right foot," stoop-shouldered "from bow-
ing my head to the dust before the general directors." It goes
without saying that Eça's hero, Teodoro, had extraordinary
fantasies about acquiring untold riches and luxury. "I was bit-
ten by the desire to be able to dine at the Central Hotel with
champagne, to clasp the delicate hands of viscountesses and, at
least twice a week, to slumber in exhausted bliss on the fresh
bosom of some Venus." Teodoro is vicariousness itself, but he is
not at all plunged into the depths of Romantic distress because
of his inability to realize his fantasies. In his own words, he is
saved from such engulfment by the simple fact that "he does
not have much imagination. . . . I did not consume myself by
madly coveting fictitious paradises born in my yearning mind
like mists rising from the surface of a lake. . . . I am a
positivist. I longed only for the rational, the tangible." As a
good Portuguese constitutionalist, he prays every night to Our
Lady of Sorrows and buys chances in every lottery. And, like

Eça, he is a bibliophile. In a recently purchased set of folios, he finds the miraculous Mandarin text, the proposal by a bourgeois Mephistopheles. The sum of well over $100 million is offered if the Mandarin is done away with by merely touching the bell at Teodoro's side; the devil offers also the unique prospect of taking part in the "transubstantiation" of all matter. "To kill, my boy, is almost always to restore the necessary equilibrium of the universe. It is the elimination of an excess here to make up for a lack there." This solid philosophy has the appropriate effect upon Teodoro; with a firm hand, he rings the bell, and Ti Chin Fu expires with a sigh in farthest China. Ringing the bell was no more difficult than summoning a waiter.

In due course, the riches arrive. Teodoro embarks on a spree, but the inevitable remorse brings with it a ghostly emblem—the dead Mandarin reappears as a vision at the most inopportune moments. Having begun to enjoy the Queirosian delights of surfeit followed by tedium, Teodoro is plagued by a "potbellied figure with the black pigtail and the yellow gown, with his parrot in his arms." Full of regrets and intent upon mortification, he leaves for China, an expansive exercise in expiation and appeasement. The plan is simple: He will arrange a regal funeral for the unhappy ghost, and furthermore he will marry one of Ti Chin's now impoverished descendants. With the aid of a cooperative Russian ambassador in Peking, he transfigures himself into the image of the Mandarin, following the best jesuitical tradition of assimilating Confucian models for the purpose of proselytizing the Word of Christ. Donning the costume of the Mandarin, he senses himself "imbued with Chinese ideas and instincts: the love of meticulous ceremonial, respect for bureaucratic formula, a tinge of cultivated skepticism." Mme Camiloff, the Russian ambassador's wife, a reader of Goethe and Dumas fils, fall into Teodoro's arms.

After a vain search for the descendants and considerable peripatetics, Teodoro returns to Lisbon only to find the same paunchy Mandarin haunting him once more, "filling the arch of the Rua Augusta" in downtown Lisbon. He then renounces the millions and returns to his former boardinghouse, begging to be delivered from his riches—"Revive the Mandarin! Give me back the peace of poverty!" The devil brushes this request aside, asserting that "It can't be done, my good sir, it can't be done." Teodoro prepares his will, a document containing a penultimate moral dictum: "Only that bread tastes good that we earn each day with our own hands. Do not kill the Mandarin!" Had the novella ended with this fortifying moral prescription, we might well associate *The Mandarin* with the moral imperatives of earlier days, but Eça ends with a final paragraph which rings out with strong Baudelairian echoes, destroying thereby an possible moralistic interpretation to the work. Here it is:

> Nonetheless, dying, I am greatly consoled by this idea: that from the North to the South, and from the West to the East, from the Great Wall of Tartary to the waves of the Yellow Sea, throughout the whole vast Kingdom of China, not a single Mandarin would remain alive if you, dear reader, could suppress him and acquire his millions as easily as I did—oh Reader, creature improvised by God, feeble work of faulty clay, my image and my brother![9]

What is the possible moral of *The Mandarin?* None at all. It is true that Eça gives us the honorable and possible moral nuance on the matter of earning one's own bread; however, the novel *truly* ends with a resigned acceptance of a base moral code: the Mandarin should not be killed, of course, but anyone would do it if they could, no? As gross as such conclusions are, they are not indicative of the peculiar brand of moral relativism that is suffused throughout Eça's next published novel, *The Relic* (1887).

It seems to be a delightful, even aery work, and it is also Eça's most devious, entertaining, and ultimately subversive work. At this juncture, among so many others, we begin to wonder what that rather ugly adjective "Queirosian" could possibly mean—it could never have the sense of direct identification that we know is correct when we speak of the Jamesian comic sense or the Dickensian vision of industrial society in *Bleak House,* let us say.

One might exaggerate the uselessness of such adjectives in Eça's case by simply saying that there is no work of him that is wholly *characteristic* of him—each story and novel seems to be created ex nihilo, above all when we speak of such fanciful flights as *The Mandarin* and *The Relic*. Each work seems to be an imaginative raid upon a series of moral propositions that have no apparent coherence among each other or even between one book and another.

For instance, in *The Mandarin*, the weight and detail of symbolic means embedded into the fabric of the work is of infinitely greater interest than the character of Teodoro, who is a purposefully drawn puppet, and who takes on meanings more related to allegory and fable than to the function of character in a Realistic novel. Teodoro, Adela, General and Madame Camiloff, and others have no human dimension, at least in the sense that Eça's theory of character would have evinced in the earlier works. Social determinants have been discarded, and rather obviously so. Society has no connection with the moral temptations proposed by a bourgeois Mephistopheles. The old apparatus or, as Eça used to call it, his "process," is not at all visible in the making of *The Mandarin* or *The Relic*. Eça de Queirós is cleaning house, and he is doing so with ancient allegorical means. *The Mandarin* reflects an imaginative economy of gesture that will be new to Eça during these years. There is a considerable degree of correspondence between the surface intent of the work and its own final realization. It is a work which is not at all reluctant to demonstrate its own luminous simplicities. At the same time, *The Mandarin* is, as we have said, thankfully lacking in any surreptitious theses of social reform, precisely those aspects that many readers have found so unsettling in such a cast of the imagination as that of Eça's.

One matter that might be worth considering is the degree of narrative omniscience in *The Sin of Father Amaro, Cousin Bazilio,* and *The Mandarin*. The earlier novels of Eça contain subjective eruptions, often in the form of a carefully adjusted family of adjectives, or in the open guise of the dreams and fantasies of Luiza or Father Amaro. These elements bring those essentially mimetic texts to another level, the oneiric. *The Mandarin* is quite different, in that the narrative voice is directly personal, an "I" which is constantly on the scene, constantly in control of the "voyages" in space and time which the narrator experiences. In the earlier works, the narrative voice was broader, more amply modified among the various characters; but it was *fixed* in the sense that it was directly associated with a sure sense of ideological and affective identity on the part of the author. This is only vaguely discernible in the new guises of *The Mandarin*.[10]

Furthermore, we might say that *The Sin of Father Amaro* and *Cousin Bazilio* are works of a satiric nature, but they are not at all ironic. In this sense, it would seem that the distinction made in Frye's *Anatomy of Criticism* is useful—the distance between satire and irony. Frye will suggest that the more evident the "functionality" of a text, the less room there will be for either ironic intent or ironic perception on the part of the reader: "The chief distinction between irony and satire is that satire is militant irony: its moral norms are relatively clear, and it assumes standards against which the grotesque and the absurd are measured. Sheer invective or name calling is satire in which there is relatively little irony: on the other hand, *whenever a reader is not sure what the author's attitude is or what his own is supposed to be, we may have irony with relatively little satire* (italics mine)."[11] This may well be the case with Eça's varying practice. The earlier works contain patterns, messages, and even open satirical thrusts which are not at all covert in their expressive intent. On the contrary, Eça is delighted to demonstrate the pedagogical intent that lurks just beneath the surface in those works.

The Mandarin is different, and so is *The Relic*. They are above all imaginative and imagined landscapes, nonreferential terrains for moral quandaries and problems. In this sense, as Eça divorced himself purposefully from the tasks and the duties of the novelist he had formulated in the Casino lecture and in his letters to Ramalho and Teófilo, Eça begins his tortuous course toward what Mario Sacramento termed "the conquest of irony," where an act of writing negates all saving instincts, all faiths.

In the earlier days, writing *was* related to faith, devotion to ideals, action through the word. But if the earlier novels depress us at all, it is probably because of our perception of the implacable power of societal authority over self in such works as *The Sin of Father Amaro* or *Cousin Bazilio.* This, in turn, must have something to do with the instinctive authorial power that pervades those works; no matter what inner disquiet a character might undergo, that same character gradually becomes anesthetized by blind tradition. As Leo Bersani has suggested on many occasions, passions can occasionally subvert the decorum of the society in a novel, but often these insistent, disruptive desires are contained by the awesome stillness of a dormant society which somehow "settles everything" at dreadful cost to ordinary human sensibility and extraordinary desire.[12] In this sense, Emily Brontë and Proust must be seen as the liberative novelists.

The acceptance of external schemes and structures in Eça's earlier novels is made clear by the implacable denouements with which both novels are brought to a close. In *The Sin of Father Amaro,* Amélia dies, of course, but Amaro thrives, "radiant, delighted at finding himself there in a Lisbon square in intimate conversation with an illustrious statesman." The count asks the young priest to view the "peace and prosperity" of the bustle in a Lisbon square: "What peace, what movement, what prosperity!" What the two priests and the count are contemplating, of course, is the depressing spectacle of the Loreto in Lisbon, with "faces, pale as chalk, testifying to the decadence of the race . . . a decrepit world . . . passing sluggishly through the square . . . with the poisonous air of a fetid sewer, the alleys of a district of crime and prostitution." [13]

An equally obtuse and repugnant set of protagonists round off the domestic drama that is *Cousin Bazilio.* In that work, on the last page as a matter of fact, Bazilio returned to England with his English friend; upon learning of Luiza's death, the former lover strikes the pavement furiously with his walking stick, cursing his own bad luck—he could have brought along his new mistress had he known of Luiza's opportune death. In both novels, the machine that is society triumphs easily over the individual fates and passions which had been so carefully delineated in the novel. There is a lesson to be learned from this, and it is not at all far from the surface of the text. Eça seems to suggest that a society feeds upon egotism; the more pugnacious and unrepentant are rewarded by society with the gift of survival itself; the sentient being (flawed though he or she may be) loses, and rather consistently in this unequal equation between man and society. A lover in a novel by Eça de Queirós seems frightened by his own erratic individuality—such individuals teeter on the brink of engulfment by the world. But they do not teeter for long; in fact, they fall. Society does triumph, inevitably so.

The Relic (1887) has often been associated indiscriminately with *The Mandarin;* Eça de Queirós consciously aided in this association, since both novels are purposefully "fantastic," both have protagonists with similar names (Teodoro, Teodorico), both are impecunious and idle at the start, and both are subject to the Lisbonese tedium which is, as we know, a special subject for Eça. Both protagonists are devious and cowardly; their dreams of riches and aggrandizement are both related to voyages to the East: Teodoro to China, in an epic of expiation and remorse; Teodorico to the Holy Land in search of a relic which will certify his inclusion into his Aunt Titi's last will and testament. This Aunt Titi is, of course, much more and less than a woman of the highest moral principles. She is a fetishist, addicted to the rituals and ceremonies of the church. Her religious life is almost totally a function of the accounterments of belief—attendance at mass, acquisition of statuary, relics, and the friendship of fawning clerics.

The Relic is a radically different work from *The Mandarin.* It is richer, infinitely more comic in its implications, a work written with a newly found eloquence that compares most favorably with the more earthbound richness of detail of the earlier works. One of the most telling signals of this new direction is the choice of principle behind the work—a range of associations which, by their very nature, bring out Eça's abundant gifts as a master of irony and duplicitous expressivity. In earlier works, the theme of hypocrisy itself was presented in a rather prejudicial light. We sensed the author's heavy hand in the final pages of both *The Sin of Father Amaro* and *Cousin Bazilio.* It is also present in *The Relic,* of course, but now the author's finger is not raised in censure—hypocrisy has moved to center stage; it is the primum mobile of all the characters; it is the comic agent for Eça's newly discovered sense of entertainment in fiction. *The Relic* occupies a singular position within the history of literary morality in Eça. The protagonist enjoys a moral ambiguity never accorded to any character before. Teodorico is not only licentious; he is a fervent anchorite to boot; and not only is he an incredulous and parasitic womanizer, but he is, also, at least in the eyes of his rich aunt, the image of piety and chastity. To say that he leads two lives would be to minimize to the extreme the delirium of hypocrisy and *arrivisme* which exemplify his desperate campaign to gain his aunt's financial favors. His life and wanderings are a system, the organization of disorganization. In this sense, he becomes one of the more alluring of Queirosian protagonists. He gains—through indeterminacy, simple fluke, and comic action—a degree of inner life not evident in earlier works.

Eça's ironic fabulation implies a multiplicity of motives, an abundance of possible moral or amoral implications. Teodorico is, happily, an inhabitant of nowhere in particular; one might say that his only dwelling place is in his rotten soul. As is the case so often with Eça's protagonists, the young man is an orphan, finding shelter and protection in the manorial splendor of his aunt's mansion. Survival is of the essence, and this implies a formidable outward display of the most supine brand of piety, accompanied by a meticulously organized program of disguise and dissimulation. In this battle for survival and subsequent possible enrichment, Teodorico's own personal integrity, never visible in any case in the novel, would be the first obstacle, and so is dispensed with summarily. The possibilities of the picaresque adventure are also explored for the first time in *The Relic;* the genre offered to Eça a tempting spectrum for the depiction of a character with no center, as it were, thrown out onto life and making what he might of it. This is the basic scheme, after all, for such otherwise dissimilar works as the *Lazarillo de Tormes, Moll Flanders* or *The Confessions of Felix*

Krull—they all exploit the possibilities of moral duplicity and relativism in order to match and even conquer the bourgeois world. Social station is gained only by one's own energies and astuteness.

In the picaresque mode, moral implications either are secondary or are often absent. The picaresque delights in blurring the wholeness and the integrity of the self, since the character so often is what he or she *gets to be,* not what he or she ever *was;* they begin as foundlings, castoffs from society. Too, the picaresque will often delight in the idea of a play of narrative perspectives, with a vision of the world that is without hierarchies, without "chains of being," without the solace of established social stations. The dynamism of the self in the picaresque lies precisely in the state of being a changeling, a hustler of sorts who is able to adapt to what the world asks him to be. We might also tend to think of the picaresque as the genre which covered the distance between appearances and essences, between the mores of a society as seen from the outside and the true mores of that same society as seen from below or from within, as seen by the disengaged egotists, the picaro. Not only are the remnants of inner virtue overwhelmed by the sheer drama and necessity of survival and endurance; outward display and rhetorical strategies begin to take over the surface and the substance of the text. For instance, at the end of the *Lazarillo de Tormes,* we know that Lazarillo has married a woman at the behest of the Archpriest, and we know that it is the Archpriest who is cuckolding Lazarillo, and that this same woman has had three children before marrying him. Here is Lazarillo, speaking of his wife: "When I sense that someone wants to say something to me about her, I cut him off and say, '. . . I swear on the sacred host itself that she is as good a woman as any in Toledo. If anyone says the opposite I'll kill him.' As a result nobody says anything and there is peace at home." The nature of the picaresque, the uneasily acquired "paz en casa" is here, and it is a lesson.

Perhaps the term "hypocrisy" is not the most useful one for a critical discussion of the thematics of *The Relic.* It might be more instructive and acute to speak of a new brand of fictional skeptiçism, gradually taking over Eça's much-vaunted "process" around this time. It would seem that Eça had gradually abandoned the possibility, in any case debatable, of empirical possession of moral knowledge as it might relate to his portraits of Portuguese society; such moral fixations as are visible in a work like *Cousin Bazilio* begin to dissolve. There seems to be a newly found recognition that the moral possibilities in fiction are fraught with reductive simplistics and that the most judicious stance for the artist lies in the suspension of moral judgment, done in the name of moral relativism and the broadest kind of warm comprehension of human folly, not just *Portuguese* folly. Age is taking its toll; in a conversation with a friend around this time, Eça described himself as "the carcass of an old cynic." [14] There seems to be little room for doubt: *The Relic* is related to the collapse of political and even religious ideals in Eça, and this in turn is reflected in the Renanian echoes of the work. Without an understanding of Renan's ferocious demythification of Jesus in his *Vie de Jésus*, a whole range of comic despair in *The Relic* might be overlooked.

True to his fervent reading of Renan, Eça will question, although regretfully, the divinity of Jesus; he will even deny it in the same way that Renan rejected the supernatural in the Gospels, "for the same reason that we reject the existence of centaurs and hippogriffs." [15] But this does not mean that Eça or his protagonists become mere debunkers and fervid rationalists a la Homais. There will be a considerably loose area available for the workings of myth among men. Renan's version will be that of a disillusioned visionary: "The world is a stage-play at once infernal and divine, a strange symphony conducted by a leader of genius, in which good and ill, the ugly and the beautiful, march in the ranks assigned to them, so as to fulfill a mysterious end." [16] In this sense, Renan's depiction of Jesus' last hours—the condemnation and crucifixion—makes Christ an exemplar of divine folly, a seer gripped by a unique and invincible idea. He is a privileged being because of the admirable lunacy of his belief. In Renan's words, "in the East, the lunatic is a privileged being; he enters the highest councils without anyone daring to stop him; he is listened to, he is consulted." [17] Individual reason is extinguished only to reappear under the guise of divine reason as promulgated by such possessed seers as Jesus. Too, in the kingdom of the Caesars, Jesus becomes the divinely inspired leveler, the democrat who undermines the authority of fixed society, a man who disdains earthly wealth and pomp. Such is the power of this revolutionary idealist; he is all-powerful through suffering, resignation, and the minimal use of earthly powers. "The triumph over force through purity is an idea that belongs to Jesus alone." [18] It is here that Renan repeats the lessons of admirable folly which Erasmus and Cervantes dramatized in an earlier age: "Nothing great has been established which does not rest on a legend." [19]

In a fine exposition of the critical significance of *The Relic,* Ernesto Guerra da Cal has rightfully denied any mimetic qualities to this novel. If there is any remainder of the earnest verisimilitude of old, it might be glimpsed in the comic truth within historical phantasmagoria that Eça has created. As he said to a friend during the writing of the work, the Holy City in *The Relic* is "my Jerusalem, not of Jesus, as devotion would require, nor of Tiberius, as History would ask for, because it really belongs to me, being a work of my imagination. History will always be a grand fantasy. . . . To reconstruct is to invent" (*OC,* III, 551). Another text of Eça is even more revealing of the disenchanted skepticism of those years. As is known, he was often wont to publish fictional "letters" under the name of his *homo duplex* and spiritual brother, the hyperaesthete Carlos Fradique Mendes. This character, formed out of the imagination of Eça and other members of the Coimbra circle, often can be thought of as a bellwether for Eça's unexpressed or at least suppressed opinions and divagations.

In one of these "letters," written by Fradique Mendes to an equally imaginary railroad planner and builder in Palestine, the apocryphal poet laments the arrival of such modern conveniences as rail transportation to the sacred realms of the Holy Land. The missive is written to this other, nonexistent M. Bertrand, an engineer who has just enthusiastically described, in what Fradique terms "a horrid letter," the maps and plans for the projected railway from Jaffa to Jerusalem. For Fradique, the Holy Land is the land of the Gospels, which of course are fables, but "which for two thousand years have given enchantment, hope . . . and energy to a good portion of Humanity. . . . Palestine was always the preferred residence of the Divinity. Therefore, nothing should intrude upon this spiritual retreat. It is painful that the smoke of Progress should stain the air which still conserves the perfume of angels' visits, and that your iron rails agitate the soil which still shows the imprint of divine steps. You smile, and accuse ancient Palestine of being an incorrigible source of illusion. But illusion, dear Bertrand, is as useful as certitude; in the formation of any human spirit, fairy tales should have as much weight as the theorems of Euclid if it is to be a whole" (*OC*, II, 1077).

This is one indication of many; all points to a strategic ideological retreat. Not only are "reality" and "illusion" the two concomitant parts of the duple structure of *The Relic,* but these two antinomies gave to Eça the complete subtitle to the work, a motto which is missing not only in the English translation but in most Portuguese editions now available, this full title being *The Relic: Over the Crude Nudity of Truth, the Diaphanous Veil of Fantasy.* Not only does *The Relic* represent a rich amplification of stylistic possibilities in Eça's work, but it presents us with a gallery of voices which elaborate this complex system of antitheses into a highly original symbiotic existence between author and hero, between creator and character, between author and his *homo duplex.* This is a narrative voice which is not only crassly ordinary and lubricious in its perceptions but is also a rarefied and delicate observer/narrator. He is many things and people in one, and he is of his own time—the nineteenth century—and also of the time of Christ and Pontius Pilate. As a matter of fact, he blithely smokes a cigarette at the moment of Jesus' death and is able to witness the final condemnation of Christ "across the centuries," as it were. But this is followed by a crucifixion scene wherein Christ does not die but becomes the innocent victim of a trick played on him by the disciples. In Teodorico's version of the events, Christ is merely drugged as he hangs on the cross; the Resurrection is depicted as a carefully calculated happening in the form of mere resuscitation, engineered for the delectation and astonishment of ignorant believers. In sum, this is a highly sardonic view of the Passion of Christ.

The historical romance offered him the latitude he so desperately needed, the novelistic privilege of presenting "the truth . . . under circumstances of the writer's own choosing or creation," to use Hawthorne's words, describing the romance. But this was a combination of theme and execution that was not at all pleasing to many of Eça's readers. They had been led to expect a certain cast of fiction from him, and he was no longer capable or willing to provide it in the manner to which they had become accustomed. *The Relic* is a classic example of how an author's previous books can blind a whole generation of readers to a new direction, a new development. In the Lusitano-American world, *The Relic* is the least understood of Eça's works; going even further, it is the work most roundly condemned by readers then and now. The reasons relate to something called *coherence,* which many critics found singularly missing from the work. For instance, in an article published in 1887, Eça's good friend Mariano Pina made the following objection to the work: "If *The Relic* were intentionally a novel, this work would be condemned by the most elementary principles of criticism, which demand that in a work of art, all the effects be *convergent.* If it were truly a novel, we would be hesitant, since we would not know that was objective [*o fim*] of the work." [20] Pina demands coherence and literary/moral principles, clear aims. Eça, on the other hand, had quite divergent ideas about fiction during the writing of *The Relic,* since it is above all a discrete and happily divergent work. It is not another opportunity for dogmatic optimism or shallow psychology.

Another critic could not decide whether the work was "a novel, a satire, or a farce—a little of all these things." Another spoke of "barefaced violations of the most rudimentary good sense in literature." Things have not changed much to this day. [21] These misunderstandings are difficult to explain; one of the many reasons that readers associate *The Mandarin* with *The Relic* is probably due to their apparent similarity of narrative schemes and narrative voice. This seems to be true; both works are constructed around a narrative "I" which is also the character gradually evolving in the text. Many years before, in a text that can only be taken as a foreshadowing of *The Relic*, Eça began to experiment with the historical voice in narration. Here is the opening sentence of his short sketch, "The Death of Jesus," dated 1870: "My name is Ezekial, I was captain of the Temple guard; I am old and ready for the sepulcher; before I go off to eternity I want to tell what I know and what I saw of a superior man" (*OC*, I, 667). Not only does the regulatory "I" direct the text itself, it is a critical voice who asks us to question from the very beginning the reliability, veracity, and verisimilitude of the text we are in the process of reading.

The Mandarin was preceded by two prefatory documents: The Letter that Should Have Been a Preface," and the short dialogue from an "unpublished comedy." Both the "letter" and the dialogue had marked theoretical pretensions. There is also a prologue to *The Relic*, but theory is eschewed; it is a text that justifies what is to come and introduces the voices that will govern the text. The narrator in this prologue gives himself wide latitude for excision and foreshortening of events: "despite the promptings of vanity, I have suppressed in the manuscript full and splendid descriptions of ruins and of customs." [22] What he will not suppress, of course, is the parodic distance between the landscape of the Gospel as seen through the refraction of blind belief and religious rapture—the realm of diaphanous fantasy—and the kingdom of crude truth which is the *other* Jerusalem of pragmatic fact and critical observation: "I found nothing but ugliness, drought, dirt, desolation, and rubbish. Jerusalem is a Turkish town of sordid narrow streets, crushed between walls of the colour of mud and stinking in the sun as the bells ring out mournfully." [23] *The Relic* is made out of such disruptive and alarming contrasts.

The two Jerusalems, so essential to the structure and inner meaning of *The Relic*, are also the comic source for the ruminations of the now aged Teodorico of the prologue, retired memoirist who is now in the process of composing (or has composed) these "restful holiday pages [*páginas de repouso e de férias*] in which reality lives, now halting and hampered by the heavy robes of history, now leaping free under the gay mask of farce." [24] The other Teodorico is, of course, not the fervent believer, but the conniving Machiavellian of farcical and blasphemous belief, nephew of Aunty Titi, Dona Patrocinio das Neves, the aged spinster who possesses that fortune which *might* be inherited by Teodorico, should she have the decency to die and should he continue to behave in a manner of which she approves. The true Teodorico, a hedonist and lazy parasite, can never make his true self known to the dreadful Aunt. Since infancy, he must feign the most supine and beatifically innocent existence imaginable. For instance, while at Coimbra, "I drank my fill of love . . . , I sauntered along singing ballads by moonlight," but every fortnight, "I wrote to Aunty in my good handwriting a humble, pious letter, in which I told her of the severity of my studies, the austerity of my habits, my many prayers and stern fasting, the sermons that were my daily food, the sweet atonement to the heart of Jesus." [25] After graduating from Coimbra, he returns to Lisbon to begin a veritable orgy of dissimulation: daily mass dressed in black, visits to churches to pray to the martyrs, luncheons with Aunty and a group of disagreeable and malevolent priests. Evenings are different: they are spent with a treacherous Spanish prostitute, but he is home by eleven, just in time for the nightly litany.

The degree and character of Aunty's religious belief are of interest: "For Aunty Patrocinio all human actions outside the doors of the churches consisted in running after men or running after women, and to her both these pleasant, natural impulses were naturally odious . . . She almost considered Nature obscene for having created two sexes." [26] In effect, Teodorico finds himself in competition with Jesus himself; as a magistrate coolly advises our hero, "You will inherit everything if your Aunt Dona Patrocinio is convinced that to leave her fortune to you is the same as to leave it to Holy Mother Church." [27] He will dispute "these wretched fleeting possessions" with "the Son of the carpenter." Just as Jesus undergoes his condemnation, Passion, death, and Resurrection, so too will Teodorico undergo a worldly variant of the same process as he voyages through the Holy Land. But before this happens, and even before the possibility of this expiatory trip to the holy shrines is even considered by Aunt Titi and her council of priests, Teodorico is dismissed in summary fashion by the Spanish prostitute, but receives in compensation a fabulous vision from the heavens:

> At night after tea I took refuge in the oratory, as in a tower of holiness, and gazed at the golden body of Jesus nailed upon His fair cross of black wood. But gradually the golden gleam of the precious metal grew dim and assumed the white color of warm soft flesh; the thin bones of the sad Messiah became rounded into forms divinely full and fair, from between the thorns of His crown sprang wanton rings of black curly hair, and on the breast, above the two wounds, arose two firm and splendid rose-tipped breasts; and it was she, my Adelia, who was there on the cross, naked, superb, smiling, victorious, holding out to me her open arms. And I did not see in this the temptation of the devil, but rather, a favor of the Lord." [28]

The peregrination to the Holy Land can only be thought of in the light of a now sanctified concept of duplicity. A traveler or pilgrim not only has his sins forgiven, but sins are also pardoned "for any pious person of his family who is certified to have been unable to perform the journey; with payment, of course, of double fees." [29] Aunt Titi's nephew, the good Teodorico, promises to bring back a relic which will guarantee her good health, and eternal life, in case she should die sometime in the future.

On his way to the Holy Land, his ship makes a stop at the island of Malta, where he meets what is to become his learned traveling companion, a Dr. Topsius, a grave Teuton who is in the process of composing a monumental volume entitled "History of the Herods." Further on, he meets a goddess in the form of a golden-haired English beauty in Alexandria—"a symbolical Cleopatra," in the words of Dr. Topsius. Just before

Teodorico leaves for Palestine, this English goddess named Mary gives him a relic of their worldly lusts, passions, and general bedroom activity—her nightdress, "still warm from my arms"; with the garment, a note dedicated to "My dear Teodorico, my fine little Portuguese, in remembrance of all our joy." [30] While clutching Mary's parcel, Teodorico suffers a premonitory vision of the triumph of Christianity, that religion brought forth by the Son of the carpenter: "all was over. Men's faces had become perpetually pale and mortified; a dark cross, crushing the earth, withered the splendor of the roses and robbed kisses of their sweetness; and the new God delighted in ugliness." [31] They arrive at Jerusalem and immediately make a visit to the Holy Sepulcher in top hat and gloves. At the shrine itself, relics are being peddled wholesale—"pieces of plank planed by Saint Joseph," among other things. The guards at the door are not there to protect the public but to "prevent the priests who celebrate rival rites there from coming to blows round the mausoleum of Jesus." [32] These are, of course, Greek Orthodox, Armenians, Copts, Maronites, "all ferociously intolerant." After bathing in the not especially cleansing waters of the Jordan, Teodorico seeks out and ultimately finds material for an appropriate relic—a crown of thorns. After consulting with Topsius concerning its authenticity, and after the "lofty science of Germany had spoken," Teodorico is sure that this is the same kind of material with which the original crown of thorns was fashioned. He then cuts off a bough and has it formed into a crown—only a few drops of blood are lacking. He is now the proud possessor of worldly and celestial relics of passion, wrapped, and unfortunately so as it turns out, in identical packages.[33]

On the plains of Jerusalem, Teodorico sleeps and is thrown back nineteen centuries. He witnesses Christ's condemnation, crucifixion, and Resurrection. At least temporarily he "loses his identity as Teodorico Raposo, a Catholic Bachelor of Law, a contemporary of gas and the *Times* and [becomes] a man of classical antiquity, of the time of Tiberius." [34] Brandishing a very contemporary cigar, both Topsius and Teodorico enter the galleries of Pontius Pilate's palace and finally reach the chambers where he and the representative of the Sanhedrin are questioning Jesus. The reasons for Teodorico's "mobility of identity" becomes clear—to a contemporary of Jesus, Christ assumes the proportions of a genial visionary, but a man without divinity, without the comforting power that chronological distance affords to ordinary men who transfigure themselves into myth. Here, Teodorico sees Christ for the first time:

> I felt neither ecstasy nor fear. It seemed as if suddenly the long weary centuries of history and religion had dropped from my mind. It did not occur to me that that spare man was the Redeemer of mankind. I became strangely anterior in time. I was no longer Teodorico Raposo . . . my identity had fallen from me . . . and I too had become one of the ancients. I was Theodoricus, a Lusitanian, . . . and the man before me was not Jesus nor Christ nor the Messiah, but a young man of Galilee who, filled with a great dream, had come down from his green village to transform the world and renew the kingdom of heaven.[35]

Jesus is accused before a bored Pilate, whose "chin is resting in his hand, looking sleepily at his scarlet boots sprinkled with stars of gold." Not only has Jesus profaned the Temple and thus revolted against Jehovah, but he pretends to be a prince of the house of David: "My kingdom is not of this world." [36] Pilate interrupts: "Thou sayest thou art a king. And what does thou here?" [37] "I came into this world to bear witness to the truth. He who desires the truth, he who wishes to belong to the truth, must listen to My voice." Pilate shrugs his shoulders: "But man, what is truth?" Jesus' answer is—nothing at all. "[He] was silent, and through the Praetorium a silence spread as though all hearts had stopped beating, suddenly filled with doubt." [38]

At the behest of the Sanhedrin, Jesus is condemned in spite of the bland protestations of Pilate: " 'Do you desire the life of this visionary? What matter is it to me? Take it. Are you not satisfied with his scourging but wish the cross also? Crucify him. But it is not I who shed his blood.' The thin Levite cried passionately: 'It is we, his blood be upon our heads.' " [39] As Christ agonizes on the cross, Teodorico curses the Temple: "while the Man of Galilee, incomparable friend of man, was dying on His cross and that voice of love and of the joys of the spirit was being extinguished forever, there stood the Temple which caused His death, gleaming triumphantly." [40] Jesus is brought down from the cross still alive, is given a drugged wine, and is placed in the tomb. According to the tale told to both Dr. Topsius and Teodorico, the Messiah is removed while still alive from the tomb, but he dies soon after. The Resurrection is promulgated nonetheless: "It is necessary, for the good of the earth, that the prophecies should be fulfilled." [41] Mary Magdalene, "in her fervent faith, will go crying through Jerusalem: 'He is risen, He is risen.' And thus a woman's love changes the faces of the world and gives a new religion to humanity." [42]

Having witnessed the end of the ancient world and having seen the legend of Christianity being born, Teodorico reenters his own age; he awakens. On the table next to his bed lie the bottles of champagne drunk to science and religion the evening before; the parcel containing the crown of thorns is at his bedside also. The servant offers either tapioca or coffee for breakfast, or perhaps both. He chooses tapioca, "to remind me of Portugal." [43]

He returns to Jerusalem for a final encounter with this geographical mélange of biblical myth and empirical, contemporary fact. Needless to say, no visit to the Holy Land, not even a parodic repetition of sacred events, would be fulfilled without a visit to the Mount of Olives, since "nowhere else near Jerusalem was there a place of such pleasant shade in which to spend a fine afternoon lazily smoking." [44] Within this idyllic grove, tended only by a silent and smiling monk, Teodorico projects yet another passionate death, this time one that might well occur soon, in the near future. He will return to Lisbon, cry "Aunty, Aunty!" and present her with the relic. "She would call me her son, her heir. And on the day following, she would turn yellow and groan and die. Delicious thought!" [45] If that were to be the case, his first act upon her expiration would be a simple act "of justice: I would run to the oratory, put out the lights, scatter the flowers, and leave the saints in mouldy darkness. Yes, I, Raposo, a Liberal, needed my revenge for having prostrated myself before their painted images like a sordid sacristan. . . . I had served the saints to serve Aunty; but now, ineffable delight, she was mouldering in her grave; . . . after fulfilling this philosophic act of justic I would be off to Paris, to enjoy myself." [46] The good friar tending the garden of the Mount of Olives asks for an alm and announces to Teodorico the time of closing. Raposo trods the Via Dolorosa for the last time, sure of his triumph: "Adieu, cesspool of Sion!"

With both relics intact, Teodorico and Dr. Topsius begin the return journey to Portugal. Near Emmaus, he hears the weeping of a woman with a starving child, who recounts a grisly tale of a Turkish rampage; Teodorico, lacking any coppers to give to the woman, throws her one of the two packages—the one containing the nightdress of the Alexandrian Mary, of course. "She could get at least two gold piasters for this luxurious, civilized piece of clothing." [47] Back on the same steamer that brought them to Palestine, he spies a nun with whom he fell in love on the voyage over; as he is about to declare his love, the boat gives a lurch; "I defiled the blue sea of Tyre and slunk away to my cabin." There is a lesson to all this, but it is not a happy one; naturally, it is a lesson of which Aunty would have approved: "So do kindred souls ever fail to meet in this world of eternal aspiration and eternal imperfection." [48] This is a very Queirosian note.

Back in Lisbon, all gather to witness the opening of the package containing the relic, this momentous event to take place in the opulent oratory of Dona Patrocinio. In this atmosphere of reverence and beatific expectation, the package is opened with considerable panache by Teodorico himself. Unhappily, there has been a confusion of relics—Mary's nightdress appears from under the wraps, "in all its shameless luxury, fold on fold," with note attached.[49] The woman at Emmaus must have been delighted with such a confusion. Amid imprecations on the order of "Swine!" Teodorico is expelled and of course disinherited. Undaunted and most anxious to survive, he becomes a maker and seller of false relics: nails from the cross, water from the

Jordan, straw from the Manger, and so on. Aunt Titi does die, and she bequeaths to him a telescope "so as to be able to consider the rest of the fortune from afar," as one of Teodorico's acquaintances so aptly puts it.[50]

After a harrowing encounter with the voice of his conscience in the form of a Christlike apparition, Teodorico apparently mends his ways, proclaiming "the uselessness of all hypocrisy." An old schoolmate named Crispin gives him a minor post in his father's linen factory. He accepts Crispin's unattractive sister in a calculate *mariage de raison*—"Love? Not love. But I think her a fine woman, I like her dowry, and I would make a good husband."[51] Like the final pages of *Lazarillo*, we find our Teodorico apparently cleansed of his youthful peccadilloes, married, a proud father, a comendador of the Order of Christ and proud possessor of a carriage and a squint-eyed wife who makes succulent *ovos queimados*. In effect, we are now at a moment that parallels exactly the apparent affirmation of a moral in *The Mandarin*, which we all recall—"Only that bread tastes good that we earn each day with our own hands. Do not kill the Mandarin!"[52] As we know, this is *not* the final lesson of *The Mandarin*: the final paragraph admits that anyone would kill the Mandarin if he or she were able to do so. *The Relic* once again establishes a possible moral and then proceeds with an even more abrupt and surprisingly amoral volte face. With a "more material perception of life," Teodorico meditates on the fatal mixup of relics and his being cast out into financial darkness: "for an instant in Aunty's oratory I had not had the courage to affirm. Yes, when in place of the martyr's crown appeared the wicked nightdress, I should have shouted without blanching—'This is the relic. I wished it to be a surprise. It is not the Crown of Thorns. It is better still. It is the nightdress of Saint Mary Magdalene. She gave it to me in the desert.' "[53] Who would have doubted such an absurdity? "My portrait would have hung in the sacristy of the cathedral; the Pope would have sent me his apostolic blessing by telegraph."[54] And of course, Ernest Renan, "the sentimental heresiarch, would refer to his dear colleague Raposo."

And all that I had lost. Why? Because, for an instant, I had lacked that shameless heroism of affirmation which stamps its foot vigorously on the earth or gently raises its eyes to heaven, and amid the universal illusion founds new sciences and religions.[55]

It would seem that Eça is a moralist manqué. In both works he has intuited, with ever increasing malice, the possibilities of fictional texts without a moral focus; that is to say, texts that trust themselves to their inner coherence and not at all to a particular society or to a specific moral intent. In each text there is a latent set of possibilities for the resolution of the moral quandaries of the heroes: they are invited to resign to the resolution of their moral dilemmas, to resign to the mediocre and the everyday, a happy and restful brand of conformity. But the point is this: in both *The Mandarin* and *The Relic*, something prevented Eça from ending those two works with literary placebos. That final *something* is the element which transfigures these texts into a more subversive and unsettling brand of "moral" fictions—they are turned upside down, as it were, by the fillip administered in the final pages. The author is no longer a judge—he knows and confesses to know "nothing at all," as the good skeptic that he is.

Eça has made his point, though; there is a relation of cause and effect between the Teodoro of *The Mandarin* and Teodorico of *The Relic*. After all, both are pusillanimous and hesitant on the matter of acts of violence. For instance, it would be difficult to imagine the protagonist of *The Mandarin* as capable of an intentional and direct assassination of the old Chinese sage. Teodoro can kill at a distance, of course—that is the tantalizing possibility. On the other hand, the Teodorico of *The Relic* is equally incapable of a deftly engineered poisoning or a happily arranged accident to finish off the dreadful Aunt. In *The Relic*, no devilish tempter points out the existence of a bell which need only be touched.

Both protagonists undergo the rigors of voyages in the East; one for the purposes of expiation and the attainment of some degree of surcease from the rigors of his accusatory conscience. On the other hand, Teodorico of *The Relic* passes through the hallowed places of the Holy Land only a ruse to gain riches and reach his true geographical and spiritual objective—*Paris*. Dona Patrocinio is the Mandarin of *The Relic's* Teodorico, and the Mandarin of *The Mandarin* prefigures her baleful yet inviting presence.

If there are any moralities to be found in these texts, they are discordant and not easily digested by the faithful, and for good reason. Moral urgency has disappeared from the Queirosian canon, and except for some hagiographical exercises in the form of the later *Legends of the Saints*, this brand of fictive moralism will disappear from the works of Eça. What replaces it is a complex series of correspondences, conflicts, and oppositions. This is a literature of low mimesis and high comic pretensions.

The crown of thorns and the nightdress are only the beginning of the Queirosian system; from this simple set of objects, a whole antinomy of discourse is established between the fictional level of Teodorico's existence (the manner of an arriviste picaro) and the equally fictional yet slightly more repugnant level of Dona Patrocinio, ferociously *contra natura*. Both relics brought from the East have the same wrappings and the same outward appearances, and both are relics of various and sometimes convergent passions: one is a signal and instrument of martyrdom for humanity; the other, a relic of a "divine" process of attaintment and conquest, reaching the highest degree of human passion and delight. One of these relics might bring Teodorico a fortune; the other might well bring him to his ruin.

It is not hard to think of Teodorico and Dr. Topsius as errant nineteenth-centruy versions of Don Quixote and Sancho, in the same way that we instinctively associate the loose Mary of Eça's work with Mary Magdalene; and both figures might be thought of as parodic dulcineas, objects of celestial desire. While Dr. Topsius searches for final meaning in the making of his "History of the Herods," Teodorico proceeds through this miasma of illusion and myth with one very Sanchoesque ideal—the finding and creation of a relic, which, in the words of da Cal, "will

open up the coffers containing Aunty's money in the same way
that Sancho searches for the concrete lucre of his fantastic isle
[of Baratraria]." [56] As in the masterpiece of Cervantes, this
seriocomic odyssey will take place in a present that is plagued
and even overwhelmed by the weight of the past and of a pre-
ponderantly Christian habit toward Platonic idealization. As is
the Christian habit, so it would seem, the elimination of fact
from the realm is a prime necessity for transcendence and the
creation of myth.

Teodorico sees not a Christ of wood, silver, or ivory. He has
seen the true body of Christ, and nothing less. This oneiric
remembrance from the vision can but contrast with the innumerable examples of Christological iconography in the new
Jerusalem of tourist-believers, and also with the primitive and
fanatic fetishism of the luminous, glowing colors of the altar in
the oratory of Aunt Patrocinio.

The initial duplicity or "doubleness" of the two relics may
well explain the nature and category of Teodorico's visionary
voyage back into the Holy City's past. It is just too easy to say
that he experienced a dream; Eça is far too much an ambiguous
consciousness by now to make such a solid affirmation. The
dream is more in the realm of a "miraculous vision," contructed
with the detail and ardor so much in vogue in such a work as
Flaubert's *Salammbô*. Teodorico alternately loses and regains his
perspective as an inquiring skeptic of the nineteenth century,
transfigured as he is out of his corporeal, bourgeois existence
into the form and witness to the birth of a new mythic system of
value and belief.

This is the reason that the idea of discordance in *The Relic*
may well be the key to a supple and undogmatic interpretation
of the work. It may be said that it is not at all a *con*cordant work;
there is no conscious effort on the part of the author to achieve
convergence, the lack of which so irritated Eça's friend Mariano
Pina, as we saw. Without a single object, the work easily makes
sinse if we read it for what it is—a historical-satirical fantasy. It
is at the very least misguided to ask for a unitive impulse when
The Relic is fundamentally incomprehensible from that point of
view.

Consider: Teodoro kills the Mandarin but recommends that no one else do the same. This counsel is given to all readers with a depressing sense of comic resignation before the spectacle of the way man is. Teodoro knows that no Mandarin would remain alive were all men to have such fortuitous opportunities given to them. The moral lesson is announced but then is immediately controverted by the pragmatic fact that it is simply not efficacious—it is not in the nature of man to refuse to commit an act so apparently minimal as that of touching a bell at one's bedside.

The Teodorico of *The Relic* loses the riches of his Aunt, not at all because he is a hypocrite per se, but because he was not so to a sufficient and necessary degree; he was not false to himself up to the very last moment of the role that he had designed so assiduously for himself. After all, a Nietzschean affirmation of the "genuine" quality of the night dress of Miss Mary would have guaranteed the fortune for Teodorico himself. He loses everything, of course, out of *the fatal intrusion of scruple* at the precise moment that the prize is unwrapped in the oratory. In *The Mandarin,* a criminal inherits a fortune with no justification but the execution of a whim; in *The Relic,* a relatively innocent schemer is disinherited by an equally whimsical act of outrage and indignation on the part of his malevolent Aunt.

A final *mise en abîme.* For the only time in his literary career, Eça de Queirós entered one of his books. *The Relic*, in a prestigious literary contest, one that had he won, would have given him the prize of some 1,000 pounds. The work received not *one* vote from the jury. The decision generated in turn an extraordinarily vituperative polemic between the unfortunate principal reader for the jury, Pinheiro Chagas, and an outraged Eça de Queirós.[57]

As for the correspondences and coincidences between literature and life, *The Relic* offers evidences of Eça's most corrosive view of his own self. On February 10, 1886, Eça de Queirós marries a woman of distinctively aristocratic lineage and one who showed considerable gifts for domesticity and order in the ménage. His father finally recognized him as legitimate just prior to the ceremony but did not feel constrained to attend.

Eça's new bride, Emilia de Resende, is curiously allied with the fate of Theodorico Raposo, his *mariage de raison*, his final ascendancy. In the words of António Coimbra Martins, the parallels are both glaring and instructive:

> "Theodorico had a friend at school by the name of Crispin; Eça also had a friend, Manuel Resende." (This is the same Resende who accompanied Eça to Egypt and the Holy Lands.) "Crispin was rich and so was Resende. Crispin had a sister named Jesuina, and Resende had a sister named Emilia. Resende knew the true feelings of Eça, but admired him, just as Crispin knew the true feelings of Theodorico, not at all conformist, not at all jesuitical. . . . But he 'passed over in silence' the sincerity of his friend. Theodorico, not at all a jesuitical type, marries Jesuina and Eça marries Emilia Resende." [58]

The person who planned it explained it in prose just before converting it into action.[59]

Needless to say, Emilia de Resende despised *The Relic*.

Notes

1. Richard Chase, *The American Novel and Its Tradition* (New York: Doubleday Anchor Books, 1957), pp. 12–13. I make use of the Chase text as the most succinct summary of the novel/romance problem. See also Northrop Frye, *The Secular Scripture: A Study of the Structure of Romance* (Cambridge, Mass.: Harvard University Press, 1976). Frederic Jameson's words on romance seem most apt here: "In the case of romance, it would seem that this genre is dependent for its emergence on the availability of a code of good and evil which is formulated in a magical, rather than a purely ethical sense. This code finds its expression in the vision of higher and lower realms in conflict. . . . Romance as a form thus expresses a transitional moment, yet one of a very special type: its contemporaries must feel their society torn between past and future in such a way that the alternatives are grasped as hostile but

somehow unrelated worlds." "Magical Narratives: Romance as Genre," *NLH*, VII (Autumn 1975), p. 158.

2. Eça de Queirós "Letter That Should Have Been a Preface," in *The Mandarin and Other Stories*, trans. Richard Franko Goldman (Athens: Ohio University Press, 1965), p. 4.

3. Ibid., pp. 3–7.

4. This paragraph contains conclusions already drawn by João Gaspar Simões, *Vida e Obra de Eça de Queirós*, 2d ed. (Lisboa: Livraria Bertrand, 1973), pp. 467–69.

5. *The Mandarin*, n.p.

6. Ibid., p. 13.

7. See the exhaustive catalogue of sources in Western literature accumulated by António Coimbra Martins in his lengthy essay, "O Mandarim Assassinado," in his *Ensaios Queirosianos* (Lisboa: Publicacões Europa-América, 1967), pp. 9–265 (!). The Chateaubriand quotation is translated from page 31 of this article.

8. See the extensive investigation of Archer de Lima, *Eça de Queiroz Diplomata* (Lisboa: Editora Portugália, n.d.), which contains verbatim many of Eça's direct reports to the Foreign Ministry in Lisbon concerning the plight of the Chinese in Cuba—Chapter VIII is especially useful. The Cuban experience was, for Eça, a nightmare alleviated only by the presence of some American families who wintered on the island and who seemed to have taken an interest in him. Eça himself characterized Havana as nothing less than that "stupid, ugly, dirty, hateful, ignoble city . . . The bad wines! The filthy hotels!" Later, in the same letter to a friend, he qualifies these insinuations, suggesting that the city and the entire island are, among other things, "a tobacco warehouse" and, furthermore, "a puddle of sweat" (*OC*, III, 499). After definitively leaving Cuba, and before returning to Lisbon, Eça traveled to the United States, visiting New York, a few cities in Pennsylvania, Niagara Falls of course, and ending in Montreal, which charmed him (*OC*, III, 500–505).

9. *The Mandarin*, pp. 11, 12, 20, 34–35, 51, 88–89.

10. See Carlos Reis, *Estatuto e Perspectivas do Narrador na Ficção de Eça de Queriós* (Coimbra: Livraria Almedina, 1975).

11. Northrop Frye, *The Anatomy of Criticism* (Princeton: Princeton University Press, 1957), p. 223.

12. Leo Bersani, *A Future for Astyanax* (Boston: Little Brown and Company, 1976), p. 83.

13. Eça de Queiroz, *The Sin of Father Amaro*, trans. Nan Flanagan (New York: St. Martin's Press, 1963), pp. 351–52.

14. As cited in Gaspar Simões, *Vida e Obra*, p. 523.

15. Ernest Renan, *Life of Jesus*, trans. Joseph Henry Allen (Boston: Little, Brown and Company, 1929), p. 13.

16. Ibid., p. 26.
17. Ibid., p. 28.
18. Ibid., p. 170.
19. Ibid., p. 266.
20. As cited in Gaspar Simões, *Vida e Obra,* p. 481.
21. Ibid.
22. Eça de Queiroz, *The Relic,* trans. Aubrey F. G. Bell (New York: The Noonday Press, 1954), p. 4.
23. Ibid.
24. Ibid., p. 7.
25. Ibid., p. 21.
26. Ibid., p. 35.
27. Ibid., p. 42.
28. Ibid., p. 53.
29. Ibid., p. 59.
30. Ibid., p. 81.
31. Ibid., p. 85.
32. Ibid., p. 97. Compare Melville's impressions of the church of the Holy Sepulchre during his visit to Jerusalem in 1857—". . . you stare for a moment on the ineloquence of the bedizened slab, and glad to come out, wipe your brow glad to escape as from the heat and jam of a show-box . . . A sickening cheat." Melville was surrounded, as was Eça, some twelve years later, by hawkers, Turkish police, ignorant pilgrims and tourists. See the fine discussion of Robert Penn Warren in his 'Introduction' to *Selected Poems of Herman Melville* (New York: Random House, 1970), p. 36.
33. Ibid., p. 123.
34. Ibid., p. 183.
35. Ibid., p. 159.
36. Ibid., p. 163.
37. Ibid., p. 164.
38. Ibid.
39. Ibid., pp. 170–71.
40. Ibid., p. 196.
41. Ibid., p. 220.
42. Ibid., p. 221.
43. Ibid., p. 222.
44. Ibid., p. 230.
45. Ibid., p. 231.
46. Ibid., p. 232–33.
47. Ibid., p. 236.
48. Ibid., p. 243.
49. Ibid., p. 265.
50. Ibid., p. 275.
51. Ibid., p. 285.

52. *The Mandarin,* p. 89.
53. *The Relic,* p. 287.
54. Ibid., p. 288.
55. Ibid., p. 289.
56. I have summarized here the eloquent argument of Ernesto Guerra da Cal in his *A Relíquia: Romance Picaresco e Cervantesco* (Lisboa: Editorial Grémio Literário, 1971).
57. I am referring to the article "A Academia e a Literatura," subtitled "Carta a Mariano Pina," in *OC,* II, 1454–62. The amusing and corrosive response of Pinheiro Chagas to Eça's article/letter is to be found in *Polémicas de Eça de Queiroz,* Prefácio e Recolha de João Luso (Rio de Janeiro: Ediçoes Dois Mundos), pp. 265–78. Chagas was to dog Eça until his death; it is no wonder that Eça called him "o homem fatal."
58. Coimbra Martins, *Ensaios Queirosianos,* p. 165.
59. António Coimbra Martins, "Eva e Eça," *Bulletin des Etudes Portugaises,* XXVIII/XXIX (1967/68), p. 288. Emilia de Resende was clearly a resourceful and energetic wife and mother, but the courtship was stiff, even painful. One of Eça's most charming letters to his future wife (dated September 14, 1885) is addressed to "Minha Senhora," to be followed by another from London, dated September 28th, addressed to "Minha querida noiva." The letter of October 7th, complains rightfully and bitterly about two persons who still don't use the 'tu' form, but who are no longer able to speak to each other "decentemente" by means of "você." Eça's marvelous correspondence with his fiancée and later wife is to be found under the title *Eça de Queiroz Entre Os Seus* (*OC,* III, 1447–1692).

4.

Fauns and Apostles, Wars and Georgics (*The Maias*)

In his study of Tolstoy's *War and Peace,* Isaiah Berlin presents a quandary that haunted his subject and, by inference, any nineteenth-century novelist. What is the relation between empirical fact and the vision of that same fact within a fictional space? Tolstoy was disturbed by the alternating demands of the two allegiances—one inevitably belied the other, and annoyingly so. Tolstoy "was by nature not a visionary; he saw the manifold objects and situations on earth in their full multiplicity; he grasped their individual essences and what divided them from what they were not . . . but he longed for a universal explanatory principle." [1] We marvel at the "unrivalled concreteness" and "perception of specific properties" in his works, but we also note a "hunger for final understanding," a longing for an apprehension of order that might elevate the mere fact to a more transcendental plane of meaning and historical destiny. [2] We might say that this drive to harmonize the irreconcilable is at the heart of the discrete making of the novel and the theoretical disquisitions embedded into the fictional fabric of the work. For Tolstoy, it would have been easier to go in one direction or another, and this discontent with the mere fact probably explains Flaubert's outburst—"Il philosophise!" In Berlin's view, there is no single solution to the dilemma. Rather, readers must recognize the dualistic vision in Tolstoy's fiction as the only path to the slippery truths lurking in *War and Peace*. At once hedgehog and fox; at once scattered, empirical, and Aristotelian while at the same time visionary, transcendental, and Platonic.

If we think of Eça de Queirós in a theoretical sense, we would more than likely think of him as a hedgehog desperately attempting to enter the undogmatic world of "colours, smells, tastes, movements, jealousies, loves, hatreds, passions"—the fictional space of the unfettered observer of all that is around us.[3] This is the world of foxy multiplicity and total freedom of which Eça often dreamed.

At the end of the third edition of *The Sin of Father Amaro*, the reader will recall that fateful reunion in Lisbon of a singular trio: Father Amaro, Canon Dias, and Count Ribamar, the latter a superb exemplar of a fatuous constitutionalist politician in the Acácio manner. They gather around the statue of Luís de Camões (1524–1580), the archetypal representative and symbol of the political and cultural hegemony of Portugal during the age of discovery and conquest. Eça thus ended his compelling novel of domestic tragedy and priestly corruption with a paragraph that attempted to bring the empirical fact to a level of dramatic historical symbolism; Camões becomes the paradigm by which the author measures for us the present decadence and moral languor of Portugal.

> And the representative of the state, the two representatives of religion, all three in line, near the railings of the monument of Camões, their heads, raised, were filled with delight at the certainty of the glory and grandeur of their country; there at the foot of that pedestal under the cold bronze gaze of that old poet, erect and noble, with his fine strong horseman's shoulders, his epic over his heart, his sword held firm;

surrounded by the Portuguese historians and heroic
poets of the past, a past gone forever, a memory almost lost.[4]

Two unworthy priests and a pompous buffoon, facing *the*
exemplar from Portugal's past. The symbolism is not subtle, but
the distance between what was and what is makes this a
noteworthy and instructive moment in Eça's fiction—after all,
what else is his writing but a dialogue between imagined past
and observed present? The choice of Camões is, of course,
peculiarly significant, not only because this particular monument was missing from the earlier *Amaro* versions, but also because of the fact that this last version was published in the year
1880, the same year in which Portugal underwent a veritable
paroxysm of civic pride and messianic hopes for a new day—
the tricentenary year marking the death of Camões himself.
Civic enthusiasm and patriotic fervor were at their height; in a
nation almost suffocated by a lethal sense of resignation before
history, many of the principal figures in the Coimbra generation made use of the tricentenary to further their own political
and cultural ideals. For instance, a committee formed of distinguished intellectuals and journalists (including Teófilo Braga,
Ramalho Ortigão, and Jaime Batalha Reis) spoke of its intentions which went well beyond the merely literary: "[We wish] to
instigate the Portuguese people to create works of art in which
the sense of tradition and national destiny might be made manifest," and, furthermore, "to join the name of Camões to the
founding of a [movement] of strong moral significance." [5] Not
unexpectedly, the celebrations took on a markedly anti
monarchist tone, and most historians of the time note the fact
that this tricentenary date, June 10, 1880, as the beginning of
the creation of the Partido Republicano, which will culminate in
the Revolution of 1910 and the definitive exile of the monarchy.

Teófilo Braga, who was one of the organizers of these sumptuous celebrations, expressed the delirious optimism which the
tricentenary seemed to release among the Portuguese people at

large: "Never in Portugal had such a grandiose or moving demonstration been seen. All wept with happiness and enthusiasm, embracing each other; there was complete peace [in the land], and all declared that the tenth of June was the beginning of a new era in the life of the Portuguese nation." [6] In effect, the tricentenary did unleash a reinvigorated generation of Regenerators. Eça de Queirós will not participate directly, but both Antero de Quental and Oliveira Martins, at one time or another, will take active part in politics, as it were, much to the resigned bemusement of Eça himself. Eça could not possibly take part, not only because he was an official employee of the foreign ministry, but because he himself reflected a brand of historical pessimism with regard to Portugal's irredeemable decadence that no temporary burst of political enthusiasm could possibly alter. His obsession with the idea of Portugal's decadence is not simply related to the collapse of the epic world represented by the figure of Camões; actually, it is more related to his ideas about a decline in the "race," to use his term, a moral debility which corroded everything touched by it, a fatal weakening of the national energies over the years and the centuries. As Eça now saw his own land, it was a country of wan specters, ghosts who inhabited the chambers and the ministries of an exhausted and demoralized shambles of a government. [7]

As Antero was to assure his listeners during his Casino lecture, "Revolution is nothing more than the Christianity of the Modern World." [8] Most observers of the then present state of Portugal lamented precisely the lack of political dynamism within the body politic, and they emphasized in their diagnostics a set of ideas which João Medina has called the literature of "A Miséria Portuguesa"—works by essayists, historians, and novelists which were governed not at all by a revolutionary stance but rather by a passive and highly pessimistic vision of Portugal's decline and decadence. It is a fact that political activism on the part of the Coimbra generation was fitful, to say the least. Antero's suicide in 1891 produced one of Eça's most heartfelt and eloquent analyses of the state of apocalyptic desperation (both political and personal) which Portuguese *intel-*

ligenzia was to undergo during those years.[9] Eça's vision of his own land, seen through the optic of exile, is lacking any sense of Oliveira Martins's or Antero de Quental's cosmic despair, but it is nonetheless corrosive:

> When I return to Portugal after a year in England, outside of all the things that I have been missing, there is one thing that strikes me, and another thing which depresses me: I am struck by the downcast countenances, and I am depressed by the anemic cast of everyone. What an appearance they have! The disjointed walk, the morbid and languid glances, complexion of the skin of a chicken, a collapse of the kidneys, the touch of lymphatic humors, the sad promenade of a wasted race in the corridors of a hospital.[10]

This is part of the sensibility within which the literature of "A Miséria Portuguesa" was constructed. For our purposes, it is symptomatic of a certain historical vision, of an organic and carefully developed theory of Portugal's triumph, apotheosis, and decline. No historian of the generation of Coimbra did more to codify and dramatize this decadentist vision of the Portuguese present than did Joaquim Pedro Oliveira Martins (1845–1894), author of *História de Portugal* (1879) and *Portugal Contemporâneo* (1881), among some twenty-five other historical studies.[11] To understand the structure of Eça's grandiose historical concept underlying *The Maias*, the work of Oliveira Martins offers not only a global vision of the dynamics of Portuguese history but also a particular conception of the history of Portugal in the nineteenth century that Eça will exploit, for it is the fundamental scheme of his fictional elaboration of the fate and destiny of the Maia family for three generations of its existence.

It is this "intense but invisible internal dialogue" [12] between Eça de Queirós and Oliveira Martins that helps us to understand, if in a somewhat rudimentary way, the parallel historical conceptions that guide the making of the three most distinguished and incisive diagnostics of fin de siècle Portugal: *História de Portugal, Portugal Contemporâneo,* and *Os Maias.*

Like most members of the generation, Oliveira Martins conceived of moral consciousness in the Kantian manner; that is, as the source of moral and social life. History is a frieze which "demands above all the direct contact with the sources, the true painting of sentiments, the faithful description of events." [13] The historian coordinates in an "impassive" manner the generating feelings and the positive acts resulting from such sentiments. Since the historian is by nature a coordinator, such an effort can in no way be thought of as an imposition upon reality, since "no formulas may transform night into day in the face of things. Society is not a mechanism, like a theater; it is an organism, like the world." [14] Nonetheless, the historian cannot be entirely passive before the events that he and his readers witness: "History is above all a moral lesson." [15] In the same manner in which Eça will make use of observation and intuition in the creation of a literature of moral judgments, Oliveira Martins will insist upon the exemplarity of the great figures of history—they are expressive of the collective will which incarnates itself in the heroes of history. Here it is Hegel who vaguely but insistently moves to the fore of Oliveira Martins's brand of passionate historiography. "The collective genius already defined in the consciousness [of the people] realizes that mystery which religions symbolize in the incarnations of God. God incarnates Himself and descends into the depths of individuals." [16] In this sense, the author considers his *História de Portugal* a sort of "introduction to a series of exemplary biographies of heroes, symbolic men who had incarnated to perfection [the history of] the nation." The dramatic traversal of Oliveira Martins will give us ample characterizations of such pivotal figures of Portuguese history as Prince Henry the Navigator, Afonso de Albuquerque, and the marquis of Pombal, not to mention an ample panorama of the Napoleonic invasions, the loss of Brazil, and the beginnings of the liberal revolution in Portugal under King João VI.

In this short list of exemplary figures and events chosen by Oliveira Martins as the focal points for his *História de Portugal,* one seminal figure has been purposefully omitted—that of King Sebastian, who took up his reign in 1568 only to end it ten years later in the sands of North Africa—at Alcácer Quibir, to be exact, with his army of some twenty-four thousand men. Sebastian has cast a shadow over Portuguese history which has never extinguished itself, even to this day. A king who confused dementia with courage, who confounded messianic (extra-) national ambitions (Africa, the Near East) with the airs of the chivalric code, Sebastian is, for Oliveira Martins at least, not only "the incarnation of the folly of the [Portuguese] people," but the generator of the perennial myth of *O Sebastianismo,* that periodic recurrence of belief in the miraculous return of a national, epic savior of the Portuguese destiny. Only through an understanding of the power of the Sebastianist myth can one understand the powers represented by the fratricidal conflict between Dom Pedro and Dom Miguel, a conflict which so dominated the political life of Portugal after João VI's death in 1826. Sebastian still haunts Portugal—not only in the Eça de Queirós of *The Illustrious House of Ramires,* with its heroic passage of the hero from Portugal into Africa, into the lands of conquest, but even in such a mute and acerbic figure as the contemporary poet and "national theoretician," Fernando Pessoa (1888–1935). Even there, in him, Sebastian lives in an oblique and yet ultimately revealing fashion.

The wealth of mythological possibilities in the historical figure of Sebastian are easy to glean from Oliveira Martins's portrait: Sebastian dreamed of being crown emperor of Africa in Fez, then proceeding on to Egypt, Palestine, and Constantinople, in the glorious tradition of the Crusaders. But there are more literary echoes to his ambitions, since there was such a passionate alliance between the inflamed imagination of Camões and the more terrestrial if no less ardent fantasies of King Sebastian. Although Camões was physically incapable of accompanying the king's troops to Africa, he learned of the cataclysm while almost moribund in Portugal—he died soon after hearing the news of the defeat at Alcácer-Quibir. Both would leave behind a prostrated nation that would soon be annexed by Philip II. As Antero de Quental had already suggested, epic becomes epitaph in the work of Camões and his *Os Lusiadas*.[17]

For these reasons, the statue of Camões, as seen through the optics of the generation of 1870—the Coimbra generation—is no mere ornament from the past; as V. S. Pritchett has seen so acutely, the epic past of Portugal and the humiliations of the present day make, in the work of Eça, a symbiotic drama of displacement between the ideal and the real, and this is the compelling force behind the fatidic cast of the historical imagination in both the theoretician of history that was Oliveira Martins and the practitioner and novelist of history that was Eça de Queirós.

The Camões tricentenary year, 1880, brought forth a euphoria that only a mirage could possibly produce, along with an even more lethal brand of political skepticism among the minority of the Coimbra generation, best summarized by a quick reading of Oliveira Martins's *Portugal Contemporâneo* of 1881, the work that begins with the death of João VI and the subsequent fratricidal battles between his sons Pedro and Miguel and that ends with a bleak portrait of a prostrate Portugal at the end of the Regeneration period, 1851–68, and a moving portrait of the disillusioned Alexandre Herculano. *Portugal Contemporâneo* shows the badge of the theories of democratic socialism, of course, but the author is implacable not only toward the conservatives, but to all parties, whose "lost aerial balloons have all fallen to earth: radicals, Jacobins, federalists, republicans, individualists, localists, *tutti quanti*.[18] In no country of Europe, avers Oliveira Martins, can one see such a lack of individual character and virtue. "The conservative classes, skeptics, living in a moral apathy which undermines dignity and even intelligence, remain dull, banal and insignificant. The revolutionaries, without the beneficial discipline of sage and savage enemies, are on the same level [as the conservatives], displaying, through their acts, the disorientation of their thought processes, the emptiness of their brains, and a virulence which demonstrates the absence of true strength, when not demonstrating the inferiority of their moral character." [19]

As for the simple question that any amateur might ask of an

historian—How did things get this way?—Oliveira Martins avoids all possible dialectical explanations except the "racial" possibility. This ethnic explication of a complex historical process is disconcerting in a historian of the caliber of Oliveira Martins, with his flair for dramatic re-creation of historical events and his intuitive psychological insight into the men of the past. But this is just the point. Eça was also wont to explain away the frightful spectacle of Portuguese history in the nineteenth century with similar references to a mythic "racial" defect. Let me quote from the final pages of *Portugal Contemporâneo*, vol. I:

> When we view illusions, one's own errors, crimes, or the most undignified or most dreadful happenings from the point of view of morals or aesthetics, they seem to us necessary when we see them related to the fatal chain of cause and effect. If we were to be asked if a radical revolution were necessary to establish the Charter, or if we were asked if it were possible to re-form national institutions without a revolution, we would answer: what was, had to be. Why? . . . It had to be, because of our Latin temperament; it had to be, because of the miserable state of degradation of the Portuguese nation. In other lands, with another people, having better blood [*havendo melhor sangue*], more judgment, and better criteria, the old structures would reform themselves without being destroyed, as is the case in Germanic Europe.[20]

With this picture of continuing and irreversible national decomposition, Oliveira Martins offers no remedies, no solutions; while such positivist historians as Teófilo Braga severely attacked the methodology and "the lack of philosophical discipline" in Oliveira Martins's work, Eça will praise him, but in terms that are related more to fictional elaborations than to a work of history. For instance, in a letter written in 1894, just before the historian's death, Eça will speak of Oliveira Martins's *Vida de Nun 'Alvares* as not being a "book, a printed object, but rather a grand living reality, in which nothing is of paper and everything is of living substance . . . and even more than one of those historical resurrections in which one always feels the mastery of the *resuscitator* in every line. While reading *Salammbô*, one never loses sight of the genius and the knowledge of Flaubert. In your *Nun 'Alvares*, the personality of the artist-historian disappears on the first impression, and one comes, or at least I came, into direct communication, in contemporaneous communication, with the objects and the men that are evoked." The only note of criticism on the part of the novelist will lie in his objection to a certain degree of overdramatization of body gesture; the novelist will ask the historian: "Were you there? Did you see it?" [21] Nonetheless, Eça's admiration is plain enough, both for the vibrant and dynamic narrative style of Oliveira Martins, as well as for the dogmatic theoretical armature with which *História de Portugal* and *Portugal Contemporâneo* are constructed.

Eça obviously took umbrage at the historian's invasions into the realms and prerogatives that apparently should belong only to the novelist; he was attracted by the possiblities of broadly drawn historical characterizations and by the visible sweep of the nation's history as it gradually evolved out of the holocaust of the Napoleonic invasions and the ferocious civil contentions between Miguelists and Pedreists. Oliveira Martins's achievement offers a greater amplitude and panoply of scene and ambition to Eça, and he took up the novelistic challenge with what might be thought of as his most imposing achievement, *Os Maias—The Maias*. This is the work which is not only his lengthiest and most carefully elaborated, but it is the work which reflects his most pressing ambitions toward historical, political, and spiritual fidelity to the continuing crisis that was Portugal during the latter half of the nineteenth century. As is always the case, Eça will be plagued by the scope and the breadth of the work, and by the seeming effrontery of attempting to transfigure a series of historical processes into fictional characters and realities, all under the guise of a massive portrait of the Maia family, beginning with its apogee in the heroic, patriarchal figure of Afonso de Maia, and then with the family's fatal decline, fall, and end in the figure of Afonso's grandson, Carlos Eduardo, an attractive but fatally flawed decadent.

Again, the sheer ambition of the project, which took some ten years of intermittent writing and revision to complete, daunted even Eça's patience and "Benedictine" assiduousness. It may well be his most perfectly formed work of fiction, but he was constantly threatened by his own critical perceptions of its possible hypertrophy and amorphousness. In 1884 he wrote to Oliveira Martins the following laconic description of his progress with the draft of *The Maias*: "I am continuing on with *The Maias*, that vast machine of al fresco painting in annoyingly monumental proportions, done with darkish colors, overblown and frivolous, all of which may well earn me the name of the Michelangelo of the insipid. Mas emfim! . . . ." [22] A vast canvas, then, but one done with a particularly restricted view of the nature of Portuguese society, one that does not at all match the monumental and synoptic ambitions of the work. Eça's portrait, his vast "machine," concentrates on a specific case in Lisbon society, since "that vast majority [of the rest of the population] doesn't count. In the end, a country is always a very small thing. . . . it is composed of a group of men of letters, statesmen, businessmen, and club members . . . the rest is landscape. The direction of a country is given precisely by this minority in the capital." [23] One of the more disenchanted characters in *The Maias* will put it more succinctly: "Lisbon is Portugal . . . . outside Lisbon there's nothing. The entire country lies between the Arcade with its ministries and São Bento with its so-called parliament. It's the most wretched breed in Europe." [24] These restrictions are fundamental to the intensity of Eça's dissection of the spiritual dissolution of Portugal. No Balzacian breadth could possibly compensate for his insights into this hermetic, disconnected group of fops, *littérateurs*, politicians, diplomats, and courtly hidalgos: they are a perfect, if limited, cast for the acute eye of the spectator-novelist.

As Eça draws them in this fresco of some 630-odd pages, they appear to be a largely sympathetic and agreeable group of languorous young men whose grip on the reality around them is tenuous, fraught as it is with their own narcissism and willful self-deception. Most of the time, Eça describes an overwhelmingly dominant masculine world of striped pants, top hats, walking sticks, abundant beards, and moustaches. In the Portuguese manner, women are either inconspicuous or simply invisible, lost in the lives of their husbands, their families, or their lovers. In particular cases, though—Maria Eduarda, the Countess Gouvarinho—the women are described with a sumptuousness and a care the author had never lavished upon his female characters in prior works. The Lisbon setting is, of course, the same scenario of tedium and listlessness which gave that dense air of entrapment to certain scenes of *Cousin Bazilio.*

The plot is a mere arabesque, forming the most minimal portion of the canvas. *The Maias* follows the fortunes of the family for three generations, the portrait beginning with Afonso, an austere and grave gentlemen of seemingly noble principles, formed in the crucible of the civil wars during the early part of the nineteenth century. As we meet this benevolent and generous spirit in the first few pages, we note a few facts that are intrinsic to his presence in the novel. A fiery Jacobin in his youth, and an intransigent enemy of injustice and political fanaticism whether from apostolic or liberal contenders for power, Afonso moves through the novel with an ineluctable sense of moral consciousness within the family and within the society at large. This moral sensibility will be sorely tried over the following two generations, for his own son Pedro will commit suicide after having been abandoned by a treacherous wife, while his only grandson, Carlos Eduardo, orphaned at an early age and brought up under Afonso's utilitarian and pragmatic eye, will in due course take as his mistress and future wife a woman later discovered to be his sister, Maria Eduarda da Maia, the striking beauty who had been abducted by her mother and mistakenly thought to have died while still a child. If this minimal plot has more than a taste of cheap theater and deus ex machina, the novel itself is at its most impressive as it carefully draws its savage insights into a world on the wane, a world formed in a verbose and retarded brand of Romanticism and governed by a grotesque parody of constitutional monarchism. Feeding on the inane and the ludicrous, Eça becomes a law unto himself in late-nineteenth-century European letters, fusing Romantic sentiment and ferocious irony, transfiguring himself into a lyric satirist. The means used in *The Maias* are as evanescent and as subtle as they were obvious in the earlier works. These new subtleties may take some time to elucidate, but it is time worth taking; *The Maias* functions with a majesty of vision, tempo, and elaboration that richly reward the unhurried reader.[25]

In spite of their carefully organized conception and at times elaborate revision, all of his earlier novels lacked a measured sense of the passage of time. In *The Maias,* the action itself has little dynamic function. An acute observer of this phenomenon has said it very well: "it is time, not action, which move the events; the characters in the novel really do grow older. When Afonso da Maia dies in his garden at Ramalhete, he is truly old, much older than in the first pages of the book." [26] This consciousness of the passing of time, of the 'weight' of the years, is probably the one single distinguishing element that is wholly new in the dense fabric of *The Maias.* This in turn not only makes for a less jerky and discontinuous flow of fictional discourse, but it alters radically the sense of irony in *The Maias,* as it might be distinguished from the ironic qualities of the earlier novels. We might now distinguish three kinds of ironic usage in the works of Eça de Queirós, corresponding more or less to three disjunct functions.[27]

For instance, in *Cousin Bazilio,* ironic usage is directed toward the eventuality and possibility of the reform of society. This is the not at all covert manipulation of observed fact and spoken commonplaces; in this sense, the admonitory journalism contained in *As Farpas* carried with it the same corrosive intent as did such openly condemnatory fictions as *Cousin Bazilio.* This is the not too subtle world of early Eça, in which error and delusion were exposed by the novelist/accuser. Yet there are other possibilities for irony in his works; irony might also be conceived as a corrective against unbridled emotion and exacerbated sensibilities—it can be an antidote to *Bovarisme.* Whereas *The Sin of Father Amaro* seems to be singularly lacking in this respect, it is more than visible in the brand of psychic undercutting of his characters that Eça practiced, above all in the case of Luiza as she proceeds toward her carefully arranged demise in *Cousin Bazilio*. *The Maias* does not at all represent a mélange of the above two possibilities, but something quite different and much richer in novelistic hue. In this work we have a gentler and more benevolent brand of ironic practice, one tinged with sympathy and comprehension. The earlier rancor and didacticism is gone. The change, if it can be called that, has been gradually evolving during the years of the making of *The Maias*. During the 1880s Eça began to realize that he too could not be considered apart from the spectacle of Lisbon in decline and that he too shared the insidious strength society gains from conventional illusions and · Acácio-like pretension and vain pomp. In this sense, the passage of time is the major coalescing agent in *The Maias*. The pressures of a now defined destiny— Portugal as eternal Parvonia—finally make its way into the militant defenses of Eça's formerly revolutionary aesthetics. The satiric edge, formerly so sharp, shows signs of wearing away. Not only is the mediocrity of Lisbon essential to what was left of the caricaturist in Eça, but also needed was the quality of fatality built into the plot: the interwoven destinies of Carlos Eduarda and Maria Eduardo, two "superior" souls, condemned to each other because of the spiritual and even genealogical similarities, had no choice but to have their destinies joined. In this sense, we have a plot of absolutely fatal denouement: amid the baseness and mindless egotism of this society, these two noble souls could not avoid finding each other. Whatever happens had to be; Oliveira Martins *dixit*. The habitat of *The Maias* is the aristocracy, but an aristocracy of what? Surely Eça's keen insight into the mirage of appearances and exterior elements of a society, those surfaces which obscure a sordid reality, led him to the name Maia itself.

It is a relatively famous Portuguese lineage, but it also suggests the veil of Maya in Schopenhauer's *The World as Will and Representation*, a work very much studied by Eça during the Coimbra years and after. No economic or cultural forces act upon Carlos Eduardo or Maria Eduarda. In this sense, the cast of characters in *The Maias* is free from the impositions of circumstance. Yet Carlos Eduardo and Maria Eduarda are not free; there is an inner magnet which draws their lives together, makes them love each other in a passionate and otherworldly way, and ultimately leaves them touched by the guilt and horror of incest. It is fate, not circumstances, that brings them together. This is the same "machine" that will bring Oedipus to his mother's bed, that will bring Siegmund to love his sister Siegelind in Wagner's *Die Walküre,* and which will force Tristan to betray King Mark and plunge into the abyss of the Liebesnacht in *Tristan und Isolde.* There is a Wagnerian shadow over *The Maias,* born of the fatal union of love and death. [28]

But the question remains: What kind of Realism is this, that speaks of mythic fates and ineluctable destinies and that brings forth the shadow of Greek tragedy and Wagnerian plot to the novelistic space that is *The Maias?* Isn't there some degree of "dissonance between the individual tragedies of brother and sister and the magisterial portrait of a collective torpor that is Portugal?" [29] Put another way, how can one reconcile the overwhelming wieght of some of the set scenes in the novel that Eça paints with such gusto—the excursion to Sintra, the horserace at the Hippodrome, the scene at the newspaper, the mock duel, the literary soirée at the theater—with the apparently incidental fact of the incest?

The answer lies at the essence of the whole meaning of Eça's novelistic symbolism, a system in which incest comes to be the most expectable and ordinary act of an aristocracy that does not deserve the name. Incest in *The Maias* is the fatidic summation of a nation enclosed within the walls of its citizens own private and individual egos, their own manors, their own circles, their own kind. In this way, the apparently mechanical plot construction is, for Eça, the ultimate revelatory *true* which describes the world in which he grew up and in which he is now growing old. But let us not go too precipitously into the final meaning of the incest in *The Maias.* The novel is a world unto itself, and like any world it should be observed from as many perspectives as one can summon.

Once again, the decline and fall of Portugal, that process

which Oliveira Martins so disconsolately described, is precisely the process and the scheme behind the history of the Maia family. Leaving aside the granitic spirit of the reigning patriarch that is Afonso da Maia, the book begins to document the decline of symbolic Portugal by describing, with a luxury of detail, a character who has not drawn the attention of critics to any great degree—Pedro da Maia, the son of Afonso and the hapless father of both Carlos Eduardo and Maria Eduarda. The destructive nature of this character, his willingness to succumb to the vortex of the passions, is quite possibly the dynamic center of the whole novel. Examining the peculiar sensibility of Pedro da Maia helps us enter into one of the darker realms of the substructure of *The Maias*—the family and the novel.

In turn, to understand Pedro, we must recall the disaster that was the marriage of his father, Afonso, to Dona Maria Eduarda Runa, "a lovely dark-eyed girl, loving and fragile." [30] We know of Afonso as the Jacobin freethinker, the virulent proponent of revolution and the destruction of the tattered feudal structure of old Portugal. But whom does this revolutionary marry? An independent and critical spirit? A soul mate? No. As soon as she finds herself in exile in England with her husband, Dona Maria shows herself to be what she most surely is—an ignorant, superstitious Catholic, a mental invalid. "Since her arrival she had lived in suppressed hatred of that land of heretics and their barbarous language . . . her piety exalted itself, exacerbated itself in that hostility she sensed all about her against the 'papists.' And it was only at night that she was content, when she went up to the attic to take refuge with the Portuguese maidservants and to say the rosary kneeling on a straw mat, and to enjoy, in that murmur of 'Ave Maria' in a Protestant country, the delights of a Catholic conspiracy." [31] Much to the disgust of Afonso, young Pedro is drilled with the catechism and inculcated with a horror of the "three enemies of the soul—the world, the flesh and the devil." [32] Afonso, though alarmed by the sheer number of Franciscans and Capuchins in his corridors, and sensing the house being converted into a "musty sacristy," does nothing, and this is a key point.

Much of the novel is already prefigured in this inexplicable situation, for Pedro himself is a product of this resignation before fanaticism. Fearful of "wind, trees and shadows," passive and weak, Pedro da Maia is a sensitive soul "whose only lively and intense feeling had been his passion for his mother." This is a young man ready neither for life nor for love. Not only does he soon become imbued with an "elderly air," but his education and upbringing have accorded him an "unbalanced nature," which will soon send him into the arms of a "goddess, the incarnation of a Rennaissance ideal, a Titian model." [33] "It was the love of a Romeo, born suddenly from a fatal and dazzling exchange of glances—one of those passions which take possession of an existence, burst on it like a hurricane, snatch away will-power, reason, human relationships and sweep them all violently into the abyss." [34] Afonso recognizes in his son the image of his own grandfather whose name "was used as a bogey in the family . . . who had gone mad, and, believing himself to be Judas, had hanged himself on a fig tree." [35] As always in Eça, genealogical observations are always to be taken at much more than face value. If Afonso senses in his hypersensitive son the image of the traitor of Christ and the unbridled engulfment of Romantic passion, we should take note; his son will fulfill this troubled premonition. Pedro will marry this "goddess" and in so doing will betray the family name at the same time, since the woman in question, Maria de Monforte, is the daughter of a disreputable slave trader and therefore a slur upon the good name of Maia. Afonso disowns Pedro, only to accept him back into the house after Maria has run off with Pedro's good friend, Tancredo. Maria bears two children: one is the future Maria Eduarda; the other is named Carlos Eduardo. Like his father, Carlos Eduardo will be a passionate traitor to the Maias' family name and, much worse, he will violate the sacred code of the family honor and break the tabu of incest. The shadow of Afonso's grandfather and his suicide falls relentlessly upon succeeding generations, from Afonso to Pedro to Carlos and Maria. But there is an implication: had Afonso married differently, the chain of fates would never have extended itself to succeeding generations. But Afonso is "typically Portuguese," and this is a "typically Portuguese" union of libertarian males and cloistered, ignorant females. Afonso is a patriarch, all right, but he is fatally flawed from the beginning. The Maias were well on the decline already; he is neither the beginning nor the end of the chain of fates.

In *The Maias* some details are superfluous, we might disrespectfully speculate that some scenes could have been dispensed with in relation to the fundamental movement of the plot. Other scenes are fundamental agents of the work and could not possibly have been excised. But the point is this— both elements, the superficial and the essential, contribute to the grand allegory that is gradually evolving within the novel and within the historical consciousness of both author and reader; the meaning of the allegory and the essence of the diagnostic of family and country are manifold. Eça has constructed a novel that is at once a grave meditation upon Portugal in world history; a symbolic expiation of the historic folly of one nation; and finally, a blinding tragedy of two souls who are at once simple in the Flaubertian sense and complex in their various statuses as representative existences, Portuguese existences. All three modes are intermingled in the sinuous and at times contradictory biographies of the principal characters. No one has full novelistic light shown on him; each one functions and even thrives in a wealth of shadow that lurks around his apparently simple substance.

This is why Afonso himself is a paradigm for the brand of subtlety and nuance Eça brings to his people in *The Maias*. There are no longer those easy Manichaean commonplaces, no more simplistic recipes for human complexity in which the author indulged before. Afonso is a paradigm because he *seems* to be a patriarch, he *seems* to be the genealogical apex from which all succeeding generations decline. But this is not true, and Eça takes pains to point out how hollow a figure Afonso really is. He is more echo than substance, more a reflection of the past than the incarnation of lost or displaced values. We know this because Eça tells us so, clearly and flatly:

> Afonso was rather short and thick-set, with strong, square shoulders. His broad face with its aquiline nose,

rosy, almost red complexion, and long, snowy pointed beard, recalled—Carlos said—a hero of old, a Dom Duarte de Meneses or an Afonso d'Albuquerque. *And the old man would laugh as he reminded his grandson jokingly how deceiving appearances were [quanto as aparências iludem].* No, he was no Meneses, nor an Albuquerque: merely a benevolent patriarch who loved his books, the coziness of his armchair, and a game of whist beside the fire. He himself would say that he was simply an egotist. [italics mine] [36]

This is it, precisely. Many readers, attempting to discern a moral paradigm or center in *The Maias,* pounce upon the figure of Afonso as the incarnation of heroic values, a latter-day reincarnation of heroic endeavor in the manner of a Camões. But Camões is a statue, not a reality. He is a creature of retrospective nostalgia and imaginative re-creation, as done up so triumphantly by Oliveira Martins. Just as Camões represented to his contemporaries an extinct breed of explorers and dynamic founders of kingdoms, the statue of Camões in *The Sin of Father Amaro* and *The Maias* produces human imitations—noble and impressive, it would seem, but in truth nothing but egotists like Afonso, who retire to their gardens and their vineyards and nurture sons who in turn nurture other sons.[37]

Carlos Eduardo starts well, under his grandfather's energetic tutelage. He is trained to be a doctor, a man of science, a figure that should pass through all national mythologies untouched, since he is a man of today, a representative of the tenets of the new age of rationalism, science, and industry. He *should be* a humanist and a pragmatist, that is; liberal European society was precisely moving in this direction—toward a democratic revolution based on ability and not on financial, spiritual, or familial heritage. But the weight of the past is great, above all in Portugal, and science does not adopt easily to the antimechanical ethos and irrationality of the old Portuguese gods.

He begins well, embarking on a practice "that will be glory to the nation." He will divide his practice into two areas: an experimental laboratory and a set of consulting rooms where most patients will be treated "with no payment, both out of charity and for experience." The planned laboratory will have "ovens for chemical work, a room equipped for anatomical and physiological research, his library, his apparatus; in fact, all the instruments for his work would be methodically assembled here." [38] The consulting rooms are no less ambitious: "A servant liveried in the French style stood on duty in a hall lined with leather seats. The patient's waiting room was gay with green wallpaper patterned with silver garlands. Plants stood in Rouen vases; there were vivid paintings on the walls and rich armchairs were grouped around a jardinière covered with collections of the Charivari, stereoscopic pictures, and albums of half-naked actresses. And to banish utterly the dismal atmosphere of a consulting room there was even a piano with its white keyboard uncovered." [39]

The intrusive aspects of a fin de siècle salon into the chaste realms of a consulting room are already ominous signs. But it must be said that Carlos Eduardo's education at the hands of his grandfather tends to try to extirpate the *dolce far niente* that seems to work its way so insidiously into the souls of all the Maias. It is good to remember that Afonso had dedicated himself to an upbringing for Carlos Eduardo that would ban all catechisms and idle theology and learning; an English tutor, Mr. Brown, would be imported over the protestations of aging aunts and worried abbots and priests. To all these conservative protests, Afonso had a simple and most bracing rejoinder: "To devil with the classics. The first duty of a man is to live. And for this he must be healthy and strong. All sensible education consists in this: to develop health, strength and the formation of good habits, to concentrate on the development of the animal and equip him with great physical superiority. Just as though he had no soul. The soul comes later—the soul is another luxury. It's the luxury of grown-ups." [40] Afonso encourages this severe ethic, but members of the household are horrified when Carlos Eduardo bursts into a salon to show "a lithography of a six-month-old fetus in its mother's womb. Dona Ana had fallen back with a scream and her fan glued to her face. . . . 'Why, it's indecent!' 'There's nothing indecent in nature,' answers Afonso. 'What's indecent is ignorance. Let the boy be! He is curious to know how this poor machine functions. There's nothing more praiseworthy!' " [41]

Dona Ana's swoon is symptomatic. "The ladies, above all, lamented that a boy who was growing up so handsome, such a gentleman, should waste his life prescribing plasters and soiling his hand with blood-letting." [42] But Carlos Eduardo proceeds on his career with the enthusiastic spiritual encouragement of Afonso, and the *appearances* could not be more auspicious. Yet there are bad omens, and we have seen at least one of them. The decorations in the consulting rooms do not seem either serious or conducive to scientific inquiry. The poison of dilettantism begins to pervade the spirit of Carlos Eduardo, this embodiment of noble self-activism in the name of science and medicine. "Literature and Art, in all their forms, absorbed him deliciously. He published some sonnets and an article on the Parthenon. He attempted to paint in oils in an improvised studio. He composed archaelogical short stories under the influence of Flaubert's *Salammbô*." [43] Later, while the consulting room and the laboratory await a guiding hand, Carlos Eduardo finds himself wavering in his vague ambitions, alternately deciding (with equal intensity) upon a "flourishing practice," "a massive compilation of an epoch-making book," "experiments in physiology that would be painstaking and rewarding." "He discerned within himself, or *imagined he discerned,* a tumultuous power, but he could not discover a way of applying it [italics mine]." [44] A friend of the family succinctly brings the problem to the fore: " 'If it lasts,' Dr. Trigueiros said with a wide, prophetic gesture, 'we have something really big here!' And so it seemed to last." But the world of *The Maias* has only one constant, and that is the mutability of everything, the changing nature of all human existence; neither Afonso, Pedro, or Carlos Eduardo is capable of resisting the wearing away of time and the destructive *accidie* of the spirit which works its way into the ambitions of the individuals and the collective will of the society at large. There is a lovely passage which documents the end of Carlos Eduardo's medical ambitions; it is a modest moment in this portentous novel, but it is no less significant than other, more flamboyant events. After the following passage, the world of medicine is barely mentioned; Carlos Eduardo imperceptibly enters into a subjective world of self-absorption from which there is no salvation.

It is, in effect, a most insidious occasion. Carlos is alone in his consulting rooms; no patients have appeared. He is reading the *Diário de Notícias*, but the columns of prose seem to be permeated with the same morose tedium which he senses around him in his consulting rooms. Soon he yawns and lets the journal fall from his hands:

> The whole slow murmur of a languid city, the soft air of that southern climate, seemed to steal little by little into the muffled room and slip across the heavy velvets, across the varnished furniture, to wrap Carlos around with indolence and sleep. His head on a cushion, he would lie there smoking in the siesta-like calm, in a fitful daydream, vague and tenuous, like the light, whispy smoke that rises from half-dead embers. Then, with an effort, he would shake off his torpor, pace round the room, open a book here and there among those on the shelves, strum two bars of a waltz on the piano and rouse himself. His eyes on the flowered carpet, he would decide at last that these two hours in the consulting rooms were an absurd waste of time!
>
> "Is the carriage outside?" he would call to the servant.
>
> He would rapidly light another cigar, put on his gloves, go downstairs, drink in a big draught of light and air, grasp the reins, and be off grunting to himself:
>
> "One more day lost!" [45]

The consulting rooms soon provide a respectable front for an adulterous relationship with the Countess Gouvarinho. As for the no less sumptuously appointed laboratory, "all that fine research equipment lay virgin and idle under the white light of the skylight. Only in the mornings a servant would go and earn his daily pennies by making a lazy round with duster in hand." [46] The missionary zeal of Carlos Eduardo, exemplar of heroic science and medicine in the service of an impoverished humanity, has ended. We are barely one hundred pages into the novel.

The consulting rooms and Carlos Eduardo's ancestral home Ramalhete become a magnet for a welter of Lisbon dilettantes. João de Ega is perhaps a counterpoise to the decaying idealism of Carlos Eduardo; certainly, his physical description seems to be one of Eça de Queirós's most painstaking and merciless self-portraits, right down to the ever-present monocle. Wearing "canary-colored gloves" on his "thin fingers," Ega visits the consulting rooms and makes an immediate impression upon the fledgling doctor, what with his "cashmere spats, hair worn long with a waved lock drawn across the forehead, the stain tie with an opal horseshoe pin in it . . . a dandified Ega, showy, decked out, artificial and powdered." [47] Like Eça himself, Ega will insist upon the secondhand nature of Portuguese culture: "Everything is imported in this country: laws, ideas, philosophies, themes, aesthetics, sciences, styles, industries, fashions, manners, jokes. Everything reaches us in packing cases by the mail-boat. Civilization costs us very dear by the time the Custom duty's paid. And then it's second hand. It's not made for us and so it doesn't fit. . . . It's a scurvy mob in this country." [48] Like Eça during the Coimbra days, João de Ega is a rabid advocate of the massacre of the middle classes, of free love, of land reform, and of the cult of Satan. His lifework, in the process of being created throughout *The Maias*, is a work to be entitled "The History of an Atom." When completed, the work will describe the universal history of Ega's atoms since the beginning of time, starting out in the primeval muck, then to a plant, then a orangutan, then on to the lips of Plato and Jesus; then "in a knot of wood in the tribune of the Convention it felt the cold hand of Robespierre." Ubiquitous and omniscient, finding itself at last on the point of Ega's pen, and "weary of its journey through Being," the atom rests as Ega writes his memoirs. "Ega's admirers at Coimbra talked of it pensively and, overcome with reverence, they said: 'It's a Bible.' " [49] Ega is also the composer of a "comedy in five acts to be entitled *The*

Swamp—written to avenge himself upon Lisbon." [50] Both works will remain, significantly enough, unfinished. When Carlos Eduardo asks about "The Swamp" much later in the novel, Ega explains that "I abandoned it. It was too ferocious. Besides, it plunged me again into the rottenness of Lisbon, immersed me in human excrement once more. It distressed me." [51] Afonso hears of this a few pages later and complains, "What, abandoned already? When was our good João going to stop writing incomplete scraps of masterpieces?" [52] João de Ega answers Afonso with a now familiar complaint, one that was very much attuned to Eça de Queirós's own feelings: "What original spirit would not lose heart, seeing all around it the dense bourgeois mass, lethargic and crassly ignorant, disdaining intelligence, incapable of interest in any noble idea, in any well-turned phrase." Carlos agrees with João de Ega, but Afonso makes a final, futile plea to his grandson's generation and their disintegration of will: "Well, you two make the revolution then. But for God's sake, do something!" [53]

Ega soon loses himself in a "cosy little adventure" with Mme Rachel Cohen, "the wife of the fellow who's the director of the National Bank." Ega, who in spite of his satanic propensities, is the kind of poet who has more than occasional recourse to the *Dictionary of Rhymes* as much as to his beloved Baudelaire, soon reaches the bottom of social degradation by being forcibly ejected from Mme Cohen's ball. Eça's description of the humiliated João de Ega brings us back to the exact source of this scene—Eça's similarly forcible exit from the ball in Leiria 20 years ago. "Ega's melodramatic furies—and it was difficult to repress a grin before that lanky Mephistopheles who strode around the room scattering the scarlet gleam of his velvet coat and shouting furiously about honour and death, with false eyebrows and a leather purse at his waist." [54]

Just before the end of the novel, years having past and too much passion spent, João de Ega and Carlos Eduardo return to Lisbon to review the past: "Do you remember when I turned up one night in perfect agony, dressed as Mephistopheles? Carlos gave a shout: 'Rachel! That's right! What had happened to Rachel, their Israelite lily?' Ega shrugged his shoulders. 'She's around somewhere, quite faded. . . .' 'Poor soul!' muttered Carlos. And that was all that was said about the great romantic passions of Ega's life." [55]

Ega not only shares more than a little of Eça de Queirós's biography but happens to participate in a whole range of literary and political opinions which mark this character as symbolic of the Eça de Queirós that was already in the process of being subsumed into another literary and political being, above all after 1888. Like Eça in his earlier literary incarnations, João de Ega will at the same time embrace Victor Hugo as he will the new wave of Naturalism. Carlos Eduardo notes this impossible mélange of contradictions between succeeding generations, recalling that Ega had in the past declared Hugo to be a "leaking bag of spiritualism, an open-mouthed shadow, a lyrical grandfather," while on this occasion he will speak of "the heroic champion of eternal truths—a bit of idealism is essential, for heaven's sake! And what's more, the ideal can be real.[56] On the one hand, Ega will stand for the exemplar of the sublime composer of pantheistic dramas; on the other hand, he will insist that "the pure form of naturalist art should be the monograph, the dry study of a human type, a vice, a passion, just as it was dealt with in a pathological sense, without picturesqueness, without style.' 'That's absurd!' said Carlos." [57]

Just as Eça de Queirós gives us an incisive self-portrait (approaching parody as it does) in the figure of João de Ega, other selves of the author are no less subject to the process of *unmasking* in *The Maias*, and authorical intrusion is, in this sense, oblique in its fond mixture of positive construction of parodic types and negative deflation of these same characters. What unifies the process in Eça's mind is the common flaw that all share with Carlos Eduardo, Afonso, and João de Ega—the self-deception and momentary illusion that give them the only stuff of life, the only impulse to continue on with life. Perhaps no character in *The Maias* was depicted with greater affection and insight than the poet Tomás de Alencar, whom we meet in the first pages of the novel while still young, "a tall, sallow young man with a black moustache and dressed in black, who was leaning on the other doorpost [of a Lisbon café] in an attitude of boredom." [58] A good friend of Pedro de Maia's in his youth and reluctant witness to the varying fortunes of Maria Monforte after her flight from Lisbon, Tomás de Alencar becomes one of the most carefully constructed of the many satirized figures in *The Maias,* one whose presence spans the whole novel, from the first pages right down to the moment where the now aged and tiresome poet sings empty praises to the extinguished Maia clan, "with their souls of lions, generous and valiant." [59] Alencar is essentially a spectral leftover from the worst of Portuguese Romanticism, both political and literary. Eça will lavish much care upon this bibulous and voluble figure, a salon poet ever ready to recite his dreadful poems on any possible occasion. Eça deftly strokes in his vapid "sincerity" and heart-on-sleeve literary ethic, not to mention his old-time courtesy, but at the same time there is a merciless satiric edge to this affectionate re-creation. The literary evening at the theater shows to what extent a whole generation in Portugal had been poisoned by the tattered rhetoric and easy manipulation of nostalgia and *saudade,* that untranslatable word for yearning and a sense of loss. But this presence is essential to the novel in many more ways than the simple matter of Alencar's literary echoes. He is the agent of communication between Maria Monforte, her daughter Maria Eduarda, and the Maia family itself, and he is also an indispensable Romantic foil for the acrimonious disquisitions on Realism and Romanticism that course through the novel. João de Ega is, of course, the revolutionary advocate for the new literature. Alencar is adamantly opposed, naturally. The supper scene at the Hotel Central is a good occasion, not at all atypical, where the matter of Zola's *L'Assommoir* is brought up. Alencar will have none of it: "Alencar immediatley begged them not to discuss that literature of the latrine at dinner. Here everyone was a clean person, a person who might enter a drawing room, were they not? So there was no point in mentioning *excrement!*" [60]

In one of the more intrusive commentaries within the entire novel, the narrator follows the above gloss with an extraordinarily explicit critique of Alencar's brand of heroic Romantic practice:

Poor Alencar! Naturalism—those powerful and vigorous works published in thousands of copies; those
harsh analyses that had taken Church, Royalty,
Bureaucracy, Finance, and all the sacrosanct subjects,
[and] brutally dissected them and displayed their diseased organs like corpses in an amphitheatre . . . all
this had fallen upon him suddenly and had shattered
the romantic cathedral at whose altar he had for so
many years served and officiated.[61]

The comment might be taken another way, of course. The
garish display of "diseased organs" may well refer to the triumphant "experimentational" ambition of a Zola. But it is Carlos
Eduardo who marks with unusual acuity the formulaic rigidity
of this quarrel between Alencar and Ega. The following, for
instance, might be taken as a literary swipe at Ega's insistence
that Naturalist art should be "the dry study of a human type";
just as Carlos Eduardo insisted upon the "absurdity" of such
pretensions a few pages back, so too will he now make an unusually equitable literary judgment: "[He] declared that the
most insupportable thing about Realism was its great scientific
airs, its pretentious aesthetics deduced from an alien philosphy,
and the invocations of Claude Bernard, experimentalism,
positivism, Stuart Mill, and Darwin, when it was simply a matter
of describing a washerwoman sleeping with a carpenter! Thus
caught between two fires, Ega thundered back." [62] If ever the
voice of the waning Realist that was Eça de Queirós around this
time is to be found among the whole gamut of opinion and
prejudice in The Maias, it is in such thoughts as those expressed
by Carlos Eduardo, not in those of João de Ega. Regarding the
general provenance and quality of the critical and literary opinions voiced in The Maias, it is an indisputable fact that the most
judicious and sage opinions on literature and art are voiced by
characters who have no literary pretensions whatsoever—
Carlos Eduardo, Maria Eduarda, and of course old Afonso
himself. The writers or poets in the novel, as typified by João de
Ega or Alencar, come across as intolerant and injudicious fools.
As Alencar proceeds to recall to young Carlos Eduardo "those

great times" when he had been young with his father, Pedro da Maia, a sense of total superannuation comes over the poet's inattentive listener. As always, the effect is produced by the language of cliché and empty idylls of the past: "Behind his poetic language Carlos sensed the old fragrance of a world that was dead." [63] And further on, "[Alencar's] shoulders slouched in his nostalgia for that lost world. And he looked very sorrowful with his poet's mane falling out from under the broad brim of his old hat and his worn, badly made frock-coat pitifully pinching his waist." [64]

None of this will prevent Tomás de Alencar from trying his hand at a brand of verse he will proudly display as "naturalistic." One of the more gruesome moments in the novel is precisely the occasion where Alencar recites a newly composed poem, done with a "realistic note" :

> At the sleeping flower and the chaste white cloud she
> gazes,
> While the smoke from the houses coils in the air
> And the donkey at her side, pensive, grazes.[65]

In case we missed the point, the poet glosses the tercet, explaining that the donkey is "stark reality . . . it's those little details of nature that you have to notice. You can see now, can't you, how you can have realism, and good realism, without coming out with obscenities? How do you like my little work?" [66]

The same horrors are committed by Alencar at the Trindade Theater reading for charity, where Ega "covered his mouth with his handkerchief, and swore that he would burst with laughter" as Alencar emotes:

> It pierces the heart!
> It astounds the conscience!
> That all the wealth of human science
> Cannot answer the dread question!
> Time passes by
> But no light appears,
> And on one side I see hunger
> And on the other indigestion! [67]

Such moments are typical of the broad program of liquidation that marks the happily destructive portraiture in *The Maias*. At the same time, Alencar has functions within the structure of the novel that bear noting. It is he who sends old Afonso the "simple story" of Maria Monforte and her situation in Paris, a story that Alencar had unfortunately "embroidered with flowers and gilded ornaments like a chapel on a feast-day." [68] After reading the report done in Alencar's typically overheated style, we note that Afonso "tossed the letter aside, less nauseated by the sordid tale than by the lyrical affectations of the writer." It is Alencar's irrepressible lyricism, in fact, that will give Maria Monforte the motive for naming her young son Carlos Eduardo. As the poet explains the matter much later, the association between his delusions and the mock-heroics of Carlos's given name seem quite apparent: "Your father wanted to call you by Afonso's name, but your mother, who had her own ideas, insisted that you should be Carlos. And it was precisely because of a novel I had lent her . . . a romance about the last of the Stuarts, that fine fellow, Prince Charles Edward, whom all of you, my lads, know well, and who in Scotland at the time Louis XIV—well, never mind!!" [69] Alencar may well be an effusive innocent, but that purposefully distracted "Well, never mind!!" reminds us of the powerful and significant prefigurations which Eça has so carefully embedded into the fabric of the text itself. In the final pages of the novel, there is a kind of apotheosis of literary and political cataclysm. Alencar encourages the hack musician named Cruges to embark upon a "great historic symphony" which would recount "the departure of Dom Sebastian for Africa. . . . Sailor's songs and kettledrums, the weeping of the people, the crashing of the waves . . . Sublime!" [70] But there is more.

Eça has given to Tomás de Alencar the final eulogy of the dead patriarch of *The Maias*: "Splendour has gone, passion has gone . . . . Afonso da Maia! Ah, I can see him now at the window of his palace at Benfica, with his white satin cravat, that noble face of a Portuguese of former times. . . . Now he has gone! My wretched heart is heavy!" [71] It does seem odd that

Alencar would be given the ungrateful task of eulogizing old
Afonso. However, the hidden meaning might be discerned a
few pages later when Alencar is praised, suprisingly and un-
stintingly, by the now disenchanted and exhausted João de Ega,
as he and Carlos Eduardo return to inspect Ramalhete after an
absence from Lisbon of some ten years. Ega's laudatory comments on the figure of Tomás de Alencar constitute one of the
most subversive moments in the book:

> Amid all the falseness of Lisbon, Alencar was the only
> Portuguese who remained genuine. Moreover, he re-
> sisted honestly the all-pervading and contagious
> meanness and trickery. And there was such generosity
> and loyalty and goodness in the man . . . and finally,
> in the state into which literature had fallen, Alencar's
> mediocre verses stood out for their correctness and
> simplicity, and touch of true emotion. All in all, he was
> a highly estimable bard! . . . Character and talent
> have sunk so low that our old Tomás, the author of
> *Flower of Martyrdom* suddenly appears with the propor-
> tions of a Genius and a Just Man, too.[72]

This is both a literary and a political diagnosis; Alencar's
poetry is related to a brand of goodness in the Portuguese
people, and *that* quality is inherent in his "mediocre verses";
goodness seems to be a literary quality to be treasured. Too,
compared with the duplicity and emotional falsity of most of
Portuguese literature, the now disenchanted protagonists of
The Maias seem to be willing to accept Alencar as both a genius
and a just man.

If there is a mixture between moral judgment and autonomous literary qualities in Ega's exhausted ruminations, surely the
cause, as it were, is related to one of the central concerns of the
book. This is where the literary opinions of Afonso de Maia
may help us explain Alencar's speech and Ega's belated admiration. Afonso has no cosmic pretensions, either in the realm of
the arts or in that of the decayed political life he was born to
witness over his long life, spanning most of the nineteenth cen-

tury as it did. However, Eça will make Afonso da Maia into something of a paradigm of literary recititude in the few declarations that he allows him throughout the novel. For instance, early in the work Afonso rails against the unbridled rhetoric and open display of verbal brilliance that he sees in the literature of the day. He will call it a "peninsular preoccupation . . . the Portuguese can never be a man of ideas because he is too concerned with form. He has a mania for the brilliance and the music of the fine phrase. If he has to falsify an idea or leave it incomplete, or exaggerate it so that his phrase can gain in beauty, the wretched fellow does not hesitate. Thought can go by the board [água abaixo], but the fine phrase must be salvaged." These are, of course, the thoughts of Eça as he expressed them in the already discussed prologue to *The Mandarin* (see pp. 151–2).

Carlos attempts to temper his grandfather's severe critical dicta, insisting that "It's a question of temperament." Carlos then proceeds to describe himself, and most succinctly: "There are inferior beings for whom the sonority of an adjective is more important than the exactitude of a system—I am one of these monsters." Afonso then replies, "Damn, you're a rhetorician!" Carlos answers this exasperated accusation with a simple inquiry: "Who isn't?" Before the luncheon is served, the primacy of word over thought is emphasized in a definitive fashion by Carlos—"Viva a bela frase!" [73]

Within the structure of *The Maias*, it would have been unthinkable for Eça de Queirós to have allowed Carlos the last word on the matter of the relation between idea and word. After all, Eça always looked upon the world as a system that does not lead toward visual or aural impressions, but rather as a design, a trope which carries forth the import of the underlying structure. In this sense, Eça has used the theoretical tenets of Realism as he understood them in order to actualize the radical presence of physical objects in his texts, to make them *mean* more. A text such as *The Maias* signifies not at all the unordered or impulsive revelation of Eça's own self—this would make of any of his texts the artifact or manifestation of chaotic, "sensitive" receptive powers. But by now his view of the function of fiction is highly distilled and objectified, relating perceptions within the imagination, uncovering relationships beneath appearances, making use of both the moral and the dogmatic faculties within his aesthetic that will subject the observed and/or imagined society to the logical and argumentative faculties that were always latent within him. In this way with fiction, things are not separate identities, not just the evidences of the rich diversity of fancy. Afonso da Maia is a synthesizer of a moral impulse within the practice of imaginative literature. It is his majestic preaching (as expressed toward the end of the novel) which might be taken as a fusion of aesthetics and morals to which Eça always aspired. This is a unique moment; here is what Afonso recommends to the people of Portugal, be they artists or simple citizens:

> Anyway, all he had to say to his country as the result of his years of experience could be condensed into three brief pieces of advice: to the politicians, "Less liberalism and more character"; to the men of letters, "Less rhetoric and more ideas"; to his countrymen in general, "Less progress and more morals." [74]

In every sense, these are Afonso's last words on these matters. His delphic recommendations only remind us again of the multiplicity of implications within *The Maias*. In his recommendations, he effortlessly moves from the personal to the social level without sensing any grand barriers between the two. He knows that the Byronic rhetoric that surrounds the passionate alliances of both his son and his grandson are not idle symptoms or temporary aberrations. They are the signs of dispersive and ill-disciplined sensibilities; he also senses, even from the opening pages of the book, that he will be the impassive and almost silent witness to a collapse into moral degeneration. Afonso da Maia's insistence on more character, more ideals, and more morals is the most obvious emblem for the symbolic function he himself must play out to the very end in the work. He must be the immovable moral axis of the novel, even though he is hollow, even though he is an imitative figure. He must be the

judicial figure from which we may measure and estimate the
degree of divergence and dissociation from the hollow ideal
which both son and grandson so mindlessly demonstrate on
every page.

We might extend the import of the symbolism of Afonso by
suggesting that the distance between himself and his succeeding generations uncovers one of the hidden themes and structures of *The Maias*—that of the relation of self to societal order.
It might be suggested, for instance, that both Pedro and Carlos
Eduardo incarnate a certain willful definition of a liberated
self—a Romantic self perhaps—and that the counterpoise to
this generational erraticism and moral laxity can only be
Afonso da Maia himself, along with the whole panoply of symbolic elements and attitudes which accompany his authority—
his townhouse, the mansion Ramalhete, his country estates, his
statuesque and imposing manner. The fact that there is little
substance in Afonso is of little import. We have an intriguing
and unequal equation between moral discipline already badly
flawed (and this in turn associated with "the family name") and
its destructive opposites—the son and grandson of a defective
Afonso, upholders of the dominion of passion over reason, of
epidermic sensibility and fancy against the deadly impositions
of moral ancestry and authority. There is an occasion in *The
Maias* where this unequal equation between Afonso and Carlos,
always out of balance, becomes stretched to its limits. No other
moment in this novel displays the central moral dilemma so
clearly; this is the moment when Carlos has decided to flee
Lisbon with Maria Eduarda; before leaving, he meditates upon
the meaning of Afonso's existence in relation to his own visionary self:

> Carlos was going off with Maria, was going off to
> achieve perfect felicity; but he was going to destroy
> once and for all old Afonso's happiness. . . . Afonso
> was a man of bygone eras, austere and pure, one of
> those strong souls which would never know a moment
> of weakness. . . . The natural espousal of souls, as
> something over and above fictitious civil laws, would

mean nothing to him; and he would never understand this subtle sentimental ideology. All the subtleties of passion, however beautiful and strong they were, would burst like soap-bubbles against the fundamental concepts of Duty, Justice, Society and Family, which stood solid as marble and upon which he had based his life for nearly a century. . . . The history of his family had thus become a repetition of adulteries and flights and dispersals under the vicious goad of the flesh!

Sobering, tormenting thoughts, ever-present and implacable, which would poison his grandfather's last years of life. But what else could he do? . . . he had rights to his happiness, by God! Rights bestowed by nature![75]

The rupture with tradition that Carlos senses within himself can be read in more formal ways. For instance, Leo Bersani has suggested that an equation composed of "disruptive desire" is counterbalanced by the "containers" of desire, the latter going under various rubrics during the nineteenth century. For Bersani, some of the variants of this containment might be termed simply the "structure" of a society, "significant form" within the work itself, societal containment, or viewing the author as a "compulsive pursuer of significant design." [76] In this sense, Carlos Eduardo's disquisition on the rights of self over familial authority fits neatly into Bersani's scheme, above all when the critic defines "disruptive desire" and a "disease of disconnectedness, a scandalous affinity with elements alien to that structure." The most frequent confrontation in the Realistic novel is between society and a hero "who refuses to accept the definitions which society proposes of his duties and satisfactions." [77] This should remind us, if it is at all necessary, that in spite of all the historical and cultural appurtenances which form such a massive imposition upon the structure of *The Maias,* we are reading a tale of doomed Romantic love, a tale of a man who makes love to his sister at first unintentionally, and then later quite intentionally, well after her identity has been revealed to him. All well and good. But the question touched upon a few pages earlier still comes back to us: What has incest, so carefully embedded into the plot, to do with the more objective ambitions of *The Maias,* with its immense, collective panorama of Portuguese society over three generations? The question has troubled many well-disposed readers. The most negative readings might imply that this lengthy documentary is essentially one which functions at cross purposes, in the sense that there is no logical or intuitive connection between the historical display and the incest theme. In fact, they could imply that the two tendencies might be working against each other. This is the possible "dissonance between the individual tragedies of brother and sister and the magisterial portrait of a collective torpor that is Portugal" which is noted by António Coimbra Martins in his superb essay on the symbolism of *The Maias.*

The incest theme is *not* at all incidental to the structure of the work; it is not a bizarre intercalation which undermines the fundamental intent. The incest between Carlos and Maria is welded into the design of plot and its elaboration. It is there because the theme was immensely useful to Eça, in the most utilitarian sense. It is a perfect vehicle for a surreptitious social critique. We should keep in mind that Eça was not alien to manipulating salacious and sacrilegious elements in his novels. We might recall, almost at random, the odd use of the Virgin's tunic in *The Sin of Father Amaro,* the "new sensation" which Bazilio so adroitly teaches to the sexual novice that is Luiza in *Cousin Bazilio,* or the devastating appearance of Mary's nightdress in Aunt Titi's chapel in *The Relic.* All of these moments are profoundly disruptive; all are occasions which move against the dominant assumptions of reverence, propriety, and general moral fastidiousness. They suggest a haven outside society where there will or would be no question of imbalance between sexual choice and the benediction of a society. Just as Carlos Eduardo imagines the fairyland that is "his" Italy where he and Maria Eduarda will live, all of Eça's "desecrators" or "disrupters" dream of secret precincts and realms where perfect felicity is achieved forever.[78]

Naturally, all of this has a long and dramatic ascendancy in the literature of European Romanticism. Chateaubriand's René, for instance, bears alarming resemblance to the character and actions of Carlos Eduardo. Both René and Carlos Eduardo have been invaded by "le vague des passions"; both are weighed down with ennui; both are nauseated by the spectacle of modern civilization. Both are seemingly cursed by higher powers; both sense themselves as superior creatures, desperately in search of the *other* that only their mirror image can give them; both seek an image "like Eve, [who] was born from a rib of Adam." Both Carlos Eduardo and René love their sisters, ineluctably and fatally; for René, she "is the only person [I] could love"; both undergo a tortured exile after their secret is revealed.[79]

At any rate, Eça makes the passion of Carlos and Maria Eduarda as something unique, a feeling never before experienced by the usually blasé and immovable Carlos Eduardo. They had to meet, not because they were two extraordinary individuals within the mediocrity of the Lisbon bourgeoisie, but precisely because they *were* brother and sister—they are mirror images of each other. Just as Narcissus disappeared into his image into the pool, so too will these two doubles of each other, so much is their self-absorption, their incapability of touching a true "other." It is Eça himself who alludes to the inevitability of this crossing of paths: "because of [their] abundant charm, they become attracted to each other quite fatally [*muito fatalmente*]. . . . Could there be anything more natural? . . . It was natural that they should get to know each other and probable that they should fall in love." [80]

This may well explain the intense degree of repugnance which Carlos feels toward the Countess Gouvarinho, a relationship fraught with unrequited passions and a considerable degree of peremptory, even cruel behavior on Carlos's part. Of course, she is importunate and even desperate in her pursuit, but that is not the heart of the matter. After meeting her in the Opera House, his desires flee from him after having exchanged scarcely three words with her in the drawing room. And it was not the first time he had experienced these false surges of desire, which invaded him almost like love and threatened, at least for a time, to engulf his entire being—only to culminate in tedium—"I'm dried out! I'm sentimentally impotent like Satan." [81] This process has been a part of Carlos's life, but this is not to be repeated with Maria Eduarda, who appears in the novel as an unearthly goddess, the untouchable divinity. There is a brilliantly insinuated prefiguration of the incest relationship during the preparations for the ball of Mme Cohen. Countess Gouvarinho will attend the costume ball dressed as Margaret of Navarre, while Carlos, *at Afonso's suggestion,* intends to dress as Françoise Premier. Margaret and François were, historically and "naturally" enough, brother and sister. [82]

In the beauty of Maria Eduarda, Carlos contemplates not a brother and sister in costume, which the possible relation between himself and the Countess implies, but *himself, through his sister.* She is the physical means by which he may love himself infinitely; she, in turn, is the medium through which Carlos may "disconnect" his self from the formative psychic authority which Afonso has so effortlessly imposed upon both himself and his son Pedro. Finally, Maria Eduarda is the emblem for the sterility of the Maia clan, the reflection of the collapse of an aristocracy that is incapable of adventuring outside the dominions of self. António Coimbra Martins has put it so well: "Hidalgos rarely leave their country estates; they care only for their stone towers and themselves. Fearful of unworthy alliances, cousins marry among themselves. Really, the competent men such as Carlos Eduardo da Maia were plagued with narcissism. The incest in *The Maias* represents this kind of narcissism, the sterility of an elite." [83]

If the destruction of the family is summarized by the ultimate transgression that is the incest between Carlos Eduardo and Maria Eduarda, the figure of Afonso remains as the still implacable reminder of the rigors of moral law and its continuity, in spite of his highly debatable character. If a summary study were to be made of the language with which Afonso is described, we would probably find a consistent system and pattern of images related to *statuary* or *ancestry,* and this in turn related to a transcendent moral order, much in the manner of the statue of the Comendadore in *Don Giovanni,* or Hamlet's ghost, for that matter. They are all equally implacable, equally unforgiving. Accompanying these images, and in a way complementary to them, the image of the mansion called Ramalhete is described as the architectural mediator between the unchanging Afonso and the mutability and decline of the family and, by implication, Portugal itself. In this sense, Afonso and his home are symbiotic, but Afonso is able to withstand decline to a more paradoxical degree than can his surroundings. For instance, in the first pages of the novel, at that moment when Pedro de Maia asks permission from his father to marry Maria Monforte, "the daughter of a murderer, a slave trader," Afonso stands before his son "stern and inexorable, the personification of family pride." [84] After their marriage and escape to Italy, Afonso is the object of Maria's loathing. She hastened their wedding and departure "just to show [Afonso] that genealogies, Gothic ancestors and family pride counted for nothing against her naked arms." [85] Pedro's friends begin to deride Afonso's display of hubris, "laughing at the obstinacy of the old-fashioned father sulking in the country, because his daughter-in-law had not got ancestors who had died at Aljubarrota!" [86] When Pedro returns to Ramalhete after having been abandoned by Maria, Eça pictures the old man as just what he seemed to be—the implacable moral arbiter of his family and his nation: "Afonso stood before his son still and mute, like a figure of stone." [87] These are the images that are always associated with Afonso's appearances in the novel. Much later, when Carlos is discussing with Ega how to inform his grandfather of his impending marriage, the grandson instinctively reveals the moral function of the grandfather: "It would take a more flexible, a more worldly character than Grandfather had to understand this case of a noble spirit caught in an implacable net of circumstances. Old Afonso was a block of granite; one could hardly expect from him the subtle discriminations of a modern casuist." [88]

In the final pages of the novel, after Carlos has returned to Ramalhete from Maria's "Hideaway" (*A Toca*), Afonso appears in the hallway, a vision from another world. Just as Afonso judged his son silently many years ago, so too will he judge his grandson: "The light emerged in front of him, and behind it his grandfather in shirtsleeves, a great, mute, livid, spectral form. Carlos stood stock-still holding his breath; and the old man's eyes fell upon him—wan red eyes full of horror which lingered on his went right through him to the very depths of his soul, reading there his secret." [89]

The next morning Afonso is dead, surrounded still with that aura of ancient grandeur, granitic in the power of his example and his silent admonition the night before: "Carlos caught up the old man's face, waxen now and stiff . . . he was dead, already cold, that body which, older than the century, had resisted the years and the storms so splendidly, like a great strong oak. There he had died alone, with the sun already high, on that rough stone table where he had lain his weary head." [90] Afonso's death is at once the realization of the ancient Maia curse and an atonement at the same time, fulfilling the ominous implications of one of Afonso's most treasured family heirlooms, that "painting attributed to Rubens . . . of a crucified Christ, his athlete's nakedness outlined against a fiery and troubled sunset" which hung for so many years in his study at the end of the corridor at Ramalhete.[91]

The curse of Ramalhete and that of the Maia family is a real thing, right from the beginning. In the first pages of the novel, the steward Vilaça attempts to dissuade Afonso from returning to Ramalhete and taking up the extensive repairs that the old manse requires, above all on the grounds that "the walls of Ramalhete had always been fatal to the Maias, 'although,' he added carefully, 'I am almost ashamed to mention such trifles in this century of Voltaire, Guizot, and other liberal philosophers.' " "Afonso laughed heartily at these words, and replied that they were all excellent reasons—but that he still wanted to live under a roof that had been in his family for generations." [92] The house itself is transformed under Afonso's and Carlos's regenerative enthusiasms. It loses its ecclesiastical air, "befitting a residence constructed in the reign of her majesty Dona Maria I," and becomes a showplace for the talents of an English interior decorator, Mr. Jones Bule. The house is the image of imported, chaotic eclecticism—Moorish divans and rugs, white marble statues, Indian vases, a fine painting by Constable, silk-covered, gilt-ornamented furniture, Japanese screens, and bearskin rugs all jostle each other to such garish profusion that the wise Vilaça is led to remark that Carlos's rooms, and by implication the whole house, were not the rooms of a doctor but those of a chorus girl.[93] In the final pages of the novel, Carlos and Ega silently walk through the shuttered Ramalhete, closed for ten years now, having become a warehouse of haphazardly stored furniture and clothing— gloves and stockings left by Maria, an old slipper of Afonso. "This is lugubrious," cries Ega, and so it is, the architectural image of the fall of the Maias.[94]

A different series of artifacts gather around the figure of Maria Eduarda and Carlos; these objects are to be found not in Ramalhete but in the "paradise" which is "the Hideaway." Within just a few pages, Eça describes a rich, almost overwhelming collection of furniture, tapestries, beds, and statuary which seem to recall the joyful disorder in Ramalhete. But The Hideaway is not Ramalhete, it is an intensely sexualized space, with its "strident air of luxury," which at first does not please Maria Eduarda, coming as it does from a "room lined with tapestries, where the loves of Venus and Mars were worked into the weave of the wool . . . the four poster bed . . . filled the room completely, a splendid, severe piece of furniture clearly destined for the voluptuous grandeur of a tragic passion of the times of Lucretia or Romeo." An owl gazes at the "couch of love with evil meditation in its two round ominous eyes." An old painting of "a livid decapitated head set in its own blood on a copper plate" also glares from the wall—"I believe it's our old friend Saint John the Baptist," says Carlos.[95] The definitive "guardian spirit" of The Hideaway completes the carefully arranged list of significant objects:

There in the centre, on a wide pedestal, was a bronze Japanese idol, a bestial god, naked, bald and obese, a broad grin on his swollen face. His belly was distended triumphantly in the indigestion of a whole universe and his two soft flabby little legs were like the flaccid flesh of a foetus. And this monster squatted in triumph on a fabulous animal with human feet that bowed a submissive neck to the ground, and in its snout and slanting eye showed the dumb resentment of its humiliation. "And to think that entire generations have come and knelt before this grotesque creature, prayed to him, kissed his navel, offered him their riches, died for him. . . ."

"Love felt for a monster is considered more meritorious, I believe, isn't it?" asked Maria.[96]

Although the idol recalls the benign contentment of a Buddha, it is purposefully more suggestive of an idol construct which dominates the humanoid figure of man who has become beast in the service of this unknown god, a bestiality that is somehow sacralized.[97] Although Maria Eduarda does not object openly to the presence of this "guiding spirit," she does protest the presence of the head of John the Baptist—" 'That horrible head!' she cried. Carlos pulled the cover off the bed and concealed the sinister painting . . . Then every sound was stilled, and the isolated house slept among its trees, a long sleep in the calm of the July afternoon." [98]

If The Hideaway does not have within it any of the ancestral objects that give Ramalhete its sense of tradition and sustaining continuance, Afonso's old manse does have an echo of The Hideaway ensconced in the garden—a statue of Venus, an object which undergoes intriguing changes over the years recounted in the novel. In the opening pages, the statue is noted by a prospective tenant, a Monsignor, who inspects the garden in its disheveled state and so decides not to rent Ramalhete: "All the house could boast was a poor untended yard at the end of a tiled terrace that had been abandoned to weeds, with a cypress, a cedar, a dried-up fountain, a tank filled with rubbish and a marble statue—which Monsignor at once recognized as the Venus of Cythera—blackening in a corner under the slow damp of the branches." [99] After Carlos Eduardo's enthusiastic renovations had been completed, the garden becomes the favorite haunt of old Afonso: "the garden had a pleasant air, with its tall, straight sunflowers near the terrace steps, the cypress and the cedar growing old together like two sad friends, and the Cytherean Venus, clean and white once again like a statue in a park, looking as though it had come from Versailles, straight out of the 18th century." [100]

Throughout the novel, both Maria Monforte and her daughter, Maria Eduarda, are carefully described by Eça in statuesque terms. Maria Monforte reminds Pedro da Maia of "the splendour of a Ceres," with her "ivory flesh" and "statuesque figure." [101] In a daydream, Carlos Eduardo imagines Maria Eduarda to be a figure "taller than any human woman, walking on clouds, with the magnificent air of a Juno climbing Mount Olympus." [102] Seeing Maria Eduarda in the streets of Lisbon reminds him of "that marvellous form vibrating with a warm, flowing, nervous grace under those rich lines of old marble." [103] He imagines her to be a "blonde Diana." [104] When Maria Eduarda makes her single and highly significant visit to Ramalhete, Afonso is of course absent, and so too is the marble statue of Venus. It has been replaced by its incarnation in the flesh, as it were.[105] The stone table on which Afonso will lie his head and die is very much in this scene, however: "They went down to the garden, which also pleased her, quiet and bourgeois as it was, with its little waterfall cascading with a gentle, babbling rhythm. They sat a moment under the old cedar beside a rustic stone table with barely discernible letters carved in it and an ancient date; Maria found the trilling of the birds in the branches above prettier than any other birds' songs she had heard; then she picked a branch to take back with her as a souvenir." [106]

In the final pages of *The Maias*, Carlos and Ega penetrate for the last time the sacred confines of Ramalhete. The garden is hardly overlooked on this *tour d'horizon*. "The garden below, sandy and clean and cold in its winter nakedness, wore the melancholy of a forgotten retreat which is no longer loved and visited. A green mould from the damp covered Venus of Cythera's large limbs [*grossos membros*]; the cypress and the cedar were growing old together like two friends in a hermitage; and more slowly than ever sung the fountain as the water fell drop by drop into the marble basin." [107] The garden has returned to its original state, but the statue has somehow lost its graceful proportions. Without the richness of summer foliage surrounding it, Venus has become almost grotesque, an unsightly figure with "large limbs." The motive behind the sudden and almost inexplicable unattractiveness of Ramalhete's Venus likes almost unperceived within that moment which may well be the most horrific and melodramatic of the novel—the paragraph of inner monologue spoken by Carlos Eduarda as he returns to Ramalhete, after having spent the night at The Hideaway, with full knowledge that he had been loving his sister, Maria Eduarda. Here is the text:

> He could feel emerging from the depths of his being a satiety, only tenuous now, yet nevertheless already perceptible, since he knew they were of the same blood—a material, uncontrollable carnal repugnance which ran through him like a shudder. First it had been the perfume she wore, which surrounded her and hung between the curtains and clung to his suit and skin, and formerly had excited him and now annoyed him—last night he'd soaked himself with eau-de-cologne to get rid of it. Then it had been her body, which he had always adored like some ideal statue, that had suddenly appeared to him as it was in reality—too big, too muscular, large-limbed like a savage Amazon [de grossos membros de Amazona bárbara], with all the abundant beauty of an animal of pleasure. [108]

As Machado da Rosa has noted, "the transposition is so obvious that no commentary is needed." [109]

In The Maias, particular objects are infused with a significance of meaning that often lies hidden within the wealth of apparently dispensable detail. We pass over, at times impatiently, the rich descriptions of the interior of The Hideaway, let us say, without realizing the sometimes portentous meaning

that they contain. The painting of John the Baptist is there for a
reason, as is the imperious owl staring at the bed, the parodic
Buddha, whatever. They are elements of the symbolic frieze
which Eça has taken such pains to install in his novel, and in so
doing they allude to an inner meaning that goes well beyond
the realm of a gratuitous catalogue or an idle display of descriptive powers. One final instance might be added in this regard.
As the two lovers visit their Hideaway for the first time, they
come upon a grandiose cabinet whose carvings and iconography might well be considered to be the pictorial representation of the complete structure that is the novel called *The Maias;*
let us inspect, with Eça, this highly suggestive artifact:

> Almost filling the far wall stood Craft's "divine piece,"
> a carved cabinet from the time of the Hanseatic
> League—a luxurious sombre affair constructed majes-
> tically: at the base four warriors armed like Mars
> flanked the doors, each one depicting in low relief
> either the assault on a city or an encampment; the
> upper part was guarded at its four corners by the four
> Evangelists, Matthew, Mark, Luke and John, inflexible
> figures wrapped in those violently agitated garments
> which prophetic winds always seem to blow; then, on
> the cornice stood an agricultural composition with ears
> of corn and bunches of grapes and ploughshares, and
> amid these objects of toil and plenty reclined *two fauns
> in careful symmetry, indifferent to the heroes and saints as
> they played their reed-pipes in bucolic rivalry.* [italics
> mine] [110]

The two outer sections form the outer boundaries of religious
faith and military prowess—the past of Portugal. In the center,
two fauns enjoy themselves in the *locus amoenus,* equally distant
from and equally indifferent to prophetic faith and martial
valor. In the same way, Carlos and Maria Eduarda will play at
life, oblivious to the ineluctable powers of faith and history. But
this may well be reading too much into this text. It could be that
this cabinet is just a cabinet, after all.

As we well know, Eça can hardly be thought of as a novelist who brandishes "significance" at every turn. The cabinet may well mean something; it may well not. In this regard, we should recall that this cabinet does make a desultory reappearance toward the end of the book, at that moment when Carlos and Eça pore through the dusty confines of Ramalhete, inspecting the detritus and trash left by time. Carlos, "pale and silent," enters the billiard room and finds most of the valuable pieces from The Hideaway accumulated haphazardly. He spies the "cabinet from the time of the Hanseatic League," as imperious as ever, at the far end of the room. The martial figures and the figures of the four Evangelists are intact. However, the two fauns have undergone both a transfiguration and the deleterious effects of careless treatment. One takes on the aspect of a satyr; the other has lost his flute: "Carlos noticed some damage to the cornice, in the two fauns which were challenging each other on the flute amid agricultural symbols. One faun had broken its goat's foot; the other had lost its bucolic flute. 'The clumsy brutes!' he cried furiously, his love of works of art sorely wounded. 'To damage a beautiful thing like this!' " [111] The two fauns, who *had* been described as resting luxuriantly, are now in altered states; one is no longer a faun; the other has lost his (or is it her?) flute. Once again, it is difficult to imagine that Eça was entirely unconscious of what seems to be a carefully contrived evolution in this repertory of subliminal symbolism.

The fate of the two fauns is central to the shattering final irony of The Maias. Maria Eduarda's past, and the simple fact that she is the daughter of Maria Monforte, has been unwittingly revealed by an acquaintance of Afonso's, one Guimarães, a resident of Paris and a firebrand of the best revolutionary French tradition. A Francophile thus exposes the moral quagmire that is the relationship between Carlos and Maria. We began the novel under the carefully prepared impression that we were about to read a coruscating satire of Lisbon cosmopolitan life. The fauns on the cabinet remind us of a single fact that may well have been lost amid the glorious detail and pomp of the text; we are reading the tragedy of two sensitive souls. Carlos has no interest in finding out about Maria Eduarda's past, and this listless lack of interest seals the incestuous circle of happenstance and fate with which the fabric of *The Maias* is woven.

Nothing else can explain the luminous summations by Carlos and Ega as they wander through Ramalhete, tinged as they are with the exhausted resignation with which the novel ends, all under the dreary rubric of "We've failed in life, my friend!" [112] Carlos accepts this diagnosis of the past, but adds to it a Bovaresque ingredient which of course has always been present in the novel, but rarely so blatantly expressed: "I believe so . . . but so do most people. That is, they fail insofar as they never attain the life they planned in the imagination. They say: 'I'm going to be like this, because it's beautiful to be like this.' But it never turns out like this, but invariably like that: occasionally better, but always different." [113] As they leave Ramalhete in the cold winter twilight, Carlos murmurs to Eça, "It's strange! I only lived two years in this house, yet I seem to have lived my whole life here." [114] This is the essence of the many-tiered meaning of the lives lived in and around Ramalhete. It sums up a life lived with passion, that only and unique element "which gives flavour and depth to life"—and at what costs! After *that* passion, Carlos falls into a brand of "Moslem fatalism," as he would have it: "to fear nothing and to desire nothing. . . . To accept everything, whatever comes, whatever eludes you, with the tranquility with which one accepts the natural changes of the weather, the stormy days and the calm ones." [115] This having been done, the ego then "deteriorates and decomposes until it reenters and loses itself in the infinite Universe." [116] These Schopenhauerian lucubrations end with the same lesson as that of Ecclesiastes: all is vanity, everything resolves in dust. "If I were told that a Rothschild's fortune or the imperial crown of Charles V awaited me down the road here if I ran, I wouldn't quicken my pace. No! I wouldn't change this slow, prudent, safe and steady step which is the only one you should have in life." [117] Shades of Theodorico's final ruminations in *The Relic!*

How long does this newly found *contemptus mundi* last? A few paragraphs. Carlos notes that he is hungry, dreams of a fine Parma ham, reminds himself of an engagement at a café with

Vilaça. Carlos and Ega scurry off down the street in hot pursuit of a passing tram:

> "We'll make it! We'll make it!" The red lantern began to move. And to catch the tram the two friends had to run desperately down the hill and along the Aterro under the light of the rising moon. [118]

1. A Postcript on "José Matias."

The Story Itself. "José Matias" is a short story written in 1897 (See Appendix for this text.) It recounts the gradual decline of a gentleman in love. In his youth, José was known as a "personable lad," much given to "general ideas," but at the same time a youthful figure who had been considered by his Coimbra classmates as "scandalously commonplace," with a correctness of bearing that was nothing less than "horrifying" to his peers. A contemplative, even quietist spirit amid the political passions of that Coimbra generation, José is noted for his utter inability to be "moved by the wounds of Garibaldi," and who inexplicably could not "groan and grow pale upon reading *Les Contemplations*"; "a pleasant companion, always cordial, and quietly cheerful. All of his unshakable placidity seems to stem from complete superficiality of feeling." José falls passionately in love with one Elisa Miranda, "the sublime Romantic beauty of Lisbon at the end of the Regeneration period." Elisa, however, is married to a morose diabetic of some seventy years, the Counselor Matos Miranda. The Miranda house and its garden are separated from José's "old blue-tiled house" by only a walled garden. For ten years, José Matias and Elisa contemplate each other from their respective homes, "throwing their letters to each other over the top of the wall," but never a stolen conversation, never "the delight of a silence shared in the shadows," never a kiss.

This "transcendent and dematerialized love" (so radiant because untouched by interference of bodies during the rapturous communication between two souls) is threatened by what might otherwise be considered a welcome event—the death of the doleful diabetic husband, Sr. Matos Miranda. José Matias's friends eagerly await his ten years' virtue to be rewarded by a prompt marriage with Elisa, after an appropriate period of mourning.

But there are ominous signs in José Matias's behavior—he is seen pacing the floor of his home, glancing toward Elisa's house with manifest "inquietude, anxiety, almost terror." "It was the kind of sidelong glance one gives at a badly secured cage in which a lion is pacing." He flees to Pôrto for what will be an extended period of rustication under the guise of mourning.

José Matias stays in Pôrto for almost one year; that is, until the announcement of the marriage of the beautiful Elisa to a well-known landowner, a virile fellow with thick black whiskers—Senhor Francisco Torres Nogueira. It turns out that Elisa had pursued José Matias to his lair in Pôrto, but he had not consented to see her. He did not wish to marry.

Elisa's new husband installs himself in the comfort and tranquility of the Matos Miranda estate. José Matias returns to his home whose garden wall he shares with that of Elisa and her husband. He continues to worship Elisa from afar, but now with subtle and excruciating differences. Instead of the rapturous beatitude that formerly flowed out of his contemplation of the divine Elisa, he now spies on her furtively, concealed from her, "with his face ravaged by anguish and defeat." Convinced as he is that she loves him and only him, and with a love that cannot possibly diminish in time, he is nonetheless destroyed by the realization that "a man, a male animal, a brute, should have taken possession of a woman who was his." "The feelings of our extraordinary Matias were those of a monk, prostrated in transcendent rapture before an image of the Virgin, when suddenly a sacrilegious beast tramps to the altar and indecently raises the Virgin's robe." (Father Amaro imagined the same act, as we will recall.) José Matias gradually turns dissolute, with scandalous extravagances and wild orgies. He begins to gamble and drink. After seven years of this, his love still intact, Elisa's second husband dies of dropsy. Both Elisa and José Matias disappear from view, she to the *quinta* of her sister-in-law for a new period of mourning, José Matias to parts unknown.

Approximately one year later they both reappear, but in decidedly differing circumstances. Elisa has taken on a married man for a lover, the robust Superintendent of Public Works, who is now the regal occupant of the bed formerly occupied by Elisa's late husbands. José Matias, on the other hand, takes up his eternal vigil in a doorway opposite Elisa's new home, since he is by now "impoverished, disheveled, alcoholic," with long hair "hanging in meager wisps from under an old derby hat." He spends some three years in fixed contemplation of Elisa's window, alternating these sacred duties with frequent portions of wine and brandy at a nearby tavern. But he could always be found, "fixing his bleary eyes on the dark facade of the house where he knew she was sleeping with another." He takes to trailing the Superintendent all over Lisbon, all in order to assure himself of the total fidelity of Elisa's new lover. "As a service to her happiness, he kept watch over the lover of the woman he loved." When José Matias finally succumbs to a congestion of the lungs, Elisa sends her lover, the Superintendent, to the funeral with a bouquet of flowers. In this way, she sends her "carnal lover to accompany her spiritual lover to his grave and to cover him with flowers." [119]

In many senses, we have seen versions of the character José Matias throughout the fictions of Eça de Queirós—all lovers in his books are irrevocably touched by *A Venus Tenebrosa,* and they rarely escape the consequences, which generally lead to their extinction. José Matias achieves a kind of ascesis of the body, and so he eternalizes the love which would only be momentary in other beings. But he is also a sensationally comic figure, the apotheosis of Romantic love a la Lamartine. At the same time, he brings to summation the whole nature of reality and its inherent contradictions which are at the core of all of Eça's fictions. We mentioned that there were many variants of José Matias in the novels, and for that matter we should look no

farther than Pedro da Maia himself, the convoluted and unbridled Romantic, fated by his passion to commit suicide after
having been abandoned by the "unworthy daughter of a slave
trader." We recall that courtship early in *The Maias*, Pedro carries on a seraphic courtship much in the manner of José Matias:
"It was not long before all of Lisbon started to talk of Pedro da
Maia's passion for the 'slaver.' Moreover, he wooed her publicly
in the old style, standing for hours on the street corner . . .
with his eyes fixed on her window, motionless and pale with
ecstasy." [120]

Nonetheless, "José Matias" contains more implications than
those suggested by its inimitable protagonist. The story is nar-
rated by an anonymous, yet highly possessive and dominating
voice—a professor of philosophy who begins the story by inviting a stranger, quite possibly any reader, to accompany him
from the church to the cemetery, where José Matias's remains
are about to be buried. The story, then, is told to the stranger
and to us within the few minutes of the carriage ride between
the church and the burial grounds. The time encompassed
within the telling, however, expands effortlessly to the same
twenty years that lie between the initial vision of the young José
Matias, "a personable lad, a gifted chap," and the final spectral
vision of the same determined lover, "huddled in a doorway
. . . shivering with cold, wearing an old yellow jacket, patched
at the elbows, stinking abominably of brandy."

"José Matias" recounts a voyage toward death in two senses.
We witness the horrific transformation of José Matias from virile youth to degraded adulator, and at the same time we note a
more imperceptive transformation, gradual and carefully regu-
lated, that is contained in the Professor's monologue as he and
his companion travel toward the graveside. This professor of
philosophy, whose apparently impulsive and disconnected discourse is the essence of the fictional text in the making, gener-
ates his "text" almost without thinking, as an afterthought to his
practice as a philosopher. We know as little about José Matias at
the end of his story as we do in the beginning; but the discourse
of his fictive professor-writer, however, brings us new knowl-

edge of the various perspectives from which the opaque enigma
that is this individual José Matias might be viewed.

These hidden perspectives behind the surface of "José
Matias" might be implicit in the philosophical texts which the
professor is in the process of writing during the many and
various years recounted in the story. These are texts which are
not *in* the story, of course; we have only the titles. Each title
occurs and is mentioned at a particular juncture in the narrative organization, and may well allude to some elementary
philosophical notions that remain dormant and yet implicit.[121]

Is it just idle happenstance that our narrator informs us on
the first page that the protagonist not only had a predilection
for "general ideas" but was "keen enough to understand my
Defence of Hegelian Philosophy?" It would seem that the title,
mentioned as it is in the beginning of this highly suggestive
story, is indicative of a defense of the dialectical process toward
knowledge, in which Matter and Spirit oppose each other in
mutually illuminating and revelatory opposition. Hegel himself, in his *Introduction to the Philosophy of History,* speaks of the
Spirit as "that which has its center in itself. It has not a unity
outside itself, but has already found it; it exists in and with
itself. Matter has its essence outside itself; Spirit is self-
contained existence." The good professor's work might have
implied this dialectical process, along with a justification of the
system of antinomies in which Matter and Spirit form the complementary elements of the mind's approach to multitudinous
and diverse reality. After all, this *is* the text of a
protoprofessor—it has all the trappings of a speculative and
tentative probing. For this reason, the *Defence of Hegelian
Philosophy* may be directly related to "José Matias" in that the
narrator makes use of the objective example of José Matias as
the "case," or the living exemplar, of one who lives out or,
better still, *undergoes* precisely this bifurcation within the self
implicit in the apocryphal philosophical text: The Spirit of the
Soul and the Matter of the Body. As has been suggested by
Maria Lúcia Lepecki, we must allow for some semantic corruption in Hegel's terminology. For *Spirit,* we should read the

"spiritual exaltation" of José Matias as he contemplates Elisa from across the garden wall, and later from his modest door-way. For *Matter,* let us read it as the "animal life" of Elisa as she cavorts in bed with the various lovers of her ample body. These are vulgar equivalents, of course, but surely philosophy has been put to worse uses. But the professor has written other books with other titles, implying other texts, with even more inviting implications.

After the death of Elisa's first husband, José Matias flees to Pôrto to escape the delicious freedom that awaits him on the other side of the garden wall. Our narrator visits José Matias in Pôrto and finds him plagued by a constant question: "What shall I do?" The narrator leaves José Matias behind in Pôrto and returns to Lisbon while Elisa arranges her estate and mari-tal future by marrying the black-whiskered landowner. Mean-while, the professor-narrator works on his "Origins of Utilitarianism." Now, what could this severe title imply within the evolution of the text?

Utilitarianism does not seem to enter into the pro-tophilosophical schemes of José Matias himself. No one could ever accuse him of base calculation or crass conduct; no one ever heard him speak of the greatest happiness among the greatest number of persons. Both José Matias and Elisa, not to mention the imperious narrator, are highly organized egos with magnificently displayed defenses and prohibitions, all coalesc-ing into a fictional system sufficient, and exactly so, to Eça's purposes. We might engage in another perversion or degrada-tion of hallowed philosophical concepts by suggesting a pecu-liar reading of the concept of greatest happiness, in the sense registered by J. S. Mill. This is a reading that would insist upon the relativity of such a concept; in the light of this fictional text, could we not think of the apocryphal "Origins of Utilitarianism" as a reflective opposite of Mill's principle? We might thereby imply that the "greatest happiness," for José Matias at least, existed only within and because of the maximum privation and pain. "The greatest pleasure would therefore be the equivalent of the greatest pain," and so we seem to be at the heart of the masochistic system which so often

motivates the characters in Eça's fiction. Total loss is total pleasure, unceasingly so.[122]

The third "philosophical" text lies embedded in the final
pages of the story, at the moment when the philosopher learns
that Elisa has acquired, not a third husband, but an energetic
and faithful lover—it is at this time that the narrator informs us
that "All that year, too, I was plugging away at my *Essay on
Affective Phenomena.*" Could we not imply that "José Matias" is,
in effect, a fictional elaboration on precisely this topic? That is
to say, a fiction and an essay in which psychological phenomena
are not referred to in any kind of abstractive mode but are
instead concretized and made real through the activities of a
fictional character, however tinged with philosophy, however
subject to occasional impositions from the world. The final consequence of "affective phenomena" may well lie in the most
exquisite irony of all in the story—the spectacle of the highly
active physical lover of Elisa attending to the burial of the extinct spiritual lover. "It's just that the material will always worship the spirit, even without understanding why, and without
deriving any happiness from it." At this moment, we might
gratefully accept the explanation of the philosopher, who now
describes himself (as he faces José Matias's grave) as a
"metaphysical;" who, among other endeavors, has "convincingly demonstrated the illusion of sensation." We might
further suggest that "affective phenomena" such as those
exemplified by José Matias's affections are those generated by
the subjective imagination, and not at all in the possible, implicit, or imagined "objective" qualities of the beloved. The
seeming spontaneity of his passion only belies the true nature
of José Matias, which is that of what Stendhal so acutely defined
as a *vaniteux,* an exemplar of imitative Romanticism. The *vaniteux,* as René Girard would have it, "cannot draw his desires
from his own resources; he must borrow them from others";
even worse, "a *vaniteux* will desire any object so long as he is
convinced that it is already desired by another person whom he
admires." [123]

From these observations, among so many others, René
Girard has clarified the apparently paradoxical process by

which the spontaneity of feeling and passion in Romantic fiction is in truth a mere camouflage for a new brand of imitational behavior, as Flaubert's Emma Bovary knew so well. The impossible system of José Matias's "love" becomes the imaginative "parthenogenesis" of an enclosed and intensely narcissistic imagination. In order for José Matias's system to continue to work its apparently inexplicable magic over himself and his observers, Elisa must remain an abstraction. This is the implacable rule which gives this story its comicity. At the same time, is it not true that all of Eça's work tends to suggest the real folly of all irrational illusion; and what happens when we take illusion as the ultimate reality, as it is for José Matias.

Girard rightly observes that Flaubert's characters lack originality, "so that being nothing in themselves, they become something, one thing or another, through the suggestion which they obey." [124] These characters can never equal the models they have chosen, but their striving gives them a dynamism and a sense of torturous "becoming" which is part of the movement of all of Eça's fiction.

In "José Matias," Eça has taken this imitative process (as much a part of *Don Quixote* as it is *Madame Bovary*) and expanded it to the most suicidal and vertiginous possibilities. After all, José Matias does not "become" anyone at the end of the story any more than he is "someone" at the beginning; the transformations occur within the narrator, within our own changing perceptions of the narrator and the protagonist, and perhaps within the imagination of the silent hearer of the philosopher's discourse. José's love is absolute, and he is determined not to alter its absolute nature by submitting it to the conditions of time and change, conditions which are dangerously implicit in the idiom of "Matter" and "Bodies." However, this absolute Spirit is condemned to communicate to the body of Elisa only through surrogates and mediators—the two husbands and the lover—who in turn become votaries of Elisa (on a slightly less exalted level, of course), but votaries upon whom José Matias imposes his own seraphic standards of devotion and fidelity. When the lover (incarnated this time as the Superintendent of Public Works) is faithful, in the eyes of José Matias,

he is able to accept the Superintendent into the fellowship of
this priesthood of love and feels, not jealousy, but tenderness.
He and other husbands may traffic in bodies; José Matias has
not done so, and must not. In this sense, "José Matias" suggests
a classic text in which the finite or the empirical fact is presented as an irrelevance in the presence of the Ideal, or the
Platonic object itself. The mode by which both Matter and
Spirit are transcended, both in "José Matias" and in so many of
the other novels, may well suggest the axis around which the
various conflicts between Eça's innate Romantic self and the
imposed Realistic practice may well be explained—by reference
to the governing ideal of his art.[125]

We might think of the dilemma in other terms—on the one
hand, the imaginative representation of a search for knowledge
or for truth; on the other hand, the creation of beauty or art
which may or may not have empirical knowledge as the basis
for such creations. Such dramatic, even dialectical opposition
between the aesthetic and the practical is, among other things, a
problematic directly related to European Romanticism and to
such works as Keats's "Ode on a Grecian Urn." The final four
lines of the second stanza of that poem are suggestive of the
kind of "eternal present" which lurks throughout so many
Romantic ambitions, and most certainly in "José Matias":

> Bold Lover, never, never canst thou kiss,
> Though winning near the goal—yet, do not grieve;
> She cannot fade, though thou hast not thy bliss,
> For ever wilt thou love, and she be fair!

Keats's poem, as do the actions of José Matias within the story
itself, come to suggest a state of permanent fixing, a state of
arrest, in a high contention between Matter and Spirit. Keats's
poem stands for the observed Urn, and is the Urn in fact, just as
the story "José Matias" stands for the ironic, supercharged
idealism which so catastrophically compels the protagonist to
deny himself as he does. He is creating a work of art; he is a
man in the process of becoming a work of art through his
selflessness. Both the "Ode on a Grecian Urn" and "José

Matias" transcend mortality and the flesh; both round out this process by coming to dwell upon the deathly redemption given by the Absolute to those who suffer the constrictions of time, mutability, and traitorous Bodies.

If, in Keats, the initial divergences between Matter and Spirit are coalesced into the final equation that is "Beauty is truth, truth beauty," it must be noted that no such luminous resolution is suggested by the last pages of "José Matias," where the acrid monotone of the narrator-philosopher continues to drolly exploit the distance between the Hegelian realms, as realized on earth in the characters of José Matias and Elisa. The only ecstasy in José Matias's life is decidedly one-sided, finding an infinity of desire only in an absolute nonexistence. For good reason, the narrator notes laconically the "illusion of sensation," the "inexplicability" of José Matias himself, "much more than a man, or still, perhaps, less than a man."

The story does suggest, on the other hand, a comic prolongation of the initial *coup de foudre,* an extension into time of "the state just prior to fulfillment—not exactly arrested ecstasy, but rather an arrested pre-ecstasy." [126] José Matias's death, a Romantic disaster if ever there was one, might be charitably seen as a rebirth in freedom, a liberation based upon nothing at all. All moral criteria are quite transcended in this opaque system; as Robert Martin Adams has suggested, it "sterilizes desire beyond the grave of its Christian connotations, good or bad, orthodox or heretical." Further, "those who disdain the world and all that is in it must have seen something beyond it which is precious indeed." [127]

"José Matias" affords us an oblique and highly restricted version of the theme common to it and *The Maias*—the obstruction of feeling, love, and passion. In *The Maias,* the incest so carefully placed into the plot structure provided the unique barrier to fulfillment and realization of the "mad" passion between Carlos and Maria. In "José Matias," the obstacles are not only the obvious ones—Elisa's various marriages and her stages of involvement outside marriage, the garden walls, and so on—but something much more deeply rooted within the baffling and opaque soul of José Matias himself. It is an inner prohibition, a pervasive tabu which makes of him, paradoxically enough, the most passionate and generous of all Queirosian lovers as well as the one unique major character in Eça's fiction who never takes his beloved to bed and, simply put, never "makes" love at all.

Notes

1. Isaiah Berlin, *The Hedgehog and the Fox* (New York: Simon and Schuster, 1953), p. 36.
2. George Steiner, *Tolstoy or Dostoyevsky* (Harmondsworth, England: Penguin Books, 1967), chap. II.
3. Berlin, *The Hedgehog,* p. 20.
4. Eça de Queiróz, *The Sin of Father Amaro,* trans. Nan Flanagan (New York: St. Martin's Press, 1963), p. 352.
5. João Medina, *Eça Político* (Lisboa: Livros Horizonte, 1972), p. 162.
6. Ibid., p. 38.
7. In the following pages, I am deeply indebted to João Medina, "Finis Portugaliae" (Estudos sobre *Os Maias*) in his *Eça Político,* as well as to Alberto da Rosa, "Nova interpretação de *Os Maias,*" in his *Eça, Discìpulo de Machado?,* 2d ed. (Lisboa: Editorial Presença, n.d.).
8. Medina, *Eça Político,* p. 36.
9. See *OC,* II, 1540–65, "Antero de Quental."
10. Eça de Queirós, "Ramalho Ortigão" (Carta a Joaquim de Araújo), *OC,* II, 1380–92.
11. These works of J. P. Oliveira Martins have been recently reprinted: *Portugal Contemporâneo,* 8th ed. (Lisboa: Guimarães Editora, 1976), 2 vols.; *História de Portugal* (Lisboa: Guimarães Editora, 1972).
12. Medina, *Eça Político,* p. 44.
13. Oliveira Martins, *História,* p. 7.
14. Oliveira Martins, *Portugal Contemporâneo,* p. 28.
15. Oliveira Martins, *História,* p. 7.
16. José Augusto França, *Le Romantisme au Portugal* (Paris: Editions Klincksieck, 1975), p. 752.
17. See Oliveira Martins, *História de Portugal,* book V, "A Catástrofe," especially parts III and IV; "Jornada de Africa [D. Sebastião]" and "O Sebastianismo." A perceptive analysis of the continuity of "Sebastianismo" can be found in Joel Serrão, *Do Sebastianismo ao Socialismo em Portugal* (Lisboa: Livros Horizonte, 1973), especially the Introduction, "O Sebastianismo na estrutura do antigo regime português."

18. Oliveira Martino, *Portugal Contemporâneo,* I, p. 29.
19. Ibid., p. 27.
20. Ibid., p. 375.
21. *OC,* III, 636.
22. *OC,* III, 528.
23. *OC,* II, 819.
24. Eça de Queiroz, *The Maias,* trans. Patricia McGowen Pinheiro and Ann Stevens. (New York: St. Martin's Press, 1965), pp. 151–52.
25. These are the thoughts of João Gaspar Simões, *Vida e Obra de Eça de Queirós,* 2d ed. (Lisboa: Livraria Bertrand, 1973), pp. 566–67.
26. Gaspar Simões, p. 566.
27. I am grateful to my student Stephen Isaacson for this deft formulation.
28. Once again, I refer the reader to the magisterial essay of António Coimbra Martins, "O Incesto d' *Os Maias,* in his *Ensaios Queirosianos* (Lisboa: Publicacoês Europa-América, 1967).
29. Ibid., p. 276.
30. *The Maias,* p. 15.
31. Ibid., pp. 17–18.
32. Ibid., p. 18.
33. Ibid., p. 23.
34. Ibid., p. 22.
35. Ibid.
36. Ibid., p. 13.
37. Patrick Gardner's elucidation of the "veil of Māyā" might well conveniently explain why Eça was to name his "family" in the way he did: "The world as idea of representation is ultimately an illusory world. . . . It does not present reality as it is in itself, i.e. as the unitary will, but only as it appears, fragmentary and broken, under the forms of the principle of sufficient reason. . . . Egoism in the practical sense certainly presupposes a view of things in which a man thinks of himself and of everyone else as distinct and separate phenomena; however, it presupposes something else as well. For one who is committed to the standpoint of egoism is committed to the further belief that he alone, out of all those innumerable others, is of importance and deserving of serious consideration." Patrick Gardner, *Schopenhauer* (London: Penguin Books, 1963), p. 264.
38. *The Maias,* p. 88.
39. Ibid., p. 89.
40. Ibid., p. 57.
41. Ibid., p. 79.
42. Ibid., p. 80.

43. Ibid., pp. 81–82.
44. Ibid., p. 88.
45. Ibid., p. 93.
46. Ibid., p. 115.
47. Ibid., pp. 94–95.
48. Ibid., p. 99.
49. Ibid., pp. 100–101.
50. Ibid., p. 268.
51. Ibid., p. 339.
52. Ibid., p. 341.
53. Ibid.
54. Ibid., p. 239.
55. Ibid., pp. 629–30.
56. Ibid., p. 118.
57. Ibid., p. 146.
58. Ibid., p. 22.
59. Ibid., p. 597.
60. Ibid., p. 145.
61. Ibid.
62. Ibid., p. 146.
63. Ibid., p. 159.
64. Ibid., p. 160.
65. Ibid., p. 377.
66. Ibid.
67. Ibid., p. 538.
68. Ibid., p. 72.
69. Ibid., p. 143. Alencar is referring, of course, to the ill-fated leader of the Jacobites, "Bonnie Prince Charlie" (1720–1788), defeated at Culloden in 1746.
70. Ibid., p. 614.
71. Ibid., p. 597.
72. Ibid., p. 624. (The translation has been adjusted slightly.)
73. Ibid., p. 225.
74. Ibid., p. 501.
75. Ibid., pp. 399–400.
76. Leo Bersani, *A Future for Astyanax* (Boston: Little, Brown and Company, 1976), p. 52.
77. Ibid., p. 66.
78. This in turn is related to the constant use of "refuges" or "hiding places" in the novels of Eça. See António Coimbra Martins, "Eva e Eça," *Bulletin des Etudes Portugaises*, XXVIII/XXIX (1967/68), p. 294.
79. Reinhard Kuhn, *The Demon of Noontide: Ennui in Western Literature* (Princeton: Princeton University Press, 1976), p. 206.
80. *The Maias*, p. 550.

81. Ibid., pp. 134–35.
82. Coimbra Martins, "Eva e Eça," p. 283.
83. Coimbra Martins, "O Incesto d' *Os Maias*," p. 284.
84. *The Maias*, p. 29. Eça's father published Petrarchan verses in a literary review entitled "O Ramalhete" during his own Coimbra days.
85. Ibid., p. 32.
86. Ibid., p. 33.
87. Ibid., p. 42. See also Machado da Rosa, *Eça, Discípulo*, pp. 393ff.
88. Ibid., pp. 456–57.
89. Ibid., p. 590.
90. Ibid., p. 591.
91. Ibid., p. 10.
92. Ibid., p. 9.
93. Ibid., p. 11.
94. Ibid., p. 625.
95. Ibid., p. 383.
96. Ibid., p. 385.
97. Coimbra Martins, "Eva e Eça," p. 322: "The idol has more of Bacchus or Baal than Buddha. And the fabulous beast represents man made beast, since he has subjected himself, like the companions of Ulysses, to Circe, to Eros or to Venus." Further on, Martins refers to the idol as a "Buddha/fetus."
98. *The Maias*, pp. 386–87.
99. Ibid., p. 7.
100. Ibid., p. 11.
101. Ibid., p. 25.
102. Ibid., p. 165.
103. Ibid., p. 180.
104. Ibid., p. 198.
105. Machado da Rosa, *Eça, Discípulo*, p. 372.
106. *The Maias*, p. 414.
107. Ibid., p. 627.
108. Ibid., p. 589.
109. Machado da Rosa, *Eça, Discípulo*, p. 355.
110. *The Maias*, p. 384. Carlos's reaction to the above description is most telling—"A complete poem from the Renaissance: fauns and apostles, wars and georgics!" (p. 384). This analysis draws on Machado da Rosa, *Eça, Discípulo*, pp. 371–72.
111. *The Maias*, p. 625.
112. Ibid., p. 630.
113. Ibid.
114. Ibid., p. 631.
115. Ibid.
116. Ibid., pp. 631–32.

117. Ibid., p. 632.
118. Ibid., p. 633. Recently, Wilson Martins has suggested a direct relationship between the theme and structure of *The Maias* and Machado de Assis's novel *Helena*, published twelve years before *The Maias*. See the excellent discussion in Martins, *História da Inteligência Brasileira*, III (São Paulo: Editora Cultrix, 1977), pp. 523–25, 535–36.
119. Eça de Queirós, "José Matias," in *The Mandarin and Other Stories*, trans. Richard Franko Goldman (Athens: Ohio University Press, 1965), pp. 145–76. Permission to reprint the story is gratefully acknowledged.
120. *The Maias*, p. 26.
121. The discussion of the "voices" within "José Matias" and the probable import of the narrator's philosophical divagations is drawn from the acute analysis of Maria Lúcia Lepecki in her fine essay, "Sobre José Matias," in *Eça na Ambiguidade* (Lisboa: Jornal do Fundão Editora, 1974), pp. 28–76.
122. Lepecki, "Sobre José Matias," p. 58.
123. René Girard, *Deceit, Desire and the Novel* (Baltimore: The Johns Hopkins University Press, 1965), p. 7.
124. Girard, *Deceit, Desire*, p. 63.
125. I have here taken over in a wholesale manner some thoughts of Denis Donoghue on the matter of "José Matias," as given in a private communication dated March 11, 1978. At the risk of suggesting an amateurish analysis, I must say I was struck by Freud's thinking on the divinization of women, as derived from his hasty conversations with Gustav Mahler: 'The 'Holy Mary Complex' was a term used by Freud for the intense idealism of the feminine which he found in Gustav Mahler. Mahler . . . worshipped the Eternal Feminine, his lofty, idealizing conception of the *mater gloriosa* being matched by a neglect of his actual wife, of which he was unaware . . . The individual who suffers from the 'Holy Mary Syndrome' vacillates between adoration of a split-off ideal and loathing of the fleshly woman." David Holbrook, *Gustav Mahler and The Courage To Be* (London: Vision, 1975), pp. 255, 261. See also Ernest Jones, *The Life and Work of Sigmund Freud* (New York: Basic Books, 1955) II, pp. 79–80. A Freudian approach toward Eça and his work is to be found in the first version of João Gaspar Simões's *Vida e Obra de Eça de Queiroz* (Lisbon, 1945) which I have purposefully not used in my study, preferring the more balanced revised version of 1973.
126. Kenneth Burke, *A Grammar of Motives* (Berkeley: University of California Press, 1969), p. 450. This phrase forms a part of Burke's "Appendix A," where the discussion is centered on the

"Ode on a Grecian Urn." The association between José Matias, his own decline and death, and its opposite—bourgeois marriage—is unknowingly summed up by Burke when he says that "we can thus see why the love-death equation would be particularly representative of a romanticism that was the reflex of business."

127. Robert Martin Adams, *Nil* (New York: Oxford University Press, 1966), p. 182. Adams's discussion of "self-fulfillment through self-annihilation, victory for will through denial of will, life eternal as a result of deliberate death, ecstasy through ascesis" is highly and uniquely applicable to the peculiar world view of the "protagonist," José Matias. He is Eça's most vaporously drawn character; nonetheless, he exemplifies the implacable characterological method used by Eça in the making of all his characters; they are normative, coherent and unified, and they are describable to the last degree. In this sense, I regret that my exposition of Eça's sense of his characters could not reflect the disruptive arguments on the subject contained in the second half of Leo Bersani's *A Future for Astyanax,* where the ambiguity, even deconstruction of character is discussed. Eça's characters cannot break out of their molds; they cannot conceive of a fragmented and discontinuous self, nor an "exuberate indefiniteness" of identity. See Bersani, *A Future . . . ,* Chapter VII, "Desire and Metamorphosis."

5.

The Temptations of Pastoral

". . . Settling down to be happy, anywhere, under a tree." *OC*, III, 1463.

It is difficult to imagine Eça, in any stage of his life, as being tempted by regressive pastoral fantasies, the writing of historical novels, or any kind of literary production that an objective observer might dismiss as the work of a chauvinist and a political reactionary. Yet this may be the case with the last two novels of Eça de Queirós. Many readers of these two novels do think of him as the exemplar of an exhausted revolutionary who has now married well, has solved to some extent his financial problems, and who has lost even the most tenuous link that he might have had with *o povo*. It is true, to some extent. Eça's final years in literature *do* seem to celebrate the hoary values of noble ancestry, heroic piety, and traditional Christian social ideals, those that are conveniently contrasted with the more disruptive ambitions of a Marx or even a Proudhon. And many readers are under the impression that Eça de Queirós, in his final years, practiced and encouraged a kind of novel with which he was nurtured in his childhood and early adolescence, and which he spent much of his adulthood demolishing with gleeful abandon in *As Farpas,* not to mention the early novels. His early critical writings and a certain substratum of such works as *The Sin of Father Amaro* and *Cousin Bazilio* denounce the empty irrelevance of such a kind of literature, above all because they were so unresponsive to the social conditions of late-nineteenth-century Portugal. The young Eça would have insisted—and most certainly did insist—that this was literary escapism, and protested against it in the most varied ways.

In reading Eça's last two novels, *The Illustrious House of Ramires* and *The City and the Mountains,* the reader must sense a change of atmosphere—as compared, say, with the dark and prophetic final pages of *The Maias.* On the surface of these two texts, the unthinkable seems to have occurred. Eça seems to have reneged the aesthetic and political ideals which had governed his fictional practice all through his career up to *The Maias.* A not completely discerning reader might well note a quite distinct softening around the edges, a real loss of satiric bite, a more uncritical and even languorous view of the ancient attractions of old Portugal. All of this is odd, and we might begin to explain it by ascribing this transfiguration to an apparent reawakening of nationalistic feeling in Eça's political presumptions. Many critics have observed that both these works relate to the fact of his continual exile from Portugal; his increasing disenchantment with France, with Paris above all; and his disillusionment at least, in his novels, with the idea of social change, not to mention social revolution. Read in this way, these two books seem to radiate a new benevolence toward traditional Portugal; we have the unsettling spectacle of an author writing in a mode which he despised in his youth and spent most of his maturity demolishing.

So the questions are these: Are these novels any kind of a literary betrayal? Has the author gone soft? Are they an anachronistic celebration? Are they reactionary? Do they celebrate country over city, traditional authority over the ideal of social justice, myth over actuality, feudal values over bourgeois democracy, the pastoral/historical novel over the urban novel of bourgeois ascendancy? These are crude questions, but they may well be worth asking; they are not easy to answer: the tentative answers to such barefaced questions do not lead automatically to the conclusion that they represent a wholesale decline. At the outset, let it be said that no works of Eça are more woefully misunderstood and misread than these last novels. They deserve more attention than they have received over the past seventy years.

Eça was fully conscious, above all in his years as a writer, that a bucolic vision represented a cast of the imagination that was divorced or at least distant from a particular reality at hand. It suggests social stasis and neofeudal orders. A bucolic text is unlikely to reflect political ideals, and above all those related to social justice. Conversely, a novel which is governed, as were Eça's in his early years, by the admirable ideals of social reform and the democratization of humanity's impulse toward a better life, is more than likely to be a text that dispenses with the solace and the nostalgia that the pastoral vision affords. A Realist must perceive the essence of social dynamics and mobility within him and his audience, while the pastoralist must equally possess the assurances and presumptions that only the values of permanence, order, and the status quo can give.

Above all, the pastoral mode functions in direct relation to optical distance from reality. One way in which we can look at the sources of Eça's late novels might involve precisely this— how bucolic pastoralism functions throughout his work, and how it reflects in a dialectical manner the opposing impulse in his fiction—the will toward revolutionary Realism and social reform.

One of the most instructive early instances of the "alienation" effect of pastoral in Eça's prose can be found in the revised travel chronicle published posthumously in the year 1926: *O Egipto*. This work is a considerably rewritten version of the travel diary Eça kept during his epochal trip to Egypt in the company of his future brother-in-law, Count Resende. In Chapter III, after Eça and his friend have left Alexandria under the Baudelairian motto, "Emporte-moi wagon, enlève-moi fregate . . . . ," they voyage through the Nile Delta by train, in the possibly fictional company of an engineer from the just constructed Suez Canal. Eça seems hypnotized by the transcendental peace of the landscape unfolding before his eyes through the window of the railway car: "I have never seen such a serene, humane, and pleasantly fecund landscape; no contrast, no violence of mountain profile. Everything is broad, flat, immense, and inundated with light" (*OC*, III, 704). Later, after having seen this timeless landscape peopled peaceably by camels, the fellah, soldiers, and mute women, Eça begins to react to this visual idyll: "Everything surprises us, as if we had entered an ancient world . . . those elongated lines, that transparence of colors, the serenity of those horizons, everything makes us feel that we are in a world that has disengaged itself from the contradictions of life, and which has entered . . . into immortality." "Instinctively, we think of Paradise, of the ancient mythological fertility. The men who live there must be strong, of sure and perfect movement, solid and well-built. Their houses must be full of abundance, their lives are surely simple and peaceful; the old people must live with a quiet placidity and a primitive goodness; they all must be openhearted, sober, tranquil, and happy" (*OC*, III, 705–6). All of this seems attractive from the distance of the train window— that is, until the engineer reminds Eça and his friend that the beauty and the peace they contemplate hides the misery and the subslavery of the class that makes such a sight possible—the fellah, the anonymous Egyptian peasant. The engineer then documents for the benefit of his Portuguese friends the hideous life of the delta fellahin: the feudal bondage, the forced marriages, the dominance of the local pasha, the imposition of arbitrary taxes on each village, the neverending baksheesh, "the animal resignation of those who do not perceive that they are unhappy." This slavery, avers the engineer, does nothing but serve the interests of European capitalism and exploitation; Egypt is a country of the dead, since it is a country that should be agricultural in nature but which is being transformed into an industrial one by rapacious European capitalists who disembark, steal their prey, and flee back to Europe. In this land of *The Thousand and One Nights,* degradation and slavery are the means that keep the delta the paradisiacal Eden it seems to be from a distance, contemplated as it is by these interested and conscientious Portuguese tourists.

The shock of recognition started here. On the one hand, a visual idyll—stasis, peace, order. On the other hand, grinding misery, impassive indifference to suffering, all under the rubric "It is Allah's will!" This discordance between visual allure of pastoral and a deeper perception of social injustice will be a constant element in Eça's conflictive response to city and country. But there are other texts which give even more acute instances of Eça's subversive yet ever present response and challenge to the temptations of pastoral.

Needless to say, this period was one of the most intense from the point of view of Eça's social action. After having returned from the tour of Egypt in early 1870, he takes up his hated post in Leiria, prepares for consular examinations, and begins his extensive collaboration with Ramalho Ortigão, that literary friendship which will produce not only the collaborative novel entitled *O Misterio da Estrada de Sintra*, but the ferocious satiric attacks which were then published as *As Farpas*. Too, the Casino lectures, under the stewardship of Antero de Quental and José Fontana, begin in the spring of 1871, and Eça will give his important lecture, "Realism as a New Expression of Art." But there are other impulses operating also. In an article written for *As Farpas*, dated September 1871, Eça will ask for a temporary truce from satire and social criticism. The reason adduced for this unexpected *tréguas* is inherent in the subject about to be taken up—the rural novel *As Pupilas do Senhor Rector* (1866) of Julio Dinis, an author who, in the words of a perceptive commentator, "was more at ease in the rural milieu that he only knew of through recuperation from illness." [1] Eça asks for a moment of uncritical peace in order to speak about the delights of Dinis's pastoral visions, and it would seem significant that this truce was asked for within the tumult of political and literary activity that the years 1870–71 represented in the life of Eça de Queirós. "He never abandoned his idealism or his native sentimentalism. Reality had for him an outward crudity that frightened him, *so that he copied it from afar*, with misgivings, rounding off the exact contours which seemed to him crude . . . his country towns are true, but they are poeticized; it would seem that he sees them and draws them only when an autumnal mist shades the outlines, turns them blue, idealizes the perspectives. A broad and true light never bathes his work. Everything is hidden under a poetic hue. . . . He was simple, he was intelligent, he was *pure*. He worked, he created, he died. Happier than we, he had his destiny affirmed, and for him *the question* was resolved. Let us pass on, then . . . beyond this serene page, we listen to the winged ironies which, like vengeful bees, buzz around in the air! [italics mine] (*OC*, III, 1087–88).

With the publication of the three versions of *The Sin of Father Amaro* and *Cousin Bazilio*, Eça elaborates fictional versions of the satiric and critical program that first found its basic formulation in the various sketches in *As Farpas*. As we know, *The Mandarin* and *The Relic* represent a divergent tendency from the former novels of analysis. By 1884, let us say, the whole authorial ethic of Eça will undergo variations and subtle contradictions. In September of that same year, Eça will meet his future wife, Emilia de Resende, with whom he will carry on that stiff courtship, ending in the *mariage de raison* at her family's country estate, Quinta de Santo Ovídio, on February 10, 1886.

Eça wrote a highly significant and amusing letter to Count Ficalho, dated September 4, 1884. He finds himself with "gastric discomfort" while on leave from his post in Bristol. The cause of the indigestion is, according to Eça, the cuisine of the hotel in Pôrto where he is staying, a cuisine "done dreadfully and pretentiously in the French manner." It is all France's fault, suggests the exasperated invalid, the result of the idiotic imitation and translation from the French that the Portuguese people have practiced over the years, "from ideas to soups." The letter continues in a tone of even greater mock fury, accompanied by an even greater dose of neochauvinistic furor. Is Eça really joking? Isn't the following paragraph a premonition of the many *boutades* against the disease of "O Francesismo" that he was to launch on so many occasions during the 1890's?

It's your fault, it is clear that it is your fault—you and
your friends the liberals, and Dom Pedro IV, and the
men of the Generation of 1820, and of the unspeak-
able Fernandes Tomás! Those people did not comprehend that this country, in order to enjoy prosperity
and health, should not have deviated from the true
national tradition, the legitimate and old-time one,
with an absolutist and paternalist King, monks, country lunches in the churchyard, broad-collared frock
coats, and a good roast pig on the skewer, and delicious baked rice for dessert. But what happened? We
wanted to be Humanitarians, read the Encyclopedia,
parrot the Rights of Man, and we made ourselves into
liberals, philosophers, mannered, *French, littérateurs,*
and we substituted the noble roasts of our grand-
fathers for the abominable *boeuf à la mode* of Jacobin-
ism. And now you see the consequences: the country
in the fine state which you know only too well, and I,
here in Pôrto, with gastric difficulties for eight days
now, taking seltzer. Beelzebub confuses Liberalism
with Liberal Sauces! (*OC*, III, 533)

If the past is beginning to assault Eça's grip upon the present,
it is doing so, not only under the pressure of his own changing
discontents with himself and his distant homeland, but also
because of a newly uncovered set of possibilities for social reform within the structure of the church. This marks the beginning of a whole range of Franciscan allusions in Eça's late essays
and hagiographies, a frame of reference within which his own
former political militancy will lose its contours and become
transfigured into another level of social action, all under the
seraphic social action of Il Poverello. Christian socialism became another alternative for the anguished conscience of the
writer. Jaime Cortesão perceived this new phase; he saw that
"Eça de Queirós underwent the influences of that triple credo
of idealism, Franciscanism, and Social Christianity. It would be
more fair and more accurate to have said: by means of that
movement the writer gained the highest consciousness of his

idealist core and took advantage of Christian Franciscanism, so basic to Portuguese religious tradition, in order to give literary expression to his old and deeply felt faith." [2] By 1897, Eça's friend Eduardo Prado announced that "God entered into the home of Eça with the birth of his first child." And that same child, many years later, declared that "My father was not the skeptic that so many say he was. He was essentially a religious person, and though he did not practice any cult, every evening he retired, closed his eyes, saying that he was 'going to communicate with God.' " Summing up, Cortesão suggests that Eça "was a Deist, in the manner of the eighteenth-century French *philosophes,* admitting the existence of God, and possibly the immortality of the soul, and deriving from that faith a rule of duty, while rejecting entirely revealed dogma." [3]

He also becomes alarmingly benevolent toward the Portuguese monarchy, a matter which upset many. In an essay of 1898 entitled "The Queen," Eça seems to signal his definitive abandonment of his former ideal of lay social progress:

> the anguishing presence of human misery, so many aged without a home, so many infants without bread, and the incapacity or indifference of monarchies or republics to bring to realization the only urgent task of the world—"a home for everyone, bread for all," *have gradually converted me into an uncertain, saddened anarchist, a humble inoffensive idealizer* . . . our poor world needs goodwill and gentleness to such an extent that I sincerely believe in the social benefit of a queen who, at times, would radiate a bit of her tenderness, her benevolence, her beauty on to customs, spirits, and laws. [italics mine] (*OC,* II, 1615–16)

If Eça's increasing pessimism concerning the viability of social change is something of a constant during his last ten years, 1890 marked an extreme moment of national disgrace and outrage. By that date, the Portuguese government had claimed all of the African lands now known of as Angola, parts of Mozambique, and all of present-day Zambia, Malawi, and Rhodesia. On January 11, 1890, the British government sent an ultimatum to Portugal requiring the immediate abandonment of most of this land, under the threat of a break in diplomatic relations and the open threat of force, a policy which was, in effect, the fruit of the energetic vision of Cecil Rhodes. The Portuguese government complied and withdrew from most of the disputed lands. Eça's reaction to the national shame represented by the British colonialist triumph was not long in coming. In a carefully worded essay entitled "The Ultimatum," Eça urges his countrymen to abandon the dark hatred of England the political intervention had unleashed, with its useless threats of boycott and the reams of chauvinistic and utterly ineffectual speeches. "What are vain protests worth? The great shout that should be heard is not 'Delenda Britannia,' but 'Servanda Lusitania!' Because it is not a question, unfortunately, of destroying England, but rather of conserving Portugal" (OC, III, 953).

The conservation of Portugal carries with it a multitude of ramifications, both literary and political. Not only will Eça resign himself to his vague brand of "Christian Anarchism," but he will occasionally suggest the opposite, in a vain outburst of patriotic fervor: what the country needs is an authoritarian dictator. In a letter to Oliveira Martins written in 1890, he envisions only one solution—a tyranny. "We need a sword along with a thought. You are capable of being the man who thinks, but where is the man who will do the slashing?" (OC, III, 615). In a later letter to Oliveira Martins, the delights of the past and the hypnosis experienced by the historian as he brings his consciousness into the depths of the past leads Eça to one of his most candid and unsettling statements of his own eroding allegiance to surrounding reality:

"Evidently, for a Portuguese citizen today, there is only one solution—which is to live in History as you have done, and forget *what is* while living with *was*" (OC, III, 628). Part of the process of losing himself in what *was* at the expense of what *is* lay in a simple yet most fortunate fact: Eça's mother-in-law died in January 1890, and he and his family inherited a goodly sum of money plus that sumptuously appointed *quinta* near Pôrto where he and Emilia de Resende had married just two years before. This estate, called Santo Ovídio, is the same idyllic retreat which will serve as the dramatic fulcrum for Eça's posthumously published novel, *The City and the Mountains*. From this point of view, his letters from Santo Ovídio (written during consular vacations) take on an air of bucolic contentment, which is a reflection, it would seem, of an altered state of mind about ancestral homes, the countryside, tradition, whatever. A good example would be his letter of May 29, 1892, to his good friend in Paris, the Brazilian *boulevardier* that was Eduardo Prado, possibly the model for the Jacinto of *The City and the Mountains*.

> Here there is a convent, asleep within its surrounding stone wall, or better, its bed of roses, since now in May roses are everywhere, and [I am] so far away from the world of business that when the doorbell rings announcing the arrival of the mail, there is as much commotion as in the old days among the monks when the news of the Court arrived in a jangle of bells from the mule's reins. I also . . . took an excursion to [the regions of the] Minho and Douro, which I had not seen for many years. This land of ours is without a doubt the masterpiece of the Great Landscape Painter in the sky. What loveliness! Everything takes on the mild look of an eclogue. Everything sings. Ditchdiggers and harvestmen sing while working, and the old wooden cart, the ancient cart of Latium, sings while carrying the brush along the narrow trails. The worst are the beds in the hostels, but in compensation, what marvelous casseroles of rice, and what divine Easter lambs roasted in the oven! I cannot comprehend how this is a *failed* country. . . . [I know that this] seems to be an epistle from an eighteenth-century judge, celebrating, in grave and fluent verses, the *joy of the countryside*.[4]

Precisely. This is another Eça de Queirós.

The rediscovery and conservation of traditional Portugal brings with it an authorial instinct which is not at all easy to characterize. For instance, readers of Eça have been led to believe by many commentators that his "late phase" was that which represented something close to a complete abdication of the principles of his earlier practice. While it is true that there are texts—letters, essays, short stories, and novels—that seem to confirm this traditionalist thesis in late Eça, there also exists a substratum of clear and level-headed critique of the kinds of literature that he was gradually in the process of evolving. This can be gauged, for instance, in an extensive letter written to Alberto de Oliveira during the summer of 1894. Oliveira has sent to Eça a short work he had just published, one of nostalgic evocation of the Portuguese landscape. But in this instance, Eça will react against it and begin a surreptitious demolition of traditionalism in literature: "Traditionalism in literature was attempted for a long time in Portugal, for some thirty years between 1830 and 1860, and it certainly did not produce that moral renovation that Portugal needs and which my friend expects from it. . . . No, my friend, miseries are not cured by resuscitating traditions . . . the duty of men of intelligence in a humiliated country has to be greater than reconstructing on paper the Castle of Lanhoso or calling all souls to come and listen to the nightingales in the poplar groves of Coimbra" (*OC*, III, 638).

1. The Illustrious House of Ramires

In this same letter to Alberto de Oliveira, Eça wryly invented a typical sentence from a historical novel in order to attempt to dissuade his reader from the practice of such anomalous genres. That sentence—"Thou liest, rogue!!" ("Mentes pela gorja, D. Vilão!!")—appears, not at all surprisingly after all, in *The Illustrious House of Ramires* as having been written by the Hamletian character Gonçalo Mendes Ramires, the protagonist and central figure of the novel, who as a child had written a

short historical romance entitled *Don Guiomar,* "a mournful tale
of love where every page resounded [with] cries of 'I faith-
! . . . Thou liest, rogue! Fetch me my black stallion,
page!' . . . And through all this vernacular emerged a sufficient number of stable-boys in light mantles, mendicant friars
concealed in the shadows of their cowls, tax-collectors laden
with leather pouches, stewards slicing fat loins of
pork . . . the novel marked a salutary return to national sentiment." [5] In *The Illustrious House of Ramires,* Gonçalo's friend
José Lucio Castanheiro has founded a magazine entitled *The
Fatherland,* where this historical romance will first be published.
This review was founded "with the lofty intention of reawakening . . . the dying love of the beauty and the grandeur and
the glories of Portugal!" Castanheiro praises the "excellent archaic flavor" of *Don Guiomar* and predicts that when "our Gonçalinho becomes acquainted with our past and our chronicles,
we shall at last have in our literature a man who really feels our
fatherland, who feels our race!" [6]

At the very least, *The Illustrious House of Ramires* is a novel
about a writer who is writing a novel, and it is a novel about the
relationship between this writer, his writing, the past and present of the nation. At the same time, *The Illustrious House of
Ramires* is a historical novel of the past and present, which contains within itself a wonderfully vibrant and parodic re-creation
of the Scottian mode in literature. A novelist begets a novel and
becomes an artist of literature and life and therein finds his own
justification for political and literary action amid an atmosphere
of overwhelming inaction and pessimism. This is one way of
putting it. But Eça's novel is more than just that. Let us think of
Gonçalo Mendes Ramires as the final heir of an illustrious family aristocracy, one whose lineage and genealogy contain the
essence of Portugal's history and tradition. Gonçalo inhabits the
family manor of Santa Ireneia, "the country seat of the Mendes
Ramires since the middle of the tenth century." [7] The author/
squire is "without doubt the most genuine and ancient nobleman in Portugal." Admittedly, the family fortunes have been
somewhat on the wane lately; Gonçalo's father "wore out the
soles of his shoes up and down the steps of the Mortgage Bank

and along the Arcade in Lisbon . . . until a Minister appointed him Civil Governor of Oliveira." Gonçalo himself, aimless and without national or personal destiny, fails his third-year examinations at the university and begins a life of amateur/*littérateur*/historian, haunted now as always by the ghosts of his ancestors who inhabit the Tower of the manse, that Tower with its "vastness and its strength, its steep steps and walls, so thick that the narrow window-slits in its density looked like corridors dimly lit . . . the bare echoing rooms with their great flagstones, their dark vaulted roofs, stone seats, the odd hole in the middle, round like a well, and on its walls still streaked with smokestains the ringed holders for torches." [8]

As a creature of his own past and uncertain future, Gonçalo lives in a confluence of exhausted present and a familial past of glory and rectitude. His past is indicated to him in an unsettling way, simply through the silence of the stones and the parapets of the tower; they tell him how insignificant and unworthy he is to continue the line of the Ramires. As a literary mind and a protonovelist haunted by this historical and familial past, and as an indolent historian enchanted with the possibilities of the historical novel as a means of sharpening the "political consciousness" of his readers, who in turn are precisely those who might help him win a local election, Gonçalo Ramires is drawn as an author who is gradually writing this grand historical novel entitled "The Tower of Don Ramiro," chapters of which are liberally quoted within *The Illustrious House of Ramires*. But this historical novel is being written for aesthetic pleasure, too. It is a means of resuscitating the grandeur of his family lineage. And, as mentioned, it is a political document which will aid his contemporary political ambitions. As a member of the present doing everything he can to vivify the past, Gonçalo expects that his novel will be the focus of sufficient publicity to turn out the vote. It is Castanheiro who reminds Gonçalo that "literature leads to everything in Portugal . . . nowadays, it is the pen, where once it was the sword, that builds kingdoms." As he becomes more and more attracted to the idea of a literary reanimation, he begins the labor of evocation of the Tower and the manor of Santa Ireneia, and of his ancestors—"huge iron-clad men with ringing voices who remained as elusive as wisps of smoke." [9]

Thus, novelist/historian/politician fuse into an entity at once meretricious and admirable, a sleazy hypocrite and a "Regenerator" of the family and of Portugal. He and his novel will be this composite created out of the materials in the family legend and the very contemporary pecuniary and political needs of him, the bereft last member of the clan. But there are terrible humiliations along the way. In order to be able to campaign for the parliament seat, Gonçalo must obtain the aid of precisely the same gentleman who, many years before, had abandoned his sister after having courted her rather assiduously. He effects this embarrassing reconciliation with this gentleman, the governor of the province, one André Cavaleiro. After the initial formalities and friendships are resumed, Cavaleiro begins yet another long and very carefully plotted repetition of yet another seduction of the sister. This process is intertwined with the writing of Gonçalo's novel and the progress of his electoral campaign. But if the behavior of Gonçalo's sister Graçinha and that of Cavaleiro can be thought of as the dumb repetition of earlier and even more inauthentic acts, Gonçalo's literary ambitions are also tainted with the fact that his imagination is exhausted before he begins the work, and he thus must depend on outright and at times surreptitious plagiarism. More copies of copies.

The novel entitled "The Tower of Don Ramiro" being composed by Gonçalo Ramires is in point of fact a secondhand gloss of a text composed by his uncle, "during the years of idleness and imagination, from 1845 to 1850 . . . a poem in blank verse called *The Castle of Santa Ireneia*. . . . [It] sang, in romantic strains, of an incident of feudal arrogance, which glorified the name of Tructesindo Ramires, standard bearer to Sancho I in the battles between Afonso II and the Princesses." [10] Thus the text that Gonçalo is in the process of assembling and writing is itself a pastiche of "the mellifluous tones of 1846 romanticism" and a newly "terse, virile prose of an excellent archaic color. . . . Would this be plagiarism? No! To whom, more than to him, a Ramires, belonged the memory of these historic Ramireses? Anyway, who nowadays knew of this poem?" [11] The process of reconstruction and resuscitation is shown to be tinged with fraudulence, borrowed phrases, and fake invention, a Queiozian process. Castanheiro, fatally and enthusiastically, characterizes this literary and political venture of Gonçalo: "The sublime deed of Tructesindo Mendes Ramires, told by Gonçalo Mendes Ramires! . . . And all in the same Tower! In the Tower, old Tructesindo does the deed, and seven hundred years afterwards, in the same Tower, our Gonçalo recounts it! By Jove, my boy, by Jove! This is really renewing tradition!" [12]

This sleight of hand is at the heart of the fundamental relationship between history and actuality in the work, between recovered text and "newly" generated text. It was V. S. Pritchett's fine intuition that brought out this peculiar element in *The Illustrious House of Ramires.* Speaking of Gonçalo's novel within the novel, he suggests that "one is tricked at first into thinking one is caught up in a rhetorical tale of chivalry à la Walter Scott; then, one changes one's mind and treats its high-flown historical side as one of these Romances that addled the mind of Don Quixote; finally one recognizes this element as an important part of psychological insight." [13] After all, Gonçalo Mendes Ramires is not an unlikable or contemptible character. As is the case with so many Queirosian prototypes, he is living in a ruined past and a worse present, but hoping all the while for a miraculous and heroic future in the blazing Sebastianist mold. He is at once weak, generous, enthusiastic, and prone to paralyzing melancholy. The generation of this empty text, his act of literary and political regeneration, is, to use Pritchett's words, "an act of personal and political therapy," since the writing and the act of borrowing and plagiarizing take his mind off the humiliations of the present—a dishonored sister; his own poverty; his own lack of simple, elementary ethics in dealing with his neighbors and his fellow citizens, ancestors of whom were happy serfs who used to look to the Tower for moral and military protection in an age gone by. Like Hamlet and Don

Quixote, Gonçalo is a dreamer who is impelled into whatever action he is capable of only under the unrelenting pressure of the past, barbaric and grand as it was and as it "is." [14]

But the actions of Gonçalo are, inevitably, of a hapless variety. As Pritchett sagely observes, these actions are both of a literary and a physical nature, both kinds feed off of a past that cannot be remembered, resuscitated, or relived. He is constantly betrayed, not only by his pusillanimity, but also by his madcap taste for the physical realization of the deeds of yore. In the end, he tries to recover "either by writing one more chapter of his novel of chivalry, fleeing to an ideal picture of himself," or just the opposite, and this is precisely the ironic fillip so often present in Eça—"his liability to insensate physical rage, always misplaced." [15]

For instance, early in the novel, Gonçalo decides to rent the Tower and the surrounding fields to a local farmer, one José Casco, "respected throughout the neighbourhood for his seriousness and exceptional diligence." [16] The price is 950 milreis, and it is agreed upon, the contract being sealed "in accordance with ancient custom" by a shake with the farmer's hand. Later in the novel Gonçalo meets another farmer, Pereira the Brazilian, who offers the sum of 1,150 milreis for the same land. Gonçalo accepts the new offer with the following blithe disclaimer: "If I had given Gonçalo Ramires' word decisively to Casco, would I be doing business with you now, Pereira, or even merely talking to you about renting the Tower? . . . Shake hands! Now we know where we are! That's giving our word!" [17] Much later even, the good Casco insists that "Your Lordship gave his word! . . . Heaven help me, I'll smash these bones of yours before I go to prison." [18] Gonçalo flees the raised crook of Casco and later has him packed off to prison because he was threatened with an assault—but a justified one, of course. After Casco's wife blurts out, "in a tumult of cries and supplication, 'They've arrested my man, they're going to send him into exile to Africa. . . . Ay my dear, dear sir, have pity!" [19] Of course Gonçalo relents; his rage is assuaged; and Casco is released forthwith.

On another occasion, Gonçalo will give us a discourse on the latent power of this seemingly dormant will of his over the declining circumstances of his family fortunes and those of Portugal: "Yet it was man's will that counted—only in the exercise of the will does enjoyment of life reside. Because, if a carefully applied will encounters submission, there is the pleasure of serene combination; if it encounters resistance, there is the greater pleasure of an interesting battle. The only state which provides no strong, virile pleasure is that inertia which lets itself be dragged mutely along in wax-like silence and passivity. But he, descended from so many famous for their strong will, had he not buried somewhere in his Being, warm and dormant like a hot coal beneath dead ashes, some spark of this hereditary energy? . . . Perhaps! With another sigh, he snuggled further into the bedclothes." [20]

The faces of his ancestors parade before his ancestral bed; they offer their weapons to him, those strong arms proven by history, "ennobled in assaults against the Moors, in elaborate sieges of castles and towns, in splendid battles with the arrogant Castilians. . . . All round the bed was a heroic glitter and a jangle of weapons. And all of them proudly shouted, 'Oh grandson, take our arms and defeat your hostile Fate!' But Gonçalo, glancing with sorrowful eyes at the flickering shadows, replied, 'Oh my ancestors, what's the good of your weapons if I lack your soul?'" [21] The next morning, armed with his father's "hippopotamus-hide whip," Gonçalo leaves the Tower for a morning's ride, only to meet two taunting ruffians nearby. He almost kills both of them, and this experience gives him a new confidence made out of this parodic repetition of his ancestor's bravery: "And now he was returning [to the Tower] like a new man, suddenly supremely virile, freed at last from the shadow that had so painfully darkened his life, the vile sluggish shadow of fear. . . . At last he was a man!" [22] Telegrams pour into this newly vitalized warrior, congratulating him "on escaping from such a terrible ambush and destroying the ruffians." [23] Because of this encounter with the two locals, he becomes even more apt for political purposes, and one with more than a few literary possibilities. In the words of one Lisbon paper, "we now await with redoubled expectation the appearance of the novel by Gonçalo Ramires, based upon an adventure of his ancestor Tructesindo in the twelfth century, and promised for the first number of *Annals of Literature and History,* the new review 'that is . . . the worthy restorer of the heroic conscience of Portugal.' Gonçalo's hands trembled as he unfolded the newspapers." As one friend says to the nobleman, "Gonçalinho, you're going to get a tremendous number of votes!" [24]

It should be mentioned that, after Gonçalo had returned to the Tower, he had experienced the kind of emotional, contradictory duplicity in which Eça so specialized. Once he sees the blood of the ruffians on the whip, he is cast back into the Portugal and the Tower of the *then*, but it is a then "now." The blood is upsetting as it never would have been for his ancestors. "He does not want to be as murderous as the knights of old. He is all for humanity and charity. He was simply trying to solve his psychological difficulty: that he had never in anything until then imposed his own will, but he had yielded to the will of others who were simply corrupting him and leaving him to wake up to one more humiliation." [25] So he becomes a politician with at least a momentary grip upon the heroism of old. With the cooperation of the governor who had jilted his sister so long ago, Gonçalo makes a heavily compromising arrangement in order to be elected deputy. But the governor, Cavaleiro, is implacable; he wishes to seduce Graçinha once again, just as in the old days. The scene shows the moment in which Gonçalo discovers his sister's infidelity, and it is one of the more harrowing scenes of humiliation in all of Eça's novels. Sooner or later, all of his characters discover the unsettling nature of life's compromises, but this does not take the sting out of the happenstance when he notices his sister in the process of being seduced by the man who is the key to his newly found political career. Gonçalo hears a murmur and a disturbed whispering: "someone was pleading, was stammering, 'No, no! This is madness!' Someone was urging, impatiently and ardently, 'Yes my love! Yes my love!' He recognized both voices—as clearly as if the blind had suddenly lifted and all the bright light of the garden had streamed in. It was Graçinha! It was Cavaleiro!" [26]

Not long after, Graçinha's husband will receive a semi-anonymous letter informing him of his wife's unfaithfulness. Gonçalo is thus thrice betrayed—by his sister, by his friend Cavaleiro, and by his other friend Dona Ana, a woman whom he had wanted to marry because of her extraordinary attractions, only to find out that she has had a lover and thus is not suitable for entrance into the glorious line of the Ramireses. Gonçalo's novel within the novel now takes a compensatory turn toward Grand Guignol—the condemned villain is placed into a pond filled with leeches. Under the imperious command of Tructesindo, the bastard villain dies an intentionally repulsive death which is minutely described with obvious relish, a la *Salammbô:*

> A shudder ran through the thick water, around the submerged thighs of the Bastard, fat bubbles swelled and from first one leech sluggishly appeared and then another and another, shiny and black, undulating and clinging to the white flesh of the belly, from which they hung, sucking, immediately fatter and shinier with the blood that was slowly flowing. . . . In the dark water floated fat clots of waste blood. . . . Thus devoured and oozing blood, the ill-fated knight emitted, amid foul oaths, curses of death and fire against the whole race of Ramires! . . . His frenzy died away in a long weary sigh—until he seemed to have fallen asleep in the thick knots of the cords, his beard gleaming with the sweat which soaked it as if with a heavy dew, and from the beard came a ghastly, white, delirious grin.[27]

In Gonçalo's subliminal imagination it is the blood shed which serves as the bridge between the barbaric, ghastly, and heroic past and the tempestuous and unconscious whipping in the present of the two young tormentors. The historical novel has never been put to more sardonic and compensatory balancing between literature and life than in the case of "The Tower of Don Ramires," that literary complement and analogue to another novel in the making, now called *The Illustrious House of Ramires,* by one Eça de Queirós.

At this point, the novel takes on a symbolic, even messianic tinge, one that is not at all unrelated to the latent Sebastianism that has occasionally lurked through the political and literary writings of Eça. Recognized as a Ramires of old, fully in charge of his noble heritage, elected deputy for the local district, Gonçalo climbs the stairs of the Tower for a final meditation, only to conclude that his life was "stupid and uninteresting . . . in comparison with others [which are] full of supreme vitality. . . . The Nobleman of the Tower, motionless on the terrace of the Tower, between the star-filled sky and the dark earth, ruminated a superior life for a long while, until he was carried away, as if the energy of the long race that had passed through the Tower were flooding his heart, and he imagined his own progress toward a vast and fertile action in which he could enjoy supremely the happiness of really living, and around him life would be created and a new lustre would be added to the old lustre of his name." [28] Gonçalo abruptly leaves for Africa, the new concessionaire of a vast tract in Zambezia. He returns to Lisbon after four years, having planted two thousand coconut trees, cocoa, rubber, and having become the possessor of "thousands" of chickens. He has also built "a big house on his piece of land near the river, with twenty windows, all painted blue." [29] But he returns to Lisbon, not at all sure that he will see Africa again; his friends welcome him back and speak of his extraordinary qualities: "His weakness, his kindness, his goodness . . . his crazes and enthusiasm, which peter out almost immediately, but at the same time his persistence and tenacity when he really latches on to an idea . . . his generosity, his carelessness, his constant expectation of some miracle occurring . . . his vanity . . . a streak of melancholy, in spite of his talkativeness and sociability." Gonçalo's friend, after summing him up with this potpourri of contradictions, "good mixed with bad," asks the final rhetorical question: "Do you know whom he reminds me of?" "Who?" "Portugal." [30]

The Illustrious House of Ramires is the work of Eça de Queirós that is most distant from the contemporary reader, not only because of the particular historical critiques that are engendered within its fictional structure, but also because of the openly allegorical intent which is enforced, perhaps excessively, by the final conversation just quoted. But it is more than a national diagnostic. What it does offer is a superbly drawn denouement of a kind that has had a long and powerful ascendancy in the work of Eça—the transfiguration of an apathetic victim to a hero, from a passive anonymity to an active consciousness. This in turn is effected by the trauma of humiliation and a resultant bouncing back—a restitution of physical and moral values related to individual dignity; a *return*, if you will, of all those values which seem to have been lost in the morass of Romantic historical mythification and economic decline during the nineteenth century. Gonçalo is a convert, but "not to the reactionary values which, in general, were identified with the countryside and the most conservative national traditions (Nobility, History, deeds of great men, etc.), but rather that which subsisted in Portugal as authentic, positive, and bearing future hopes [for the nation]." [31] In this sense, Gonçalo's relation to his own past and his own Tower is not that different from that of Hamlet in relationship to Elsinore. How to act? How to save oneself and one's nation? How to *be* and thereby avoid nonbeing? Through the alchemy of individual reform, Gonçalo breaks out of the dark conclusions that so paralyzed the readers of many of Eça's works and certainly those of Oliveira Martins. In the same way, he breaks out of the exhausted limitations of his caste and his class; he abandons the "traditional agrarian routine"; he walks out of the comfortable clubs of Lisbon and the revolving door of constitutionalist politics. Whatever Eça may have thought then of the colonial rule of Portugal in Africa, there is no doubt that those who went to Angola and Mozambique served him as the possible models for one kind of regeneration of the exhausted spirit of the peninsula. In this sense, the African adventure of Gonçalo is nothing but a pretext for the dispensation and actualization of moral and physical energies for which there was no room at all in the hardened, neofeudal structures still extant as part of the monarchic legacy and heritage of nineteenth-century Portugal. In a way, Gonçalo tries to live up to Afonso's dictum: "Less liberalism and more character"; the acquisition of character and consciousness, then, is most of the drama that is so axial to Eça: How to escape from the past and the deadened present? How to *be*?

2. The City and the Mountains

If the "African" solution for the quandaries of Gonçalo seems to suggest to the modern reader a rather heavily imposed deus ex machina to end *The Illustrious House of Ramires*, these same readers might be equally alarmed by the apparently simplistic thesis and novelistic structure that underlies Eça de Queirós's last novel, posthumously published, entitled *The City and the Mountains*. Although all sorts of misunderstandings and misreadings of Eça's novels have cropped up over the years, *The City and the Mountains* presents the modern reader with an even more inviting occasion for misunderstanding and misreading. And the reasons are not hard to find, above all if we study the heartfelt and highly favorable reception of the novel *within* Portugal and contrast these readings with the rather unfavorable tenor taken by most readers outside Portugal. Foreign readers, then and now, have read the work as if it were the final and most convincing artifact that proves Eça's decline as a novelist. In this sense, it is read as a novelistic argument, based upon a flaccid and highly nationalistic, not to say chauvinistic, brand of reactionary pastoralism. Contemporary readers of the book continue to sense a discernible weakening of powers, and they aver that not much can be said for it except for its value as a documentation of a decline in literary fortunes. Above all, it seems to be considered unfavorably because of the supposedly simplistic nature of the thesis, and this thesis, everyone continues to say, is what governs the book. Here is V. S. Pritchett's summary: "This particular novel savages Paris as the height of city civilization, a wealthy Utopia; it argues for the return to nature in the Portuguese valleys." [32] It is to be understood that this is the argument of the novel, the ultimate meaning of the novel. Miguel de Unamuno, a fervent admirer of most of Eça's work, noted that *"The City and the Mountains,* a book in which its author made a reconciliation with his people, did not satisfy me. It is a book of exhaustion. And the repentance from the cold crudity with which he formerly lacerated his country . . . is a repentance of attrition, and not of contrition."[33] Within Portugal, as João Medina has noted in his overview of the critical reception of this work, it was received with a sense of relief by most readers. For once, Portugal was depicted with a fervor and an admiration which few readers of Eça's works had come to expect, unless, of course, they were privy to the immense, even radical change of posture toward Portugal that began operating in Eça's sensibility after the publication of *The Maias. The City and the Mountains was* deemed to be an act of "reconciliation," which is a decorous way of saying that most readers considered it to be an act of recantation. The former sarcasm and iconoclasm, not to mention the revolutionary socialism, had apparently disappeared or lost its clear contours and was replaced, thankfully enough for most readers, by the repentant novelistic voice of a prodigal son who has recovered his homeland in the mind, and who was anxious to return to the world of traditional Portugal—and to an "agrarian, retrograde and humble Portugal" at that.

This theory also matches a neatly curvaceous critical scheme, as João Medina has also noted; beginning with *The Sin of Father Amaro* and *Cousin Bazilio,* and on through *The Mandarin* and *The Relic* to *The Maias,* the reader will note an ever increasing degree of excoriation of Portugal—that is to say, of Lisbon society.[34] After *The Maias,* one might also perceive, following this convenient argument, that the two final novels of Eça de Queirós, products as they are of Eça's increasing disenchantment with liberalism, democracy, socialism, and French society above all, are works that give off a new and infinitely more benevolent air toward the reality that was Eça's Portugal—Lisbon society, that is. Whether these last two novels have anything to do with the Portuguese countryside is another matter, as we shall see. And to this argument, it must be admitted that many of Eça's letters, occasional essays, and conversations during the 1890s *do* give evidence of an increasingly intense reevaluation of the nature of Portuguese society, precisely that same society that had sent him into such literate furies on so many prior occasions.

What is most unsettling in all this is that these arguments simply cannot be dismissed, and they must have at least some validity. If a Pritchett can so flippantly characterize *The City and the Mountains* as he has, then the work must be at least minimally suggestive of the argument he gives us. That thesis, if you will, begins with the depiction of an exiled Portuguese aristocrat, resident in his mansion on the Champs-Elysées, who represents to the ultimate degree the surfeit of Eça's late view of Paris and of civilization in general. Eça's protagonist (hardly a hero), Jacinto, lacks nothing in the realm of culture in his sumptuously appointed manse. It is a veritable stockroom, in the manner of Hearst and/or Citizen Kane, of the well-known film by that name, that ostentatiously displays the newly found values of conspicuous consumption and even more conspicuous waste; La Belle Époque is about to be born. Surfeit, luxury, and infinite gadgetry are the cardinal elements of this mansion, and such an item as Jacinto's bathroom is no exception; on the contrary, it is a comic microcosm of the macrocosm that is this mansion, this receptacle of man's industrial genius:

> In these marble vaults were two jets of water, each graded from zero to one hundred degrees; two showers, one of fine and the other of wider jets for the hair; a sterilized fountain for the teeth; a frothy jet for shaving; and still more discreet little buttons, which, if touched, would discharge spouts, squirts, singing cascades, a light summer dew, a cool floating mist, or hot steam, according to one's requirements. From this terrifying retreat, where slim tubes held, in discipline and servitude, so many kinds of boiling, spouting, and violent waters or vapours, Jacinto would emerge.[35]

The supercivilized protagonist is surrounded by a wealth of objects and devices that denote the veritable state of the art of contemporary mechanical inventions and conveniences. The

house has both a theaterphone and a lecturephone so that performances and lectures may be heard in the salon without having to venture out into the traffic. There is a ticker tape to keep
Jacinto up on his worldwide investments, a primitive type-
writer, "the most sumptuous array of mechanisms, apparatuses,
model engines, gadgets, syringes, tubes, platings, cogwheels,
tweezers, lancets, along with every possible frigidity or rigidity
of glass or metal that modern invention could supply." [36] Jacinto's library is a "majestic product of Reason and the Imagination," all arranged according to the material and spiritual values they might contain. Thus, "Hobbes was heavy, bound in
thick black leather on the lowest shelf. Plato on the top shelf
shone white and pure. In the center of the vast hall began the
various Universal Histories." [37] In other nooks and crannies,
whole spaces were devoted to the natural sciences, poetry,
whatever—the sum of the world as it was then, in short. Most of
the books are unread.

As always with Eça, boredom and tedium in society are at the
heart of his characters, and the Jacinto of *The City and the Mountains* is no exception. He mulls over his inertia, complains of his
uselessness, dreams of another life, but in the end relishes the
delights of Paris as only a resident exile can. Jacinto is also an
amiable fellow, wallowing in self-consciousness and languid
immobility. His house is a gaudy warehouse, and he is the Ob-
lomov of this realm. Too, it is not to be denied that he is talented, likable, and intelligent. As his friend (who is also the
perspicacious narrator of the novel) Zé Fernandes informs us,
"his intelligence wound itself through the densest philosophies
with the ease of a lustrous eel through the clear waters of an
aquarium." He possesses an even temper and disposition;
somehow, things have always fallen his way. He dabbles in
theosophy and esoterica, and assiduously cultivates his person
because he is convinced that "man is only greatly happy when
he is highly civilized"; the formula is expressed in the following
equation: "Absolute Knowledge × Absolute Power = Absolute
Happiness." [38]

Paris *is* civilization. It is so for Jacinto, just as it was for Eça
when he finally achieved his lifelong dream of a consulate in

Paris, in 1888. And similar to Eça, Jacinto clings to Paris. Con-
comitantly, Jacinto professes a disdain, even hatred of nature.
A walk in a carefully tended forest or *bois* is more than enough
to send him into a state of sheer terror. "Caught between the
unconsciousness and impassivity of Nature, Jacinto would
tremble with terror at his fragility and his isolation. . . . What
is more, when confronted by Nature, he suddenly experienced
the complete incapacitation of all his faculties of superiority. . . . All intellectuality became sterilized in the country;
only bestiality prevailed." [39]

Within his palace, however, he is the apparent master of this
comic and bizarre "all-mechanized home," a self-sufficient
world, a living monument to the triumph of ingenuity, reason
and inventiveness of nineteenth-century man. Zé Fernandes
professes to admire all this immensely. Unlike Jacinto, who was
born in Paris of an ancient and long-exiled Portuguese family,
Zé Fernandes is very much a part of the then contemporary
Portugal, since he is true landed gentry in Portugal, and has
long ago established himself as something of a gentleman
farmer or, at the very least, a small landed proprietor. But his
secure station within Portuguese society does not mean that he
is not seduced by the extraordinary allure of the Champs-
Elysées mansion. "Everything seemed to transmit Universal
Forces. Nature bowed to the discipline of my friend and entered his household with docility." [40] But the world of the
machine is bound to have its imperfections; Jacinto soon
realizes, with the aid of the critical acumen of Zé Fernandes,
that he is the slave of his mechanical paradise. A fish especially
baked for a grand duke gets stuck fast in the dumbwaiter, while
the above-described bathroom explodes with Vesuvian rum-
bles, inundating the whole house. Friends tell Jacinto of their
passionate interest in viewing the spectacle: "It's thrilling. All
the beautiful cloth spoilt, and the carpets. . . . I'm dying to see
the ruins." [41]

As his valet ruefully admits, "his excellency suffers from surfeit." [42] In effect, the futility of his existence finally overwhelms
him: "Oh Zé Fernandez, that's all our industry is worth! What
impotence! What impotence!" [43] Wrapped in a silken bathrobe,

he plunges into Ecclesiastes and Schopenhauer for confirmation of his total indifference to everything, but there is a moment of illumination, even conversion, as Jacinto and Zé view the prodigious panorama of all Paris from the terrace of Sacré-Coeur; this may well be one of the most pivotal texts in the continuing dialogue between city and country in Eça.

> Look, Jacinto! It was in the City that Man lost his strength and the harmonious beauty of his body: he became withered and lean, or obese and drowned in his own grease, with bones as soft as rags, with eyeglasses, wigs, and dentures of lead, bloodless, without brawn, twisted and hunchbacked—a being in whom a horrified God would find great difficulty in recognizing the slim, sturdy, noble Adam of his creation. . . .
> How can you ever have happiness in the City for these millions of beings who are forever rioting in the breathless occupation of *wanting, needing,* and *desiring,* and who never satisfying the need or desire, incessantly feel the disappointment, despair and defeat of it? The most genuinely human feelings become dehumanized in the city. . . . Friendships are never more deep than alliances of common interest . . . which will snap at the first sign of rivalry or pride. . . . But what the City most destroys in Man is his intelligence, because it either imprisons him within the pale of banality or else forces him out into the wastes of eccentricity and extravagance. . . . Man himself appears an anti-human creature without beauty, without strength, without freedom, without true feeling, like a slave or an imprudent mime. . . . And there, my fine Jacinto, you have the long and the short of a fine City! . . .
> "Yes," he said, with a sigh, "The City! It may well be a perverse illusion after all." [44]

A landslide on his ancestral lands in Portugal requires Jacinto's presence, and he reluctantly takes leave of Paris and his manse to supervise the reconstruction and the reordering of his estate. "When we were in front of the Arc de Triomphe he turned his head and murmured: "It's a very grave thing to be leaving Europe." [45] Once in Portugal after a trip full of Spanish vicissitudes, Jacinto is entranced by country life, although he still feels isolated from the rest of the Continent. Portugal is not Europe. But he begins a remarkable new career as a feudal philanthropist and a budding country squire; tenants' houses are repaired; a school is established for the peasantry in the Tolstoyan manner; and "all along the sierra the popularity of Jacinto grew. In that 'God bless you, sir!' with which the women addressed him as they passed and turned to follow him with their eyes, there was an almost reverent feeling, a sincere desire that God should indeed protect and bless him all his days." [46] He marries a young cousin of Zé Fernandes, the very image of country maidenhood: "Her cheeks, from walking about in the sunny garden were suffused with a delicate pink, and her pale dress, slightly opened at the neck, showed up the splendid whiteness of her skin against the pale gold of her curly hair— and the smile of pleasure which lit up her face enhanced the beauty of her large, soft, dark eyes." [47] Two children are born. Zé comments that "I definitely realized that Jacinto was a changed man and that a perfect balance had established itself at last in his soul." [48] Some years later, Zé Fernandez makes an epochal return visit to Paris and the now dormant mansion on the Champs-Elysées. The Paris of Proust is now seen to be a moral sewer, a mechanicized nightmare, the last gasp of hyper-civilization: "Every night, at the theatre, I met the everlasting Bed, which was presented as the centre and goal of life, attracting, more strongly than the dung-hill does the fly, a swarm of erotic stupefied humanity buzzing with a senile hum." [49] He goes to a lecture at the Sorbonne, where a professor is speaking on the "Institutions of the Middle Ages": "His clear and elegant speech was drowned by yells, roars and stampings. It was a bestial, tumultuous hooting." [50] Zé inquires of an old man sitting nearby asking, " 'What is the matter with them? Are they fed up with the lecturer, or is it politics?' 'No,' said the man, shaking his head and sneezing, 'it's always like this now. They don't want ideas, I think they want songs. It is a general love of filth and scoffing [*amor da porcaria e da troça*]." ' [51] Horrified by the Paris that has now become infernal and bestialized, Zé takes definitive leave of Paris: "Well, goodbye and until never again. You will not catch me again slopping around in your vice and mud or in the rottenness of your vanity. What is good about you, your intelligence and elegant clarity, I shall receive all that at home by post. Goodbye!" [52] Having escaped this "putrid civilization," and having undergone the convulsive processes of Parisian *gouffre* and *spleen*, Zé journeys back to the eden that is Portugal, or so it would seem, and the novel ends on a tone of mellow pacificism:

> And indeed it did seem to me, as we made our way along the lanes and through the quiet cultivated countryside, that my Prince Jacinto, sunburned by the noonday heats and the wind of the mountains, and that sweet and loving mother, my Cousin Joaninha, with her two first-born, and I—were at last all treading an everlasting, solid earth. And now, with our souls at peace with God, we could serenely and securely climb toward the Castle of Great Happiness.[53]

Is Zé ironic? Is he sincere? Has he, in fact, converted to the Quixotic pastoral ideals that are so energetically espoused by Jacinto? All of this has to do with the ultimate meaning of the novel, and that cannot be considered until we have thought a bit more about the narrative structure and Zé Fernandes's own role as teller of tales and also as critic of the Quixotic protagonist. He is, for our purposes, a very useful Sancho Panza. But for the moment, let us consider the previous few pages above as a rough résumé of the novel, composed as they are to reflect the idea that *The City and the Mountains is* a thesis novel, and that most readers have found it so. Aside from the already mentioned opinions of Miguel de Unamuno and V. S. Pritchett, one might add more fuel to the fire by mentioning the all-too-obvious opinions of Jacinto do Prado Coelho, who qualifies the work as a "reactionary novel" pure and simple, while others found it to be a text of "far too simple a moral lesson." Ernesto Guerra da Cal sees it as the "loving ironization of the two contradictory poles within the soul of Eça de Queirós; one, centrifugal and cosmopolitan (Fradique Mendes), the other centripetal, ruralist ("the poor fellow from Póvoa de Varzim")— symbols of the two fundamental facets of the Lusitanian spirit—bucolism and exoticism." [54]

In all these formulations, there seems to be a central concern and a central belief, and that might be summarized by saying that there is a progression visible in the work, and this essentially means that Jacinto's return to Portugal is at once a regression while at the same time constituting itself as a *conversion and partial revision of Jacinto's personal values and his mode of existence in the world*. Another possible reading, one that has appealed to the subtlest and most discerning readers of the book, and which demands the most minute attention to Eça's ironies as he passes them through his narrator, Zé Fernandes, is one that presents an essentially ambiguous and nondoctrinaire reading and can best be summed up with the following formula: *Return to country—no modification of the protagonist Jacinto*.[55] Of the few critics who have gradually led us toward this last possible reading, that of António Sérgio deserves attention. It is Sérgio's thesis that "in *The City and the Mountains* the City is not the real evil, nor is it the technical progress of modern civilization, the way it seems to the protagonist. Technical advances, to an *active* mind . . . are simply instruments of future action; and the true sage or the true artist has a qualitative concept of human culture. But our Jacinto? . . . In his way of thinking, it is a simple accumulation of inert information, of null experience. The disease of Jacinto lies in this accumulative, passive, and inert idea of the culture of the spirit (and the desolation which accompanies it). It is not in Civilization, it is not in Paris, it is not in the City. He doesn't suffer from satiety, he suffers from the tedium of an indolent life; he suffers from the boredom of mental sterility. . . . The true antithesis of the book is between inertia and the pursuit of goals [*ociosidade e ocupação*]. And the proof of this lies in the fact that when he takes up residence in the country, he begins to become active, the tedium disappears, and thus the redemption of the character." [56] But is Jacinto truly redeemed?

In this illuminating but still possibly erroneous reading, *The City and the Mountains* and the characters therein relate back to the overwhelming presence of tedium and dilettantism so rampant in all the earlier novels. Jacinto is the final apotheosis of the diseased spirit that so destructively characterized Luiza; Fradique Mendes himself; Carlos da Maia; Craft; Teodorico— even Afonso da Maia, the apparent representative of rural values as he inhabits in country estate Santa Olavia. No one escapes from *dolce far niente* in the works of Eça de Queirós. His characters are *passionate,* but that is not a good thing. This means that they have little resistance before the iron character of life itself, its forward rush, its implacability. They are all subjective slaves to their senses and their bodies, and they are egotists with only the most uncertain grip upon the nature of the reality which surrounds them. In Sérgio's formulation, Jacinto is yet another character lacking in what so many of Eça's characters lack—creative and unified action, the will made manifest in the service of a higher goal than that of passing the time away as best one can on this earth. These "higher goals" are those shared, in Eça's most exalted view, by saints, social reformers and revolutionaries, and artists with a humane consciousness of their mission as artists. These are the men and the women who use their talents for the greater good of humanity. Let us not forget the fact that while Eça was composing *The City and the Mountain* he was also in the process of writing his relatively neglected *Legends of the Saints,* works which propose a complementary and highly activist view of the possibilities for Christian social action.[57] One of these legends, that of Saint Christopher, is modeled upon the highest ideal ever imagined by Eça for man's destiny on earth—that of the acts and action of a holy revolutionary, in the way that Christ was a revolutionary for his time, all in the name of the nameless and the humble. Sérgio's point is well taken. The only redemption for man is to be found in generous and high-minded action; it is the only antidote to the tedium of the ego and of "civilization." This means that these generous actions will always run the risk of being pure folly, tilting at windmills, the utopian vision. No matter. It is better to do something than to do nothing; it is better to try to live than to take the road of annihilation. And this is part of the mixed, secret meaning of *The City and the Mountainss.*

Once again we pose the question still not answered: Does Jacinto undergo a radical transformation of his self and of his own conscience/consciousness in his regressive return to Portugal, or is the character unchangeable, the same in Paris as in the beatifically pastoral Tormes? The arguments in favor of the latter view have recently been presented in a brilliant essay by the Brazilian critic Maria Lúcia Lepecki. In this view, which seems to be a unique interpretation, there is no quick conversion to pastoral values, there is no easy thesis, there are no facile polarities. This apparently simplistic or "reactionary" novel is found to be one of the most oblique and ambiguous works ever written by Eça. Let us see if this interpretation of *The City and the Mountains* makes any sense, and let us see if the rather coarse plot résumé above can be proven to have presented a false and highly misleading interpretation of the novel, as was most certainly this writer's intention at the beginning of the discussion—just for the sake of argument, let's say.

Perhaps the final meaning of the novel might be expressed by means of the following formulation: *if there is a thesis to the novel, it is constantly contradicted by the minute verbal insinuations carefully inserted into both parts of the novel, and these are always expressed by the dominant narrative voice in the novel, Zé Fernandes.* The narrator belongs to Jacinto's class; they both have had, more or less, the same kind of languid upbringing; they have no economic pressures facing them; and they both accept without much discussion the same code of social and moral values, although one has much more of a critical intelligence than the other, as we will see. It is understandable that Zé finds himself incapable of criticizing openly either Jacinto's life-style in Paris or the pastoral fantasies of Jacinto as he "progresses" or "regresses" into the state of rural aristocrat, with adoring peasants at hand at all times. However, the one link that is established, and it is a critical one, is that which Zé Fernandes carefully establishes between ourselves as readers and himself. *We* are the ones who know infinitely more about Zé's true feelings toward Jacinto than does Jacinto himself. Subtly, Zé takes us into his confidence, he winks at us from the page. In this way, we may more objectively view the apparent transformation from boulevardier to country gentleman in Jacinto. It should be said that Zé is not in the least reluctant to give us negative information, even pejorative characterizations concerning Jacinto, who is constantly addressed as "my Prince," but often in terms that are not flattering to Jacinto. Jacinto is protected from undue barbs, but we get them all. According to Lepecki's statistics, the word "Prince" occurs some 103 times in the first half of the novel, but on approximately 65 of these occasions, the word is accompanied by "negative or ironic adjectives." A "negative climate" is thereby established, let us say. This is to be understood in the context of the novel, since Eça takes great pains to establish the discontent of Jacinto in Paris; he wants us to consider this particular prince as something less than regal. In the second half of the novel, set in the bucolic Tormes, one might expect that the negative associations already established in the Paris adjectivizations would disappear, since the narrator has already assured us that "Jacinto was a changed man." [58] As Lepecki notes, such a change does not occur. The ironic characterizations continue apace and, if anything, gain in semantic power and critical bite. For instance, in that ludicrous moment when Jacinto is trying to convince Zé that a tree converses with man ("Why, it is a most sublime conversationalist!"), Zé reacts: "I smiled and agreed. All he said was very specious and far-fetched [*rebuscado e especioso*]." [59] There is also a grotesque moment where Jacinto asks a question concerning his tenants that in itself is a good index of the final meaning of Jacinto's odyssey toward his Ithaca: "Hunger? Can he be hungry? Do people here suffer from hunger?" [60] Zé informs us that the peasant "Silverio smiled at such candid ignorance of life in the sierra." [61] As Jacinto finally realizes what everyone else knows—that there always has been and always is hunger in the Portuguese countryside—Zé treats him paternally: "I patted his shoulder." Jacinto is convinced that he can cure the eternal hunger so rampant in the countryside by means of his good works and Tolstoyan regimes for the peasants, but Zé tells *us* otherwise: "I did not disillusion my Prince, and we both climbed happily up the steps of the old mansion." [62] As for the endlessly drawn plans for immense vegetable gardens, irrigation canals, grape arbors, cheese factories, and henhouses, Zé informs us that "none of these fabulous projects ever took a more definite form than we gave it in our enjoyable confabulations, or on the papers whereon Jacinto drew them, which kept on accumulating on the table in a heap between the brass inkstand and the flower-vase. . . . For the rest it more than satisfied my Prince, *who was rather of an imaginative than an operative case* [italics mine]." [63] All of this is summed up in the unusually stern admonition delivered on one occasion to Jacinto by Zé himself:

> "My son," I would say, "I may not be more than a very small landed proprietor, but with me it's not a question of knowing that the land is *beautiful* or the soil is *good*. Listen to what the Bible says: 'You will plough the soil in the sweat of your brow.' It does not say, '*You will contemplate it in the heat of your imagination*' " [last italics mine].[64]

Jacinto marries only because Zé has jogged him temporarily out of his world of fantasy: "And all this Tormes business, Jacinto, this reconciliation of yours with Nature and your renunciation of all the falsities of civilization, is all very pretty—but damn it all, one must have some women about! He agreed, laughing *languidly*, as he lay back in his garden chair" [italics mine].[65]

In sum, it is fair to say that Jacinto is and will remain an *iludido*, whether in Paris or in Tormes—deceived, deluded, a victim of his own ego, subjectivism, and self-pity. The abyss between Jacinto and the world is complete, since he is incapable of mental dynamism and lacks the critical spirit that is necessary for one to percieve the world as it is; furthermore, he is incapable of simple humane sharing. The hunger that he finally discovers around Tormes is alleviated more for aesthetic reasons than anything else; Joaninha enters Jacinto's life for similar reasons—external and superficial in both cases. If Schopenhauer afforded some justification for the *tedium vitae* he experienced in Paris, it surely is significant that Jacinto's readings in Tormes include Virgil (as a source of practical country knowledge!) and *Don Quixote* (as a sourcebook for his own folly). Zé Fernandes is content to associate his own self with Sancho Panza in this Portuguese Barataria, and it may well be that the renowned "Quixotization of Sancho" commented upon by Salvador de Madariaga finds its match in *The City and the Mountains,* since Zé at times seems to fall under the spell of Jacinto's faulty world view; the zealously chauvinistic "goodbye" to Paris is a case in point here.

If there is a philosophy behind Jacinto's newly found pastoral values, it is surely related to the suffocation of consciousness, a true sense of culture, and the *active* reasoning faculties. The countryside has taught him nothing but these ludicrous bromides:

> "What these hills and trees counsel our wakeful, agitated souls to do—is to live in a vague dream, to covet nothing, to rebel against nothing, to let the world roll on without expecting more from it than a rumour of harmony which lullabies them and helps them to go to sleep at last in the hand of God. How does it seem to you, Zé Fernandes?"
>
> "Perhaps. But then it would be necessary to live in a monastery with the temperament of a Saint Bruno, or to have an income of a hundred and forty thousand a year and the gall of certain fellows like yourself [*o desplante de certos Jacintos*]." [66]

At times, Zé Fernandes can be counted on for vigorous rectification.

Obviously, there will always be some degree of discrepancy between the apparent intentions of a novel and the way in which it evolves dynamically, as the text itself progresses. It may be said that *The City and the Mountains* is an unusually subversive text in this sense, since the narrative explodes whatever easy theses readers might be impelled to divine from the text. I should say that the narrative "should explode" such easy theses, but it is apparent over the years that it certainly has not. Really, the book does not contain the simple contrasts that most have seen in it. Quite the contrary, Eça has plunged us into a dense and highly ambiguous critique of alienation and moral obtuseness, as practiced by members of the declining aristocracy who are variously unconscious or oblivious to the political and social elements that will soon impel Portugal into the creation of the republic in 1910, some eleven years after *The City and the Mountains* was drafted. There are no solutions in the novel, and there is no Arcadia in it either, although most readers seem to have found one. We know there is no promised land, above all because Zé Fernandes is ever present in the novel, and he assures us fitfully (if we are willing to perceive his message) that Jacinto is yet another Queirosian *iludido*, a man who makes of himself the measure of all that surrounds him, and he does this "in a desperate attempt to survive in a time and in a place that are no longer his, and in a reality which never has been his, above all because Jacinto [and the class that he represents] never knew either his own time or his own place." [67] It is the measure of Eça's tragic relation to Portugal that the above words, applied as they are to Jacinto, may also describe Eça's own desperation during the years of final disenchantment and despair in Paris, equally exiled as he was from a distant and increasingly cherished Portugal, and a now all too proximate and highly detested Paris, and France itself.

The breach between Eça and his fictions is finally closed.

Notes

1. José-Augusto França, *Le Romantisme au Portugal* (Paris: Editions Klincksieck, 1975), p. 591. By the way, the epigraph for this chapter, " . . . Settling down to be happy, anywhere, under a tree" is Eça's English phrasing in a letter to his fiancée (*OC*, III, 1463).
2. Jaime Cortesão, *Eça de Queiroz e a Questão Social, Obras Completas*, III (Lisboa: Portugália, 1970), p. 16.

3. Ibid., p. 18.
4. *Cartas de Eça de Queiroz* (Lisboa: Editorial Aviz, 1945), p. 333. Throughout this chapter, my remarks on pastoral owe much to the discerning study of Leo Marx, *The Machine in the Garden: Technology and the Pastoral Ideal in America* (New York: Oxford University Press, 1964).
5. Eça de Queiroz, *The Illustrious House of Ramires,* trans. Ann Stevens (Athens: Ohio University Press, 1968), p. 9. It should be kept in mind that Eça's one major translation done in his maturity is his version of Sir H. Rider Haggard's *King Solomon's Mines,* published with no reference to Haggard's authorship in *OC,* II, 835–979.
6. Ibid., p. 10.
7. Ibid., p. 5.
8. Ibid., p. 291.
9. Ibid., p. 20.
10. Ibid., p. 15.
11. Ibid.
12. Ibid., p. 17.
13. V. S. Pritchett, "Iron Comedian," *New York Review of Books,* April 9, 1970, p. 3
14. Ibid.
15. Ibid.
16. *The Illustrious House,* p. 19.
17. Ibid., p. 56.
18. Ibid., p. 109.
19. Ibid., p. 138.
20. Ibid., pp. 236–37.
21. Ibid., p. 239.
22. Ibid., p. 247.
23. Ibid., p. 262.
24. Ibid., p. 265.
25. Pritchett, "Iron Comedian," p. 3.
26. *The Illustrious House,* p. 214.
27. Ibid., pp. 273–75.
28. Ibid., pp. 294–95.
29. Ibid., p. 305.
30. Ibid., p. 310.
31. João Medina, *Eça, Político* (Lisboa, Seara Nova, 1974), pp. 97–98.
32. Pritchett, "Iron Comedian," p. 3.
33. Miguel de Unamuno, "El Sarcasmo Ibérico de Eça de Queiroz" in *In Memoriam* (Lisboa: Parceria Antonio Maria Pereira, 1922), p. 179.
34. Medina, "D. Jacinto em Itaca," in *Eça, Político,* pp. 113–54.
35. Eça de Queiroz, *The City and the Mountains,* trans. Roy Campbell (Athens: Ohio University Press, 1967), p. 28.

36. Ibid., p. 20.
37. Ibid., p. 22.
38. Ibid., p. 11.
39. Ibid., p. 14.
40. Ibid., p. 22.
41. Ibid., p. 38.
42. Ibid., p. 70.
43. Ibid., p. 36.
44. Ibid., pp. 74–76.
45. Ibid., pp. 108–9.
46. Ibid., p. 178.
47. Ibid., p. 201
48. Ibid., p. 202.
49. Ibid., p. 213.
50. Ibid., p. 214.
51. Ibid.
52. Ibid., p. 215.
53. Ibid., p. 217.
54. As cited in Maria Lúcia Lepecki, *Eça na Ambiguidade* (Lisboa: Jornal do Fundão, 1974), p. 93.
55. Ibid., p. 96.
56. See António Sérgio, "Notas Sobre a Imaginação, A Fantasia e o Problema Psicológico-Moral na Obra Novelística de Queirós," in *Obras Completas,* VI, ed. Castelo Branco Chaves et al. (Lisboa: Livraria Sá Costa, 1976).
57. This point has been most thoroughly made by Cortesão in his *Eça de Queiroz e a Questão Social.*
58. *The City,* p. 202.
59. Ibid., p. 143.
60. Ibid., p. 168.
61. Ibid.
62. Ibid., p. 174.
63. Ibid., p. 162.
64. Ibid., p. 159.
65. Ibid., pp. 174–75.
66. Ibid., p. 144.
67. Lepecki, *Eça na Ambiguidade,* p. 147.

A Concluding Note

Ending a book on Eça de Queirós would seem to require at least as much courage as starting one. It is even more daunting to think about his qualities today in the light of both the fin-de-siècle novel and the then contemporary beginnings of the modern novel as exemplified by such authors as Gide, Proust, Joyce, and Mann, above all because any such attempt inevitably takes on the color of partisan pleading and apology—the kind of argument that critical advocates of particular provincial authors and literatures continually impose upon readers in the United States and in England, more often than not to no avail. The authors and literatures in question remain unread. Either Eça is an overlooked author who properly belongs to a cosmopolitan tradition, or he is an exotic, interesting because he so resembles the great authors of his time. But each possibility is only a partiality; to appreciate a writer like Eça, we must see him as he was, a fusion of several cultures.

Is Eça a great writer? F. R. Leavis found himself able to constitute what he called "the great tradition" of the English novel by naming five authors: Jane Austen, George Eliot, Henry

285

James, Joseph Conrad and D. H. Lawrence. Many observers have taken Leavis to task for what might be thought of as high arbitrariness in the selection of his novelistic tradition; surely it is more helpful to view Leavis' study as a noble, stern effort to establish a criterion with which all other English novelists should be read. He helps us place other novelists, he aids us in taking their measure. In no sense does he infer that we should read no other authors but the five, or that his own opinions are not subject to change. For instance, it is common knowledge that, although Dickens was given short shrift in *The Great Tradition,* a subsequent re-reading of all of Dickens led Leavis (in collaboration with Q. D. Leavis) to dedicate a full-length study to Dickens as a novelist. In sum, it can be said that Leavis' tradition is a broad and generous one, inviting us to read other novelists even though they do not meet the excruciatingly high standards of achievement that he asks for and finds in the five novelists he examines. Eça de Queirós does not attain the level of richness, breadth and originality of Leavis' quintet, nor can he be rudely compared to his French contemporaries. Eça was fully aware of his inadequacies, and, if we are honest and sympathetic readers of his work, we know them also. There are others means available to us as we try to place Eça de Queirós as a European novelist. Suppose we examine what Leavis says about Benjamin Disraeli and his novels. On the first page of *The Great Tradition,* Leavis enumerates several Victorian novelists who were, as he wrote, undergoing a revival (of which he clearly disapproved). As he discusses these novelists, Disraeli among them, he states that he will *not* study them: although, and here he is indeed talking about Disraeli, "he is not one of the great novelists, he is so alive and intelligent as to deserve permanent currency . . . his own interests as expressed in these books—the interests of a supremely intelligent politician who has a sociologist's understanding of civilization and its movement in his time—are so mature." [1]

These few words about Disraeli must strike a sympathetic

[1] F. R. Leavis, *The Great Tradition* (New York: The New York University Press, 1963), pp. 1–2.

note in the mind of any reader of Eça de Queirós, for they bring to mind not only the achievement of Eça but also what Eça himself wrote about Disraeli just a few months after Disraeli's death in 1881. In that essay, we see not only what Eça saw in Disraeli but what Eça saw as the idealized figure of the artist; of, therefore, himself. For Eça, Disraeli was "a perpetual paradox in action" in whom nothing seemed to be lacking—"he had a fantastically clever mind, an iron will, the serene courage of a hero, an inexhaustible vein of irony, a crepitating fire of eloquence, the absolute knowledge of men, brilliant penetration into the depths of character and temperament, a subtle power of persuasion, an irresistible personal charm—and all this contained (as in a luminous atmosphere) within a brilliance, a richness and impressiveness and unexpectedness that was, or effectively seemed to be, his own peculiar nature." Eça's statements on Disraeli's novels are no less self-revelatory: "Characters, landscapes, interiors, the very movement of the adventure—all this is bathed in a serene, graceful light. Portraying things as he did outside social reality, and not having to present the sombre shadows, he could exclude from his vast paintings all that is hard in life, all that is brutal and ugly and evil and stupid—all the various forms of human baseness. He wrote for a wealthy society, a noble, literary and refined society, and he showed them a world of crystal and gold, spinning round in a beautiful harmony, bathed in rosy hues." This vision of Disraeli as the creator of escapist fantasy is one aspect of both Disraeli and Eça. But there are darker tones and firmer outlines in both Eça and Disraeli, and Eça does not pass over them in his estimation of the English novelist: "I have insisted on this unreal aspect of Lord Beaconsfield's books. However, a man like this, a former dandy, a critic and a statesman accustomed to governing, an observer by necessity, could not help but accumulate a large experience of characters and society; and this experience would naturally have emerged in his portraits of life. And there it is in fact; amid the great symbolic creations of an imagination run riot (*Tancred, Lothair, Sibyl*), a very real world moves, sketched in bold, accurate strokes, figures of flesh and blood represented with singular vividness in design and color. They are the secondary characters, his politicians, his plotters, his men-of-letters, his fashionable women, his elegant lords. But even for readers who do not frequent London society, and do not know the originals, these characters are interesting—because they are alive . . . these people make a sharper impact, like the profiles of real humanity, emerging from a mist of mythology." [2]

It is time to think about Eça's stature within European literature—after all, some eighty years have passed since his death. To say that few people outside Portugal and Brazil have read him is to say nothing at all, since, as we noted many pages ago, literature in the Portuguese language makes its way with considerable difficulty in the Anglo-Saxon world. Let me start by saying that there is a grand and generous spirit of fabulation in Eça's work. Moreover, it contains the peculiar, magnetically attractive power of a satiric genius, a recognizable current that we sense, not in the fullness of characterization in any one of the hundreds of his characters, since there are really no heroes as such in his work, but rather in the suppleness and blistering wit with which he drew the collective portrait of the Portugal that he knew. It is a certain tone in Eça, a feeling for an acerbic yet humane vision that gives off touches of grandeur even in the least of his novels. Not at all an effusive soul himself, his work overflows with rich, warm perceptions of the foibles of society—these same satiric nuances and ceremonies are the unique catalysts of his critical imagination. And it *is* a world of his imagination, in spite of all the ambitions toward mimesis and documentation; this is a richness born, paradoxically, of his own bereft and isolated self, his maddeningly self-imposed exile from Portugal for so many years, his dogged sense of apprenticeship and inadequacy as compared with French and English masters whom he considered both as his ideal and his collective nemeses. And we should never pass over, even in his most modest works, the simple delights of the story; not at all

[2] Eça de Queirós, *Letters from England*, Trans. Ann Stevens. (Athens: Ohio University Press, 1970), pp. 81–103.

an advocate of the then avant-garde, Eça is a happily old-fashioned teller of tales.

We easily recognize Eça now as a reflector and observer of some of the principal cultural obsessions of fin de siècle European culture. He is a part of the grand whole that is the Realist and Naturalist novel in Europe. But just as we acknowledge his presence in a European cultural identity, we must also note his obstinate sense of inner bifurcation, his waywardness, his insistence on something that is peculiarly Portuguese about himself and his writing, since he was born into a provincial national tradition which he both detested and represented. Refusing to resign himself to the role of passive imitator of a central corpus of European fiction, and refusing all the more to continue a vapid kind of Romantic evocation of the glories of the national past, Eça's work was born out of a double cultural parricide: against 'old' Portugal, against France. His pages are the summary of how he triumphed over the national syndrome, when so many of his contemporaries and predecessors had failed. In his luminous and sardonic way, he is distinct from any of his continental contemporaries.

In so many of his pages, he makes much of his own sense of estrangement and alienation; he constantly feeds on his own emotional sterility. He *almost* tells himself and his peers within Portugal to give up the game, to resign themselves to settle for the fate of being provincial. His characters are immobile and weighted down with *accidie; he* never stopped. Thus, his writing displays the critical virtues of both action and contemplation; he saw all human enterprise as badly flawed, and for that reason eminently worth any amount of energy that might be poured into just those same flawed enterprises.

As a novelist, Eça de Queirós still has to find his place among the masters of nineteenth-century European fiction. Except for Turgenev, no other writer of his time dramatized so magisterially the quandary provoked by opposing and at times mutually destructive cultural forces that operated within a writer born into the peripheries of Europe and magnetized by the spiritual and cultural hegemony of France and England. And on the whole, Eça de Queirós gives us, and with abundance, a moving and compelling portrait of an artist who was a self-sufficient creator of a novelistic universe.

He is a major figure in nineteenth-century European literature, a master who deserves more than the few readers he has now. I hope I have done something to change that situation.

Appendix

José Matias

Translated by
Richard Franko Goldman

A FINE AFTERNOON, my friend! I'm waiting for the funeral of José Matias—José Matias de Albuquerque, the nephew of the Visconde de Garmilde . . . you surely must have known him—a personable lad, blond as an ear of corn, with a neat cavalier's moustache above the undecided mouth of a thinker . . . a gifted chap, elegant in a rather fine and restrained way. And an inquiring mind much given to general ideas and keen enough to understand my *Defence of Hegelian Philosophy*! But this picture of José Matias goes back to 1865. The last time I saw him, on a bitter January afternoon, he was huddled in a doorway in the Rua de São Bento, shivering with cold, wearing an old yellow jacket, patched at the elbows, and he stank abominably of brandy. . . .

But, my friend, I recall one occasion when José Matias

291

stopped over in Coimbra on his way from Porto, and I dined
with him at the Paço do Conde! And there was Craveiro, who
was then working on his *Ironies and Sorrows of Satan,* to deepen
the gulf between the Purist and the Diabolic schools, and who
recited that so lugubriously idealistic sonnet of his, beginning:
In the cage of my breast, my heart. . . . And I still remember José
Matias, with a splendid necktie of black satin arching out from
his white linen collar, smiling wanly without taking his eyes off
the candles in their holders, at that heart roaring in its cage. It
was a night in April with a full moon. Afterwards we all strolled
with our guitars toward Choupal and the bridge. Januário sang
feelingly one of the romantic plaints of those days:

> Last evening, when the sun set,
> You regarded in silence
> The mighty torrent
> That boiled at your feet. . . .

And there was José Matias, leaning on the parapet of the
bridge, with his eyes and his soul lost in the moonlight. . . .
Why don't you come along and see this interesting lad to the
Prazeres Cemetery? I have a carriage, a licensed public hack, as
is suitable for a professor of philosophy. . . . What? . . . because you have on light trousers? Oh, my good friend! Of all
the manifestations of sympathy, none is more grossly material
than black cloth . . . and the man we are going to bury was of
an extremely spiritual character!

Here is the coffin being brought out of the church. . . . Just
three carriages to accompany it. But the fact is, my friend, that
José Matias actually died six years ago in his unspoiled splendor. The one we are taking away now, half decomposed inside
that wooden box covered with yellow lace, is a drunken relict
without a name or a story, who was killed in a doorway by the
February cold.

The person with gold-rimmed spectacles, in the coupé? . . .
I don't know him, friend. Maybe a rich relative, one of those
who show up at funerals, with the relationship correctly ob-

served with crêpe, since the deceased is no longer importunate or compromising. The fat man with the ugly yellow face in the victoria is Alves Capão, who runs a periodical in which, unfortunately, philosophy is hardly conspicuous; it's called *A Piada*.[1] What did he and Matias have to do with each other? I don't know. Maybe they got drunk together; maybe José Matias contributed lately to the *Piada*, or maybe underneath that fat and that literature, both equally sordid, there is concealed a compassionate heart. Here is our carriage. . . . Shall I lower the window? Have a cigar? I have matches.

Then, too, José Matias was an upsetting type for someone like me who likes to see life evolve in a logical way and who claims that the grain grows integrally from the seed. In Coimbra we always considered him a scandalously commonplace character. His horrifying correctness perhaps contributed to that opinion. Never a pulled thread in his cape; never a spot of dust on his shoes; never a hair out of place on his head or his thin moustache, the neat alignment of which was our despair. Aside from this, he was the only intellectual in our passionate generation who didn't rage over the miseries of Poland, who didn't groan and grow pale on reading *Les Contemplations,* and who seemed unmoved by the wounds of Garibaldi. And yet, in this same José Matias there was no insensibility or harshness or egoism or lack of affability. On the contrary. A pleasant companion, always cordial, and quietly cheerful. All of his unshakable placidness seemed to stem from complete superficiality of feeling. And in those days, it wasn't without reason or aptness that we nicknamed this youth, so mild, so blond, so easygoing, Matias Squirrel-Heart. And after he graduated, as his father had died, then his mother, a gentle and charming woman from whom he inherited 50 contos,[2] he left for Lisbon to brighten up the solitary life of an uncle who adored him, the General Visconde de Garmilde. You doubtless remember that

[1] Alves Capão—*A Piada.* An elaborate play on words. *Capão,* literally, means *capon. Piada* is a malicious joke, a taunt—perhaps rendered in modern American as "wisecrack." But it also means cackling or chirping.
[2] *50 contos.* A large sum. The reader may take the 1875 *conto* to be roughly the equivalent of $1000.

perfect classical type of a general, always with terrifically waxed moustaches, pink military trousers stretched desperately tight by straps to the glistening boots, and his riding whip under his arm, ready for action, eager to thrash the world! A grotesque warrior . . . and deliciously good. The general lived at that time in Arroios in an old blue-tiled house, with a garden in which he passionately cultivated superb beds of dahlias. This garden inclined gently upward to an ivy-covered wall that separated it from another garden, the large and beautiful rose garden of Counsellor Matos Miranda, whose house, with an airy terrace between two little yellow turrets, stood at the top of the hill and was known as the Parreira.[3] You know, my friend (at least by reputation, the way one knows Helen of Troy or Inés de Castro), the beautiful Elisa Miranda, Elisa da Parreira. . . . She was the sublime romantic beauty of Lisbon at the end of the Regeneration period.[4] Though actually Lisbon hardly ever saw her except through the windows of her large calèche, or on an occasional evening of illumination on the Passeio Publico in the midst of the dust and the crowds, or at the two balls of the Carmo Assembly of which Matos Miranda was a highly respected director. Whether she was simply inclined to stay at home like a provincial lady, or because of her being part of that serious bourgeoisie which in those days in Lisbon still kept the old rigid and strait-laced customs, or because of the paternal restrictions placed on her by her husband, who then was seventy and diabetic—the goddess rarely emerged from Arroios to be seen by mortals. The one who did see her with easy frequency and almost unavoidably from the moment he settled in Lisbon was José Matias. Since the *palacete* of the general lay at the foot of the hill below the garden and the house of Parreira, the divine Elisa could not appear at a window, cross the terrace, gather a rose among the rows of boxwood, without being deliciously visible, all the more so since no tree made a curtain of dense foliage in the two sun-drenched gardens. My friend has

[3] *A Parreira*. Literary, The Trellis or the Trellised Vine.
[4] Regeneration period. The two chief political parties of Portugal in the period were the "Historicals" and the "Regenerators." They alternated in power.

doubtless warbled, as we all have, those hackneyed but immortal lines:

Era no Outono, quando a imagem tua
À luz da Lua. . . .
(It was in autumn, when thine image,
In the moonlight. . . .)

So, just as in the strophe, poor José Matias, coming back from the beach at Ericeira one October, saw Elisa Miranda one evening on the terrace, in autumn, in the moonlight! You have never laid eyes, my friend, on anything approaching that rare type of enchantress á la Lamartine. Tall, slender, well-rounded, worthy of the Biblical image of the palm tree in the breeze. Black hair, thick and lustrous, in wavy tresses. A complexion like perfectly fresh camellias. Dark eyes, liquid, bewitching, melancholy, with long lashes. . . . Ah, my friend, even I, who was then laboriously annotating Hegel, even I adored her for three exalted days and wrote a sonnet to her after meeting her one rainy afternoon when she was awaiting her carriage at the door of the Seixas house. I don't know if José Matias dedicated sonnets to her. But every one of us, his friends, soon noticed the mighty, profound, and absolute love which, beginning with that October night in the moonlight, took possession of the heart that we in Coimbra had described as a squirrel's.

It is to be understood that so proper and modest a man did not give vent to his sighs in public. However, as far back as the time of Aristotle, it was observed that love and smoke cannot be hidden; and from our self-contained José Matias love soon began to emerge like wisps of smoke through the chinks of a closed house that is burning furiously. I well recall one afternoon when I visited him in Arroios on my return from the Alentejo. It was a Sunday in July. He was on his way to dine with a great-aunt, one Dona Mafalda Noronha, who lived in Benfica on the Quinta dos Cedros where Matos Miranda and the divine Elisa also were in the habit of dining every Sunday. I even believe that it was only in this house that she and José Matias ever met; at least it was the only place that offered the conveniences of sheltered paths and shady nooks. The windows of José Matias' room overlooked his garden and the garden of the Mirandas; and when I entered he was still slowly getting dressed. Never, my friend, have I looked on a human face so transfigured by the most serene and untroubled happiness. He smiled radiantly as he embraced me, with a smile that came from the depths of his illuminated soul, and he kept on smiling gently as I told him all about my troubles in the Alentejo; he smiled ecstatically as he referred to the heat and distractedly rolled a cigarette; and he continued smiling, in raptures, as with ceremonious care he chose a white silk tie from a drawer of his dresser. And all the time, irresistibly, in a manner already as unconscious as blinking, his smiling eyes, calm and tender, kept turning toward the closed windows . . . so that, following this happy beam, I soon perceived the divine Elisa strolling idly on the terrace of the Parreira, wearing a light dress and a white hat, thoughtfully putting on her gloves, and also looking up at my friend's windows, which were blazoned with gold from a slanting ray of the sun. José Matias meanwhile continued to talk, or rather to mumble, without losing his fixed smile, in a pleasant but disconnected manner. His entire attention was concentrated on his mirror, on the coral and pearl pin to fasten his necktie, on his white collar which he adjusted and buttoned with the devotion that a newly ordained priest, in the pure exaltation of preparing for his first Mass, might bring to robing himself in amice and stole in order to approach the altar. Never have I seen a man sprinkle eau de cologne on a handkerchief with such profound ecstasy! And after putting on his jacket and pinning a superb rose to his lapel, it was with ineffable emotion and with a sigh he could not hold back, that he solemnly opened the windows wide. *Introibo ad altare Deae!* I remained discreetly buried in the sofa. And, my friend, believe me! I envied that man at the window, motionless, rigid in his sublime devotion, with his eyes, his soul, and all his being riveted on the terrace, on the white lady putting on her light gloves, and as indifferent to the world as if the world were merely the pavement that she trod and covered with her feet.

And this spell, my friend, lasted for ten years, always as

splendid, pure, distant and immaterial! Don't laugh! . . . certainly they met at Dona Mafalda's quinta; certainly they wrote to each other, overflowingly, throwing their letters to each other over the top of the wall separating the two gardens; but never, over they ivy of the wall, did they manage the delight of a stolen conversation or the still more perfect delight of a silence shared in the shadows. And they never exchanged a kiss . . . no doubt about it! A fleeting and hungry touching of hands under the shade trees at Dona Mafalda's was the exaltedly extreme limit that their wills set to their desires. You find it hard to understand how two fragile beings could go on in this way for ten years in such terrible and morbid renunciation. . . . Yes, to be sure, they were not given an hour of freedom or a little gate in the wall so that they might lose themselves. For the divine Elisa really lived in a convent, the bolts and bars of which were shaped by the rigidly secluded habits of the diabetic and gloomy Matos Miranda. Moreover, in the chasteness of this love there was also much moral nobility and a superior finesse of feeling. Love spiritualizes man—and materializes woman. This spiritualization was easy for José Matias who (we can't be under any illusions about this) was born distractedly spiritualistic. But the human Elisa also derived a delicate pleasure from the idealistic adoration of this monk who, with his trembling fingers enmeshed in a rosary, never dared to touch the robe of the transfigured Virgin. *He* . . . of course! he found a superhuman charm in this transcendental and dematerialized love. And for ten years, like the Ruy Blas of old Victor Hugo, he went along dazzled and fascinated in his radiant dream, a dream in which Elisa actually dwelled within his soul in a fusion so perfect that she was consubstantial with his own being. Will you believe that he gave up smoking, even when he was riding horseback by himself in the surroundings of Lisbon, the moment he discovered one afternoon at Dona Mafalda's quinta that smoke bothered Elisa?

And this real presence of the divine creature in his own being caused José Matias to take up new and odd ways stemming from his hallucination. As the Visconde de Garmilde dined early, in the traditional style of old Portugal, José Matias supped, after the performances at São Carlos, at that delightful and cherished Café Central, where the sole seems to have been cooked in heaven, and where in heaven, too, the Colares seems to have been bottled. And he never supped without a profusion of candelabras lit up and the table piled with flowers. Why? Because Elisa was also supping there, invisibly. Hence those silences observed with a devoutly attentive smile. Why? Because he was always listening to her! And then I remember him taking down from the walls of his room three classical engravings of daring Fauns and vanquished Nymphs . . . ideally, Elisa was present in these surroundings, and he had to purify the walls, which he ordered hung with light silks. Love impels one toward luxury, especially a love of such elegant idealism, and José Matias was splendidly prodigal in providing luxury that she could share. He could not, in decency, travel with Elisa's image in a rented hack or permit the august vision to come in contact with the straw-covered seats of the parterre at São Carlos. He therefore rode in carriages of refined and sober style, and subscribed to a box at the Opera, where he installed for her a pontifical armchair in white satin, embroidered with gold stars.

Beyond this, as he discovered that Elisa was generous, he related himself to her in this and became sumptuously generous himself. There was no one in Lisbon at that time who scattered 100-milreis notes with more easy gaiety. And he thus rapidly ran through 60 contos for the love of this woman to whom he never gave so much as a single flower.

And during all this time, what of Matos Miranda? The good Matos Miranda, my friend, didn't cast a shadow over either the perfection or the tranquillity of this happiness. Could the spirituality of José Matias have been so absolute that as soon as he became interested in her soul, he was indifferent to the use of her body, that low and mortal covering? I don't know. It could be true that the worthy diabetic, so serious, always with a scarf of dark wool, with his greying whiskers, his heavy gold-rimmed spectacles, did not bring to mind disquieting pictures of an ardent husband, whose ardor, fatally and involuntarily, would be shared and consumed in passion. But nevertheless I never understood—I, a philosopher—the almost affectionate consideration of José Matias for the man who could, even disinterestedly, by right, by custom, watch Elisa undoing her white silk ribbons. Could it be that he was grateful to Miranda for having discovered this divine creature on a back street in Setúbal (where José Matias never would have found her), and for keeping her in comfort, amply fed, beautifully clothed, conveyed about in well-sprung calèches? Or could José Matias have received that usual avowal:—"I am not yours, but neither am I his"—that is such a consolation for one's sacrifices, since it so flatters the ego? I don't know. But one thing is certain: that magnanimous disdain of his for the corporeal presence of Miranda in the temple inhabited by his Goddess, gave the happiness of José Matias a perfect wholeness, the unity of a crystal that sparkles from every facet with equal purity, without a scratch or a streak. And this felicity, my friend, lasted ten years. . . . What a scandalous luxury for a mortal!

But one day the whole earth trembled for José Matias in an earthquake of incomparable horror. In January or February of 1871, Miranda, already weakened by diabetes, died of pneumonia. Along these same streets, in a lumbering hired carriage, I followed his well-attended and elaborate funeral, complete with Ministers, as Miranda belonged to the Institute. And later, taking advantage of the rented carriage, I visited José Matias in Arroios, not out of perverse curiosity, nor to offer him indecent congratulations, but so that he might have at his side on that staggering occasion, the moderating influence of philosophy. I found with him, however, an older and closer friend, the brilliant Nicolau da Barca, whom I have also already accompanied to this same cemetery, where now repose under headstones all those comrades with whom I once built castles in the sky. . . . Nicolau had arrived at dawn from Velosa, his quinta at Santarém, summoned by a telegram from Matias. When I entered, a servant was busy packing two enormous trunks. José Matias was leaving that night for Porto. He was already wearing a traveling suit, completely black, with shoes of tan leather; and after shaking my hand, while Nicolau mixed a grog, he continued to wander about the room, silent, as if stunned, with an air that seemed to be neither emotion, nor joy decently disguised, nor amazement at the sudden transformation of his destiny. No! If the good Darwin doesn't deceive us in his book, *The Expression of the Emotions,* the only emotion that José Matias felt and expressed that afternoon was embarrassment. Across the way at the Parreira, all the windows remained closed in the sadness of the gloomy afternoon. Nevertheless, I caught José Matias casting rapid glances at the terrace, glances in which were manifested inquietude, anxiety, almost terror! How shall I put it? It was the kind of sidelong glance one gives at a badly secured cage in which a lion is pacing. The minute José Matias went inside to his bedroom, I murmured to Nicolau over the grog: "Matias is doing absolutely the right thing in going to Porto. . . ." Nicolau shrugged his shoulders: "Yes, I think it's most delicate . . . I approve. . . . But only for the months of deep mourning. . . ." At seven o'clock we accompanied our friend to the Santa Apolónia station. On our way back we philosophized inside our coupé as a heavy rain beat down. I smiled with content: "A year of mourning, and then great happiness and many children . . . it's a complete poem!" Nicolau elaborated: "It's a poem completed in delicious and juicy prose. The divine Elisa will be left with all her divinity, plus Miranda's money, some ten or twelve contos of income. . . . And you and I, for the first time in our lives, may contemplate virtue rewarded!"

* * *

My dear friend, the months of strict mourning passed, and then others, and José Matias did not stir from Porto. That August I found him installed on a permanent basis in the Hotel Francfort, where he was whiling away the scorching days smoking (for he had gone back to tobacco), reading novels by Jules Verne, and drinking cold beer until evening, when the air freshened, at which time he dressed, perfumed and primped himself to go to dinner at Foz.[5]

And despite the fact that the end of the mourning period and of the maddening wait was approaching, I did not observe in

[5] *Foz.* S. João de Foz, a resort near Porto.

José Matias either any finely suppressed rapture or any irritation against the leisurely pace of Father Time, that ancient who is sometimes so slow and halting. On the contrary! The smile of radiant certainty that lit up his face in the old days with a beatific glow was replaced by an expression of worried seriousness, all lines and shadows, the expression of someone who is debating in his mind an irresolvable choice, always present, gnawing, and painful. Would you like my opinion? That autumn in the Hotel Francfort, it always seemed to me that José Matias at every instant of his waking life, even while pouring down cold beer, even while putting on his gloves to get into the calèche that would take him to Foz, was in anguish, asking his conscience: "What shall I do? What shall I do?" And later on, one morning at breakfast, he really amazed me when he opened the paper and exclaimed with a rush of blood to his face: "What! It's already the 29th of August! Good God . . . already the end of August . . . !"

I returned to Lisbon, friend. The winter passed, very dry and clear. I worked on my *Origins of Utilitarianism.* One Sunday on the Rossio, when they were already selling carnations in the tobacco shops, I caught a glimpse of the divine Elisa inside her coupé, wearing red feathers on her hat. And that same week I ran across in the *Diario Illustrado* the brief, almost hesitant announcement of the marriage of Senhora Dona Elisa Miranda. . . . With whom, my friend? With the well-known landowner, Senhor Francisco Torres Nogueira!

(At this point my friend clenched his fist and pounded the cushions in amazement.) I too, at the time, clenched both my fists, but only to raise them to heaven where the deeds of earth are judged, and to cry out furiously, with a roar, against the falsity, the crooked and perfidious inconstancy, against all the deceiving indecency of women, and especially of that Elisa, infamous beyond all women! To be in such a hurry, when barely out of mourning, heedlessly to betray that noble, pure, intellectual Matias! And with his love of ten years, so patient and sublime!

And after I had raised my fists to heaven, I pressed my head between them, and shouted: "But why? . . . why?" For years she loved this young man rapturously and with a love that had been neither disillusioned nor fulfilled, since it remained suspended, immaterial, and unsatisfied. Was it ambition? Torres Nogueira was an amiable do-nothing like José Matias, and derived from his mortgaged vineyards the same 50 or 60 contos of income that José Matias now received from the excellent and debt-free lands of Uncle Garmilde. And so . . . why? Undoubtedly because the thick black whiskers of Torres Nogueira appealed to her more than the tentative blond down of José Matias! Ah! Saint John Chrysostom rightly taught that woman is a dung heap of impurity, mounting to the gates of hell.

Well, my friend, while I was raging in this way, one afternoon on the Rua do Alecrim I met our friend Nicolau da Barca, who jumped out of his carriage, pushed me into a doorway, excitedly grabbed my poor arm, and, choking with excitement, exclaimed: "Have you heard? It was José Matias who refused her! She wrote, she went to Porto, she wept . . . he didn't even consent to see her! He didn't want to get married . . . doesn't want to get married!" I stood there staggered. "And what about her . . . ?" ". . . spurned, furiously besought by Torres, tired of being a widow . . . with those fine thirty years behind her . . . what the devil! . . . poor thing, she got married!" I raised my arms to the ceiling of the patio: "And what about that sublime love of José Matias?" Nicolau, his close friend and confidant, swore with unanswerable certainty: "It is still the same . . . infinite . . . absolute! But he doesn't want to get married! " We stared at each other, and then we separated, shrugging our shoulders in that resigned amazement proper to prudent souls before the unknowable. But during all that night I, a philosopher, and yet an imprudent spirit, probed the action of José Matias with the needle of my expressly sharpened psychology; and by dawn, worn out, I concluded, as one always concludes in philosophy, that I was up against a first cause, by definition unknowable, on which the point of my instrument would be broken without any advantage to him, to me, or to the world.

After the divine Elisa married, she continued to live in the Parreira with her Torres Nogueira in the same comfort and tranquillity as she formerly enjoyed with her Matos Miranda. In the middle of autumn José Matias returned from Porto to Arroios and the large house of Uncle Garmilde, where he installed himself in his old quarters with the balconies overlooking the garden already blooming with dahlias that now no one looked after. August came, quiet and hot, as always in Lisbon. On Sundays, José Matias dined with Dona Mafalda de Noronha in Benfica, alone, because Torres Nogueira was not acquainted with the respected lady of the Quinta dos Cedros. The divine Elisa, dressed in light colors, strolled in the afternoons in her garden among the rosebushes. So that the only change in that lovely corner of Arroios seemed to be that Matos Miranda now was in his fine resting place in the Prazeres Cemetery, and Torres Nogueira in the excellent bed of Elisa.

There was, however, one tremendous and grievous change—in José Matias. Can you guess how this unfortunate creature passed his barren days? With his eyes and his memories and his soul, with his whole being pinned to the terrace, the windows and the gardens of the Parreira. But it was no longer from wide-open windows in open ecstasy, with a smile of unquestioning beatitude; it was from behind drawn curtains, through a narrow slit, concealed, furtively stealing glances at the white ripples of the white dresses, with his face completely ravaged by anguish and defeat. And do you know why he suffered so, this poor soul? Simply because Elisa, spurned by his unopened arms, ran immediately without struggle and without scruples to other arms more accessible and willing? . . . No, my friend! Now please note the subtle complexity of his passion. José Matias remained devoutly convinced that Elisa, from the bottom of her heart, from those blessed spiritual depths that are affected by neither the demands of convention, nor the decisions of pure reason, nor the promptings of pride, nor the emotions of the flesh—loved him and only him, and with a love that would never diminish, never change, a love that would flourish in all its luxuriance without being nourished or tended, like the ancient Mystic Rose. What tortured him, my friend, what put deep lines in his face in the space of a few months, was that a man, a male animal, a brute, should have taken possession of a woman who was his! And that in the most holy and socially approved fashion, under the benign auspices of the Church and the State, this man was dirtying with his thick black whiskers, as often as he wanted, those divine lips that he had never dared to touch in his superstitious reverence and near terror of her divinity! How shall I put it? The feelings of our extraordinary Matias were those of a monk, prostrated in transcendent rapture before an image of the Virgin, when suddenly a sacrilegious beast tramps to the altar and indecently raises the Virgin's robe. You're smiling . . . what about Matos Miranda? Well, my friend, that one was fat and morose and diabetic, and he was already installed in the Parreira with his diabetes and his corpulence when Matias first knew Elisa and dedicated his heart and his life to her forever. But Torres Nogueira, that one, burst brutally into this pure love of his with his black whiskers, his beefy arms, his vigorous attraction of an old bull tamer . . . and lay hold of this woman— to whom, perhaps, he revealed what a man is!

But . . . what the devil! He had refused this woman when she offered herself to him in the freshness and the generosity of a feeling that no disdain could afterwards wither or lessen. What do you expect? It's the amazing spiritual twistedness of that Matias! At the end of a few months he had *forgotten*, absolutely *forgotten*, his insulting refusal, as if it had been some slight conflict of material or social interests that had taken place months ago in the North, and from which time and distance had removed the reality and the slight bitter taste. And now, here in Lisbon, with Elisa's windows facing his and the roses of their adjoining gardens scenting the shadows, the real grief, the present grief, came from the fact that he held a sublime love for a woman whom he had placed among the stars so as to contemplate her in the purest adoration, and that a dark-skinned brute with black whiskers had plucked this woman from among the stars and had flung her into bed!

An intriguing case, don't you think so, my friend? Ah, I thought a great deal about him as a matter of philosophical duty. And I came to the conclusion that Matias was a sick man suffering from hyperspirituality, from a violent and putrid spiritual inflammation which made him recoil in terror before the material facts of marriage, of bedroom slippers, of the way people look on waking in the morning, of bellies distended for six months, of babies howling in wetted cradles. And now he was screaming with rage and torment because a certain gross materialist next door was getting ready to find Elisa acceptable in woolen camisoles. An imbecile? No, my friend, an ultraromantic, insanely remote from the basic realities of life, who never suspected that bedroom slippers and soiled diapers are objects of superior beauty in a house where the sun comes in and where there is love.

And do you know what aggravated this torment more furiously? It was the fact that poor Elisa still showed the old love for him. What do you think? Devilish, no . . . ? At least, if she didn't still feel the old love intact in its essence as strong as formerly, and as unique, she retained an irresistible curiosity about poor Matias and she repeated the gestures of love. . . . Perhaps it was merely the fatal circumstance of the adjoining gardens! I don't know. But from September on, as soon as Torres Nogueira had left for his vineyards at Carcavelos to supervise the harvest, she began again from the edge of the terrace, from above the opened roses and dahlias, that sweet dispatch of gentle glances with which for ten years she had enraptured the heart of José Matias.

I don't think that they exchanged correspondence over the wall of the garden as they did under the paternal regime of Matos Miranda. The new Senhor, the robust man with the black beard, imposed discretion and reserve on the divine Elisa even from a distance, from the vineyards of Carcavelos. And quieted down by this young and robust husband, she now felt less need for any cautious meeting in the warm shadows of night, even had her moral refinement and the strict idealism of José Matias permitted them to take advantage of a ladder against the wall. Besides, Elisa was basically honest, and she preserved a sacred respect for her body—knowing it to be so beautiful and so thoughtfully constructed by God—more than for her soul. And who knows? Perhaps this adorable woman belonged to the same fine race as that Italian marchesa, Giulia de Malfieri, who kept two lovers at her sweet service: a poet for romantic delicacies and a coachman for coarser necessities.

Anyhow, my friend, let's not psychologize any more about her, who is still alive, except as concerns the one who is now dead for her. The fact is that Elisa and our friend insensibly fell back into their old ideal union across the flowering gardens. And in October, as Torres Nogueira was still tending to the vineyards in Carcavelos, José Matias once again ecstatically opened his windows wide in order to contemplate the terrace of Parreira.

It would seem that so rarefied a spirit, recapturing the ideality of his old love, should have also rediscovered his old and perfect happiness. He reigned in the immortal soul of Elisa . . . what should it matter to him that another was in possession of her mortal body? But no! The poor boy suffered painfully. And to ease the sharpness of these torments, he ended up—he, so calm, and with such a gentle harmoniousness in his ways—by turning into a wild man. Ah, my friend, what a tumult and a whirlwind of life! Despairingly, for a year he turned Lisbon upside down, giddily and scandalously. Some of his extravagances of that period are legendary. Do you know the one of the supper? A supper given for thirty or forty of the filthiest and most vicious women picked up in the blackest alleys of the Bairro Alto and the Mouraria,[6] whom he afterwards ordered to get on burros and whom he led, riding in front solemnly and sadly on a great white horse, holding an immense whip, to the heights of Graca to greet the rising sun!

But all these alarums didn't dissipate his sorrow—and it was then, that winter, that he began to gamble and drink. All day long he stayed locked up in his house (and without doubt behind drawn blinds, since Torres Nogueira had returned from his vineyards), with his eyes and his soul fastened on the fatal terrace; then, at night, when Elisa's windows were darkened, he set out in a carriage, always the same one, Gago's, played roulette at the Bravo, then went on to the "Cavaliers' Club" where he gambled furiously until it was time for a late supper in a private room of a restaurant, with bunches of candles lit up

[6] *Bairro Alto* and *Mouraria*. Slum quarters of Lisbon.

and Colares and champagne and cognac flowing in desperate torrents.

And this fury-driven life lasted for years . . . seven years! All the lands left to him by his Uncle Garmilde were gone, mostly in gambling or drink, and all that remained to him was the large house in Arroios and the loans he had raised by mortaging it. But suddenly, he was no longer seen in any of the gambling dens or drinking places. And we learned that Torres Noguiera was dying of dropsy.

At this time, because of some business of Nicolau de Barca's, who had sent me a worried telegram from his quinta at Santarém (a complicated business about a letter), I went to see José Matias in Arroios at ten o'clock one warm night in April. The servant, as he was leading me through the poorly lit corridor, already stripped of the handsome cabinets and carved pieces from India that had belonged to old Garmilde, explained that the master had not finished dining. . . . And I still remember with a shudder the feeling of desolation the poor fellow gave me. He was in the room that opened onto the two gardens. In front of the window, which was covered by damask curtains, the table was resplendent with two candelabras, a basket of white roses, and some of Garmilde's noble silver service; and alongside, stretched out at full length in an armchair, with his white collar undone, his pale face drooping on his chest, an empty glass in his limp hand, José Matias seemed to be asleep or dead.

When I touched him on the shoulder, he raised his unkempt head with a start: "What time is it?" I spoke loudly, in a gay tone, to wake him up, and had just told him that it was late, that it was ten o'clock, when he hurriedly filled up his glass with white wine from the nearest decanter, and began to drink slowly with his hand shaking . . . shaking. And then, pushing back the hair from his damp forehead, he asked: "Well, what's new?" Distractedly, without understanding, as if in a dream, he listened to the message sent by Nicolau. Finally, with a sigh, he twisted a bottle of champagne in the bucket in which it was cooling and filled another glass, murmuring: "What a heat . . . what a thirst . . . !" But he didn't drink; he raised his heavy body from the cane-bottomed armchair and made his way unsteadily to the window from which he first violently pulled back the curtains and then opened the window itself. He stood there stiffly, as if immobilized by the silence and the dark quiet of the starry night. I kept my eyes open, my friend! Two windows in the Parreira house were open to the mild breeze and shone with bright illumination. And this strong light enveloped a figure in white, in the long folds of a white nightgown, standing at the edge of the terrace as if lost in contemplation. It was Elisa, my friend! Behind her, at the back of the lighted room, her husband was doubtless breathing with difficulty in the oppression of his disease. She, motionless, was resting, sending a gentle glance, perhaps even a smile, at her dear friend. The miserable wretch, fascinated, hardly breathing, was drinking up the charm of that beneficent vision. And between them, in the softness of the night, rose the scent of all the flowers of the two gardens. . . . Suddenly, and in haste, Elisa withdrew, summoned by a groan or a complaint of poor Torres. And soon the windows were closed, and all the light and life went out of the house of the Parreira.

Then José Matias, with a rending sigh of overflowing torment, staggered back, clutching so anxiously at the curtain that he tore it down, and he fell helplessly into my extended arms. I dragged him to a chair, limp and heavy, like a dead man or a drunk. But coming to for a moment, to my astonishment this extraordinary man opened his eyes, smiled a patient and weary smile, and murmured almost calmly: "It's the heat . . . this awful heat! Wouldn't you like some tea?"

I excused myself and took myself off—while he, stretched out in the armchair and indifferent to my departure, was shakily lighting an enormous cigar.

* * *

Good Lord! Here we are already at Santa Isabel! What a hurry these brutes are in to transport poor José Matias to the dust and the worms! Well, my friend, soon after that strange night, Torres Nogueira died. The divine Elisa, during this new mourning period, retired to Corte Moreira, the quinta of her sister-in-law, also a widow, near Beja. And José Matias disappeared entirely, sank out of sight, so that I had no news about him, not even rumors—all the less since the close friend through whom I might have heard something, our brilliant Nicolau de Barca, had left for the Island of Madeira with his last remaining fragment of lung, hopelessly ill, to fulfill the classical obligations, one might say the social obligations, of a consumptive.

All that year, too, I was plugging away at my *Essay on Affective Phenomena*. But one day at the beginning of summer, I was going down the Rua de São Bento, with my eyes raised looking for Number 214, where the library of the Morgado de Azemel was being catalogued, when whom do you suppose I saw on the balcony of a new corner house? The divine Elisa, poking lettuce leaves into a canary cage! And so beautiful, my friend! A little more rounded, more well-proportioned, ripened and delicious and desirable, despite having celebrated her forty-second birthday in Beja! But this woman came from the same family as Helen, who forty years after the siege of Troy was still fascinating mortal men and immortal gods. And, by a curious coincidence, through Seco—that is, João Seco, of the library, who was cataloguing the Morgado's [7] collection—I learned the most recent part of the story of this admirable Helen.

The divine Elisa now had a lover . . . but only because she could not have him, with her usual correctness, as a third and legitimate husband. The lucky young man whom she adored was, in fact, married . . . married in Beja to a Spanish woman who, after a year of marriage and a few affairs on the side, had departed for Seville to observe Holy Week with piety, and to sleep in the arms of a very rich cattle breeder. Her husband, a peaceable Superintendent of Public Works, remained in Beja where, as a sideline, he gave some sort of lessons in some sort of drawing. Well, one of his pupils was the daughter of the lady of Corte Moreira; and there at the quinta, while he was guiding the little girl's pencil, Elisa met him and fell in love with him with a passion so undeniable that she hastily snatched him from

---

[7] *Morgado.* A landed proprietor, by inheritance, roughly equivalent to the English "Squire."

the Public Works and dragged him to Lisbon, a city rather more favorable to scandalous pleasure than Beja, and one in which one can hide away. João Seco comes from Beja, where he spent Christmas, and he was well acquainted with the Superintendent and the ladies of Corte Moreira; and he caught on to the romance when, from the windows of No. 214, where he was cataloguing Azemel's collection, he recognized Elisa on the corner balcony, and the Superintendent nonchalantly coming through the doorway, well-dressed, well-shod, with light gloves, and with every appearance of being infinitely happier in private works than in public ones.

And from that same window of No. 214 I came to know him too, the Superintendent. A handsome fellow, solid, light-complexioned, with dark beard, an excellent number from the standpoint of quantity (and perhaps also from that of quality) to occupy a widowed heart and, perhaps, as the Bible has it, an idle one. I was often at No. 214, as I was interested in the catalog of the library, since the Morgado de Azemel, through the ironic operation of inheritance, possessed an incomparable collection of eighteenth-century philosophers. Several weeks later, coming out from the books one night (for João Seco worked at night), I stopped a bit further along the street near an open doorway to light a cigar, and in the glimmering light of the match I glimpsed José Matias, huddled in the shadows. But what a José Matias, my good friend! To get a better look at him, I struck another match. Poor José Matias! He had let his beard grow, a wispy, characterless, dirty beard, soft as yellowed cotton; he had let his hair grow too, and it was hanging in meager wisps from under an old derby hat. All of him, for that matter, seemed diminished and shrunken inside his rumpled long jacket of nondescript material and his black trousers, in the large pockets of which he kept his hands in the traditional pose, so infinitely sad, of idle poverty. In the shock of pity that I felt, I could hardly stammer: "Here you are! You! What has happened?" And he, with his polished courtesy, but curtly, so as to get rid of me, and in a voice that much brandy had roughened: "Oh, I'm here waiting for somebody." I didn't pursue it, but went on my way. Then, farther along, stopping, I confirmed what I had suspected at first glance—that the dark doorway was situated directly opposite the new house and the balconies of Elisa!

And so, my friend, José Matias lived for three years huddled in that doorway!

* * *

It was one of those courtyards of old Lisbon, without a concierge, always left open, always dirty . . . one of those caverns on one side of the street from which no one would ever chase away the hidden victims of poverty or grief. Next door was a tavern. Invariably, at nightfall, José Matias came down the Rua de São Bento, glued to the walls, and, like a shadow, disappeared into the shadow of the doorway. At this hour Elisa's windows were already alight, in winter shrouded by fine mist, in summer open once more and breathing out repose and calm. And on these windows, motionless, with his hands in his pockets, José Matias remained fixed in contemplation. Every half-hour, stealthily, he found his way to the tavern. A glass of wine, a glass of brandy—and then, very softly, back to the darkness of the doorway, back to his ecstasy. When Elisa's windows were dark, even throughout the long night, even through the black winter nights—he remained, shriveled up, numb with cold, pounding his worn soles on the pavement or at the back of the courtyard sitting on the stairs, fixing his bleary eyes on the dark façade of the house where he knew she was sleeping with another.

At the beginning, when he wanted to smoke a hurried cigarette, he climbed up to the deserted landing so as to conceal the light that would reveal him in his hiding place. But later, my friend, he smoked incessantly, leaning against the doorpost, puffing cigarettes feverishly, so that the tip would glow and light him up! And you see why, my friend? Because Elisa had already found out that inside that doorway, humbly adoring her windows, with the same soulfulness as formerly, was her poor José Matias . . . !

And will you believe that after that, every night, either through the windows or leaning from the balcony (with the

Superintendent inside, stretched out on the sofa, already in his slippers, reading the evening paper), she remained gazing at the doorway, very quietly, without any other gesture, with that same old and silent look as she used to send from the terrace over the roses and the dahlias? José Matias, recognizing this, was enraptured. And so he desperately kept his light alive, like a beacon, to guide her beloved eyes through the darkness, and to show her that he was always there, frozen with cold, but all hers, and faithful.

In the daytime he never went near the Rua de São Bento. How could he dare with his jacket torn at the elbows and his worn-out shoes? For this young man, once so fastidiously and soberly elegant, was now literally in rags. Where did he dig up even the small change for wine and for a dish of *bacalhau* [8] in the tavern? I don't know. . . . But let us sing the praises of the divine Elisa, my friend! With great delicacy, and in a roundabout and ingenious way, she, being rich, tried to set up an allowance for José Matias, now indigent. A piquant situation, what? The grateful lady setting up stipends for her two men— her bodily lover and her spiritual lover. The latter, however, guessed the origin of the dreadful charity, and refused it— without revulsion or wounded pride, but rather as if deeply moved, and even with a tear fluttering on his brandy-inflamed eyelids.

But only when the night was fully dark did he dare enter the Rua de São Bento and slip into his doorway. And can you guess how he spent his days? Spying on, following, sniffing after the Superintendent of Public Works! Yes, my friend, with an insatiable, frenetic, atrocious curiosity about this man whom Elisa had chosen! The two previous ones, Miranda and Nogueira, had entered Elisa's bedroom openly by way of the church door, and for other human reasons in addition to love: to possess a home, perhaps have children, and to have stability and tranquillity in life. But this man was merely the lover whom she elected and whom she kept only for making love to her, and in this union there seemed to be no rational motive beyond the

---

[8] *Bacalhau.* Smoked cod, a staple food of poor Portuguese.

meeting of two bodies. He could not, for this reason, get enough of studying this man, his face, his clothes, his habits, so anxious was he to understand perfectly what kind of man this was whom, to fulfill herself, Elisa had preferred among all the throng of mankind. For propriety's sake, the Superintendent lived at the other end of the Rua de São Bento, opposite the market. And this part of the street, where the eyes of Elisa could not surprise him in his rags, was the haunt of José Matias from early morning, so that he could watch and nose out this man when he returned from Elisa's house still warm from the comfort of her bedroom. Nor did he abandon the watch later, but cautiously, like a thief, followed in his tracks at a distance. And I suspect that he followed him like this, less out of a perverse curiosity than to make sure that among the temptations of Lisbon, which are terrible for a Superintendent from Beja, he remained physically faithful to Elisa. As a service to her happiness, he kept watch over the lover of the woman he loved!

A furious refinement of spirituality and devotion, my friend! Elisa's soul was his and forever received his eternal devotion; and now he desired that the body of Elisa should not be less adored, nor less faithfully, by the one to whom she had entrusted it. But the Superintendent found no difficulty in remaining faithful to a woman so beautiful and so rich, who wore silk stockings and jewelled earrings, and who dazzled him. And who knows, my friend? Perhaps that faithfulness, a corporeal homage to the divinity of Elisa, was for José Matias the last happiness that life yielded. I have that idea because one rainy morning last winter I ran across the Superintendent buying camellias from a florist on the Rua de Ouro; and across the way, on a corner, José Matias, ghastly looking and falling apart, was gazing at the man with tenderness, almost with gratitude! And perhaps that same night in his doorway, shivering and pounding his soaking shoes, with his yearning eyes fixed on the dark windows, he was thinking: "Poor little girl . . . poor Elisa! I am very happy that he brings her flowers!"

This went on for three years.

Finally, my friend, the day before yesterday João Seco

showed up at my house in the afternoon, out of breath, to say: "They have just taken José Matias to the hospital on a stretcher, with a congestion of the lung!"

It seems that he was found at dawn, stretched out on the pavement, wrapped up in the thin flopping jacket, gasping and with death written on his face, but turned so as to be able to see the balcony of Elisa. I ran to the hospital. He was dead. . . . With the doctor on duty, I went up to the ward. I lifted up the sheet that covered him. Underneath his torn and dirty shirt, hung from his neck by a string, he had worn a small silken pouch, also torn and dirty. Doubtless it contained a flower, or a lock of hair, or a piece of lace of Elisa's, from the time of the first enchantment and of those afternoons at Benfica. I asked the doctor, who had known him and was sorry for him, whether he had suffered.—"No. . . . He was momentarily in a coma, then he opened his eyes wide, exclaimed '*Oh!*' with an expression of great surprise . . . and that was all."

Was that the cry of his soul in the shadow and horror of dying? Or was it his soul triumphant in the recognition that it was at last immortal and free? You don't know; neither did the divine Plato know; nor will the last philosopher on the last afternoon of the world.

Here we are at the cemetery. I think we ought to help hold the trappings of the coffin. . . . Really, it's quite odd to see that Alves Capão following our poor spiritualist so sorrowfully. . . . But—Holy God!—look! Over there, waiting, at the door of the church, that sympathetic fellow, in a dress coat and light cloak. . . . It's the Superintendent of Public Works! And he's carrying a large bunch of violets. . . . Elisa has sent her carnal lover to accompany her spiritual lover to his grave and to cover him with flowers! But, oh, my friend, let's believe that never indeed would she have asked José Matias to scatter violets over the corpse of the Superintendent! It's just that the material will always worship the spirit, even without understanding why, and without deriving any happiness from it, and will always treat itself, despite the pleasures it receives from itself, with brutality and scorn. A great consolation, my friend—this Superintendent with his bunch of flowers—for a metaphysician who, like myself, has written commentaries on Spinoza and Malebranche, who has rehabilitated Fichte and convincingly demonstrated the illusion of sensation! For this alone it was worth taking to his grave that inexplicable José Matias, who was perhaps much more than a man . . . or still, perhaps, less than a man. . . .

You're right, it's cold . . . but what a beautiful afternoon!

Bibliography

A. The Major Novels

"O Crime do Padre Amaro." 1st ed. Lisboa: *Revista Occidental,* 1875.

O Crime do Padre Amaro ("Edição definitiva"). 2d ed. Lisboa: Tipografia Castro e Irmão, 1876.

O Crime do Padre Amaro (Nova edição inteiramente refundida e recomposta). 3d ed. Pôrto c Braga: Libraria Internacional de Ernesto Chardron, 1880.

O Crime do Padre Amaro (Edição crítica organizada por Helena Cidade Moura, baseada nas versões do 1875, 1876, 1880). Pôrto: Lello e Irmão, 1964. 2 vols.

O Primo Basílio. Pôrto e Braga: Livraria Internacional de Ernesto Chardron e Eugenio Chardron, 1878.

"O Mandarim." Pôrto e Braga: Livraria Internacional de Ernesto Chardron, 1880.

A Relíquia. "Sobre a Nudez Forte da Verdade—O Manto Diafano da Fantasia." Pôrto: Livraria Internacional de Ernesto Chardron, Casa Editora Lugan e Genelioux, Sucessores, 1887.

Os Maias. "Episódios da Vida Romântica." Pôrto: Livraria Internacional de Ernesto Chardron, Casa Editora Lugan e Genelioux, Sucessores, 1888.

A Ilustre Casa de Ramires. Pôrto: Livraria Chardron de Lello e Irmão, 1900.

A Cidade e as Serras. Pôrto: Livraria Chardron de Lello e Irmão, 1901.

317

B. *Partial or Complete Collections*

Obras de Eça de Queiroz, I. Pôrto: Lello e Irmão, 1966
  O Crime do Padre Amaro (3d ed.)
  A Cidade e as Serras
  Prosas Bárbaras
  Contos
  O Primo Basílio
  A Ilustre Casa de Ramires
  A Relíquia
Obras de Eça de Queiroz, II. Pôrto: Lello e Irmão, 1966
  Os Maias
  Cartas de Inglaterra
  Ultimas Páginas
  As Minas de Salomão (translation of novel by Sir H. Rider Haggard)
  Correspondência de Fradique Mendes
  Ecos de Paris
  Cartas Familiares e Bilhetes de Paris
  Notas Contemporâneas
Obras de Eça de Queiroz, III. Pôrto: Lello e Irmão, 1966
  A Capital
  O Conde de Abranhos
  *Alves e C.*ª
  Correspondência
  O Egipto
  Cartas Inéditas de Fradique Mendes
  Uma Campanha Alegre
  O Mistério da Estrada de Sintra
  Eça de Queiroz Entre os Seus
*Obra Complete,** I. (Organização Geral, Introducão, Explicacões Marginais e Apêndices de João Gaspar Simões. Fixação do texto de Helena Cidade Moura. Fixação Ortográfica de Joaquim C. Marques). Rio de Janeiro: Companhia José Aguilar Editora, 1970.
  A Correspondencia de Fradique Mendes
  O Crime do Padre Amaro
  O Primo Basílio
  A Capital
  A Relíquia
*Obra Completa,** II. Rio de Janeiro: Companhia José Aguilar Editora, 1970.
  Os Maias
  A Ilustre Casa de Ramires

* N.B. This edition remains substantially incomplete.

A Cidade e as Serras
O Conde de Abranhos
*Alves e C.*ia
O Mandarim
Contos

C. *Books Containing Some Materials So Far Uncollected in the*
Obras Completas

Machado de Rosa, A., ed. *Prosas Esquecidas* (de E. de Q.) Lisboa:
Editorial Presença.
  I. Farsas
    "O réu Tadeu"
    "Onfalia Benoiton"
    "O Misterio da Estrada de Sintra"
    "O Crime do Padre Amaro" (1875 ed., abbreviated)
  II. Crítica, 1867
  III. Articles from *O Distrito de Évora,* 1867
  IV. Polêmica, 1867
  V. *Farpas,* 1871
Cartas de Eça de Queiroz. Lisboa: Editorial Aviz, 1945.
Novas Cartas Inéditas de Eça de Queiroz. Rio de Janeiro: Editora Alba,
  1940.
Folhas Soltas (Palestina, Alta Siria, "Sir Galahad," Os Santos). Ed.
  Maria d'Eça de Queiroz. Pôrto: Lello e Irmão, 1966.

D. *Translations* *

The Sin of Father Amaro. Trans. Nan Flanagan. London: Max
  Reinhardt, 1962. New York: St. Martin's Press, 1963.
Cousin Bazilio. Trans. Roy Campbell. London: Max Reinhardt, 1953.
  New York: The Noonday Press, 1953.
The Mandarin and Other Stories. Trans. Richard Franko Goldman.
  Athens: Ohio University Press, 1965. London: The Bodley Head,
  1966.
The Relic. Trans. Aubrey F. G. Bell. New York: Alfred A. Knopf,

* The author is grateful to Max Reinhardt and The Bodley Head, possessor
of world rights to these translations, for permission to quote from these works
and to reprint in its entirety Richard Franko Goldman's translation of "José
Matias," from *The Mandarin and Other Stories.*

MCMXV. New York: The Noonday Press, 1954 (With an Introduction by Francis Steegmuller). London: Max Reinhardt, 1954.
The Maias. Trans. Patricia McGowen Pinheiro and Ann Stevens. London: The Bodley Head, 1965. New York: St. Martin's Press, 1965.
The Illustrious House of Ramires. Trans. Ann Stevens. London: The Bodley Head, 1968. Athens: Ohio University Press, 1968.
The City and the Mountains. Trans. Roy Campbell. London: Max Reinhardt, 1955. New York: Noonday Press, 1956. Athens: Ohio University Press, 1967.

E. World Bibliography of Eça de Queiroz

da Cal, Ernesto Guerra. *Bibliografía Queiroçiana Sistemática y Anotada e Iconografía Artística del Hombre y la Obra,* a four-volume Appendix (some subdivided) to his *Lengua y Estilo de Eça de Queiroz.* Coimbra: Por Ordem da Universidade, 1954.
   I. *Bibliografía activa.* Coimbra: Por Ordem da Universidade, 1975.
   Novelas: Ediciones y traducciones
   Obra breve diversa
   Obra póstuma
   Obra inédita o perdida
   Correspondencia particular
   Obras traducidas por E. de Q.
   Varia
  II. A y B *Bibliografía pasiva.* Coimbra: Por Ordem da Universidade, 1976. Fuentes secundarias: Escritos sobre la Vida y la Obra de E. de. Q.: Libros, monografías, ensayos, artículos, reportajes, entrevistas, encuestas, documentos, cartas y sueltos periodísticos.
 III. *Obras Artísticas Derivadas de la Figura y de la Creación Literaria de E. de Q.*
   1. *Artes de la representación*
     A. Adaptaciones de obras de Eça a medios de comunicación colectiva.
      a. Teatro
      b. Cine
      c. Televisión
      d. Radio
     B. Bibliografía
   2. *Literatura*
     A. Ficción, ensayos, crónicas, epistolografía ficticia, pas-

tiches, parodias y entrevistas basados en la obra o la persona de Eça

B. Poemas inspirados en la persona o la obra de E. de Q. o dedicados a él
   a. Serios
   b. Burlescos, satíricos y festivos

C. Bibliografía

3. *Sub-Literatura.* Historietas de dibujos, adaptaciones literarias, pedagógicas y de lectura infantil, etc.

4. *Artes plásticas y gráficas*
   A. Iconografía del escritor
      a. Esculturas
      b. Retratos
      c. Caricaturas
   B. Iconografía de la obra: Ilustraciones y otras interpretaciones artísticas de escenas y personajes
   C. Bibliografía iconográfica

IV. *Marginalia*
   1. *Monumentos y lápidas dedicadas a la memoria del Escritor*
      A. Bibliografía
   2. *Escenarios queiroçianos reales y ficcionales*
   3. *Fuentes de información sobre los actos públicos de celebración del er Centenario del Nacimiento del novelista y de otros homenajes*
   4. *Programas sobre E. de Q. en la radio y la televisión*
   5. *Sociedades eçófilas*
      A. "Círculo E. de Q.," de Lisboa
      B. "Clube do Eça," de Rio de Janeiro
      C. Otras Sociedades
   6. *Sobre la cuestión de la propiedad literaria de las obras del escritor*
   7. *Sobre algunos de los editores y traductores de Eça*
   8. *Esoterismo en relación al novelista: Astrología y espiritismo*
   9. *Miscelánea*

ÍNDICES

Tomo II.
  I. Índice de Láminas del Tomo 2º
  II. Índice General de Materias del Tomo 2º.

Tomo III.
  I. Índice de Láminas del Tomo 3º
  II. Índice General de Materias del Tomo 3º

Tomo IV.
  I. Índice General de Láminas
  II. Índice Onomástico de Toda la Obra
  III. Addenda et Corrigenda

F. Other Works Consulted

Adams, Robert Martin. *Nil.* New York: Oxford University Press, 1966.

———. *Stendhal: Notes on a Novelist.* New York: Minerva Press, 1968.

Batalha Reis, Beatriz Cinatti, ed. *Eça de Queiroz e Jaime Batalha Reis: Cartas e Rocordações do Seu Convívio.* Pôrto: Lello e Irmão, 1966.

Berlin, Isaiah. *The Hedgehog and The Fox.* New York: Simon and Schuster, 1953.

Bersani, Leo. *A Future for Astyanax.* Boston: Little, Brown and Company, 1976.

———. *From Balzac to Beckett.* New York: Oxford University Press, 1970.

Burke, Kenneth. *A Grammar of Motives.* Berkeley: University of California Press, 1969.

Cabral, Antônio. *Eça de Queiroz: A Sua Vida e a Sua Obra,* 3d. ed. Lisboa: Livraria Bertrand, 1945.

Chase, Richard. *The American Novel and Its Tradition.* New York: Doubleday, 1957.

Cidade Moura, Helena. "Tres Versões do Crime do Padre Amaro— Algumas Variantes." *Ocidente* (September 1961).

Clark, Priscilla P. "Stratégies d'auteur au XIXᵉ siècle" *Romantisme (Revue du Dix–Neuvième Siècle),* Nos. 17–18, 1977.

Clements, Robert J. "The City and The Mountains" *Saturday Review of Literature,* September 9, 1967, p. 24.

Coimbra Martins, António. *Ensaios Queirosianos.* Lisboa: Publicacões Europa–América, 1967.

———. "Eva e Eça" *Bulletin des Études Portugaises,* XXVIII–XXIX (1967/68).

Cortesão, Jaime. *Eça de Queiroz e a Questão Social.* Lisboa: Portugália Editora, 1970 (vol. XIX of his *Obras Completas*).

da Cal, Ernesto Guerra. *Lenguaje y Estilo de Eça de Queiroz: I, Elementos Básicos.* Coimbra: Por ordem da universidade, 1954.

Demetz, Peter. "Eça de Queiróz as a Literary Critic." *Comparative Literature,* XIX (Fall 1967), 289–307.

Dumas fils, Alexandre. *Affaire Clémenceau.* Paris: Michel Lévy Frères, 1872.

Figueiredo, Fidelino de. *História da Literatura Realista (1871–1900).* São Paulo: Editora Anchieta, 1946.

França, José Augusto, ed. *As Conferências do Casino no Parlamento.* Lisboa: Livros Horizonte, 1973.

———. *Zé Povinho na Obra de Rafael Bordalo Pinheiro.* Lisboa: Livraria Bertrand, 1975.

———. *Le Romantisme au Portugal.* Paris: Klincksieck, 1975.

Frye, Northrop. *The Secular Scripture.* Cambridge: Harvard University Press, 1976.

Garis, Robert. *The Dickens Theatre.* Oxford: At the Clarendon Press, 1965.

Gaspar Simões, João. *Vida e Obra de Eça de Queirós.* 2d ed. Lisboa: Livraria Bertrand, 1973.

Gide, André. *Prétextes.* Paris: Mercure de France, 1963.

Girard, René. *Mensonge romantique et vérité romanesque.* Paris: Bernard Grasset, 1961. Trans. Yvonne Freccero, *Deceit, Desire and the Novel.* Baltimore: The Johns Hopkins University Press, 1965.

Girodon, Jean. "Eça de Queiroz et Balzac." *Revue de littérature comparée,* XXIV (1950), 298–308.

———. "Eça et Courbet." *Bulletin des Études Portugaises,* XXIV (1963), 89–101.

———. "Eça de Queiroz et *Madame Bovary.*" *Biblos* (1949), 210–27.

———. "Fiches Queiroziennes." *Bulletin des Études Portugaises,* XVII (1966), 189–220.

———. "O Egypto d'Eça de Queiroz." *Bulletin des Études Portugaises* XXII (1959–60), 129–86.

Graña, César. *Modernity and Its Discontents.* New York: Harper and Row, 1967.

Holbrook, David. *Gustav Mahler and The Courage To Be* (London: Vision, 1975).

Jameson, Frederic. "Magical Narratives: Romance as Genre" *New Literary History,* VII (1975), 135–63.

Kuhn, Reinhard. *The Demon of Noontide: Ennui in Western Literature* Princeton: Princeton University Press, 1976.

Larbaud, Valery. "Écrit dans une cabine du Sud-Express." *Oeuvres.* Paris: Gallimard, 1957, pp. 947–58.

Leavis, F. R. *The Great Tradition.* New York: New York University Press, 1964.

Lepecki, Maria Lúcia. *Eça na Ambiguidade.* Lisboa: Jornal do Fundão, 1974.

Levin, Harry. *The Gates of Horn: A Study of Five French Realists.* New York: Oxford University Press, 1963.

Lima, Archer de. *Eça de Queiroz Diplomata.* Lisboa: Portugália Editora, n.d.

Machado da Rosa, Alberto. *Eça Discípulo de Machado?* 2nd ed. Lisboa: Editorial Presença, n.d.; 3rd ed., 1979.

Martins, Wilson. *História da Inteligência Brasileira,* Vols. I–VII. São Paulo: Editora Cultrix, 1977–1978.

Medina, João. *Eça Político.* Lisboa: Seara Nova, 1974.

——. *Eça de Queiroz e o Seu Tempo.* Lisboa: Livros Horizonte, 1972.

Menezes, Djacir. *Crítica Social de Eça de Queiroz.* Rio de Janeiro: Departamento de Imprenta Nacional, 1950.

Moog, Vianna. *Eça de Queirós e o Seculo XIX.* 5th ed. Rio de Janeiro: Civilização Brasileira, 1966.

Nunes, Maria Luisa. "Techniques and Functions of Character Drawing in the Three Versions of *O Crime do Padre Amaro.*" Diss., City University of New York, 1973. There is a translation into Portuguese—Pôrto: Lello e Irmão, 1976.

Oliveira, Alberto de. *Eça de Queiroz: Páginas de Memórias,* (2nd ed.) Lisboa: Portugália Editora, 1945[?].

Oliveira, César. *O Socialismo em Portugal (1850–1900).* Pôrto: Edição do autor, 1973.

Oliveira Martins, J. P. *História de Portugal.* 16th ed. Lisboa: Guimarães Editora, 1972.

——. *Portugal Contemporâneo.* 8th ed. Lisboa: Guimarães Editora, 1976.

Pritchett, V. S., "Iron Comedian," New York Review of Books, April 9, 1970. Reprinted in *The Myth Makers: Literary Essays* (New York: Random House, 1979).

Reis, Carlos. *Estatuto e Perspectivas do Narrador na Ficcão de Eça de Queirós.* Coimbra: Livraria Almedina, 1975.

Renan, Ernest. *The Life of Jesus.* Trans. Joseph Henry Allen. Boston: Little, Brown and Company, 1929.

Sacramento, Mario. *Eça de Queirós: Uma Estética da Ironia.* Coimbra: Coimbra Editora, Limitada, 1945.

Salgado, Jr., Antônio. *História das Conferências do Cassino (1871).* Lisboa: 1930[?].

Saraiva, António José. *As Ideias de Eça de Queiroz.* Lisboa: n.p., 1946.

Seeleye, John. "Some Green Thoughts on a Green Theme." *TriQuarterly* (Winter/Spring 1972), 576–638.

Sérgio, António. "Notas sobre a Imaginação, a Fantasia e o Problema

Psicológico-Moral na Obra Novelística de Queirós." *Obras Completas.* VI. Lisboa: Livraria Sá da Costa Editora, 1971.

Serrão, Joel. *Do Sebastianismo ao Socialismo em Portugal.* Lisboa: Livros Horizonte, 1973.

Sire, Dominique. "Une Première Ébauche du Roman *O Primo Basílio*—Le manuscrit de Tormes." *Bulletin des Études Portugaises et Bresiliennes.* XXXIII/XXXIV (1972–73), 245–64.

Solana, Rafael. "Leyendo a Queiroz." In *Musas Latinas.* México: Fondo de cultura económica, 1969, pp. 83–232.

Sousa e Costa, Júlio de. *Eça de Queiroz: Memórias da Sua Estada em Leiria.* Lisboa: Livraria Sá da Costa, 1953.

Steiner, George. *Tolstoy or Dostoyevsky.* Harmondsworth, England: Penguin Books, 1967.

Stevens, James R. "Eça and Flaubert." *Luso-Brazilian Review.* III, no. 1 (May 1966).

Warren, Robert Penn. (ed.) *Selected Poems of Herman Melville.* New York: Random House, 1970.

Index

327